Knowledge,
Power,
and Practice

COMPARATIVE STUDIES OF
HEALTH SYSTEMS AND MEDICAL CARE

For a complete list of titles in this series, please contact the
Sales Department
University of California Press
2120 Berkeley Way
Berkeley, CA 94720

Knowledge, Power, and Practice

The Anthropology of Medicine and Everyday Life

EDITED BY

Shirley Lindenbaum AND Margaret Lock

UNIVERSITY OF CALIFORNIA PRESS

Berkeley / Los Angeles / London

The publisher gratefully acknowledges permission
to use material from the following publications:

Donna J. Haraway, "The Biopolitics of
Postmodern Bodies: Determinations of Self in
Immune System Discourse," *differences: A Journal
of Feminist Cultural Studies,* vol. 1, no. 1 (1989):
3–43.

John and Jean Comaroff, *Ethnography and the
Historical Imagination* (Boulder, CO: Westview
Press, 1992), 215–233.

University of California Press
Berkeley and Los Angeles, California

University of California Press
London, England

Library of Congress Cataloging-in-Publication
Data

Knowledge, power, and practice: the anthropology
of medicine and everyday life / edited
  by Shirley Lindenbaum and Margaret Lock.
      p.   cm. — (Comparative studies of
health systems and medical care ; no. 36)
    Includes bibliographical references and index.
    ISBN 0-520-07784-9 (cloth)
    ISBN 0-520-07785-7 (paper)
    1. Medical anthropology. I. Lindenbaum,
Shirley. II. Lock,
  Margaret M. III. Series.
  GN296.K58 1993
  306.4′61—dc20   92-28208
                           CIP

Printed in the United States of America

1 2 3 4 5 6 7 8 9

The paper used in this publication meets the
minimum requirements of American
National Standard for Information Sciences—
Permanence of Paper for Printed Library
Materials, ANSI Z39.48-1984♾

Contents

Preface

The essays in this book were originally produced for a symposium sponsored by the Wenner-Gren Foundation for Anthropological Research held in March, 1988, in Cascais, Portugal. The participants, who came from Africa, Canada, France, the United Kingdom, Venezuela, and the United States, exemplified both geographical and theoretical diversity.

The aims of the conference were twofold: The first purpose was to reflect upon the historical development of medical anthropology and to consider the directions in which it is currently headed. To this end two earlier reviews of the literature were circulated in advance, one written by Horacio Fabrega in 1971, and the other by Allan Young in 1982. Both authors were present at the conference. Second, all participants were asked to write a paper linking three domains of anthropological inquiry which are often treated separately: human biology, the cultural construction of knowledge, and relations of power. In addition, each paper was to be based on research concerned with some aspect of health, illness, or affliction, providing a basis for discussion of the ways in which different kinds of data and different analytic approaches might be integrated and considered as a whole. When such topics become key issues for investigation, the disciplinary division between human biology and cultural anthropology is eroded.[1]

Many anthropologists during the past few years have lamented the stillbirth of a theoretically informed medical anthropology. One explanation for the apparent lack of theory may be that medical anthropologists for too long accepted without criticism the foundations of biomedical knowledge. Quick to recognize that knowledge and practices of other places and other times are culturally constructed, we have been slow to turn the mirror on contemporary Western medicine and Western social science. The encounter with non-Western medicine thus contributes to our understanding of the basic categories of our own medical beliefs and practices, providing grounds for considering the aura of naturalness that surrounds these institutions and activities.

It was significant, then, that when the conference participants were asked shortly after their arrival in Cascais to give brief introductory biographies, so many chose to insert the disclaimer that they viewed themselves primarily as anthropologists and not as medical anthropologists. In various ways we each affirmed the view that there is nothing inherent in the study of health, illness, the human body, or medical systems that makes it radically different from the comparative study of politics, law, or economics. It was agreed that our subject matter is neither simply medicine as an institutional body of scientific knowledge nor the human body as an unproblematic product of nature, but rather is a study of the creation, representation, legitimization, and application of knowledge about the body in both health and illness.

In taking this stand, participants distanced themselves from that large group of medical anthropologists who accept biological and biomedical data as an assemblage of incontestable natural facts. Those present were, of course, preselected on the basis of their interests and earlier publications, and it was no surprise—indeed it was required—that their presentations should draw on contemporary theory in the social sciences. In carrying out this mandate, the participants showed that health and illness can be subjected to rigorous anthropological analyses, which, in turn, feed back into current debates about theory in anthropology and the human sciences in general. At this moment, grand theory and systematizing that seek to produce universal explanations are hotly contested by an approach that recognizes multiple, competing interpretations and places emphasis instead on the cultural and historical contextualization of data. Toward the end of the week in Portugal it became apparent that medical anthropology, in common with contemporary anthropology in general, not only stimulates a radical questioning of metatheory but also leads to the reconsideration of certain basic concepts such as the "body," "health," or "aging," which are usually understood as natural categories.

Because of its applied stance and the urgency and emotional nature of much of its subject matter, medical anthropology has the potential to contribute in a special way to the parent discipline. Often confronted with human affliction, suffering, and distress, fieldwork in medical anthropology challenges the traditional dichotomies of theory and practice, thought and action, objectivity and subjectivity. The very nature of the subject matter forces the researcher to seek out a position of informed compromise from which it is possible to act.

As is apparent from their titles, the papers focus heavily on the cultural construction of illness, illness experience, the body, and medical knowledge. We are informed about the competing discourses that contribute to these constructions, including the ways in which medical knowledge is produced in the clinic, the laboratory, the medical school, and public meetings. Everyone who contributed to the symposium was highly sensitive to the relationships of hierarchy and dominance that privilege certain kinds of knowledge. All the papers seek in one way or another to call into question the unexamined authority usually assigned to contemporary biomedical knowledge. However, while at first glance it may seem that "biomedicine" or "science" is our target, these are but way stations en route to a more distant goal, an identification of the processes by which dominant voices and institutional forms come to exercise their control.

Allan Young was perhaps the first medical anthropologist to assert that "*all* knowledge of society and sickness is socially determined" and that what we need is a "critical understanding of how medical facts are *predetermined* by the processes through which they are conventionally produced in clinics and research settings. Thus, the task at hand is not simply to demystify knowledge, but to critically examine the *social conditions of knowledge production*" (1982:277), a task equally applicable to historical times, "exotic" places, or the offices of biomedical practitioners. When such an approach is complemented by a critical epidemiology of the social origins of distress and illness, as well as its interpretation and management, medical anthropology becomes a powerful tool for reassessing what is taken as natural and normal in connection with the human body. This subversive exercise places medical anthropologists alongside others who are attempting to contribute to anthropological theory concerning issues of power and inequality. Thus the question is not simply one of how the world is meaningfully constructed by individuals in any one society, but how individuals embody and come to accept as natural a world that is constructed disproportionately by those in positions of power (Asad 1979).

By reflecting on the way in which medical knowledge is created, it becomes clear that medicine is no unitary thing, just as there is no single form of anthropology. As Peter Wright, one of our invited discussants, observed, different practices produce different kinds of knowledge. Our discussions displayed a variety of anthropological interests, various methods of research, and the many forms of communication available to convey our findings. We asked, what should be our units of analysis: life histories or episodes? What is our point of entry into a problem, and what difference does it make if we begin, say, with the amniotic fluid or with the sick person?

Just as medicine is not to be regarded as a single kind of enterprise, biomedicine should not be seen as a bounded system. Critical of such a view, Peter Worsley has stressed the need to focus also on more general issues, such as misfortune, abnormality, and chance, of which illness and subsequent medical responses are but one small part. From this perspective it is possible to discern similarities in medically related knowledge and behavior through space and time, dissolving the distinction between "scientific" and other types of medicine (Worsley 1982:326).

In addition to a reluctance to question biomedical categories, many medical anthropologists have romanticized the medical domains of other cultures (as the Jefferys note in chapter 1). Such studies tend also to emphasize a unity of society and nature as inherent in the preindustrial order. However, as both Worsley (1982) and Roger Keesing (1987:161) have indicated, cultural beliefs constitute not only explanations and meanings but also an ideology by which means certain political and economic realities are legitimated. In the case of medicine, an account of the control of medical knowledge and the way it is selectively applied can demonstrate "the manner in which social interest becomes seamlessly incorporated in the set of tacit assumptions about reality" (Comaroff 1982:50). This is as true for the Azande (McCleod 1972) as it is for postindustrial societies East and West (Kleinman 1982; Lock 1988; Young 1980).

The conference papers indicate clearly that medical anthropologists are finely tuned to the problems of representation, to the introduction of competing narratives, and to a study of the way in which individual narratives, informed by various ideologies, are the products of a dialogue between observer and observed. More than dialogue, however, narratives are produced in institutional contexts that give legitimacy to narrative ideas and provide some voices with more resonance than others.

In common with other branches of anthropology, therefore, the production and form of the text was a topic of creative discussion. Medical anthropologists draw upon a storehouse of textual sources, from the machine-produced image of the fetus to the poetry of patients. As Gananath Obeyesekere, another invited discussant noted, the language of the conference at times still carried the imprint of positivism. We spoke of factors, variables, and biotic components, as well as narratives, epistemes, and symbolic forms. Medical anthropology challenges us to create a closer association between the languages of biology and culture as we speak about body and mind, matter and symbol. But as Obeyesekere further noted, the languages to be fused are not equal. The metalanguage of biology is widely accepted, and assumed to be "factual," but anthropological concepts must inevitably be contextualized and tend to be understood as signaling epiphenomena in many situations. The papers given at Cascais demonstrate that one important task for medical anthropologists is to call attention to the way in which *both* anthropological concepts *and* the language of biology are culturally and historically situated, each the product of historical separation, before any reconciliation between the two can take place. However, although there was agreement that knowledge of all kinds, including that of the basic, human, and applied sciences, is created in particular contexts and in changing arrangements of power, there was also an understanding that the anthropologist seeks to avoid a descent into the abyss of endless deconstruction.

There was no romantic denial of the power of biomedicine which, it was acknowledged, possesses information, insight, and technological devices that are often therapeutically more effective than alternate approaches. Nor was the existence of biological reality, frequently painful and debilitating, denied, but it was assumed that when efforts are made to explain, order, and manipulate this reality, the cultural construction of biological categories must be considered. Furthermore, our discussions revealed that the time is apparently long overdue for a more fruitful engagement between medical anthropologists closely allied with the health care system and those who are more academically oriented: between those who use the empirical approach of the applied medical sciences and those who largely reject empiricism and opt at the same time to "keep their hands clean."

At some point most medical anthropologists are required to enter into the urgency of practice, which requires ethical sensitivity and considerable self-reflection (a situation compounded for the physician-anthropologist, as the chapters by Horacio Fabrega and Gilbert Lewis illustrate). A commitment to practice, however, need not rule out a central concern with ideology, which was a focus of inquiry for all conference participants, whether they arrived at their positions by way of Bourdieu, Marx, Freud, or Foucault. (While all the participants hold academic appointments, perhaps half also work as consultants in applied settings). The anthropological imperative to explore the conceptual frameworks of medical ministries resulted in a number of revisionary accounts, not in the sense of unmasking knowing misrepresentations of social reality, but of determining the processes by which certain forms of knowledge achieve a moral legitimacy and appear to be part of the natural order. Like our colleagues in other arenas, medical anthropologists investigate the circumstances that have produced a world that appears to be without history and structure (Polier and Roseberry 1989). Medicine, and to a lesser degree anthropology itself, were thus subjected to critical scrutiny.

While it is true that all of the participants identified themselves primarily as anthropologists, there is no doubt that medical anthropology leaves its imprint on the substantive areas of study. Although the authors in this volume pitched their tents in the medical school and the clinic, and established residence in Papua New Guinea, Nigeria, Canada, Italy, the United States, and India, their concern was with stance, not space (cf. Fox 1991:96). As the papers here illustrate, medical anthropologists are looking anew at the relations among biology, knowledge production, and cultural context, trying to capture the imprint of social forces and then deconstructing these traces by examining the meaning attributed to symptoms and the eruption of psychic alienation. They are also documenting resistance to ideologies of bodily control, and learning how different practices change modes of knowing and conceptions of the self. Issues of concern to general anthropology thus gain new vitality by moving them to a different field site, at once familiar but now conceptually different, since the body itself, with its insistent subjectivity, provokes us to inquire into the historical processes whereby biological and cultural phenomena are mutually determined.

Note

1. In addition to the contributors to this volume, the symposium was enlivened by the presence of two distinguished discussants, Gananath Obeyesekere and Peter Wright, as well as by George Armelagos, Diana Long, Nancy Scheper-Hughes, and Nicole Sindzingre. We also discussed a paper by Bryan Turner, who was unfortunately unable to attend. Pamela Smith was a superb conference Monitor. Lisa Chisholm of the University of California Press showed exceptional care and sensitivity to the material in her copy editing of all the essays.

References

Asad, Talal
    1979   Anthropology and the Analysis of Ideology. *Man* 14:607–627.
Comaroff, Jean
    1982   Medicine: Symbol and Ideology. In *The Problem of Medical Knowledge: Examining the Social Construction of Medicine,* Peter Wright and Arthur Treacher, eds., pp. 49–68. Edinburgh: University of Edinburgh Press.
Fox, Richard G., ed.
    1991   *Recapturing Anthropology: Working in the Present.* Advanced Seminar series. Santa Fe, N.Mex.: School of American Research.
Keesing, Roger
    1987   Anthropology as Interpretive Quest. *Current Anthropology* 28:161–169.

Kleinman, Arthur
    1982   Neurasthenia and Depression: A Study of Somatization and Culture in China. *Culture, Medicine and Psychiatry* 6:117–189.

Lock, Margaret
    1988   A Nation At Risk: Interpretations of School Refusal in Japan. In *Biomedicine Examined,* Margaret Lock and Deborah R. Gordon, eds., pp. 391–414. Dordrecht, Netherlands: Kluwer Academic Publications.

McLeod, Malcolm D.
    1972   Oracles and Accusations Among the Azande. In *Azande Themes,* A. Singer and B. V. Street, eds., pp. 158–178. Oxford: Blackwell.

Polier, Nicole, and William Roseberry
    1989   Tristes tropes. *Economy and Society* 18:245–264.

Young, Allan
    1980   The Discourse on Stress and the Reproduction of Conventional Knowledge. *Social Science and Medicine* 14B:133–147.

Young, Allan
    1982   The Anthropologies of Illness and Sickness. *Annual Review of Anthropology* 11:257–285.

Worsley, Peter
    1982   Non-Western Medical Systems. *Annual Review of Anthropology* 11:315–348.

Part One

The Cultural Construction of Childbirth

Introduction

The Cultural Construction of Childbirth

In the past few decades, anthropologists, sociologists, and historians have proposed the notion that categories of illness and disease are culturally constructed: created by human beings in particular social settings and at particular times. The constructionist theme concerning the local production of knowledge about childbirth and its medicalization is introduced here by Roger Jeffery and Patricia M. Jeffery, Patricia A. Kaufert and John O'Neil and Rayna Rapp.

In many ways, the first two chapters form a related, if contrasting, pair. Childbearing practices in Bijnor, India, are examined in the context of women's other work roles, their ownership of property, and a wide array of social and kinship relations. In chapter 1, the Jefferys find no evidence of conflict concerning childbearing knowledge and birthing practice. The work of the midwife is devalued—more so than most of women's work—and she is credited with neither esoteric knowledge nor special skills. The experiences of childbirth and midwifery in Bijnor are thus in keeping with the low status of women as producers, bringers of wealth, and reproducers, three work roles that may be valued differently in Indian society at different historical times. By placing the Bijnor midwife in her specific social and historical context, the Jefferys correct earlier literature on midwifery in medical anthropology that tends to romanticize non-Western birthing practices.

The Inuit of the Canadian Northwest, on the other hand, still respect the work of their own birth practitioners. However, their status is being actively challenged by the Canadian Department of Health, which has implemented a policy of evacuating a pregnant woman prior to confinement so that the birth will occur in a hospital. Moreover, as Kaufert and O'Neil show in chapter 2, the roles of midwives and women's work shift rapidly with changes in the political economy.

By the 1980s the resident English or Australian midwife, with her skills and simple equipment, supported by a few Inuit midwives trained in Canada, was supplanted by complex machinery and hospital staff in distant urban locations. In contrast to Bijnor women who give birth among close kin, Inuit women are now removed from their communities by the institutional demands of high technology and its possessors, but not without protest. Inuit mothers understandably resist the intrusion that hinders their ability to give meaning to their own birthing experiences and to define a sense of community regeneration.

These two cases illustrate the different ways in which health care "medicalizes" social life. In early forms of neocolonial expansion, social life and imagination are infused by health ideologies and practices that do not appear to supplant indigenous views and behaviors, a pattern that also holds true for health care in nineteenth-century South Africa, as Jean Comaroff describes in a later chapter. In subsequent phases, sophisticated technologies provide fewer opportunities for accommodation, and rural people are forcibly placed in urban centers of technology and ideological production. In each case we are privy to what may be a more widespread process of ideological "accommodation": therapeutic knowledge once thought to be situated in the creative margins of "precolonial" societies is later oriented toward a central locus of technical authority. Although state medicine has left a deep imprint in Africa, for example, the outcome remains in dispute in the northwest territories of Canada, where State representatives passionately contest the validity and authority of local knowledge. In rural Bijnor, where the presence of the central government and modern technology are less obtrusive, the knowledge and meaning of childbirth still nest in a metamedical context of the gender and caste hierarchies that give them shape.

The chapter by Kaufert and O'Neil introduces a second constructionist theme developed by several other contributors to this work: the notion that different perceptions of risk stem from different versions of reality. For the Canadian gynecologist, risk is statistically measured, allowing comparison across time and populations. Inuit women, on the other hand, take their measure from the number of successful births remembered in their own communities and from their own reproductive experience, resulting in a risk factor that does not seem to them to be very high, and one that does not outweigh the loneliness of birthing in an alien environment.

Competing languages of risk are explored also in chapter 3, Rayna Rapp's discussion of the cultural meaning of prenatal diagnosis. Following amniocentesis, women in a New York clinic evaluate risk information provided by genetic counselors and choose whether or not to continue with a pregnancy. Their decisions are based on a variety of local influences—the proximity and judgment of male partners, kin, and friends, the place of a particular pregnancy in the women's reproductive histories, the weight of religion in their lives, and the blemish of a potential disability in the eyes of their own communities. Local meanings of disability vary greatly, as the parents of disabled children, their advocates, and activists indicate. The cultural meaning of diagnosis emerges as the product of a number of overlapping discourses—genetics, health economics, social work and sociology, bioethics, and feminism, as well as the language of the new workforce of genetic counselors and the women who consult them—a construction forever in the making. The voices of the pregnant women have so far only been faintly heard.

1

Traditional Birth Attendants in Rural North India

The Social Organization of Childbearing

Roger Jeffery and Patricia M. Jeffery

Anthropological knowledge produced in connection with midwifery and childbirth has often been used for political purposes in both western Europe and North America. On the one hand, negative assessments of indigenous childbearing practices are taken as one indicator of women's low status and used as a stick to beat colonial regimes or colonized peoples. On the other hand, non-Western methods of childbirth are examined in order to compare them with what are taken to be the ill effects of technologically controlled childbirth in formal medical settings. The first approach (called a biomedical perspective by Carol McClain [1982:26]) focuses on the disasters—on rates of maternal and neonatal mortality and on the experiences of doctors in Third World hospitals often faced with the effects of undiagnosed obstructed labors and long delays before hospitalization. The second (which McClain calls a sociocultural perspective) looks for social and psychological evidence of supportive environments, or for beneficial techniques (massage, positions during delivery) which are absent from standard Western practice.[1]

Both approaches tend to allow Western medical concerns to propose the agenda. The first sets out to modernize the traditional, but has often been accused of ethnocentrism (see, for example, Jordan 1987). The second calls for the insertion of traditional techniques into technocratic obstetrics, but often relies on a romanticized borrowing from the past of "exotic" cultures (Macintyre 1977). The recent advocacy by the World Health Organization of training programs for traditional birth attendants as a means of improving the conditions of maternal and child health around the world belongs to this second category (Maglacas and Simons 1986).

We are concerned with two features common to these otherwise contrasting perspectives: first, a tendency to homogenize midwifery by underplaying or ignoring cultural variation; and second, a propensity to detach pregnancy, the birth event, and the postpartum period from their social moorings. In this chapter we wish to argue for strengthening what has been a minority position, one that examines childbirth and midwifery as practices within specific social and economic contexts, especially by locating women in production and reproduction. In other words, we advocate a position that looks for the bases of variation.

One reason for the relatively stereotypical view of midwifery in anthropology is its narrow selection from the many studies undertaken, and particularly its focus on the more detailed, anthropologically oriented accounts that tend to celebrate indigenous midwives or birthing systems. The burgeoning of such studies followed the growth of feminist perspectives in social science, in which the proper task of feminist anthropology was considered to be the recovery of women's knowledge and sources of power and influence. Sheila Cosminsky (1982), Brigitte Jordan (1983), Carol Laderman (1983), Carol MacCormack (1982), and Lois Paul and Benjamin Paul (1975), for example, describe childbirth among Mayan Indians or neighboring tribes in Guatemala, Sierra Leone, and Malaysia. We do not question the value or conclusions of these excellent reports. We do, however, point to the disadvantages of generalizing from such a relatively narrow set of social contexts. McClain's literature review of 1982, for instance, summarizes the earlier reviews by Ford (1945), Montagu (1949), Spencer (1950), Mead and Newton (1967), and Oakley (1977), which draw their material from a wide geographic range, but which deal predominantly with small-scale, relatively isolated communities or tribes, often slash-and-burn agriculture or hunter-gatherer societies.

Although this research potentially grants every separate cultural form its own significance, it has tended to downplay the densely populated, settled agricultural regions where most of the world's women live. Accounts of Han Chinese childbearing, or childbearing in Indo-Gangetic plains India, Pakistan, and Bangladesh are relatively rare. Such regions have been characterized in terms of their dominant agricultural practices as male farming systems (Boserup 1970) illustrating the Eurasian model of plough agriculture (Goody 1976), and have been associated with hierarchical social systems and relatively restricted roles for women. Both of these authors have been criticized for their inability to deal with cultural variation within these broad regions. Nevertheless, they offer a useful vantage point from which to develop an understanding of how childbearing experiences vary, and along which dimensions, in different social settings.

In what follows we will argue that the nature of midwifery in any society must be understood in the context of a wide set of relationships that include the society's range of medical resources (even if childbirth is not usually perceived as a medical event) and people's understandings of anatomy and physiology, as well as the ability of women to enter healing roles, their access to different kinds of healers, and the access of healers to them. Midwifery is also affected by the particular constraints on the organization of delivery and by the roles adopted by those who are permitted to attend a birth. These childbirth events are set in a wider context of the dominant symbolic understandings of the childbirth process and of women's other work roles, their kin relationships, and their access to property. As a result, childbearing women have differing abilities to organize resources on their own behalf, whether these are in the form of social support, cash, or access to scarce knowledge. In this dense context we find differences in the roles of specialized birth attendants, the evaluation of what they do, and their opportunities to develop specialized knowledge. That is, the practice of midwifery in any one place is conditioned by a wide set of social, economic, and symbolic considerations that give it particular shape and meaning.

If societies are placed on a continuum according to the degree of women's subordination, north Indian society would be located toward the "most subordinated" end. As we argue below, this is closely tied to women's childbearing experiences and the status of traditional birth attendants.[2] Many aspects of childbearing in north India confound the generalizations in the anthropological literature on childbirth and midwifery in non-Western societies. For example, traditional birth attendants are usually described as supportive and sisterly, in contrast to the presumed Western model of professional medical domination. What we describe below, however, is a third model—midwifery as a perfunctory service (Goffman 1968:285). The north Indian traditional birth attendant and the hierarchical biomedical expert are thus located at polar extremes, with the sisterly relationships of Yucatan midwives (Jordan 1983) occupying a middle position. Further, we would predict that conditions similar to those we outline below will obtain in many other areas, and may even be the predominant non-Western pattern in terms of the numbers of women involved.

Our data come from recent research in Bijnor District in the state of Uttar Pradesh in north India. The research was based in two adjacent villages (one Muslim, one Caste Hindu and Harijan) less than five kilometers from the bed of the River Ganges. We also conducted a survey in eleven other villages in the District, interviewing 301 recently-delivered women.[3] In the base villages, maternity histories were collected from all 236 ever-married women. Of those currently pregnant or recently-delivered, forty-one key informant women and their husbands were chosen to provide a wider range of detailed information on their work, aspects of kinship and gift-exchanges, and reproductive behavior. Patricia also attended births in the two villages and accompanied one woman who finally delivered in the local women's hospital. This material is complemented by interviews with twenty-four women identified as birth attendants in the two base villages and the eleven survey villages.

In her critique of Western obstetric techniques, Oakley contrasts "preliterate societies" and "modern industrial societies," distinguishing five aspects of childbearing: cultural definitions of pregnancy and childbearing; who controls the management of childbirth; the location of labor and delivery; labor and delivery positions; and the degree and kind of intervention in birth and the emotional and social supports for the laboring woman (Oakley 1978:18). Her portrait of childbearing in "preliterate societies" contrasts sharply with the picture of the passive laboring woman in the West, who gives birth in unfamiliar hospital surroundings away from supportive kin and friends, and who is subject to expert medical management of her birthing experience and the intervention of alien medical techniques. Oakley's framework provides the basis for our discussion below. We begin briefly by describing the role of traditional medical systems in childbearing, and the social and economic location of the typical childbearing women in this part of north India.

Women and Medicine in India

India, like China, has one of the most sophisticated medical systems to have survived to the present day. Long traditions of literacy—in Sanskrit and Arabic—and a large, wealthy clientele have supported elite practitioners' schools in *Ayurveda* ("the science of life") and *Unan-i Tibb* ("Greek medicine"). The classical texts offer only partial insight, however, into the nature of everyday medical practice. Understanding the relationship of these systems of medicine to the medical care given to and by women remains a major problem.

The classical texts and recorded practice mention only male practitioners. Some hints support the idea that *vaids* and *hakims* (Ayurvedic and Unani healers) were unlikely to play a substantial part in childbirth. Indeed, they might have given a prior claim to Brahman priests to provide amulets or to pray for recovery. But some classical texts discuss gynecological and obstetric issues, and some hakims in Bijnor prescribe remedies for infertility or for the inability to bear a son, or to accelerate labor. Direct consultations on matters of pregnancy or delivery, however, seem to have been very uncommon, both in the distant and recent past. Respectable women were constrained by issues of shame, for poorer women, their poverty was an additional hurdle, and all women had limited time for medical consultations. In the nineteenth century, at least, it seems that in north India women in need might have their symptoms described by another woman or by a related man, but male healers could not touch or examine a pregnant or delivering woman.[4] The only female folk healers described in the census or in the reports of British medical administrators are *dais,* a term that usually translates as "midwife," or more recently, traditional birth attendant.[5] Dais are well represented in contemporary north India: in Uttar Pradesh they are reported to attend over 90 percent of all deliveries, whereas in south India they attend fewer than half.[6]

Women, Property and Kinship

An appreciation of the position of young married women contributes to setting the context of midwifery in Bijnor. This can be done in terms of three key roles: as wealth-bringers, workers, and bearers of children.[7] Even in landowning families, a woman rarely owns productive property in her own right. Access to any parental land (the main rural resource) is effectively foreclosed when women leave home at marriage. Marriage establishes patterns of gift giving in which a woman acts as a conduit for wealth (usually in nonproductive forms: jewelry, clothing, foodstuffs, and sometimes cash) from her parents or brothers to her husband and his parents. A young married woman rarely controls the distribution of these resources and she cannot reclaim them if the marriage ends. Such gifts, and a woman's dependence on her brothers to continue to send them if her position with her in-laws is to remain secure, effectively prevent a woman from insisting on her legal right to a share in any productive property when her parents die. Further, marriage migration severs women from supportive relationships with their natal kin and the friends of their youth. Young married women control very few material and social resources.

Regardless of their class position, young married women work long hours at hard labor, but their work is devalued. Wherever possible, a young married woman is excluded from work in the field, except to labor on the land owned by her marital kin or as part of a kin-based work group. Her contribution to agricultural production (winnowing, threshing, grinding) is done inside the domestic compound, and is usually ignored or described by men as light and unimportant. Most women have specific responsibilities for many other tasks such as cooking, cleaning, and rearing young children, as well as the maintenance of court-yards, huts, and grain stores, the collection of fuel, and the conversion of cow-dung into fuel or fertilizer. Men regard this work as demeaning. Women's work is thus trivialized and brings them little credit, yet a woman who wishes to visit her parents may have trouble negotiating leave unless another woman is available to take her place. Women's employment outside the domestic enterprise is rare: young women should not do such work, and men will often deny that it happens. Even when women work outside the home, they rarely gain access to the pay they earn.

As a potential bearer of children, a young woman is carefully chaper-oned in her natal village. She has little say in whom she marries. She must observe norms of respect and seclusion during adolescence to achieve a respectable marriage at a proper age—norms designed to en-sure a sexual purity not demanded of a young man. Her standing with her in-laws begins at a very low level; she provides sexual services for her husband and offers work and respect to her mother-in-law. Inadequacies or resistance may be met with beatings. Her capacity to bear children is vital for the future well-being of her husband's household since sons, in particular, support their aged parents. The birth of a child begins to raise her status and secure her position, a process that culminates (if she is lucky) in her becoming a mother-in-law herself. The failure to bear a child has serious implications for a young married woman, but the pro-cess of childbearing is itself fraught with many problems.

Cultural Definitions of Pregnancy and Childbearing

Three concerns shape women's views of pregnancy and childbearing: shame, pollution, and issues of vulnerability and danger.

Shame

It is important for a married woman to bear children, but matters connected with sexual and gynecological functions are considered *sharm-ki-bat,* matters of shame and embarrassment. As a sexual being, a young married woman must not publicize her sexual relationship with her hus-band. She should be demure in his presence, and neither of them should hint at their sexual activities, either verbally or through body language. Pregnancy and childbirth, however, provide dramatic and conspicuous evidence of sexual intercourse. During pregnancy, a woman should cover her body even more assiduously. Other people's allusions to her condition should be met with a discreetly bowed head. The act of giving birth is also profoundly shameful, entailing as it does the exposure and even touching by others of body parts that should always be concealed.

Childbirth Pollution

During pregnancy, the mother nurtures the fetus with her own blood. At the moment of transition to motherhood, she loses some of this blood, which is considered much more polluting than menstrual blood. *Sutak* (the blood of childbirth) or more prosaically *maila* or *gandagi* (dirt, foulness, filth) is the most severe pollution of all, far greater than menstruation, sexual intercourse, or that of death. Only a profuse flow removes the defilement and causes a complete cleansing. Following the birth, the newly delivered woman (*jacha*) remains impure (*a-sudh* among Hindus and *na-pak* among Muslims) or simply dirty and defiled (*gandi*) and can herself be poisoned by this blood. Some defilement (*gandagi, maila*) also adheres to the baby: Hindus and Muslims alike consider the baby's first hair to be contaminated by contact with the mother's blood, and the hair is shaved off during the first year. Touching the amniotic sac, placenta, and cord (known collectively as the "lump"), delivering the baby, cutting the umbilical cord, and cleaning up the blood are all the most disgusting of tasks. Considered defiling work (*ganda kam*), these practices are the concerns of the dai.

After the birth, the dai presses the jacha's belly and tells her to bear down to make the placenta deliver quickly. If it is slow to arrive, she may massage the belly. Half the dais said that they simultaneously insert their other hand into the vagina and tug the cord robustly, but the others said that this causes sepsis. The dai cuts the cord only after the placenta has been delivered, since the cut cord could vanish inside the jacha's tubes and spread the poison in the placenta throughout her body.

In some aspects of childbearing, Hindu and Muslim practices differ. For example, Hindus invariably wait for the dai to arrive to cut the cord. One socially isolated woman, totally alone when her baby was born, was found by a neighbor who massaged her until the placenta delivered, and then helped her onto her bed. Neither woman cut the cord, but waited for the dai, who arrived over an hour later. Muslims, on the other hand, do not necessarily leave the cord uncut if the baby is born before the dai arrives. An old Faqir woman in the Muslim village will cut cords for a certain payment. Three other women will also cut cords, but only if no dai is present, and they are not paid or considered to be dais. Nonetheless, many Muslim women say cutting the cord is the dai's right, and this is one of the tasks for which she is paid.

Touching the jacha and baby is also defiling-work. Following the birth, the dai gives the jacha some old cloth or a lump of dried mud to clean herself. Women feel disgust at touching a newborn baby and the infant's preliminary cleaning is the dai's responsibility. The dai bathes the jacha to remove pollution, handles the placenta, and cleans the dried mud floor. During labor she will mop up any feces, vomit, and waters (*pani*), tasks too defiling for the laboring woman's marital kin. After the birth the dai also chips away the stained portions of the floor and puts the pieces into an old basket, along with the placenta and any rags used during the delivery. She then repairs the broken floor with fresh mud and diluted cattle dung.

Dealing with the jacha's soiled cloths and the jacha's and baby's excreta is also defiling, although not as polluting as delivering the placenta or cutting the cord. Since there are no domestic latrines and people usually defecate in scrubland or in the fields, a pit is dug in the Hindu jacha's house for her excreta and soiled cloths, and someone also cleans up the baby's excreta and washes its cloths. Dais prefer to avoid this work, but have little choice if they wish to be paid for cord cutting. If the dai does not perform this defiling work, it may be done by the jacha's mother-in-law. Only two Hindu women, both Harijans (so-called untouchables) did the work themselves. By contrast, the Muslim jacha takes responsibility for this task. Some said there was no need to employ another person, since the baby did not defecate for several days, or that they were not "dirty" enough to warrant paying for a dai. In the Muslim village, domestic compounds have dry latrines and jachas use them (at least after the first day), leaving their soiled cloths there to be collected by the Sweeper. They also clear up the baby's excreta and wash its soiled cloths.

Because she endangers them, the jacha has restricted contact with others. People avoid touching her, and those wearing amulets believe that entering the jacha's house would destroy their efficacy. Fear of childbirth pollution makes the jacha temporarily untouchable, even to the Harijans. Food cooked by a jacha is also considered dangerous, more so for a man than for his children, and a jacha is absolved from cooking. Sexual intercourse with a jacha would also affect a man's health, though informants were unspecific about the symptoms that would ensue. Another woman usually sleeps with the jacha to prevent the husband approaching, though rarely for the specified number of weeks.

Vulnerability and Danger

Many features of menstruation, pregnancy, and delivery are understood in terms of humoral contrasts, especially *garm-thand* ("hot-cold"). A profuse flow of blood after birth is necessary for cleansing, but blood is garm and the blood loss that upsets proper balance makes the woman vulnerable. Thand could lodge in her tubes, expressed as shivering fever with diarrhea.

Since mustard oil is garm, women consider an oil massage beneficial, but this rarely occurs and few dais report massaging the baby before bathing it. Dais complain that their clients are too miserly to pay the extra for such services. The jacha and baby are bathed in warm water, however, often with mustard oil added. Water is poured over the woman, she is rubbed vigorously, and hot compresses are applied to her shoulder and knee joints (the particular sites where thand penetrates). Nowadays, few Muslim jachas are bathed daily, as there is no resident dai, and women do not bathe for several days unless they are helped to do so by their mother-in-law. The jacha's diet is also carefully regulated to ensure that she does not succumb to thand.

Other people can pose a threat to the jacha and baby, who are both vulnerable to *asar* (spirits) and *nazar* (evil eye). The safety of mother and child is ensured by keeping them inside the house for several days, and within the domestic compound for perhaps several weeks. Evil influences are reduced by the careful regulation of visitors, especially menstruating women whose shadows endanger the newborn. Some Hindu households place an earthenware tub containing a small fire outside the door and tie a sprig of *neem* (margosa) leaves above the lintel. Those entering pause to let the fire drive evil influences away. Muslims are no more welcoming to guests. At most, people make very circumspect comments about the jacha and baby to avoid activating the envy of the evil eye. Evil spirits are frightened by an iron sickle on the floor at the bedhead, or by a lamp burning through the night.

The placenta is also a potent source of danger to the newborn baby. In the Muslim village, all placentas are interred in the household midden pit on the village outskirts, for a placenta is "not a thing to be buried inside." It must be hidden so it cannot be unearthed by a barren woman who, wishing to conceive, uses it for her own magic, but harms the baby in the process. Among Hindus, practice is more varied. Caste Hindus generally ask the dai to bury placentas inside the house. A small pit is dug in the floor, the placenta is buried, and a fire is lit on top to ward off evil. In some cases a boy's placenta is said to be buried by the mother's bedhead, while a girl's is buried by the foot (as befits the children's relative status). Others say that boys' placentas are buried inside and girls' outside, since magic is unlikely to be practiced on them. Following the Caste Hindu key informants' last deliveries, only two placentas were buried in the midden, both those of girls with elder siblings. The dai follows her clients' practice when dealing with placentas.

Thus, although a new baby's arrival may be a matter for celebration, local understandings are reflected in the pejorative terms used for the birth process. The belief that the jacha is a danger to herself and to others, the belief that she is in a state of vulnerability, and the view of childbirth as shameful all affect other aspects of the birth experience.

Attending Birth and Managing Labor

The social construction of birthing practices is further accentuated by considerations of shame and pollution that influence the selection of the laboring woman's attendants and determine those who must not attend her during delivery.

Childbirth is unsuitable for male involvement. Male healers are rarely consulted during pregnancy and are very unlikely to play any part in the delivery unless some crisis occurs. Male involvement demeans the man and shames the woman. When a Hindu woman recently allowed the male health center pharmacist to deliver her child by forceps, Muslim husbands said that their wives would not be allowed such treatment even if they were near death: "*Purdah* must not be broken." Further, the normal distancing between a woman and her male marital kin is exaggerated when she is in labor. If the husband needs to fetch something in the room he does it quickly, averting his gaze and remaining aloof. The laboring woman's other male marital kin remain outside. Indeed, if the woman is in labor during the day, the menfolk working in the fields may be unaware of her situation.

Moreover, a woman's male and female natal kin should not have direct involvement in her pregnancy and delivery. Childbearing is "a matter for the in-laws." A woman should not visit her parents or brothers while obviously pregnant, since this would present them with evidence of her sexual activity. It is even more shameful for them to attend the birth, and it would be unthinkable for the woman to call her father or brothers to her side. Considerations of shame also exclude female natal kin, especially her mother and sister. Unlikely to be called from another village, they too may not know that their daughter or sister is in labor.

Unmarried girls who should not learn about shameful matters before marriage are also excluded, and barren women may be kept away for fear of mishap, although there is no consensus on this. The delivery is thus attended by married women from among the laboring woman's close marital kin and from neighboring households. While the mother-in-law is alive she is central; otherwise her position may be taken by the laboring woman's sister-in-law (husband's brother's wife) or her husband's aunt (husband's father's brother's wife). An older woman may sometimes be assisted by her daughter-in-law or married daughter. More distantly related women come and go, the largest crowd being present for the birth itself. Several others stay throughout the birth process, taking turns to support or simply to watch. A laboring woman is rarely alone.

The social management of childbirth in Bijnor becomes readily apparent during a slow labor. The senior attendant may examine the laboring woman's belly to assess the baby's presentation and ascertain that it is still moving and to check the strength of the pains. She may also try to hasten delivery by using domestic remedies drawn from a repertoire known to most adult women. The attending women may suggest various measures, citing past cases where they seemed beneficial. The laboring woman, however, plays little part in this discussion. She may refuse a chosen treatment, but management of the labor is not in her hands.

The woman's mother-in-law (or other senior attendant) usually calls the dai when she considers the labor well established. In Bijnor there is often only one accessible dai, but if there is a choice, the decision rests with the senior attendant rather than with the laboring woman. In villages without a resident dai, women must rely on men to fetch a dai from beyond the village. Within the village, a woman will fetch her. In the Hindu village most women rely on a Muslim *Julaha* (weaver) widow from a neighboring village, who recently replaced a Hindu *Chamar* (leatherworker) dai when she died. A Chamar widow in the Hindu village also attends a few births under duress, although she resists being defined as a dai. In the Muslim village, women call on two Muslim *Qasai* (butcher) dais from another village, both with government training. They serve a cluster of villages and complain that they are being undercut by untrained dais.

After the dai's arrival, the senior attendant remains central in the conduct of the delivery and in decisions about whether labor should be accelerated, what the laboring woman's position should be, and so on. Certainly the dai voices her opinion, but her suggestions are not always heeded and she does her work under the watchful (and sometimes critical) eye of the other women. Even after the birth, the senior attendant reserves the bulk of decision making for herself and expects the dai to carry out tasks under her direction. She provides the thread for tying the cord, but the dai ties it. She decides what the cord should be cut with, even rejecting the dai's suggestions on occasion, but leaves the dai to do the job; she then instructs the dai about burying the placenta.

It is thus inappropriate to regard the dai as a "midwife" in the contemporary Western sense. Even in the absence of medically trained personnel, the dai does not have overriding control of the management of deliveries. Furthermore, the laboring woman herself rarely plays an active part, but merely responds to the instructions of her senior attendant and the dai.

Location of Labor and Delivery

Hospital deliveries are very rare and generally occur only when the life of the laboring woman and her baby seem to be threatened. The majority of deliveries are home births. This needs to be specified more clearly, however.

Young married women in effect lead double lives: as controlled daughters-in-law subject to surveillance in their marital villages, and as carefree daughters cherished in their natal villages. It can be said that the mother-in-law (*sas*) is a legendary ogre and the word *susri* (a de-based form of sas) is a term of abuse. Nevertheless, young married women were appalled at our suggestion that they might find it congenial to give birth with their mother in attendance; shame outweighs any benefits. At the time of delivery, a woman should be in her "own" (i.e., her husband's) house, her natal kin excluded from the birth and from subsequent celebrations. Their role is to provide food and gifts for the jacha and her marital kin.

This restriction of women to their husband's house during childbirth is unusually rigid. In Punjab to the west, Madyha Pradesh to the south, and in eastern parts of Uttar Pradesh, it is common for at least the first birth to take place in the woman's natal village, although negotiating a later delivery away from the husband's house may also be difficult (Brown et al. 1981, Gideon 1962, Jacobson 1980:80, Karve 1968:403, Luschinsky 1962:94, Thompson 1984:268–269). But in Bijnor, even those few married women living in their natal village (with the wife's kin or as within-village marriages) give birth in their marital home. Muslim women in within-village marriages are attended by their female marital kin, not mothers or sisters, except in cases of obstructed delivery or where the woman is isolated from her marital kin.

Labor and Delivery Positions

Women's labors are not merely monitored but managed. One means of doing this is to alter the laboring woman's position. Some dais said the woman herself decides what is the most comfortable position, but others often intervene and suggest that the woman adopt a prone or upright position. One dai said:

> Some women crouch on bricks as that makes them stronger and the baby can be born faster. Other women stay on the bed and I hold their legs and push their heels against their buttocks. That way the woman gets strength and the mouth of the uterus opens quickly. (Dai #4)

Other dais said the force of contractions could be increased by pressing down on the woman's belly, or by raising the woman's head so that the baby's head presses more firmly against the cervix. The woman's legs may be lifted onto a pair of bricks, or she may walk around for a while inside her house.[8] Several dais believe delivery is hastened if they help the woman squat beside the bed, her feet placed slightly apart on a pair of bricks; in this position the woman gains the strength to push and the baby shifts forward from the lower gut where it is believed to be in danger of becoming wedged. Despite these descriptions of the many possible positions to be adopted, two-thirds of the key informants lay down under a quilt during their last deliveries. Most had been in that position throughout labor, though a few had squatted on bricks for a brief time.

After reading the literature on childbirth, we did not expect to find that most women deliver lying on their backs. For example, Jordan (1987:314) writes that "traditionally, women in developing countries go through labour and give birth in upright or semi-upright positions, such as sitting, squatting, half-reclining, kneeling or standing, and often adopt several of them in sequence." Similar generalizations are provided by others (Newton and Newton 1972:165–167, Ford 1945:58, Mac-Cormack 1982:14, Blanchet 1984:87), although in Punjab "care was taken that the patient was flat on her back, knees drawn up, and the belief prevailed that shifting of position led to trouble" (Gordon, Gideon, and Wyon 1965:737). Several of our informants said that squatting during delivery exposes the woman and encourages defecation. Nevertheless, a third of the key informants did squat on bricks and felt the delivery had been speeded by this method.

Other Interventions in Labor and Delivery

In local understanding, menstrual blood accumulated during pregnancy causes a build-up of such "heat" (*garmi*) that uterine contractions are triggered and the mouth of the uterus opens. Anxious that the process should not be too protracted, the attending women use various means to assess progress. They discuss the intensity of pains and compare the duration of labor with the woman's earlier deliveries. Women describe very varied experiences, from sporadic light pains or severe pains for several days to precipitate deliveries after only a few hours. When severe pains begin, the woman lies on the bed designated for delivery, her head slightly raised on a pillow, her knees bent and her heels pressed against the sides of the bed. During pains, an attending woman squats behind her on the bedhead supporting her shoulders, while another may squat at the foot, keeping her bent legs upright.

The dai squats on the foot of the bed. She has no instruments, nor does she shave the woman's pubic hair, perform an enema, or wash herself or the laboring woman, for cleansing (*safai*) occurs after birth, not before.[9] The dai touches the woman's genitals and inserts a hand inside her body—shameful and defiling work—which other women would be appalled to do. (Women often use the words *chut* and *ghosri* (vulva) as terms of verbal abuse). The dai keeps the laboring woman concealed under the quilt and uses her left, inauspicious hand[10] for an internal examination to assess cervical dilation, to check that the baby's head is engaging properly, and to see if a dry vagina might impede the baby's transit. The dai's information contributes to the general discussion about the progress of labor. If there are severe pains without cervical dilation, or dilation with the easing of pains, a range of domestic or "country" remedies (*ghar-ka-ilaj, desi ilaj*) may accelerate labor, or in local terms "amplify the pains" (*dard barhana*).

Some Hindu families call a *pandit* to say prayers, and some Muslims send money to the mosque or ask that the *Qu'ran Sharif* be recited over lumps of *gur* (unrefined sugar), which the laboring woman then eats. None of our key informants has done this, but several had had amulets retied during labor. Others reported that a metal sieve containing grain and a small amount of money (1.25 rupees = $.09 U.S.) was circled around their head, and then placed under the bedhead to absorb the inauspiciousness thought to be slowing labor.[11] Balls of gur may also be circled around the woman's head and placed under the bedhead. A small sickle under the bedhead is considered beneficial as well. To encourage her cervix to release the baby, a woman's plaited hair may be undone, for loose hair is a potent symbol of sexual "heat" associated with the opening of the cervix during intercourse. Lids may be lifted from earthen cooking tubs, and the grain store or trunks may be unpadlocked, especially if the woman had placed something inside them while pregnant.[12]

If pains become less rapid and intense, women say they have become "cold" (thanda). To avert this, the woman is warmly wrapped in an old quilt (which also provides concealment). No heavily pregnant woman should be present in case she "cools" the pains by drawing them to herself. If such precautions fail, steps are taken to "heat" the pains again. Occasionally, the dai is asked to insert a vaginal pessary to stimulate pains, dilate the cervix, and make the birth easier by moistening the vagina. More commonly the woman is given "hot" foods. In wealthy households, the attending women prepare warm milk with almonds, hot milky tea, or (less often) hot milk with clarified butter, eggs broken into hot milk, dried grapes, or gruel made from a "hot" ingredient. Generally, however, sweetened hot water or hot water with ginger and *ajwain* (medicinal seeds) are used to reactivate pains.

During one-third of the key informants' last deliveries, no domestic remedies were used because labor was satisfactory, because the baby was born before any remedy was given, or because no suitable ingredients were available. One-fifth had nothing to eat, but squatted to encourage delivery, and the remainder used a combination of techniques, including an injection of oxytocin. Male medical personnel called in for this task usually performed no examination beforehand.[13]

There are no remedies for reducing the discomfort of labor. Intense pains are thought necessary to ensure a speedy delivery, and women are considered shameless if they make noises audible to people outside. Since pain is inevitable, they should merely "call on God's name." The laboring woman's silence is considered very important in other parts of South Asia as well; crying out draws attention to her shame (Gideon 1962:224, Luschinsky 1962:94, McGilvray 1982:57–58, Thompson 1984: 273–274).

This account suggests that women obtain little emotional or social support during labor and delivery. As they are in a polluting state, few other women will touch them. The company of mothers and sisters is expressly excluded. Childbearing thus generates little solidarity among women. As C. S. Thompson (1984:308) argues for central India:

> The rituals surrounding birth make female physical sexuality seem low status and degrading. Birth isolates women from one another, from their own caste mates and it is not seen as a source of prestige or power.

We do not wish to exaggerate this picture, but we would suggest that laboring women in Bijnor appear to have less social and emotional support than indicated in most of the other anthropological accounts we have read.

Midwives or Menials?

Childbearing is a necessary part of a woman's marital career, but it is profoundly polluting, and women regard their bodily functions with distaste. Women are capable of doing the dai's work, but are inhibited by its demeaning nature. Nevertheless, someone must cut the cord and remove the placenta. While all women who give birth are subject to defilement, only a few are obliged to earn their keep by doing defiling work for other people. This is reflected in the dais' accounts of their own work.

Financial independence is a problematic condition for a woman in north India: women should be dependent on their menfolk. In Bijnor only a very poor woman with no male support, or one who depends on a man whose earnings cannot fully keep his family, seeks employment. The few job opportunities for rural women, such as agricultural labor, domestic work for rich peasants, or craft-work, are low in status and poorly paid. Some women, therefore, become self-employed dais, unattached to the government health services. Almost all village dais in Bijnor say they began work out of economic necessity.

> How can I think this work is good or bad? I work hard and I do no wrong. But if it was bad, what could I do? I do it because I have to. (Dai #8)

Most village dais are landless Harijans or Muslims. Some are childless, but most have grown sons who could not or would not support them. Generally, widowhood or the husband's incapacity has led them to work to "fill the stomach."

> I used to go out very little and I never liked to take food and water in other people's houses. I used to be very careful about cleanliness. But then my husband died—so, I became a dai. (Dai #3)

> I must think well of work which gives me bread to eat. But I work as a dai out of necessity. Would I do this work or would my sons be laborers if we owned land? (Dai #17)

The dais thus present their work as undesirable. They see themselves as unwilling recruits, dragged to their first delivery when another dai was unavailable, not seeking out clients, but going "just where I am called." The work is more despised than most other occupations available to them:

> When I became a dai my sons thought very badly of it. But I replied that without work, how could I eat—unless they provided my food and clothes? At that they became silent. But one son-in-law is still angry that I do this work. Since I started it he has never visited me. (Dai #14)

Most dais, indeed, report objections from their kin: two said that their own relatives had refused to eat food they cooked since they became dais.

Dais who were widowed young may practice for many years, but many become dais relatively late in life. This reflects in part the age at which women are likely to lose male support. Further, the mobility of women in childbearing years is restricted by considerations of propriety and because domestic obligations in their marital home bind them in ways that are incompatible with providing obstetric services. Moreover, pregnant women should not attend deliveries, and menstruating women endanger the newborn. Thus, postmenopausal women are the most likely candidates. Consequently, village women do not expect or achieve long-standing relationships with individual dais, but call on a succession during their childbearing years as dais become senile or die. The dai's weak financial condition compels her to seek the work that erases the respect otherwise due to her age.

Few dais are literate or have any formal midwifery training. Some Bijnor dais do come from families in which being a dai is part of a family tradition. Just under half reported learning to deliver babies by accompanying a relative (usually the mother or mother-in-law). The others, however, had simply watched a few deliveries. Village dais are thus not viewed as having esoteric knowledge or specialized techniques. Their distinctiveness rests on willingness to accept payment for the unpalatable work of cutting cords.

The dai's main tasks occur during delivery. She has little involvement in prenatal or postnatal care. Nor is she likely to administer remedies for abortions or infertility. Most reported attending births only in their own village, though a few had worked in neighboring villages. Muslim and Caste Hindu dais often claimed not to attend Harijan deliveries because the defilement was too great. Some non-Muslim dais denied attending Muslim births. Caseloads were generally between twenty and forty births a year, though some dais reported as few as ten, and a few over sixty. Such restricted clientele limits their experience and keeps income low—15–30 rupees ($1.13–2.25 U.S.), plus some grain and sometimes cloth at each delivery. Several dais had additional sources of income, such as weaving cloth, basket making, laboring on cane crushers, or working as Sweepers removing night soil, taking on tasks too defiling for their caste superiors.

Historical sources rarely describe dais or give details about women's experiences of childbearing.[14] Thus, we can only speculate about how dais' skills and status might have changed in the wake of the major changes in agricultural life since the mid-1960s. It is possible that restricted employment opportunities have persuaded more women from families without traditions of dai practice to take up this work. Further, as urban facilities have expanded, the prenatal, abortion, and infertility work of dais may have declined. Yet elderly women (including dais) generally deny any reduction or enhancement in the skills of village dais. Some urban dais have reputations as wisewomen healers, but whatever they may have done in the past, women healers are not now birth attendants. The average woman in rural Bijnor is attended in childbirth by a dai such as we have described.

Most dais, then, are regarded as low status menials, necessary for removing defilement, with no special delivery techniques. Their lowly status is reflected in several ways. Most Hindu dais are Harijans who perform other defiling-work, and their presence is generally anathema to Caste Hindus (and many Muslims too). Muslim and Hindu women rarely mix socially and, because of their dietary practices, many Caste Hindus regard Muslims as little better than outcastes. Thus, in relation to most of her clients, a Harijan or Muslim dai starts with grave social disadvantages. Moreover, by virtue of performing her work, a Harijan dai may become polluted even in the eyes of her own relatives, a double stigma that is reflected in her clients' behavior. Many people admit a dai to their home only for the delivery and for subsequent cleansing work.

Once the jacha has a purifying bath, physical contact between her and the dai ceases (unless they are related). However, some Muslim dais are less despised in the eyes of their Muslim clients. The dai formerly in the Muslim village, for instance, was said to remain with a newly delivered woman performing everyday work for up to a week—even cooking for the household. Similarly, dais who now serve the Muslim village visit freely, although their attempts to find out if women are pregnant are often resented.

After the birth, the payment to the dai further underlines her inferiority. She is expected to accept the cash given to remove inauspiciousness, but risks acquiring the bad luck herself. During the following days, she is paid in installments for cutting the cord, burying the placenta, and bathing the jacha, payments specifically for the removal of defilement. She is not paid for advice, and she receives nothing if the baby is stillborn. Among Hindus a stillborn baby's cord is not cut; Muslims expect the dai to cut the cord of a stillborn baby, but they do not pay her. If the dai withdraws from the case before the birth, she is not paid. Few dais receive customary payments from their clients—after harvests or at marriage, for example—and their low level of income further weakens their bargaining position. Dais report acrimonious negotiations over pay, and after each delivery Patricia attended, the dai was abused and sworn at for claiming "unreasonable" fees. Several dais reported the promise of payments which were never fulfilled. The dai, then, is not a respected professional who can propose a standard fee for service or enforce claims.[15]

Safety and Risks

Since childbirth is socially defined as undesirable, it is not surprising that women who become dais do not claim competence to deal with complicated cases. Dais have no obstetric equipment (apart from the scissors to cut the cord), though they do examine the woman manually, both internally and externally. They fully understand the importance of recognizing complications and try to assess if the baby is correctly positioned—inverted or obstructed. Several dais said they could turn a baby even during labor. Others said this was impossible, although they might try to deliver a footling but not a breech presentation. Dais also recognize the danger of waning contractions and cessation of movement by the baby (in their terms, the woman's belly becoming thanda). But they have no stethoscopes and no means of detecting fetal distress other than by feeling the woman's belly. Equally, dais themselves said they could not remedy such problems as hemorrhage or failure of cervical dilation, nor could they arrest premature labors, induce labor in an over-long pregnancy, or cope with prolapsed cords and placenta previa.

Altogether, dais have very modest perceptions of their capabilities, as do their clients. Dais said that they only like to deal with normal presentations; their clients describe them as cord-cutters (nal-katne-wali). If dais perceive a problem, they are likely to withdraw from the case; for this reason, they claim to have few mishaps.

Of course, this is not to criticize individual dais for being unsupportive. They appreciate that their reputation (and livelihood) is imperiled by maternal or fetal deaths. For the vast majority of normal deliveries, the village dais suffice. However, the forceful way problem deliveries are handled exposes the limitations of obstetric care available to rural woman.

> There used to be no treatment for a woman having trouble during delivery. She might be in labor for eight or ten days without being given anything. Often the woman's lips would go blue with clutching the bed so tightly. There are country medicines, but there is no *hakim* in this village. Everyone just lived by God's grace. (Dai #20)

In the old days, people said, the outcome depended on God's will. Since about 1960, however, Western medicine has become increasingly accessible through government health services and independent (often untrained) private practitioners. Nowadays, the dai may call in a medical practitioner or recommend that the laboring woman go to the hospital. But this does not necessarily improve the conditions of childbirth. The practitioners' main technique, an injection of oxytocin given in standard units without a preliminary examination, causes rapid, painful contractions and a high risk of afterpains, and, when the woman is not ready to deliver, is a threat to the life of mother and child.

Conclusion

Several aspects of our account of the dai in north India depart significantly from the generalizations that have become commonplace in the
literature on midwifery and childbearing in non-Western contexts. These
stereotypes, which have been part of a critique of alienating, medicalized
birthing practices in the West, tend to divert attention away from variations that exist in non-Western birthing practices. We began this chapter
by arguing that the social meanings of childbirth and its management must
be understood in terms of women's position in relation to property ownership and their position as workers and childbearers in specific social and
economic contexts. In the space available, we chose to focus on the childbirth event itself and on the role of traditional birth attendants as exem-
plars of how wider social and economic considerations relate to the social
organization of childbearing.

Our account is relevant for those planning to use trained traditional
birth attendants in the provision of primary health care. Portraits of the
dai in north India similar to our account can be gleaned from several
contemporary sources, especially from evaluations of the dai training
programs initiated recently by the government of India (Gandhi and
Sapru 1980, Ghosal, Hiramani, Gupta, et al. n.d., Ghosal, Hiramani,
Srivastava, et al. n.d.). The conditions of childbearing that we have
sketched prevail throughout much of north India and the neighboring
regions and affect millions of women. Moreover, the problems of maternal and child health appear to be more widespread. India, with one-fifth
of the world's population, accounts for almost half of the world's maternal deaths each year, with a disproportionate number occurring in the
northern plains. In Uttar Pradesh alone, between fifty and one hundred
women die in childbirth or from related causes each day, and about eight
hundred of the ten thousand or so children born each day will not
survive to the end of their first week.[16] It is in this context that the vogue
for training traditional birth attendants has taken hold.

Our research, however, leads us to question the efficacy of dai training programs in north India. Most dais are elderly and any benefits from
training them will be short-lived. Moreover, their social standing is such
that they are not plausible channels for the dissemination of general
health information; several of the trained dais we knew found they could
not incorporate their training into their obstetric practice. Indeed, this
has been a recurrent feature of dai training programs in India since the
nineteenth century (Jeffery et al. 1985). More fundamentally, however,
we would argue that the focus on the dai represents a maldiagnosis of
the problems to be remedied. Certainly, there are obstetric crises that
the village dai cannot handle, but the main sources of maternal and child

health problems are not located there but in the lack of economic and social leverage that childbearing women have over their lives. The lowly dai is just another symptom of these wider realities so poignantly reflected in mortality statistics. Consequently, we consider that dai training programs are not the envisioned panacea for providing maternal and child health services in non-Western settings.

We can well understand why the more positive views of midwifery in non-Western societies have become so widely accepted. They are a refreshing departure from earlier ethnocentric accounts that devalued women's knowledge and expertise. They also provide an attractive (if flawed) foil for debates about Western obstetric practice. Nevertheless, a challenge to this new orthodoxy is timely. By linking variations in childbirth practices, social status, and the differential contributions of women to production and reproduction, we hope to contribute to a better understanding of the bases of these variations.

Acknowledgments

We are grateful to the Economic and Social Research Council (U.K.) and the University of Edinburgh for funding the research on which this chapter is based. Our thanks also go to numerous colleagues who have commented on drafts of this chapter.

Notes

1. McClain also distinguishes those anthropologists who treat midwifery and childbirth as part of a cultural, holistic analysis, and who explore issues of symbolic relationships (particularly in interpreting ritual observances) from those who either stress the sociocultural definitions of childbearing in order to make health workers more sensitive to the values of their clients, or who stress the biomedical risks attached to various "traditional" childbearing practices (McClain 1982:46–50).

2. We can do little but speculate about conditions at the other end of the spectrum. Browner and Perdue (1988) provide a cautionary note: in a relatively egalitarian society they found no separate sphere of women's knowledge with respect to pregnancy and childbirth.

3. More details of this research can be found in Jeffery et al. 1989.

4. For some British accounts see J. E. Mistry 1936; National Archives of India 1872, 1887; J. Robertson 1846. See also Jeffery et al. 1985.

5. The word dai can also mean a wet nurse, and some Muslim dais claim that they are due the same respect the Prophet Muhammad showed his wet nurse.

6. A summary statement of patterns of attendance at childbirth for the different Indian states can be found in Registrar-General of India 1983.

7. General overviews of the position of women in north India can be found in Agarwal 1988; Dyson and Moore 1983; Karve 1968; Mandelbaum 1988; see also Sharma 1980.

8. The foot of the bed is sometimes raised to prevent a miscarriage.

9. We are not endorsing these practices, but mention them merely to show that the dai's internal examinations are the only interventions different from those of the other women present.

10. The left hand is used for all tasks considered "dirty," such as washing the genital area after defecating or touching the genitals in sexual intercourse; the right hand is kept "clean" for eating, gift-giving, etc.

11. Raheja (1988:72, 82–83) notes how one-and-a-quarter is a quantity frequently used as a means of removing inauspiciousness ("bad luck") and passing it on to others—in this case, the dai.

12. Hershman 1974 provides an extended discussion of these relationships.

13. More information on the use of oxytocin injections can be found in Jeffery et al. 1989, chap. 5.

14. See, for example, the references in note 4 above.

15. For instance, the relative value of sons and daughters is reflected in the lower payments made to the dai when a girl is born—but that is another story.

16. In Uttar Pradesh, the rural population was about 91 million in 1981 and about 93 million in 1982 (Gupta 1982). The crude birth rate in Uttar Pradesh was 40 per 1,000 population in 1982 and the perinatal mortality rate (stillbirths and deaths of children under one week per 1,000 live births and stillbirths) was 80 (Registrar-General of India 1985). On the basis of these figures, we have estimated that there are about 10,200 births each day, 820 of whom will die by the end of their first week. Estimates of maternal mortality in India range from 500 to 1,200 per 100,000 live births (World Health Organization 1986). In Uttar Pradesh, the higher estimates are almost certainly nearer the mark than the lower ones.

References

Agarwal, Bina
     1988   Who Sows? Who Reaps? Women and Land Rights in India. *Journal of Peasant Studies* 15(4):531–581.
Blanchet, Therese
     1984   *Women, Pollution and Marginality: Meanings and Rituals of Birth in Rural Bangladesh.* Dhaka, Bangladesh: Dhaka University Press.
Boserup, Ester
     1970   *Woman's Role in Economic Development.* New York: St. Martin's Press.
Brown, Penelope, Martha Macintyre, Ros Morpeth, and Shirley Prendergast
     1981   A Daughter: A Thing to be Given Away. In *Women in Society,* Cambridge Women's Study Group, pp. 127–145. London: Virago.
Browner, Carole H., and Sondra T. Perdue
     1988   Women's Secrets: Bases for Reproductive and Social Autonomy in a Mexican Community. *American Ethnologist* 15(1):84–97.

Cosminsky, Sheila
1982   Childbirth and Change: A Guatemalan Study. In *Ethnography of Fertility and Birth,* Carol P. MacCormack, ed., pp. 205–229. London: Academic Press.
Dyson, Tim, and Mick Moore
1983   On Kinship Structure, Female Autonomy and Demographic Behaviour in India. *Population and Development Review* 9(1):35–70.
Ford, Clellan S.
1945   *A Comparative Study of Human Reproduction.* New Haven: Human Relations Area Files Press.
Gandhi, H. S., and R. Sapru
1980   *Dais as Partners in Maternal Health.* New Delhi: National Institute for Health and Family Welfare. Mimeographed.
Ghosal B. C., A. B. Hiramani, Y. P. Gupta, U. Srivastava, and S. P. Verma
n.d.   *Dais Training Scheme in Himachal Pradesh—An Evaluation.* New Delhi: Central Health Education Bureau.
Ghosal B. C., A. B. Hiramani, V. P. Srivastava, U. Srivastava, S. P. Verma, and A. Sarkar
n.d.   *Dais Training Scheme in Haryana—An Evaluation.* New Delhi: Central Health Education Bureau.
Gideon, Helen
1962   A Baby Is Born in Punjab. *American Anthropologist* 64:220–234.
Goffman, Erving
1968   *Asylums.* Harmondsworth, England: Penguin.
Goody, Jack
1976   *Production and Reproduction.* Cambridge: Cambridge University Press.
Gordon, John E., Helen Gideon, and John B. Wyon
1965   Midwifery Practices in Rural Punjab, India. *American Journal of Obstetrics and Gynecology* 93:728–737.
Gupta, R.
1982   *Census of India 1981. Series 22 Uttar Pradesh, Paper-1 of 1982: Final Population Totals.* Lucknow: Director of Census Operations, Uttar Pradesh.
Hershman, Paul
1974   Hair, Sex and Dirt. *Man* 9:274–298.
Jacobson, Doranne
1980   Golden Handprints. In *Unspoken Worlds: Women's Religious Lives in Non-Western Cultures.* Nancy A. Falk and Rita M. Gross, eds., pp. 73–93. New York: Harper and Row.
Jeffery, Patricia M., Roger Jeffery, and Andrew Lyon
1985   *Contaminating States and Women's Status.* New Delhi: Indian Social Institute.
Jeffery, Patricia M., Roger Jeffery, and Andrew Lyon
1989   *Labour Pains and Labour Power: Women and Childbearing in India.* London: Zed Books.

Jordan, Brigitte
1983   *Birth in Four Cultures.* 3d ed. Montreal: Eden Press.
Jordan, Brigitte
1987   High Technology: The Case of Obstetrics. *World Health Forum*
         8:314–320.
Karve, Irawati
1968   *Kinship Organisation in India.* 3d ed. Bombay: Asia Publishing
         House.
Laderman, Carol
1983   *Wives and Midwives: Childbirth and Nutrition in Rural Malaysia.*
         Berkeley, Los Angeles, London: University of California Press.
Luschinsky, Mildred S.
1962   The Life of Women in a Village of North India. Ph.D. diss., Cornell
         University.
MacCormack, Carol P.
1982   Biological, Cultural and Social Adaptation in Human Fertility and
         Birth: A Synthesis. In *Ethnography of Fertility and Birth,* Carol P.
         MacCormack, ed., pp. 1–23. London: Academic Press.
Macintyre, Sally
1977   Childbirth: The Myth of the Golden Age. *World Medicine* 15
         (June):17–22.
Maglacas, A. Mangay, and John Simons, eds.
1986   *The Potential of the Traditional Birth Attendant.* Geneva: World
         Health Organization.
Mandelbaum, David G.
1988   *Women's Seclusion and Men's Honor: Sex Roles in North India,
         Bangladesh and Pakistan.* Tucson: University of Arizona Press.
McClain, Carol
1982   Toward a Comparative Framework for the Study of Childbirth: A
         Review of the Literature. In *Anthropology of Human Birth,* Marga-
         rita A. Kay, ed., pp. 25–59. Philadelphia: F. A. Davis.
McGilvray, Dennis B.
1982   Sexual Power and Fertility in Sri Lanka. In *Ethnography of Fertility
         and Birth,* Carol P. MacCormack, ed., pp. 25–73. London: Aca-
         demic Press.
Mead, Margaret and Niles Newton
1967   Cultural Patterning in Perinatal Behaviour. In *Childbearing: Its So-
         cial and Psychological Aspects.* Stephen A. Richardson and Alan F.
         Guttmacher, eds., pp. 142–244. Baltimore: Williams and Wilkins.
Mistry, Jerbanoo E.
1936   My Experience of the Harm Wrought by Indian Dais. Extracted in
         Vera Anstey, *The Economic Development of India,* pp. 489–491. 3d
         ed. London: Longmans Green.
Montagu, Ashley
1949   Early History of Embryology. *Ciba Symposia* 11:4.
National Archives of India
1872   Home, Public 266-67-A.

National Archives of India
  1887   Home, Medical, August 32-A.
Newton, Niles, and Michael Newton
  1972   Child-birth in Cross-cultural Perspective. In *Modern Perspectives in Psycho-Obstetrics,* John G. Howells, ed., pp. 150–172. Edinburgh: Oliver and Boyd.
Oakley, Ann
  1977   Cross-cultural Practices. In *Benefits and Hazards of the New Obstetrics,* Tim Chard and Martin Richards, eds., pp. 18–33. London: Heinemann.
Paul, Lois, and Benjamin Paul
  1975   The Maya Midwife as Sacred Specialist. *American Ethnologist* 2:707–726.
Raheja, Gloria G.
  1988   *The Poison in the Gift.* Chicago: University of Chicago Press.
Registrar-General of India
  1983   *Survey on Infant and Child Mortality 1979.* New Delhi: Office of the Registrar-General of India.
Registrar-General of India
  1985   *Sample Registration System 1982.* New Delhi: Ministry of Home Affairs, Office of Registrar-General of India.
Roberton, John
  1846   On Hindu Midwifery. *Edinburgh Medical and Surgical Journal* 65(167):308–319.
Sharma, Ursula
  1980   *Women Work and Property in North-West India.* London: Tavistock.
Spencer, Robert F.
  1950   Primitive Obstetrics. *Ciba Symposium* 11(3):1158–1188.
Thompson, Catherine S.
  1984   Ritual States in the Life-cycles of Hindu Women in a Village of Central India. Ph.D. diss., University of London.
World Health Organization
  1986   *Maternal Mortality Rates: A Tabulation of Available Information.* 2d ed. Geneva: World Health Organization.

2

Analysis of a Dialogue on Risks in Childbirth

Clinicians, Epidemiologists, and Inuit Women

Patricia A. Kaufert and John O'Neil

This essay deals with the relationships between epidemiological constructs and social experience, between discourse and "empirical realities" (Good 1985), and between the act of research and its context. Like Ronald Frankenberg (writing elsewhere in this volume), we are interested in "the diverse possible meanings and uses of the concepts of risk and of the body in narratives and styles of narrating" (Frankenberg 1988). Hence, our focus is not birth, but people talking about birth and the risk of birth. In her work on women and breast cancer, Sandra Gifford (1986) has shown how risk is a construct which can take on a different content and meaning depending on whether the language being used is epidemiological, clinical, or lay. While making the same distinctions, our concern is also with the ways in which these three languages of risk may be used to affirm or challenge existing relationships of power and control (Harword 1988; Nash and Kirsch 1988) or to express deeply held feelings of vulnerability and responsibility.

Medical anthropology has the curious problem of sharing a research field with other disciplines that claim it as their own. In the area of childbirth and obstetrics, clinical researchers and epidemiologists are the dominant disciplines. For most epidemiologists, risk exists as a statistical construct, a product of analyzing aggregate data in a particular way (Imber 1988). Clinicians abstract the vocabulary of the epidemiologist, the epidemiological language of risk, from its place in scientific discourse and insert it into their own arguments about childbirth. Obstetricians, for example, use a lowering of risk as the justification for new forms of technical or clinical intervention into the birthing process.

Groups such as the Canadian Medical Association (1987) use risk to legitimate their opposition to home births or midwifery. Conversely, those who would challenge medical control also employ the vocabulary of risk. Midwives claim that their less interventionist, less technological mode of delivery reduces risk to both mother and child. Supporters of home birth tell tales of iatrogenesis and attribute risk to hospital birthing practices. Relative to epidemiologists, these other groups add a more political, a more emotionally suffused content to their languages of risk, whether clinical or lay. A form of immorality is imputed to those who demand a home birth or a midwife. Obstetricians are held morally accountable for unsatisfactory birth experiences. Rather than simply a statistical artifact, risk in these other languages becomes an emotional issue, a matter of moral behavior.

An exploration of the three languages of risk (clinical, epidemiological, and lay) will be developed through the analysis of a debate over risk between a physician and a woman from one of the Inuit communities of the Canadian Arctic. Their exchange will be explored as one episode in a longer historical narrative. For questions of risk are central to a discourse that both is a reflection on the realities of childbirth in the North and is itself constitutive of these realities.

We are using the term "language" as "shorthand for not only the words but also [for] concepts, values, symbolic forms" (Harwood 1988:101). We are also separating "language" from "discourse," using the latter term to describe a form of historical conversation about childbirth which has engaged clinicians and nurses, Inuit women, politicians, and midwives for the past twenty years. This conversation, or discourse, has been conducted through conferences and policy discussions, the drafting of administrative regulations, the publication of research papers and government reports, letters, memos, and media interviews, and community meetings. But it has also been expressed through the bodies of pregnant women sent away from their communities to give birth in southern hospitals.

In the process of examining these three languages, we have also become engaged in a reflection on the nature of anthropological knowledge relative to the knowledge claims of the epidemiologist. Epidemiology is based on the assumption that the acquisition of knowledge depends on adherence to certain rules of scientific method. Researchers must show they have kept these rules by describing the provenance of their data, the methods of their collection, and the forms of their analysis. By contrast, most anthropologists prefer a minimalist approach when discussing the methodological underpinnings of their work, and their sense of what constitutes data is eclectic. Anthropologists, however, are deeply disturbed by the ways in which epidemiologists decontextualize their data, objectify their subjects, ignore questions of meaning. The differences between epidemiological and anthropological knowledge becomes delicate when a project is applied (as is this one) and when the anthropologists involved have a political commitment (as in this case) to communicating beyond the boundaries of their own discipline.

We are concerned with the morality of our ends as well as with the legitimacy of our knowledge (Richters 1988). As is the case for other chapters in this volume (by Ronald Frankenberg and by Roberto Briceño-León), this one belongs within the category of "applied" rather than "pure" research. It also represents an "actively political, critical, and committed anthropology" (Scheper-Hughes 1988). For our objective is to assist change by providing a forum for all those engaged in the debate over the evacuation of pregnant women—particularly for those who have been relatively the most powerless and the most unheard, the women of the communities.

Background

The material is taken from a project which looked at the impact of evacuation for childbirth on Inuit women living in the Keewatin, an area of 225,000 square miles along the western coast of the Hudson Bay. A population of approximately 3,950 Inuit live in seven communities, which range in size from just under 200 to 1,100 people and are between 200 and 800 miles north of Churchill, Manitoba. Churchill itself is 600 miles north of Winnipeg, the provincial capital of Manitoba. Between 1970 and 1985 the annual number of births for the area increased steadily, ranging from 126 in 1971 to 168 in 1985.

Each community had a small health center, called a nursing station and staffed by one to four nurses. These stations were administered and maintained by the Medical Services branch of the Federal Department of Health and Welfare until 1988, when control was transferred to the Department of Health of the Northwest Territories.[1] A thirty-bed community hospital served both the town of Churchill and the Keewatin, with serious cases sent to a tertiary care center in Winnipeg. Under a contract with Medical Services, the Northern Medical Unit of the University of Manitoba had been responsible since 1970 for visits by Winnipeg-based specialists (including obstetricians) to Churchill and to the communities. The Northern Medical Unit also provided general practitioners based in either Churchill or Rankin Inlet who made regularly scheduled visits to each community.

Routine antenatal care was provided at the nursing stations with most women being seen by a visiting physician at least once or twice during pregnancy. According to official policy, all births should occur in a hospital. Women were sent to either Churchill or Winnipeg two to three weeks before their expected date of confinement; a few left their communities much earlier. Until the late 1970s, most nursing stations had at least one nurse-midwife on their staff. High-risk women were sent to hospitals in Churchill or Winnipeg, but low-risk women were delivered in the nursing stations. An official change to a policy requiring that all women be evacuated for childbirth occurred in the early 1980s. Some babies were still being delivered in the nursing stations, usually because the birth was premature or because evacuation was being deliberately avoided by women who arrive at the nursing station already in labor.

A woman might refuse to leave, but the pressures on her to agree to hospitalization were more extreme than those faced by women opting for a home birth in a southern Canadian city. At the time of this project in 1986, nurse-midwives were increasingly rare in the Keewatin. The nurses staffing the nursing station were often young, frequently without extensive experience or training in obstetrics, and usually unwilling to provide anything other than emergency obstetric care. Traditional Inuit midwives still lived in the communities, but they were old and had not assisted at a birth for many years. Aside from having to face birth without an experienced midwife, a woman who refused evacuation risked acquiring a reputation as noncompliant and irresponsible. This consequence was not trivial. Refusing to give birth in the nursing station meant challenging a relatively powerful institution and the sole source of health care for a woman and her family.

Having little other choice, Inuit women have been generally compliant, although also complainants. References to women's objections to evacuation are scattered throughout official reports and research papers dealing with obstetric policy in the North during the 1970s and early 1980s. While the problems that evacuation for childbirth caused women were often sympathetically acknowledged (loneliness, fear, worries about their families), official policy became increasingly committed to hospital as the only safe place of birth. The number of women allowed to birth in the community nursing station dwindled steadily throughout the late 1970s and into the early 1980s.

During the period when low risk women were still allowed to deliver in the community nursing station, negotiation over whether someone should be sent south for childbirth occurred in conversation between a particular woman and a particular health professional. Risk was individualized and decisions were contained within the clinical setting. Once policy changed in the late 1980s to one in which all women were to be hospitalized for childbirth, the issue of evacuation moved from the private arena of the nursing station into the public forum of the community meeting. Criticisms intensified partly because of this change in policy, but also because of political developments in northern communities. Evacuation policy was becoming more rigid at the same time as local pressure for an expanded role in health policy and decision making was increasing.

The Northern Medical Unit responded to the increasingly vocal criticisms of evacuation policy by putting together a team of investigators. This team included representatives from the University of Manitoba (clinicians, an anthropologist, and a sociologist), health administrators from Medical Services, and Inuit representatives. The anthropologist, John O'Neil, worked with local health committees and village councils to arrange a series of public meetings. These were held in each of the communities in 1986 and were attended by other team members. The purpose of these meetings was to explore the problems of evacuation as seen by people living in the Keewatin. For the same reason, a number of interviews were completed with Inuit women and with a small group of health professionals and administrators (two obstetricians, two general practitioners, three health bureaucrats, and three nurses). Finally, a search was made for archive materials and reports.

The materials collected during this year formed the basis for a research proposal that was submitted to Health and Welfare, Canada and funded in 1987. The design for this project combined traditional ethnographic methods with those of the epidemiologist. Questions about risk in childbirth (its existence, its causes, how it should be managed) were at the center of the debate over evacuation and also became the center of this research. Directly or indirectly, much of the work of the project was committed to the measurement, calculation, and general evaluation of all forms of risk associated with evacuation, whether to the mother, the child, her family, or the wider community. This chapter shares in this focus on risk, although we are concerned here not with issues of measurement, but rather with risk as a "concept," a "value," a "symbolic form" (Harwood 1988:101).

This essay is based not on the research project itself but on the interviews and archive materials collected in 1986 as background to the research proposal. At the core of the essay is a piece of dialogue taken from the transcript of one of the community meetings in which a woman and a physician debated the issue of risk in childbirth. At one level, the meaning of what they said was immediately accessible. At another, their dialogue can be understood only within the wider context of the meetings themselves. These meetings, however, were simply an episode within a longer historical discourse about childbirth. Our discussion starts, therefore, from a review of this discourse, proceeds to a description of the meetings, and arrives finally at an analysis of the dialogue and of the three languages of risk.

The Discourse on Childbirth

In a discussion which deals also with childbirth and obstetrics, Good (1985:249) argues that "particular human realities are uniquely constituted as a discourse and through discursive interactions, even as they articulate with structural features and empirical realities outside of language." The "structural features and empirical realities outside of language" which "articulate" with the discourse on childbirth in the Keewatin include the Arctic climate, the vast distances, the problems of travel, the small, scattered communities. Transportation of patients, physicians, nurses, and all products generated by the daily practice of Western medicine (blood and urine samples, drugs and vaccines, medical records and test results) is by plane. Flights are few and expensive. The weather may close off communities for days at a time.

In terms of the historical development of the discourse on childbirth, the ecological reality of the Keewatin is unchanging, but technological developments modify relationships to this environment within the area of medical care. During the 1970s, aircraft and landing strips were upgraded. Planes for emergency medical flights became better equipped and more easily available. The arrival of faster pressurized aircraft made it safer to transport a woman in labor. Sending patients out for tests and consultations or getting physicians into the commmunities was routinized (Kaufert et al. 1987). The consequences for obstetric policy were both direct (pregnant women could be evacuated more easily) and indirect (perceptions of accessibility changed). As it became logistically easier to transport women south for childbirth, it became ideologically more and more difficult for administrators to allow birth to continue in the communities.

The decision in the early 1980s that all women from the Keewatin must be evacuated to southern hospitals was the culmination of a relatively rapid history of medicalizing Inuit childbirth. During the war years and throughout the 1950s and early 1960s, a few births to women from the Keewatin occurred in the military hospital in Churchill or at the Catholic mission hospital in Chesterfield Inlet. As late as 1965, 66 percent of Inuit births occurred outside hospitals or nursing stations (The Annual Report on Health for the Northwest Territories 1966) dropping to 7 percent by 1969. Given the problems of compiling such statistics, the exactness of these figures is questionable, but they do indicate the dramatic speed of government intervention.

Construction of the nursing stations started in 1960 and was completed for each community by 1970. In 1971, a government report commented proudly on this achievement, "The accessibility of the population to medical facilities is now far superior to that of the provinces. The
territorial and federal governments are to be congratulated on this
achievement" (Report on Health in the Northwest Territories, 1971).

This passage contains two themes central in the discourse on childbirth
as constituted by government. The first is the comparison with southern
Canada; the second is the note of self-congratulation. Canada-wide standards and statistics were to become the "gold standard" or bench mark
against which northern statistics were measured. Comparisons of infant
and perinatal mortality rates became particularly important as these rates
were recognized internationally as indicators of community well-being.
The gap between the rates in the north and in southern Canada justified
government intervention in childbirth. The decline in rates then became
the public proof of the virtue of government policy. For these reasons,
the discourse on childbirth has always been as much about politics as
about medical care.

The federal government, acting through Medical Services, seems to
have been willing to invest heavily in the provision of obstetric care.
Each of the annual reports on health in the Northwest Territories
throughout the 1970s opened with a comparison of the year's neonatal
and perinatal mortality rates with those for the previous year and those
for Canada as a whole. Keeping down the mortality rate became a
critical objective. A perinatal mortality review system was set in place as
early as 1971. Research projects in perinatal epidemiology were frequent. Some were published (Baskett 1978; Murdock 1979; Blackshaw
1981) and some not, but each contributed its piece on death and the
prevention of death to the discourse on childbirth.

The collection of vital statistics was a haphazard process in the 1950s
and 1960s. Exact figures will never be known, but the assumption that
perinatal mortality rates were very high is probably correct. Changes in
the migration patterns of the caribou resulted in starvation among many
inland groups. In the Keewatin, people gave up their previously nomadic life and moved into coastal communities. Housing conditions,
sanitation, and nutrition were poor in these new settlements. Levels of
infectious disease (particularly tuberculosis) were high. People became
dependent on government services and vulnerable to government control. The government response to the tuberculosis epidemic, for example, was to send infected individuals south for medical care. This policy
may have saved some lives, but many died in the sanitorium and others
remained permanently lost to their families. The costs to the communities in terms of disruption and demoralization were extremely high.

Memories from the sixties and early seventies thread through the discourse on childbirth. The paternalistic overtones to the official voice are still traceable to a conviction that government "saved" the Inuit from starvation and extinction. Conversely, opposition to evacuation is still emotionally colored by memories of people sent south with TB, never to return.

At the time the nursing stations were being built, Canada was one of the few countries in the world in which midwifery was not legal; nevertheless, midwives became the lynch pin of obstetric policy in the Keewatin throughout the 1970s. Imported from abroad, they provided prenatal care to all women and delivered low-risk women within the community nursing station. Although her reign was brief, the figure of the midwife has mythic status in the folklore of northern health care. It is a myth that is reworked depending on who has invoked it and why. At the meetings we held in 1986, health officials presented the midwife as anomalous within the Canadian health care system, a foreign import, a temporary expedient. She was described as useful in her time, but underskilled in the context of modern obstetric care. We were presented with another version when interviewing health professionals who had worked in the Keewatin during the early 1970s. In their account, the midwife was often an heroic figure, self-reliant, independent, resourceful, possessed of skills that others (particularly the new, young Canadian physicians and nurses) lacked. The following quotation is taken from an interview with a health administrator who had worked for some years in the North:

> When there was no ultrasound technology you relied on your hands and nature and questions and that type of thing, and there was nothing to compare except the total information you got. You took the best guess and tried to manage on that. . . . The younger nurses are probably glad that there is technology, because they themselves do not have a lot of obstetrical experience. For the experienced nurses it is frustrating. They feel that the reasons for coming North and pursuing this type of community health career is being eroded by all the new gadgets and all the new directions the program is taking. There is no thrill anymore for a nurse-midwife.

While often singing a praise song to the passing of the midwife, older health professionals also saw her as extinct.

Women in the communities were more ambivalent in their descriptions of the midwife. She was a positive figure when at the center of the stories women told about their experiences of childbirth in the nursing stations, but midwives were also recalled as the representatives of government, as authority figures. Despite this ambivalence, women complained bitterly about the disappearance of the midwife, seeing her as the key to the returning of birth to the community setting. Many of the statements made by Inuit women in favor of midwives could have been taken directly from a debate over the legalization of midwifery which was taking place simultaneously in southern Canada. The difference was that other Canadian women supported midwifery as a matter of principal. Inuit women were talking from their own memories of birthing in a nursing station attended by a midwife.

Just as the discourse contained different images of the midwife, there were also different images of the nursing stations. The nursing stations were larger and better equipped in 1986 than they had been in the early 1970s. Seen from the perspective of the community, they would seem to have become safer as a place of birth. The same period, seen through the eyes of health professionals, was marked by a progressive widening of the technological gap between southern hospital and northern nursing station. Many of the new techniques in obstetrics adopted in the 1970s and early 1980s were dependent not only on equipment but on an array of support services and the presence of staff trained to operate the new machines. The actual process of inducing labor, for example, was technically possible in the nursing stations, but use was restricted by medical regulation to physicians with six months of obstetrical training, effectively excluding nurse-midwives. Once induction became common practice in the south, birthing without the availability of induction became unacceptable and the nursing station thus became unacceptable as a place of birth.

Most of those professionally involved in northern health care believed that an association between birth in a nursing station and an increased risk of mortality was well established. But as in the debate over home versus hospital births in the United Kingdom, the presumption of a causal linkage is not only nonproven, but unlikely to be ever established (MacFarlane and Mugford 1984). The number of births are too few and the range of variables too many for any form of retrospective analysis. The alternative might be a controlled comparison of the relative risk of nursing station versus hospital birth, but such a study is unlikely as no health professional would accept such a trial as ethical. Belief in the power of technology to preserve life and, conversely, in lack of technology as a cause of death are too strong.

As the example of induction shows, the discourse on childbirth was not created in some northern vacuum, but was responsive to changes in obstetric policies and technologies occurring elsewhere. For example, another characteristic of the new technologies was that they often substituted for existing skills based on training and experience, particularly the skills of the nurse-midwife. Trained in settings dominated by the new technologies, nurses and physicians became doubly unskilled. Unless specializing, they could not use the new machines, but neither did they know how to work without them. If sent to the Keewatin, they not only lacked any sense of being competent to manage birth alone and without the new technologies, but they tended not to trust the competence of others to do so. The pride in her craft of the nurse-midwife was seen as both misplaced and anachronistic. Nursing station births became philosophically unacceptable.

Many of the other issues in this discourse are familiar, recognizable from the epidemiological and obstetric literature, or from the writings of feminists and/or social scientists. Northern health professionals and administrators drew on the same arguments to justify hospitalization for women from the Keewatin as were used to defend hospital birth for all Canadian women by the Canadian Medical Association (1987). Criticisms of hospitalized birth by Inuit women were similar to those made in a report on the future of midwifery (Ontario Task Force on Midwifery 1987). Yet the similarities, while real, were also deceptive, obscuring the extent to which an issue might be qualitatively different or unique to the North. Criticisms of hospitalized birth that separates birth from the context of family and community is common in the writings of Canadian feminists on childbirth (Romalis 1985): when Inuit women talked about separation, they meant leaving their homes for two to three weeks rather than a few days. Accustomed to living in a social space in which almost everyone is known, these Inuit women had to accomplish birth in a place where scarcely anyone was familiar. A sense of alienation in face of technological intervention in the birth process is a common theme in the social science literature, but Inuit women rooted their criticisms in a philosophy of birth as a natural process which was particular to their own traditions. Loss of control by women over the birth process is also central to feminist analyses of power and patriarchy, but loss of control over birth for Inuit women was, in addition, an expression of a wider system of colonial relationships.

The power of the federal government in shaping obstetric care in the Keewatin included the ability to decide on obstetric policy and then enforce compliance with this decision. Resistance did occur. Both nurses and Inuit women told stories of women who evaded evacuation by arriving at the nursing station already in labor. Nurses sometimes plotted with such women, officially planning an evacuation, but preparing for a birth at the nursing station. While these are acts of individual political resistance, the incidents were too isolated and unorganized to count as rebellion (Martin 1987). Nevertheless, they were part of a tradition of opposition which is as much part of the discourse on childbirth as research papers and government reports. The meetings were an opportunity, however, for expressing political dissent in a public forum. Part of the discourse on childbirth, these meetings also signaled the reconstruction of this discourse, including giving a stronger public voice to the community than in the past.

The Meetings: Knowledge and Methodology

The title of this chapter with its reference to a "dialogue" literally describes what happened at the meetings that John O'Neil organized in 1986. The health professionals on the team (physicians, nurses, administrators) explained and defended current obstetric policy. Inuit participants presented their own views on childbirth and the problems of evacuation. Giving a piece of dialogue from one of these meetings ontological status as research data marks the difference between epidemiological and anthropological forms of acquiring knowledge. Doing interviews and searching archives for written materials is standard research practice—even among epidemiologists. The use of public meetings as a source of research data is not. Yet, seen from the viewpoint of one anthropologist, public meetings—such as these in the Keewatin—constitute the "ideal stuff of social research" (Frankenberg 1984). Frankenberg argues that meetings offer a unique opportunity to observe as the "opaqueness of social connections becomes transparent" (Frankenberg 1984). On these particular occasions the connections between risk, language, and discourse became "transparent."

As a source of data, these meetings break most of the methodological rules governing epidemiological research. Compared to the products of the standard survey with its questionnaires and measures pretested for validity and reliability, the transcripts lack structure. Participants in the meetings were not representative (in any statistical sense) of either their community or their professional group. Control over who would attend the meetings, who would speak, what questions they would ask, or the content of what they would say, was loose or totally absent. One or two women who spoke were not even Inuit, although they had lived in a community for many years and had married Inuit men. Contributions by women under thirty were rare, although they were the ones most affected by the present policy. Not only did few young women speak, but the meetings were not generally attended by the young physicians and nurses directly responsible for health care in the communities.

These data are not only "soft," "subjective," and "nonrepresentative" (all attributes of opprobrium when applied to data by epidemiologists), they deal with a topic that was highly controversial, highly political, and deeply emotional. During the period of this research project, obstetric policy in the Keewatin attracted the attention of the local and national media and a television program critical of evacuation was widely shown in the Keewatin. A number of the people attending these meetings were to appear in this program, speaking for one position or another. Most importantly, the meetings were held in the middle of a gradual process of transferring medical services from the control of the Canadian Federal Government to the control of the Northwest Territorial Government. It was a period when all health issues (including evacuation for childbirth) were highly politicized. Furthermore, many of the people at the meetings had stakes of one sort or another in this transfer and in the issues of local control and decision making which were involved.

Rather than being the objects of research (as in epidemiological survey), those in attendance (women as well as physicians and researchers) were engaged as actors in a drama, using the gatherings to lobby, to challenge, to answer back. Many were actively engaged in the debate over evacuation, whether in the formulation or implementation of current policy, or as its critics. No one was truly neutral, including other members in the visiting research team as well as ourselves. People were both partisan and passionate. Whether Inuit woman or non-Inuit health professional, they were emotionally engaged by the issue of childbirth and the question of where it might safely take place, southern hospital or community nursing station.

The languages in which people spoke about risk (whether clinical, epidemiological, or lay) reflected who was speaking, to whom they were speaking, and the historical and political context of what they were saying. Who had the right to define which risks were important was discussed in terms of the relationships (political, social, and economic) within and between collectivities (health professionals, Inuit communities, government agencies). Unspoken, yet assumed between speakers and listeners, was a common and wider awareness of the North, its environment, its political and social present, and its histories.

Observing what happened at the meetings and listening to what was being said provided insight into the place of risk in the debate over childbirth which was not available from an analysis of epidemiological data. The larger research project (now complete) included the collection of the standard data of perinatal epidemiology. Information has been abstracted from the medical records of all the women who gave birth from 1979 to 1985, allowing us to calculate the risks of prematurity, or low birth, or cesarean section, or perinatal and neonatal mortality rates. While providing measurements of risk as an epidemiological concept, these data can tell nothing of the construction and manipulation of risk as political and moral construct. For insight into this dimension of risk, we had to listen to what people were saying to each other and to us.

The Dialogue on Risk

As illustration, we have chosen an exchange between a physician and a woman at a meeting in Arviat (a community which was still called Eskimo Point in 1986). After listening to complaints about evacuation, the clinicians on the research team countered by talking about mortality rates and the risks of birth in nursing stations. Arguing that she could not recall a single mother or child dying during the previous sixteen years, a woman continued,

> I feel we're being high pressured when you start talking about maternal and infant deaths, because I have not as far as I can recall, experienced or heard of anyone dying in childbirth in Eskimo Point.

Answering her comment, the physician replied that

> In a community like you had here five years ago, with the service you had, it was estimated that the death rate would probably be about twenty per thousand deliveries. . . . What I'm going to point out is that you'd have to have all those thousand deliveries here before you'd have the twenty. So you're looking at one death in five [years], maybe.

Woman: Including births in Churchill and Winnipeg, as well as Eskimo Point.

Physician: Yeah, I'm talking about the Keewatin.

Woman: So it's really hard to isolate.

Physician: So the reason why you didn't have one here in five years is fairly obvious.

Woman: Or sixteen years.

Physician: Or sixteen years.

Woman: That's quite a long time. What we're saying is that we don't think it's quite as risky as you think it is.

Physician: We can give you the risk. The risk is twenty per thousand.

Woman: According to your statistics.

In a later exchange, the physician also talks about maternal death:

Physician: In the twenty-five years seeing on average, or working in hospitals where they deliver somewhere between two thousand and three thousand deliveries a year, I've seen seven mothers die.

Woman: In a period of twenty-five years.

Physician: Yes. But I have seen seven die.

The first passage can be read simply in terms of the difference between lay and professional languages, or between subjective, experientially based knowledge and objective scientifically based knowledge. In the second exchange, however, it is the physician who is talking in terms of subjective experience, his experience as a clinician of seeing seven women die. With the addition of this second exchange, this small piece of dialogue contains all three languages of risk; namely, the epidemiological, the lay, and the clinical.

The physician is following a tradition, well-established in the Keewatin, of counting deaths. He uses rates and number to invoke the language of epidemiology, repeating "twenty per one thousand" as if his numbers are sufficient to end all argument. For this physician, as for most health professionals, mortality rates are objective, the product of scientific fact, indisputable. A physician would not ask the same questions as an epidemiologist or statistician, such as, "Are these 'twenty' deaths occurring only after live birth or are stillbirths included?" "Do they occur within the first eight or twenty-eight days?" "Must a fetus have reached a certain weight or been carried a certain number of days to be counted as a death?" "What are the reliability of the data on which these rates are based?" In epidemiological terms, "twenty per one thousand" has no meaning; it is a pseudorate.

For anthropologists, the rate of "twenty per one thousand" is simply a statistical conceit with meaning only in epidemiological discourse, and only through its relationship to other sets of numbers. David Armstrong (1986) and Peter Wright (1988) argue that all perinatal and neonatal mortality rates are artifacts. Their meaning is ambiguous, contingent on the context in which they are used, changing with a shift in the wording of a definition. Rates are not so much untrue as the "picture of 'reality' which statistics show is out of focus" (Armstrong 1986:230).

The question then becomes, why are these rates being used in this dialogue in this particular fashion? The simplified form of epidemiological language can be seen as an attempt to convey complex information to a lay audience. In this exchange, however, the woman sees it in quite another way. She talks about "being high pressured," about "things not being quite as risky as you think." Her approach is to challenge the physician, rejecting his numbers. Rather than seeing his use of the rates as informative, she interprets the situation in terms of power and politics. She sets death as a statistical risk against the absence of death in her own experience. In replying, the clinician switches to another language, the clinical language of risk.

The Clinical Language of Risk

In the exchange, the physician countered the woman's appeal to her experience by citing his own experience of seven women who had died in childbirth. At one level, his statement appears out of context; none of these seven women were from the Keewatin. At another level, it is the expression of the sense of vulnerability and responsibility that is integral to the language of risk as used among medical professionals working in the North. These feelings provide the emotional power in their opposition to childbirth in the nursing stations.

When interviewed about evacuation for childbirth, both physicians and nurses would initially quote perinatal and neonatal mortality rates. Just as the physician cites the maternal deaths he has seen throughout a lifetime of practice, they soon turned to case examples to illustrate the dangers of childbirth. Rather than being derived from statistics as in the epidemiological language of risk, clinical risk is compounded from a few cases of actual disaster and a somewhat higher number of cases in which disaster was averted. The following quotation is taken from an interview with a nurse describing a case in which a woman went into premature labor and the weather was too bad for the planes to fly:

> We could have gotten her out if the weather cleared, but we couldn't and she could have died, the baby could have died.

Although neither died, the vividness of this experience remained intense. Speaking about births in the nursing stations, she continued,

> There is no blood here. There is no back-up. We don't have forceps, nobody knows how to do forceps deliveries. We don't have emergency OR, if you have a big head or a breech.

An obstetrician who had worked many years in the Keewatin expressed the same concerns about being isolated and without equipment:

> An unexpected birth of an infant of less than 1000 grams at Repulse Bay is seldom going to result in a survivor when the tertiary care centre is almost 2000 km from the nursing station. A patient that has a moderate abruptio placenta is unlikely to have a surviving infant when a Caesarean Section cannot be done for several hours. (Bradford 1984)

Referring to older women and their reluctance to leave when previous births have been uncomplicated, the same obstetrician commented,

> Although it's rare, they are the ones who go bad on you, they are the ones with the retained placenta, the bad pph [postpartum hemorrhage] and that's the trouble. . . . People who argue against deliveries in nursing stations, this is what it really boils down to, the third stage [of labor]. I think the third stage is the biggest [danger] with hemorrhage risks to the mom, leave aside the baby. Most of the other risks to the mom can usually be picked up with half reasonable antenatal care. The third stage is the one time you just can't [predict].

His fear of the postpartum hemorrhage was shared by others. Both physicians and nurses talked about the unpredictability of the hemorrhage, its suddenness, the necessity for an immediate response. One physician explained,

> You can't predict them and when you have a really bad hemorrhage, it's terrifying.

Another said,

> I can well remember my first severe postpartum hemorrhage. . . . Unless you do something, she is dead.

The fear of the woman bleeding to death rarely derives from experience. While hemorrhages occur, maternal deaths from this cause are now rare, and none occurred among women from the Keewatin. (Indeed, there was no record of a maternal death from 1971 to 1985.) Yet fear of the postpartum hemorrhage was a leitmotif, a theme which recurred whenever medical people talked about births in nursing stations. The combination of birth, blood, and death is universally and emotionally powerful, but the idea of seeing a woman bleed to death and being unable to do anything catches particularly at the medical imagination. Medical ideology requires that physicians define themselves as objective, scientific, their actions unswayed by emotion. Yet the emotionally charged experience is very much part of the practice of medicine. Daniel Montano, Donna Manders, and William Phillips (1990) show that having a patient die of breast cancer makes it more likely that a physician will screen other women for cancer. The death of seven women has forever colored childbirth as a dangerous happening for this obstetrician.

Reflecting on the relationship between clinical experience and the sense of risk, a young physician commented,

> I think though that physicians tend to remember those negative events and don't sort of always allow the real pattern of things to emerge and to realize that most deliveries will be normal . . . a memory of a really horrendous postpartum hemorrhage stands out and we are afraid of it ever happening again.

Talking with health professionals suggested that fear was also related to feelings of helplessness, coupled with more general concerns about competence and being able to cope in an emergency. As both Charles Bosk (1979) and Mary-Jo DelVecchio Good (1985) have shown, a reputation for competence is an important resource for physicians, easily spoiled, and made or marred through medical gossip. (This is also true for nurses.) The network of people working in health care in the North is small; anything that goes wrong with a birth would be known and any death would be a matter for formal review. The individual working in a nursing station, alone or with one other, is more exposed than the person who works in a hospital where the burden of responsibility is more often shared. The language of clinical risk, therefore, is based partly on the fear of being seen as responsible, but much more on seeing oneself as responsible.

The Inuit Language of Risk

People at the meetings challenged the philosophical or ethical assumptions that are at the foundation of arguments about risk in childbirth among not only obstetricians but also physicians, nurses, and administrators working in the North. Following Sandra Gifford (1986), we initially used the term "lay" for the third language in this discourse, but that term simply separates it from the languages used within the medical profession. More appropriately we should have referred to an Inuit language of risk. What was said at the meetings was rooted in Inuit culture and experience, not in some generalized, nonmedical view of the world.

Elders at the meetings (a number were traditional midwives) took the history of childbirth to a time before the settlements, settling it in a landscape of hunting and traveling, summer camps and snow houses. They presented the traditional ways of birth as safe. While this claim may be more ideological than factual, the circumstances of the fifties and sixties were traumatic and also unique. We have no way of knowing the degree of perinatal loss experienced under these more traditional conditions. Whatever the historical reality, the Inuit presented a view of birth as naturally safe, in contrast to clinicians who saw birth as inherently dangerous. Speaking through an interpreter, an old woman commented,

> You mentioned something about the death rate. She's not too concerned about that because . . . she's had fourteen children she delivered on her own, and she's never, never seen any children dying . . . that the mothers have never, she's never seen anybody dying.

Inuit assumptions about the general "riskiness" of human existence (including assumptions about risk in childbirth) were linked with the physical environment in which they lived and with their recent history and cultural traditions. A woman talking about risk and living in the North said,

> But living in an isolated community, where we put ourselves at risk for any number of life-threatening situations . . . we live here, this is our choice to

live here, if anybody feels that they can't live with that risk then they probably [should] move elsewhere. The possibility of losing a child simply because of the place that we live is a sobering thought, and it's a terrible thing, but still it's our choice to live here.

This language of risk was rooted in a view of a traditional way of life in which people had survived in a harsh and dangerous world by their own competence and self-reliance. Older women described managing birth totally alone, or talked about helping other women birth. Competence was linked with the possession of knowledge.

Back then, the women had the knowledge to take care of a woman in labor . . . we were informed by our elders on what to do and what not to do. (Meeting at Rankin Inlet)

The implicit comparison is drawn between the present situation, in which health professionals claim a monopoly over obstetric knowledge and this traditional time when information about childbirth was disseminated throughout the community, passing from one generation to the next. To be without knowledge is to be at risk; to be dependent on others is to be at risk. Hence, the assertion of the competence of traditional ways, as in this statement:

Inuit people do not believe that having a child, being pregnant, birthing is a disease. It's not an illness. It's a way of life, a normal function of a human being. And in the sense that it's not a disease, then they don't think that you absolutely have to be in the hospital . . . They [the Inuit] have delivered babies before for centuries and centuries.

Risk is not denied, but accepted as part of the reality of northern life. The underlying philosophical concept is expressed in the following quotation:

Can you guarantee me my life tomorrow? . . . There's always risk. I mean you wouldn't live if you didn't live with risks.

Reclaiming the right to provide a place of birth within the community is a symbolic as well as a real demand for control over community health and well being. Pressure for a more responsive system was part of the wider demand for increased community control over health care. It was also a reflection of a drive toward the preservation and reaffirmation of traditional beliefs in relation to pregnancy and childbirth. For these Inuit elders the task was to move the debate over evacuation away from the specific question "how much risk is acceptable to you?" to the more general question "what kind of society do you want?" (Frankenberg

1988, citing Douglas). The following quotation is taken from one of the community meetings:

> Nowadays we are told, like to forget about our Inuit traditional ways and my concern is that when there's a healthy pregnancy couldn't the mother have her child in her home town with the older Inuit women who have been midwives and with a younger person who has never had experience in delivering babies to help her along, to watch and to observe. Because that would teach the younger generation what our ancestors used to do . . . That's just been forgotten now because they are not allowed to do that here anymore.

Conclusion

Neonatal and perinatal mortality rates have been used/misused to justify the shifts and changes of obstetric policy in the North. It is this difference between risk and death as a subjective experience and death as an epidemiological artifact which partly explains the exchange between the woman and the physician. The epidemiological language of risk determines the medical view, and this medical view—as expressed by the physician—determines obstetric policy. But to understand how epidemiological language achieved its dominance in this case one must look at the complexities of the relationship between discourse and "the structural features and empirical realities" of childbirth in the Keewatin. These realities include the ecology of the North, but also the immediate history of medical and political relationships between Inuit communities and the Canadian federal government.

The fact that the medical profession relies on arguments of risk to the fetus to elicit compliance by individual women, or to persuade governments to invest in obstetric care, is scarcely surprising. But there is an additional dimension to the politics of obstetric care in the Keewatin. The imposition of evacuation for childbirth in the name of reducing risk was but one aspect in these communities, albeit a powerfully symbolic one, of a general political dependence on government-provided medical services.

A feminist may find in the displacement of the traditional midwife and the nurse-midwife another example of the extension of patriarchal control into the domain of women. Alternatively, a follower of Foucault might see the history of obstetric care in the Keewatin as the product of medical institutions extending oversight and control over childbirth into the North. Yet, the assumption of medical control over birth is equally an expression of the power relationships of an "internal colonialism" (Dacks 1981; O'Neil 1986): in this light, opposition to evacuation becomes a political act, a gesture of rebellion. Each of these interpretations has its own validity, yet none quite captures the emotional and political complexity of the discourse on childbirth.

In this essay we have taken one small piece of dialogue and used it as a key to this wider discourse. The exchange between the physician and the woman deals partly with the difference between risk as a subjective experience and risk as a statistical artifact. The woman's definition of risk is community based and acquired through experience. She sees the rates quoted by the physician as theoretical constructs, lacking local validity. The physician dismisses her claims as irrelevant for a definition of risk which is objective, scientific, expressible in numbers. Yet, it is the physician who moves the discussion into the emotional subculture of the debate by invoking the images of the seven dying women. We are presented with two ways of constructing birth and death-in-birth. For the woman, risk is the occasional threat of danger in childbirth accepted as part of a natural process. For the physician, risk in childbirth is a constant and frightening element in his clinical life. The woman does not grasp the emotional force behind the physician's objection to birthing in the community; he fails to understand why the place of birth is for her a political issue. Ultimately, the conversation is about politics because it is about power. The question is who has the power to define risk and to insist that their view should prevail over those of others. Should it be the woman or the physician, the Inuit community or the federal government?

Acknowledgments

This research was supported by grants from the National Health Research and Development Program (6607-1412-49) and a Health Scholar award to John O'Neil (6607-1379-48). The authors are grateful for the assistance of their co-investigators on the project, Drs. Brian Postl, Michael Moffatt, Patrick Brown, and Bernard Binns, Ms. Rosemary Brown, and particularly our Inuit collaborators, Eva Voisey and Peter Ernerk. However, the conclusions expressed here are those of the authors, and not necessarily shared by our co-investigators. We also thank the people of the Keewatin region for taking the time to discuss the issues described here with us. We are grateful to our Winnipeg and northern research staff, and in particular to Dr. Penny Gilbert, Ms. Jackie Linklater, Ms. Charlotte St. John, and Ms. Nellie Kusugak.

Note

1. Up until 1988, medical care in the Keewatin was the direct responsibility of the federal government. Local health centers were called "Nursing Stations,"

with a primary care, clinical emphasis, and all employee and contractual arrangements for medical consultants were with the federal government (i.e., Northern Medical Unit contracts). Since April 1988, the government of the Northwest Territories has been fiscally and politically responsible for most health services and regional health boards operate most facilities, employ health workers, and establish contractual relationships with medical consultants. Local medical clinics are now called "Health Centres" in an effort to symbolically broaden their mandate from a clinical to a community health perspective.

References

Annual Reports
    1964,   *Report on Health Conditions in the Northwest Territories.* Medical
    1969,   Services, National Health and Welfare Canada, Yellowknife,
    1975   Northwest Territories.
Armstrong, David
    1986   The Invention of Infant Mortality. *Sociology of Health and Illness*
            8(3):211–232.
Baskett, T. F.
    1978   Obstetric Care in the Central Canadian Arctic. *British Medical Journal* 2:1001.
Blackshaw, S.
    1981   Perinatal Mortality: Churchill and the Keewatin Zone, 1975–1979. *University of Manitoba Medical Journal* 51:9–12.
Bosk, Charles L.
    1979   *Forgive and Remember—Managing Medical Failure.* Chicago: The University of Chicago Press.
Bradford, C. R.
    1984   A Decade of Inuit Obstetrics. Unpublished MS.
Canadian Medical Association
    1987   Obstetrics 1987. A Report of the Canadian Medical Association on Obstetrical Care in Canada. *Supplement to Canadian Medical Association Journal,* March 15.
Dacks, Gurston
    1981   *A Choice of Futures: Politics in the Canadian North.* Toronto: Methuen.
Frankenberg, Ronald
    1988   Risks: Corporeal and Social; Responses: Sociological and Biological. Medical Anthropology and the Prevention of Cardiac Incidents and Highway Accidents. Paper prepared for Wenner-Gren Foundation for Anthropological Research—An International Conference no. 106, Analysis in Medical Anthropology, March 5–13, Hotel do Guincho, Lisbon, Portugal.
Frankenberg, Ronald
    1984   Incidence or Incidents: Political and Methodological Underpinnings of a Health Research Process in a Small Italian Town. In

Social Researching—Politics, Problems, Practice, Colin Bell and Helen Roberts, eds., pp. 88–103. Boston: Routledge & Kegan Paul Publishers.

Gifford, Sandra M.
1986   The Meaning of Lumps: A Case Study of the Ambiguities of Risk. In Anthropology and Epidemiology, Craig Janes, Ron Stall and Sandra Gifford, eds., pp. 213–246. Dordrecht, Netherlands: D. Reidel Publishing Company.

Good, Mary-Jo DelVecchio
1985   Discourses on Physician Competence. In Physicians of Western Medicine, Robert Hahn and Atwood Gaines, eds., pp. 247–267. Dordrecht, Netherlands: D. Reidel Publishing Company.

Harwood, Alan
1988   A Discussion About "Discourse." Medical Anthropology Quarterly 2(2):99–101.

Imber, Jonathan
1988   The Impact of Doctors on the Definition of the Abortion Issue in the U.S. Paper prepared for presentation at the Social Sciences Look at Medical Ethics conference, June 12–14, McGill University, Montreal.

Kaufert, Patricia A., Penny Gilbert, John O'Neil, Rosemary Brown, Patrick Brown, Brian Postl, Michael Moffat, Bernard Binns, and Lyn Harris
1987   Obstetric Care in the Keewatin: Changes in the Place of Birth 1971–1985. Paper prepared for presentation at 7th International Congress on Circumpolar Health, June 8–12, Umea, Sweden.

Macfarlane, Alison, and Miranda Mugford
1984   Birth Counts—Statistics of Pregnancy and Childbirth. London: Her Majesty's Stationery Office.

Martin, Emily
1987   The Woman in the Body—A Cultural Analysis of Reproduction. Boston: Beacon Press.

Montano, Daniel, Donna Manders, and William Phillips
1990   Family Physician Beliefs about Cancer Screening—Development of a Survey Instrument. The Journal of Family Practice 30(3):313–319.

Murdock, Alan I.
1979   Factors Associated with High-Risk Pregnancies in Canadian Inuit. Canadian Medical Association Journal 120:291–293.

Nash, June, and Max Kirsch
1988   The Discourse of Medical Science in the Construction of Consensus Between Corporation and Community. Medical Anthropology Quarterly 2(2):158–171.

O'Neil, John D.
1986   Colonial Stress in the Canadian Arctic: An Ethnography of Young Adults Changing. In Anthropology and Epidemiology, Craig Janes, Ron Stall, and Sandra Gifford, eds., pp. 249–274. Dordrecht, Netherlands: D. Reidel Publishing Company.

Ontario Task Force
  1987   *Report of the Task Force on the Implementation of Midwifery in Ontario.* Ontario Ministry of Health.
Richters, Annemiek
  1988   Fighting the Pests of Our Times: Medical Anthropology and Cultural Hegemony. *Medical Anthropology Quarterly* 2(4):438–446.
Romalis, Shelly
  1985   Struggle between Providers and Recipients: The Case of Birth Practices. In *Women, Health, and Healing,* Ellen Lewin and Virginia Olesen, eds., pp. 174–208. New York: Tavistock Publications.
Scheper-Hughes, Nancy
  1988   The Madness of Hunger: Sickness, Delirium and Human Needs. *Culture, Medicine and Psychiatry* 12(4):429–458.
Wright, Peter W. G.
  1988   Babyhood: The Social Construction of Infant Care as a Medical Problem in England in the Years Around 1900. In *Biomedicine Examined,* Margaret Lock and Deborah Gordon, eds., pp. 299–329. Dordrecht, Netherlands: Kluwer Academic Publishers.

3

Accounting for Amniocentesis

Rayna Rapp

Multiple Beginnings

Here are three amniocentesis stories, drawn from my New York–based fieldwork, any one of which raises the problem of how to understand the development and routinization of prenatal diagnosis:

On Tuesdays, Alfredo returns to the lab around three o'clock in the afternoon. On this particular Tuesday, there are four fluids in the specimen case he carries, two from Woodhull Hospital in Bushwick, Brooklyn, and two from St. Luke's on Manhattan's Upper West Side. Susan, the head of the lab, assigns one fluid each to Shedeh, Tom, Doris, and Moira. Shedeh will team up with Doris, who is still in training, to make sure all steps of the lab protocol are followed as the samples are logged and numbered, spun down, siphoned, divided, fed, and incubated. The fluids (or soup, as the lab techs call it) will be fed at six days and again at eleven. At fourteen days, there should be enough fetal cells in metaphase ready to read. By that time, the techs will have completed staining, scoping, photographing, and karyotyping cells from the earlier cases on which each was working. Turnaround time at the lab is twenty-one days, and it would be shorter if there were more technicians. The techs cooperate on cutting and scoping under time pressure, completing one another's karyotypes, rushing results, and feeding one another's soup. Seated on swivel chairs at the microscope, or around the cutting table, they talk about baby showers and lunch menus, rock concerts and New York rents as they work. Moira declares that "her" current fetus is a wimp: "It's got a wimpy Y and the bikini on the X is pretty gross."

Wimpy or not, this fetus is 46XY, which will be reported as a normal diagnosis. I am at the cutting table, struggling to tell number 13 chromosomes from number 14s, listening attentively to lab banter, and wondering what is happening to the woman from whose pregnant belly these "wimpy" fetal cells have been drawn.

Upstairs, Elena is answering telephones, directing patients calling for results to various genetic counselors; Henrietta is the most reassuring, the least likely to tell a twenty-one-week pregnant woman to call back in another week. She'll walk downstairs, trace a sample from the day it was logged to the scope on which it is being read, and try hard to get information she can share on the phone: "The chromosome studies aren't completed yet, but the biochemical results are just fine, and we should have the chromosomes by Friday. Call back, it's okay to call back." But in this case, Mrs. Ramirez speaks only Spanish, and Henrietta doesn't. Iris Mendez, the Sarah Lawrence student on an internship, may do the phone work, or Elena will take matters into her own hands—pestering, then translating for one of the counselors who says she is too busy to take on the case.

Mrs. Ramirez is a Honduran immigrant domestic worker who settled in East Harlem three years ago. Before coming to New York, she had three children, the last in a hospital. Before she registered at St. Luke's prenatal clinic in her fifteenth week of this pregnancy, she had never heard of "the needle test." Now she is having amniocentesis. Why and how has this "choice" to use a new and very expensive reproductive technology been made? What must I learn about migration, medicine, and motherhood to understand how amniocentesis becomes routinized for both the lab techs and women like Mrs. Ramirez?

In February, Tom found something ambiguous on the number 9 chromosomes of the sample he was scoping. Susan told him to check forty cells from all three flasks, rather than twenty from two. But the ambiguity persisted; it wasn't an in vitro artifact, or a random find. He, Susan, and the techs discussed it, and then called Dr. Judith Schwartz, the geneticist in charge of the lab. Judith agreed: there was additional chromosomal material on the top, short arm of the number 9 chromosomes. She called it "9P+": 9 for the pair of chromosomes on which it was located, P to designate the short arm, and plus to indicate additional chromosomal material. First she scanned the literature for an interpretation. Then she phoned the head obstetrician at Woodhull's prenatal clinic in charge of the case and made an appointment for the woman to be called in.

A week's research revealed nothing on "9P+," but twelve clinical reports on "trisomy 9," the closest diagnosis to which Judith could assimilate her case. The move to stabilize a label and an interpretation was not frivolous: the added material (the "plus" on the p arm) had banding patterns that suggested it was a partial replication of the #9, a trisomy-manqué. After careful reading, many phone consultations with colleagues, and a meeting with Malve, the genetic counselor who had done the intake interview with the patient at Woodhull, Judith sent Malve off to explain the problem. The patient listened, and decided to keep the pregnancy. Malve was upset by her decision, and thought she hadn't understood what Judith's research revealed: in all twelve cases she could find of trisomy 9, the babies were born with visible and structurally significant physical anomalies and some degree of mental retardation. She asked Judith to counsel the patient directly. Judith did. And the patient kept the pregnancy.

The baby was born in early June, and in late July, Judith Schwartz contacted the new mother through her obstetrician, asking if she would be willing to bring her child to the genetics laboratory for a consultation. The mother agreed. On a Wednesday afternoon, the "trisomy 9" came visiting: he was a six-week-old Haitian boy named Étienne St.-Croix. His mother, Veronique, spoke reasonable English and good French. His grandmother, Marie-Lucie, who carried the child, spoke Creole and some French. The two geneticists spoke English, Polish, Hebrew, and Korean between them. I translated into French, ostensibly for the grandmother and mother. Here is what happened:

Judith was gracious with Veronique but after a moment's chit-chat asked to examine the baby. She never spoke directly to the mother again during the examination. Instead, she and Maxine, the other geneticist, both trained in pediatrics, handled the newborn with confidence and interest. Malve took notes as Judith measured and consulted with Maxine. "Note the oblique palpebral fissure and micrognathia," Judith called out. "Yes," answered Veronique in perfect time to the conversation, "he has the nose of my Uncle Hervé and the ears of Aunt Mathilde." As the geneticists pathologized the mother "genealogized," the genetic counselor remained silent, furiously taking notes, and the anthropologist tried to keep score. When the examination was over, the geneticists apologized to the baby for any discomfort they had caused him, and Judith, herself a practicing Jew, asked the mother one direct question. "I notice you haven't circumcised your baby. Are you planning to?" "Yes," Veronique replied, "we'll do it in about another week." "May we have the foreskin?" Judith queried. "With the foreskin, we can keep growing trisomy 9 cells for research, and study the tissue as your baby develops." Veronique gave her a firm and determined "yes," and the consultation was over.

Walking Veronique and Marie-Lucie to the subway to direct them

home to Brooklyn, I asked what Veronique had thought about the experience: from the amniocentesis to the diagnosis to the genetic consultation.

> At first, I was very frightened. I am thirty-seven, I wanted a baby, it is my
> husband's second marriage, my mother-in-law is for me, not the first wife,
> my mother-in-law wanted me to have a baby, too. If it had been Down's,
> maybe, just maybe I would have had an abortion. Once I had an abortion,
> but now I am a Seventh Day Adventist, and I don't believe in abortion
> anymore. Maybe for Down's, just maybe. But when they told me this,
> who knows? I was so scared, but the more they talked, the less they said.
> They do not know what this is. And I do not know, either. So now, it's my
> baby. We'll just have to wait and see what happens. And so will they.

How do geneticists, genetic counselors, pregnant Haitians and anthropologists come to their interpretations of inherently ambiguous situations? How are the intersecting discourses of "genetics," "marriage and
family life," and "medical anthropology" constructed, and how do they
express contradictory processes?

In this business, you don't always find your own informants. Sometimes, they find you. Lauretta is working as a legal secretary when I
bump into her at the gym. When she asks what I'm doing, I describe my
amniocentesis research. "Boy," she says, "I've got someone you *must*
talk to. She's the head secretary at my law firm, she's got a little boy
who's mongoloid, and she knew, she knew in advance, and decided to
keep him." "Please ask her if she'd talk with me, confidentiality guaran-
teed," I reply, scribbling down my name and phone number. The next
day, when I answer my phone, a pleasant and self-assured woman says,
"Hi, I'm Pat Carlson, and Lauretta told me to call you. I'd love you to
meet my boy Steven, he's six and he's got Down's, but I should warn you
first, I'm against this amniocentesis business and abortion of these kids."
Two days later, I spend three hours with Pat and Stevie in their modest
row-house apartment in Queens. Pat was thirty-seven when she acciden-
tally got pregnant, and decided to keep the baby. "It was my best shot at
ever having a second child. My first one was already eighteen, she didn't
want this, but ever since I divorced her father, I knew I wanted another
marriage, another baby. I couldn't get the marriage, but I got the kid."
Pat's obstetrician recommended amniocentesis because she was over
thirty-five and without much reflection she undertook the test. When the
results came back positive, no one was more shocked than she. Her OB
wanted to perform an abortion right away, but she stalled for time. The
more she thought, the more ambivalent she became.

> I did some research, I visited this group home for adult retardeds in my
> neighborhood. You know, it was kind of nice. They looked pretty happy,

they had jobs, they went bowling. I thought about it. Maybe if I was married, maybe if I had another shot at it. But this was it: take it or leave it. So I took it. I called the Mormons back. Oh, I hadn't been to temple for years. But I knew, in my heart of hearts, they'd convince me not to have an abortion. And they did. One man, he just came and prayed with me, he still comes. Stevie gets a lot of colds, I can't always make it to temple. But when we don't make it, he comes over and prays with us. And the Down's support group, that's helpful too. They told me about schools, and special programs. Stevie's doing really well, he'll learn to read this year, I know he will. And if he doesn't, that's okay, too. This kid has been a blessing, he makes me ask myself, "why are we put here on earth?" There must be a reason, and Stevie's reason was to teach love, to stop haters dead in their tracks. Everyone who meets him loves him. They may start out talking behind his back, but pretty soon, they're rooting for him, 'cause he's such a neat kid. He's taught me a lot about love, and acceptance. So when I see a girl who's pregnant, I always tell her about Stevie, I always say, 'don't have that test, you don't need that test to love your baby the way it is.' Oh, for some of them, maybe abortion is a good thing, I don't know. But for me, Stevie was just what I needed.

How can I account for Pat's "choice" in a way that preserves her agency while noting the power of religion, class, gender ideology, and personal reproductive history in it? How can I describe the shifting powers of sexual mores and medicalization in American culture as they both construct and constrain the range of what she might "choose"?

The Problem of the Excluded Middle

> If anthropology can be said to have one foot in the sciences and one in the humanities, medical anthropology is thus doubly marked. . . . [It] must find a workable bridge linking biology and culture, matter and symbol, body and mind, action and thought. Medical anthropologists are challenged . . . to resolve the central issues in anthropological theory . . . and to contribute to contemporary discussions concerning the status of science as a component of culture.
>
> (Lindenbaum and Lock 1993)

Like all fields of critical inquiry, medical anthropology must simultaneously construct and deconstruct itself. The field seems balanced on a fulcrum, seesawing between biology and history, medicine and meaning systems, epidemiology and emic explanations. This construction tempts us to investigate an amalgam of the body biological and the body politic. When we begin with this orientation, the terrain on which our investigation rests appears stable: we can describe or measure how biology and culture intersect, assuming that each "factor" is distinct, if interactive.

Yet we also know that such bounded representations of biological and social bodies are deeply linked to nature/culture oppositions in the history of Western thought. Deconstructing such antinomies is a prerequisite for providing more powerful accounts of how illness and health operate in the lives of our informants, as well as in the disciplines of medicine and medical anthropology. Antinomies of nature and culture exclude precisely that "middle ground" on which the contest for the meaning and management of illness and health is constructed. It is not a coincidence that such antinomies also position "science" or "medicine" on the high ground of the theoretical seesaw, thus silencing competing interpretations or reducing them to ethnosciences. Binary formulations leave medical anthropologists remarkably free to construct an external role for themselves: we view ourselves as participant-*observers* with license to describe the relation between the parts, rather than observing *participants* in the social phenomena our narratives help to construct.

This triple exclusion—of the middle ground on which contests for meaning occur, of all other interpretations as less-than-scientific, and of medical anthropologists as "outside" their objects of study—became especially clear to me as I began to study the routinization of amniocentesis beginning in 1983. Combing the literature on "patient reactions to prenatal diagnosis," I found four overlapping medical discourses: geneticists spoke of the benefits and burdens their evolving technical knowledge conferred on patients (a discourse that has rapidly intensified as the Human Genome Initiative gets under way); health economists deployed their famous cost/benefit analysis to suggest which diseases and patient populations should be most effectively screened; social workers and sociologists interrogated the psychological stability and decision-making strategies of "couples" faced with "reproductive choices"; and bioethicists commented on the legal, ethical, and social implications of practices in the field of human genetics. Later, a fifth discourse, penned by feminists who are on the whole opposed to the new reproductive technologies as a "male takeover" of motherhood, was added to the literature (Arditti, Duelli-Klein, and Minden 1984; Baruch, d'Amato, and Seager 1988; Corea 1985; Rothman 1986; Spallone & Steinberg 1987; Stanworth 1987). Absent from the published texts were descriptions of the multilayered and contradictory processes by which a new reproductive technology was being produced, a new work force and patient populations created, or a language articulated to describe the impact of these processes on representations of pregnancy, maternity, children, and family life.

Yet if we return to the stories that open this chapter, we can identify many mutlilayered forces at work. They include (at least) the following seven processes, in narrative order:

First, it is important to analyze "laboratory life." The laboratory labors through which prenatal diagnoses are constructed are carried out by a class-stratified, multiethnic new work force, most of whose members are women. From the Puerto Rican driver to the Iranian, Polish Catholic, Southern African-American, and suburban Jewish lab techs, to the Polish-Israeli-American and Korean-American geneticists, this is a work force that resembles the multinational make-up of New York's population. Brain drains, civil wars, labor migrations, upward and downward mobility: these world-scale political economic forces structure the possibilities of who becomes a worker in the scientific labor force. During the two months that I "interned" at the lab, three of the twelve technicians left and were replaced. One Lebanese, one Chinese, and one U.S.-born white Anglo-Saxon were succeeded by an Armenian-Iranian, a Southern African-American, and a New York–born Puerto Rican.

This rapid turnover in the labor force of medical technology is business-as-usual, according to the two geneticists who run the lab. And genetic counseling, too, is a field where job mobility is fast and continuous. During the three years that I have been observing their rounds, five lab counselors have filled two and a half permanent slots, and three to five student interns pass through the lab each year. Work culture is thus based on medical language, and there is little continuity for long-term connections through which counterdiscourses might develop.

The world of prenatal diagnosis is distinctly female. Not only are pregnant women the clients for this new reproductive service, but virtually all the workers in this "industry" are female as well. Most lab technicians are women. Geneticists working in this field are disproportionately women, and more than 98 percent of all genetic counselors are female. This new "allied health professional" has been created in the last fifteen years explicitly to serve as "interface" between the DNA revolution and the public who will reap its consequences. Janus-faced experts in a technical and rapidly changing science, genetic counselors balance between science and social work, speaking both epidemiology and empathy to their clients. Trained in aspects of molecular genetics which many physicians do not understand, they are situated in the medical hierarchy like social workers. The cytogenetics, human genetics, molecular genetics, and counseling labors that construct prenatal diagnoses are often described as appropriately "feminine" because they focus on pregnancy, and the nine-to-five working hours do not disrupt family responsibilities. A new field of employment on the frontier of genetics thus emerges with job descriptions, prestige, and pay scales that reproduce familiar gender hierarchies.

Second, we need to consider the recruitment of highly diverse female patient populations. While nationally amniocentesis is becoming something of a pregnancy ritual for white, middle-class families in which women have delayed childbearing to further education and careers, in New York City the situation is somewhat different. The Prenatal Diagnosis Laboratory of the Health Department was set up in 1978 explicitly to offer amniocentesis to low-income, hence disproportionately non-white, women. The lab is subsidized by both the state and city of New York. It accepts Medicaid and all third-party insurance, and has a sliding-scale fee that begins at zero. The amniotic fluid samples it analyzes reflect this economic outreach to the urban poor: the lab population is approximately one-third Hispanic, one-third African-American, and one-third white; half are private patients, and half are seen at public clinics, according to the racial/ethnic categories provided by both the city and state health departments.

But these categories undoubtedly conceal as much as they reveal. At the present time, "Hispanic" includes Puerto Ricans and Dominicans long familiar with city services, as well as the "new immigrants" of Central America, many of whom are drawn from rural backgrounds, are desperately poor, and are often undocumented, and also middle-class, highly educated Colombians and Ecuadorians who may be experiencing downward mobility through migration. African-Americans include fourth-generation New Yorkers, women whose children circle back and forth between the city and rural Alabama, and Haitians who have lived in Brooklyn for only a few months. "White" encompasses Ashkenazi and Sephardic Jews, Irish, Italian, and Slavic Catholics, Greek and Russian Orthodox adherents, and Episcopalian and Evangelical Protestants, "as if" being neither black nor brown places them in a homogenized racial category. The categories themselves thus freeze a "racial map" that ignores the historical complexity of identity endemic to New York and many other urban areas in contemporary America. Despite historical insights into the process by which such a map has been created and promulgated, it is nearly impossible to escape its sociological boundaries while conducting and describing fieldwork in New York City.

New York City's Health Department has historically been a leader in providing maternal and child health services, at least since the Progressive Era, providing the most liberal, expansive, and often the earliest nutritional, well-baby, and family planning services (Duffy 1968; Rosenberg 1976, 1987; Rosenkrantz et al., 1978; Rosner 1982). But this cutting edge, then and now, is also a double-edged sword. Services and surveillance, routine care and social control are inextricably linked in extending public health measures to the poor. It is not only "their" well-being, but "our" cost-effectiveness which is continuously at issue. There is thus no way to separate eugenic and choice-enhancing aspects of prenatal diagnosis when provided by public health planning and moneys.

Third, science itself can be viewed as constructed by social and cultural processes (e.g., Latour 1987; Traweek 1988; Woolgar 1988). There is an immense lumpiness to science once one steps through the looking-glass into the laboratory. The neutral and distanced discourse of medical journals, the triumphalism of the Tuesday *New York Times* "Science" section, the reassuring "commonsense solutions" of the Phil Donahue show all occasionally claim to evaluate progress in human genetics. But none can contain the ambiguities of the DNA research frontier. There is an anxiety-provoking plethora of "information" disembedded from any cultural context for its interpretation that genetics currently represents. Prenatal diagnosis provides a proliferation of information for consumers without guideposts, for doctors to deploy as stage directions in a play whose acts are as yet unwritten, for technicians in search of metaphors. All participants are constantly negotiating a system of interpretation for both producers and consumers of "scientific knowledge." The laboratory is at once the factory of prenatal diagnoses and an empire of signs. While medical genetic discourse claims universal authority, it continuously confronts the contested nature of much of its findings, and the diversity of interpretations to which even "universal biological facts" lend themselves. The path connecting "scientific information" to "medical policy," "counseling protocols," and "popular culture" is rocky at best.

Fourth, we should note that the relationship between science and religion is unstable in many ways. Not only do different religions hold diverse stances toward reproductive technologies (Office of Technology Assessment 1988) but practitioners within religions may vary widely in their interpretations of official doctrine and personal adherence. Mrs. Ramirez, whose story opened this essay, is a practicing Catholic, but she would consider abortion of a fetus with a serious disability despite church teachings. One of her co-religionists from Ecuador expressed it succinctly:

> Could I abort if the baby was going to have that problem? God would forgive me, surely, yes, I could abort. Latin Catholics, we are raised to fear God, and to believe in His love and mercy. Now, if I were Evangeli-

cal, that's another story. It's too much work, being Evangelical. My sisters
are both Evangelicals, they go to church all the time. There's no time for
abortion for them. (Maria Acosta, 41)

Many Hispanic Catholic women reported multiple early abortions. To
them, *late* abortion was a mortal sin. Finely honed, female-centered
theological distinctions and practices are carved out of a monolithic
theology. Likewise, "Protestants" display a wide array of beliefs and
practices. Some of these differences can be linked to specific churches.
Fundamentalists are most likely to preach against the test and Pat Carlson beat a beeline to her Mormon roots when she wanted to be talked
out of an abortion following a positive prenatal diagnosis. Mainline
groups like Episcopalians, Dutch Reformists, and Methodists are either
silent or supportive on the topic of amniocentesis.

But very often, women insisted they were not expressing an official
church teaching, but a personal interpretation. Lynthia Cato, Barbadan-
born and recommended for the test at the age of forty-one, refused it,
telling me in a subsequent interview that it was against her belief. When
I queried what that was, she warned me not to confuse her "denomina-
tion" (Seventh Day Adventist) with her "creed" (personal) in which a
female deity bestowed healthy pregnancies on those whose behavior
merited them. Two Latin American evangelicals who swore they would
never consider abortion nonetheless underwent amniocentesis. In almost identical words, each told me she "wanted medicine to help reveal
what miracles God had in store." Sometimes, a woman will discuss a
meaning-behind-the-meaning of her religious discourse. When I interviewed her following an amniocentesis, Puerto Rican–born Maria-
Carmen Trujillo indicated her instrumental interests in the fervent
pentacostalism espoused by her visionary husband. Outside of his ear-
shot, when I queried about her church attendance, she told me of his
former prison sentence for drug sales, and his marital infidelities. If
pentecostalism and having a baby "for him" would stabilize his presence
at home, she would gladly participate in both projects. "Family reform"
here overrides more obvious religious referents.

All of the Jews I interviewed were positive about amniocentesis.
Many expressed this sentiment: "Why not use the miracles of modern
technology to make life better?" As one couple said, after terminating a
Down's syndrome pregnancy, "We're crying over our losses, it really
hurts, but it's better this way. Modern medicine is a blessing, even when
it brings you the hardest lessons of all." But my sample includes only a
few Orthodox women and families, where the issue is more highly contested. And genetic counselors at Mount Sinai Hospital have helped to
initiate a successful screening program that works through traditional

marriage brokers in the Crown Heights's Hasidic community where many families are known to carry Tay-Sacks disease. The *Chevra dor Yersurim* (Organization for the Generations) recruits more participants for Tay-Sacks screening than any medical institution. Here, reinforcement of patriarchal authority to arrange marriages goes hand in hand with state-of-the-art prenatal screening.

These many stories should alert us to the fact that religions continue to proliferate and make claims on personal, ethnic, and communal identity throughout American cultural life. Far from representing a "culture lag" that science will soon overtake, religious adherence might better be viewed as a continuous aspect of contemporary social life (Harding 1987). Religious identity provides one resource in the complex and often contradictory repertoire of possible identities a pregnant woman brings to her decision to use or reject amniocentesis. There is no definitive "Catholic," "Jewish," or "Protestant" position on reproductive technology, when viewed from the pregnant woman's point of view. Rather, each pregnancy is assessed in light of the competing claims on maternity the individual acknowledges and to which she responds.

Fifth, both maternalist and medical discourses require careful deconstruction. The debates (between "pharmocrats and feminists," in Gena Corea's felicitous phrase) over whether the new reproductive technologies, including amniocentesis, offer progress or degradation to family life are phrased "as if" motherhood were being revolutionized. The discourse of maternalism—technocratic or resistant romantic, the one aligned with science, the other with nurture—obviously holds ideological weight in the words of a Pat Carlson or a Veronique St.-Croix. But it is not the only or overriding basis on which a decision to use or reject amniocentesis, or pursue its consequences, is made. The dramatic discourses of modern pregnancy as allied with either nature or culture too often echo each other. Each sounds like a unified voice, but the women with whom I have spoken are always polyphonic.

Every pregnancy is embedded in its own specific context: the proximity and judgment of male partners, mothers, sisters, and friends all weigh heavily on an amniocentesis decision. Many women told me they brought their partners to see the sonogram: "Frank just isn't as committed to this pregnancy as he should be," commented white middle-class psychologist Marcia Lang, "but once he sees the baby moving, I know he'll get excited." Juana Martes, a Dominican home care attendant, also thought men should see the sonogram that accompanies the test: "When the little creature moves, they begin to know what women feel, how they suffer for it to be born, and then they respect their wives." Ecuadorian-born Coralina Bollo felt pressured into having the test by her U.S.-born husband; Flora Blanca had to keep her decision to have it secret from her disapproving *companero*. Laura Escobar's Egyptian-born Muslim husband Ibrim reluctantly agreed to the test, stressing that he didn't believe in abortion. He *knew* God would protect his unborn child. Laura turned to me, and in Spanish (which her husband does not speak) said, "When God provides a problem, he also provides the cure."

The fact of decision making involved in amniocentesis reveals the existing gender negotiations within which a specific pregnancy is undertaken. There is a complex choreography of domination, manipulation, negotiation, and, sometimes, resistance in the gender tales women tell about their decisions to use or reject this piece of reproductive technology.

The place of a particular pregnancy in a woman's romantic, marital, and reproductive history also influences the use or rejection of the test. Frankie Smithers, an African-American school teacher, was forty-one when she married for the second time:

> I thought I was done having babies, into the changes, I thought I'd already changed when I found out I was pregnant. But Ron never had any children; he really wanted a baby. "Okay," I thought to myself, "here goes another one, just one more. But only if it's healthy. I've taught those kids in special ed., they're cute and everything, but that's more than an old lady like me getting on to a second marriage is going to take on." So I told him, "Yes, so long as we have that test." And that was that.

Mary Fruticci, a white housewife, forty-three, described her fourth pregnancy as an accident. A practicing Catholic, she had amniocentesis because she and her husband could imagine enough love and money to raise one more child, but not if it were seriously disabled. After a prenatal diagnosis of Down's, she said,

> I share a lot of feelings with the Right-to-Life Movement. I've always been shocked by the number of abortion clinics, the number of abortions, in this city. But when it was *my* turn, I was grateful to find the right doctor. I sent him and his staff roses[1] after it was all over. They helped me to protect my own life, and that's a life, too.

Images of pregnancy "as if" it were located exclusively in the domain of either technical medicine or timeless maternal identity both exhibit similar rhetorical errors. The seeming universality of pregnancy is continuously undermined by its concrete historical and local embeddedness.

Sixth, disabilities, like pregnancies, are socially constructed. Pat Carlson's decision to continue her pregnancy after a prenatal diagnosis of Down's syndrome is quite a rare event: 90 to 95 percent of women receiving this diagnosis go on to terminate their pregnancies. Likewise, a diagnosis like Tay-Sacks disease carries an abortion rate that is almost 100 percent, although prenatal diagnosis of a similarly recessively transmitted disease, sickle cell anemia, probably leads to abortion only 40 percent of the time.[2] Different rates of abortion seem linked to at least two factors: the knowledge pregnant women and their supporters have about the condition's consequences (which vary, of course, by disease), and the local values (suggested by religious, familial, and ethnic experiences) they hold about it. One genetic counselor encountered two patients, each of whom chose to abort a fetus after learning that its status included XXY sex chromosomes (Klinefelter's syndrome, which affects growth, fertility, and possibly intelligence and learning abilities). One professional couple told her, "If he can't grow up to have a shot at becoming the President, we don't want him." A low-income family said of the same condition, "A baby will have to face so many problems in this world, it isn't fair to add this one to the burdens he'll have." And a Puerto Rican single mother who chose to continue a pregnancy after getting a prenatal diagnosis of Klinefelter's said of her now four-year-old son,

> He's normal, he's growing up normal. As long as there's nothing wrong that shows, he isn't blind or deaf or crippled, he's normal as far as I'm concerned. And if anything happens later, I'll be there for him, as long as he's normal looking.

It is important not to romanticize "immigrants" or "ethnic families" in interpreting these statements. What is being expressed in these acceptances or rejections of specific disabilities is their local meaning. The Puerto Rican mother who accepted her Klinefelter's son was adamant that she would have chosen to abort had the diagnosis been spina bifida. That would have been a diagnosis with which she was familiar, and which she considered to entail a great deal of stigma and maternal sacrifice.

From a patient's point of view, most diagnoses are inherently ambiguous (Rothman 1986). An extra chromosome spells out the diagnosis of Down's syndrome, but it does not distinguish mildly from severely retarded children, or indicate whether this particular fetus will need open heart surgery. A missing X chromosome indicates a Turner's syndrome female (who will be short-statured and infertile), but cannot speak to the meaning of fertility in the particular family into which she may be born. Homozygous status for the sickle cell gene cannot predict the severity of anemia a particular child will develop. All such diagnoses are interpreted in light of prior reproductive histories and experiences, community values, and aspirations that particular women and their families hold for the pregnancy being examined.

And some constituencies contest the powerful medical definitions of disabilities that predominate in contemporary American society. The disability rights movement points out that socially constructed attitudes of stigma and prejudice, not absolute biological capacities, lie behind the segregation of disabled children and adults.[3] Many disability rights groups focus on legal and policy solutions to their members' problems, often using a civil rights perspective. The discourse of civil rights influenced a series of federal laws in the mid-1970s and the recent "Americans With Disabilities Act," which explicitly deployed models developed in the battles against racial discrimination to mandate access to education, housing, employment, and public facilities for disabled citizens. The movement contains many divided allies and is continuously debating such questions as the relation of mental to physical disabilities and the ethics of prenatal diagnosis for any or all disability. But virtually all members of and advocates for disabled groups insist on the social, rather than the medical, definition of the problems they must confront.

This position has a certain irony, for it is based on a truth that medicine itself helped to produce. Prior to antibiotics, infant surgery, and deinstitutionalization, Down's syndrome children had a mortality rate of over 50 percent in their first years. "Spina bifida" is a new label that agglomerates diverse open neural tube defects (encephalocele, hydrocephalus, myelomeningocele, anencephaly), most of which led to stillbirth or newborn death until about thirty years ago, when neonatal surgery—especially shunting for hydrocephalus—was developed. The medical practices that saved such newborns also constructed them as permanent and incurable patients, trapped in a discourse of medical management. It has taken competing voices—from the disability rights movement, from the family support networks, from the professional "special education" sector—to contest the powerful medical definition of disability.

Those competing voices are particularly poignant when they articulate parental hopes and aspirations for children born with a stigmatized difference. Most of the parents I have interviewed through two of New York's Down's Syndrome Parents' Support Groups speak a double discourse. On the one hand, group members are continuously advocating for their children, learning about and demanding the most advanced resources to help them. In this mode, "mainstreaming" figures as an ideal: "high-functioning" Down's syndrome children should be enabled to benefit from connections with nondisabled children at school, and in extracurricular activities. This position is particularly well depicted in the currently popular prime time television serial "Life Goes On." The

Down's Syndrome Parents' Support Group sponsored a meeting at which a video tape of a thirteen-year-old boy with DS making his bar mitzvah was featured. All around the room, Caribbean and Hispanic mothers, Catholics and Protestants, commented on Mitchell's achievements in Hebrew as he read the Torah. Everyone was appreciative of the good speech therapy as well as the family love that underwrote this event. The Education Committee of the DSPSG rated the performance of various committees on the handicapped and private schools, according to the excellence and availability of programs for children with Down's syndrome. After two years of advocacy, committee members convinced one Manhattan Catholic parochial school to support an enclosed classroom for children with DS. They have funded not only a special education classroom teacher and a part-time speech therapist and occupational therapist but even an educational psychologist who specializes in problems of developmentally delayed children and their families. The children are mainstreamed for lunch, some physical education activities, and some after-school programs.

Mainstreaming is viewed by many parents and educators as a two-way street, of value to the nondisabled as well as the disabled. It is here that the second discourse (also voiced by Pat Carlson) is articulated. Disabled children are described by most families in the support group as having a special lesson to teach. It is a lesson of acceptance and love of difference, a replacement of "less than" by "other than."

> Our kids are very musical; they sing from their souls. When Kenny was a toddler, he couldn't speak, people would get so frustrated with him, he'd get so upset. But he would dance, and sway to the music, and you'd see the light of love in his eyes. I read somewhere that there's a community for retarded people in the mountains, somewhere in Europe. They play music, and they run a farm. Kids like this are very loving, they're good with animals, it's like the music of the universe is inside of them. If only the rest of us could listen, maybe they could teach us to hear it better. (Judy Kaufman, white nurse, mother of a seven-year-old with DS)

> I want Adam to be a messenger of God's love. God made him for some reason, it's not ours to know, but everyone who meets him learns a little more about it. You can never get angry at people who are sincere, who really try, once you meet Adam. It's not being smart, it's being loving that makes you a human being. (Bonnie d'Amato, white secretary, mother of a five-year-old with DS)

> There are some benefits from having a child like this. Robin will never show guile, she will never be deceitful, she will always give and return love completely innocently. I would never say that about my other children. (Mary Thompson, white actress, mother of a three-year-old with DS)

These views are not, however, articulated by all parents. While most activists in the support group spoke the language of both achievement and acceptance, these activists were also from solidly upper middle-class backgrounds. Aspirations for children with Down's syndrome often sounded different, when spoken by women from less privileged backgrounds who had not become activists:

> What does it mean to have this child? That I will be a mother forever, that this one will never leave home. That's okay, I'm glad I'll have him with me forever. Only I worry if I die before he does. I don't want anything else from the schools, there's no point in that. He's happiest right here at home, where I can take care of him. (Anna Morante, Puerto Rican hospital orderly, mother of an eight-year-old with DS)

> All those groups, those films and stuff, I don't know if that really helps Malik. In fact, it *don't* help Malik. What good does it do to put all those fancy white kids on television? Oh sure, it's an inspiration, I bet the Reagans, they sit home nights watchin' it. Gives 'em a good excuse not to worry when they cut the social services back. Those films don't say that the kids got parents who can pay for speech therapists, foot doctors, special computer tapes in their homes. Not my son, why don't they put my son on the television? Then people would see what it's really like. (Leila Robertson, African-American welfare mother of a seven-year-old with DS)

The discursive and material resources available for families of disabled children vary greatly along the fault lines set up by race, class, religious, and ethnic differences in contemporary America. Disability is socially constructed, reflecting not only the hegemonic claims of medicine and counterclaims of families and activists, but cross-cutting differences within the very category of "disability" as well.

Seventh, medical anthropologists must account for their own presence in the problems they study. Why should an anthropologist learn to cut karyotypes in a basement laboratory on First Avenue, follow genetic counselors through their rounds at Harlem hospital, and take the E train to Queens for home visits? Without indulging in a narcissistic exercise, it seems evident that this investigation into the social impact and cultural meaning of prenatal diagnosis is supported by almost twenty years of feminist mobilization in the discipline of anthropology. "People like me" teach women's studies courses, as well as anthropology courses, where the contradictions generated around the concepts of "reproduction" or "motherhood" glide across disciplinary boundaries. They also surface in our personal lives. Members of the same generation who produced the field of "feminist anthropology" often delayed childbearing for the establishment of education and careers, and now we study comparative reproduction. That a cultural anthropologist who has sustained two amniocenteses should query the power of medical discourse and the meaning of cultural differences in this experience seems an obvious next move.

These seven proliferating processes make it difficult to ever completely frame our "unit" of analysis. Some of the layers described here are clearly local and particular—for example, the funding priorities of New York City's health department or the existence of a permanently and luxuriantly polyglot class of working poor women in the city. Other forces pertain more generally to the political economy of advanced capitalism, where scientific discourse and practices deeply influence contemporary cultural representations of health and illness, pregnancy, disability, and gender. And all layers are, of course, historically contingent.

Endings Are Really Beginnings

In the "middle ground" partially described above, science (in medicine and medical anthropology) cannot provide stable, authoritative discourses against which to measure all other cultural practices. For scientific knowledge, like the other cultural discourses and social practices described above, is also historically contingent. To say that accounts of science (or pregnancy, or ethnic diversity, or anything else) are historically contingent is not to deny their power to intervene in what used to be called "the real world," nor to collapse this discussion into rampant relativism. The temptations of pure relativism can be avoided if the study of power relations, rather than pluralism, lies at the heart of the investigation.

This focus on power is one that was often given to me by the people who consented to be interviewed for this study, for they frequently provided insightful comments on the force fields within which their own options and possibilities were inscribed. In the narratives of pregnant women and mothers of disabled children, for example, television looms large. Sonograms provide images of the fetus in utero on a television screen. These images of floating fetuses, beating hearts, and imagined sex organs all have multiple medical, religious, and political interpretations for parents-to-be and the health professionals who orchestrate the viewing (Rapp 1991). Televisions provide multiple viewing points for the cultural problem of prenatal diagnosis. When I asked where women had first learned about amniocentesis, many respondents without advanced formal education answered, "Dallas." In 1986, it took three episodes for the drama of a prenatal diagnosis of Down's syndrome to unfold on the show, with a predictably genderized outcome: "the mother" wanted to keep the pregnancy, "the father" pressured for an abortion, "the resolution" was a miscarriage, rather than a decision. My seven-year-old daughter has accompanied me part of the way on this intellectual journey, learning to identify children and adults with Down's syndrome from her avid addiction to watching "Life Goes On" on Sunday nights. And when I asked Pat Carlson, whose story opens this essay, what would make her son Stevie's life more integrated, I expected an answer about "education" but I got one about television. "Pampers commercials," she replied. "Why Pampers?" I asked. "If they can show all those black and brown kids on TV ads these days, why can't they just show kids like Stevie?" Pat asked. Television is not a neutral presence in the life ways of health care workers, pregnant women, or families with Down's syndrome members. It may well be the most powerful panopticon through which the "information revolution" is constructed, represented, and enforced. The power of television vibrates through any "history of the present" in contemporary American culture.

Power relations are, of course, historically contingent. If, for example, the Chinese invent an earlier fetal sex chromosomal detection technology via maternal-fetal blood centrifuge to mediate the contradiction between their one-child family policy and a patriarchal kinship system, it will surely echo through protocol studies funded in Washington, D.C. down to the basement of the Prenatal Diagnosis Laboratory in New York City. There, visiting Chinese geneticists will undoubtedly enhance international scientific cooperation by teaching it to American colleagues. If the Reagan and Bush appointments to the Supreme Court do, indeed, augur the piecemeal reversal of legal abortion in the United States, prenatal diagnosis might fall victim to our particular, contemporary politicization of the court system. However, a more likely scenario would have to take into account powerful national polls indicating that over 80 percent of Americans support legal abortion when the fetus is defective, a consensus that makes disability rights activists desperate. This hypermedicalization of abortion rights, which posits a "grave fetal defect" as the only basis for a legal abortion, lies at the heart of *Doe v. Bamgaertner,* a legal case generated in Utah explicitly to test *Roe v. Wade.* Geneticists and genetic counselors were brought in to the construction of the oppositional brief to describe the arcane range of possible, diagnosable fetal conditions on the one hand, and the subjective meaning of "grave" on the other. The cultural contest over abortion rights thus includes medical experts as liberals; a century ago, physicians served as strategists for campaigns to illegalize the procedure. As this moment in struggles over reproductive rights plays itself out, we can imagine that abortion services could become severely restricted and entirely remedicalized, and prenatal diagnosis would become one obvious and popular route to ending an undesired pregnancy.

Finally, power must remain central to any analysis of the permanent condition of heterogeneity that characterizes the culture of advanced capitalism. The relation of world-structured power domains and local cultures is intimately tied to this question of heterogeneity. If advanced capitalism has enormously homogenizing tendencies that threaten to engulf and flatten cultural particularities, it also sets up uneven conditions for the continuous production of cultural heterogeneity. I want to claim this as a historical as well as contemporary truth. Had I been studying childbirth in New York City at the turn of the century, it would have been Lithuanian holdouts against hospitals, rather than Haitian incomprehension of genetic testing that I would have been querying. There is no way out of this problem. And it has for me a politics that needs underlining. At least two concrete goals flow from this understanding. The first, a familiar theme in medical anthropology, is that health care professionals who often come from the dominant culture can never escape confrontation with multicultural rationalities. They may, however, be able to learn about cultural differences. Genetic counselors, unlike doctors, are new health professionals in a small and still-developing "woman's" field. Helping them to pluralize would be a service to wo*men*, rather than wo*man*, I imagine. Their commitment to medical discourse and dominant representations of pregnancy and motherhood makes this task a difficult one, but many conscientious counselors are committed to exploring how best to serve underserved, often minority, patient populations (Marfatia, Punales, and Rapp 1990; cf. Rapp 1988).

Second, we need a discussion of what popular scientific literacy might mean, especially but not exclusively for diverse American women, given the gender biases, racial prejudices, class structures, and attitudes toward disability which serve as effective barriers to restructuring the power dynamics of scientific discourse as it shapes American cultural life. While one subtext of the present account is to demedicalize prenatal diagnosis and disability, another, paradoxically, is to suggest that many, perhaps the majority, of women whose lives it affects *still lack access* to the discursive tools and social services on which both scientific literacy and a truly "informed consent" might rest. Historically contingent accounts lead us back to the problem of coping with diversity in a complex society that simultaneously and continuously produces, reproduces, and then denies its own heterogeneous nature. Beyond its theoretical recognition, what are we to do with the abundant inequalities and differences a critical, feminist, medical anthropology must represent amongst American women?

Acknowledgments

The fieldwork on which this paper is based has been funded by the National Science Foundation, the National Endowment for the Humanities, the "Changing Gender Roles" Program of the Rockefeller Foundation, and the Institute for Advanced Study, Princeton. I am grateful for their support. Hundreds of women have shared their amniocentesis experiences with me, and scores of health professionals have enabled my work to move forward, all believing that the analysis of this technology from patients' points of view is important. Without their trust and help, none of my work would have been possible. I have changed all names to protect confidentiality. I also want to thank Donna Haraway, whose continuous encouragement has been a source of energy and inspiration. The first draft of this chapter benefited from readings by Donna Haraway, Shirley Lindenbaum, and Joan Scott.

Notes

1. At the time of this interview, roses were being bestowed by activists in the Right-to-Life movement on politicians who supported constitutional amendments and related strategies to outlaw abortion.

2. These statistics were compiled from the Laboratory's "positive diagnosis" files covering the last five years. There is no national monitoring of either amniocentesis or abortion following positive prenatal diagnosis, although the Council of Regional Networks of Genetic Services is currently developing a national data base. The best comparative figures, which approximate those of the Lab, are provided by Hook 1981.

3. For a popular, inspiring, and highly controversial digest of disability rights activism, see *The Disability Rag*. Other resources by and for disabled people and their supporters include *The Exceptional Parent* and the *Siblings Network Newsletter,* and newsletters published by many of the groups organized around specific disabilities (e.g., *National Down's Syndrome Society Newsletter; Neurofibromatosis Newsletter*). Social scientific analyses of the impact of disabilities on family life are provided by Gliedman 1980; Feathertone 1981; Goffman 1963. Personal narratives concerning the lives of families with disabled children appear in Featherstone 1981 and Jablow 1982. Stray-Gundersen 1986 combines perspectives by parents and health professionals.

References

Arditti, Rita, Renate Duelli-Klein, and Shelley Minden, eds.
    1984   *Test-Tube Woman: What Future for Motherhood?* Boston: Routledge & Kegan Paul.
Baruch, Elaine H., Amadeo F. D'Amado, and Joni Seager, eds.
    1988   *Embryos, Ethics and Women's Rights.* New York: Harrington Press.

Corea, Gena
    1984   *The Mother Machine.* New York: Harper & Row.
Duffy, John
    1968   *A History of Public Health in New York City.* New York: Russell
            Sage Foundation.
Featherstone, Helen
    1981   *A Difference in the Family: Living With a Disabled Child.* New
            York: Penguin.
Goffman, Erving
    1963   *Stigma: Notes Toward the Management of a Spoiled Identity.* Engle-
            wood Cliffs, N.J.: Prentice-Hall.
Gliedman, John, and William Roth
    1980   *The Unexpected Minority: Handicapped Children in America.* New
            York: Harcourt, Brace, Jovanovich.
Harding, Susan
    1987   Convicted by the Holy Spirit. *American Ethnologist* 14:167–181.
Hook, Ernest B.
    1981   Rates of Chromosomal Abnormalities at Different Maternal Ages.
            Obstetrics and Gynecology 58:282–285.
Jablow, Martha
    1982   *Cara: Growing with a Retarded Child.* Philadelphia: Temple Univer-
            sity Press.
Latour, Bruno
    1987   *Science in Action.* Cambridge, Mass.: Harvard University Press.
Lindenbaum, Shirley and Margaret Lock, eds.
    1993   Preface. In *Knowledge, Power, and Practice: The Anthropology of
            Medicine and Everyday Life.* Berkeley, Los Angeles, Oxford: Uni-
            versity of California Press.
Marfatia, Lavanya, Diana Punales, and Rayna Rapp
    1990   When an Old Reproductive Technology Becomes a New Reproduc-
            tive Technology: Amniocentesis and Underserved Populations. *Birth
            Defects* 26:109–126.
Office of Technology Assessment, Congress of the United States
    1988   *Appendix F: Religious Perspectives in Infertility: Medical and Social
            Choices.* Washington D.C.: Government Printing Office.
Rapp, Rayna
    1988   Chromosomes and Communication: The Discourse of Genetic Coun-
            seling. *Medical Anthropology Quarterly* 2:143–157.
    1991   Constructing Amniocentesis: Medical and Maternal Voices. In *Un-
            certain Terms: Negotiating Gender in American Culture,* 28–42 Faye
            Ginsburg and Anna Tsing, eds. Boston: Beacon.
Rosenberg, Charles
    1976   *No Other Gods: On Science in American Social Thought.* Baltimore:
            Johns Hopkins University Press.
    1987   *The Care of Strangers: The Rise of America's Hospital System.* New
            York: Basic Books.

Rosenkrantz, Barbara Gutmann, and Elizabeth Lomax
    1978   *Science and Patterns of Child Care*. San Francisco: W. H. Freeman.
Rosner, David
    1982   *A Once Charitable Enterprise: Hospitals and Health Care in Brooklyn and Cambridge*. New York: Cambridge University Press.
Rothman, Barbara Katz
    1986   *The Tentative Pregnancy*. New York: Norton.
Stanworth, Michelle, ed.
    1987   *Reproductive Technologies* Minneapolis: University of Minnesota Press.
Spallone, Patricia, and Deborah Steinberg, eds.
    1987   *The Myth of Genetic Engineering and Reproductive Progress*. Elmsford, N.Y.: Pergamon.
Stray-Gundersen, Karen, ed.
    1986   *Babies with Down Syndrome*. Kensington, Maryland: Woodbine House.
Traweek, Sharon
    1988   *Beamtimes and Lifetimes*. Cambridge, Mass.: Harvard University Press.
Woolgar, Steven
    1988   *Science: The Very Idea*. London: Tavistock.

Part Two

The Production
of Medical Knowledge

Introduction

The Production of Medical Knowledge

As the chapters in the preceding section illustrate, medical knowledge is the product of a particular place at a particular time. But how is it produced? Does the production of new knowledge simultaneously change the conception of the self? And what is the relationship between ideology and scientific knowledge? These questions are addressed by the authors of the next three chapters.

Byron and Mary-Jo Good examine the way in which medical schools transform students into doctors. Taking us through the process of learning medicine, they show us how a specific approach to the human body transforms the student and the student's view of sickness, a simultaneous reconstitution of subject and object. Two key symbols of American medicine, competence (associated with the natural sciences) and caring (associated with the humanities) are shown to replicate the cleft in Western culture between technology and humanism, or science and culture. The concept of caring in American medicine (apparently not an important category for the midwives of Bijnor) may stem from a contemporary recognition of the inability of biomedicine to cure most prevalent afflictions.

As suffering patients become "cases," and as powerful technologies create alternate ways of seeing, student physicians acknowledge a change in themselves. It should be noted, perhaps, that although immunology introduces a notion of the body as a postmodern object, students here still speak an older language of mechanism and function. The postmodern reading of the body mapped as a system of recognition and misrecognition (described later by Donna Haraway) has not yet displaced an earlier image of a machine that needs fixing, an image embedded in popular culture and sustained in the anatomy lab. As the accounts of Inuit midwives, prenatal diagnosis in New York, and menopause in Japan (presented later by Margaret Lock) show, alternate and popular languages may retain their power to mold the way we perceive and experience bodies.

Two chapters direct our attention to the production of knowledge in medical practice. Allan Young discusses treatment of a condition recently recognized in psychiatry—posttraumatic stress disorder (PTSD)—in a clinic in which nearly all therapy consists of talking. Knowledge about the condition is produced in three stages: in the patient's narrative, in the therapists' account and interpretation of the narrative, and in propositions and paradigms that result from the therapists' analysis. Dwelling on the role of ideology in the production of medical knowledge, Young acknowledges that discourse and ideology share the same technical language and the same assumptions. He distinguishes, nevertheless, between ideology and discourse. Ideologies, or local systems of knowledge embedded in particular institutions and productive processes, are shown to depend on discourse to naturalize their object (in this case PTSD). At the same time, discourse depends on ideology to provide an institutional base. Thus, discourse and ideology (from the anthropologists' perspective) are separate but intersecting systems of knowledge. This insight allows us to evaluate the ways in which behavior changes results from ideological propositions voiced by figures of institutional authority, in addition to the sense of efficacy that may be conveyed by the therapeutic model.

Lorna Rhodes' ethnography of an emergency unit in a mental health center pursues similar issues of theory and practice. Where Young finds that commitment to a single institutional ideology establishes the ground rules for action and for the production of knowledge, however, the medical staff in this emergency unit move between different layers of ideology, old and new. The contradictions that arise in day-to-day practice stimulate individual staff members to find creative solutions in different contexts, giving a fragmented, somewhat postmodern shape to theory and action.

By considering the institutional, community, and group contexts in which languages are "born," these three chapters locate the fields of power in which the production of knowledge and ideology takes place. They also open up for inspection the apparently seamless relationships among language, knowledge, ideology, and practice.

4

"Learning Medicine"

The Constructing of Medical Knowledge at Harvard Medical School

Byron J. Good and Mary-Jo DelVecchio Good

Introduction

These chapters represents a set of early reflections on a study of medical education and the structure of medical knowledge which we are undertaking in the context of a major curricular reform at Harvard Medical School. Although the larger project examines historical, structural, and phenomenological aspects of medicine and medical education at Harvard, the focus of this paper is rather narrow. Our goal is to raise theoretical and methodological questions about the study of medical knowledge through an examination of the learning of medicine during the early months of the preclinical or basic science years in the medical school. We will argue that anthropological analysis of medical knowledge and of the learning of medicine requires an examination of the structure and phenomenological emergence of the very specialized medical "worlds" to which that knowledge has reference.

Prior to the mid-1970s, anthropological analyses of Western medicine and physicians picture biomedicine in terms of idealized contrasts to traditional healing systems and traditional healers. A particularly clear example of this is found in Horacio Fabrega and Daniel B. Silver's classic account of the Zinacanteco healing system (1973:218–223). Western biomedicine and Zinacanteco healing are presented as a series of contrasts. Diametrically opposing views of the body, the nature of disease, the role of the healer, the nature of the healer/sufferer relationship, and the sources of efficacy all demonstrate the extent to which biomedicine represents the reductionism, individualism, and mechanistic thinking of Western societies. Elegantly stated in these pages, this rather stereotyped characterization of biomedicine as an ideal type that stands in opposition to rather romanticized views of healers reflects a view widely shared in many studies of healing, even today.

Although recent anthropological studies of medical institutions and ethnographies of medical practice demonstrate great diversity within current biomedicine, the literature on medical knowledge continues to outline and criticize an idealized "biomedicine." Much of this work analyzes its "tenacious assumptions" (Gordon 1988), its philosophical underpinnings, and its structure as "formal knowledge" (Freidson 1986). Critical analyses are applied to particular dimensions of medical knowledge: biomedicine, it is held, objectifies the patient and the disease, constituting both decontextualized and asocial objects of the medical gaze. Disease is thus entified and treated as a dimension of human biology rather than as socially produced misery or human suffering. Biomedicine shares biological reductionism and the mind/body dualism with much of Western culture since the Enlightenment. It reflects an "empiricist theory of language." It reproduces social conventions rather than value-free understandings of the natural world. Although anthropological studies of medicine have begun to join historical and ethnographic research with critical analysis of medical knowledge (e.g., Armstrong 1983; Arney 1982; Young 1980), analyses still tend to focus on biomedicine as a conceptual category.

The observations of this literature are often difficult to reconcile with recent ethnographic studies of "physicians of Western medicine" (Gaines and Hahn 1982, Hahn and Gaines 1985). These studies portray physicians in practice as a much more diverse lot than their characterizations appear in much of the literature on medical knowledge. Subspecialties are found to be culturally distinctive (see, e.g., Cassell 1987 on surgeons); classic internists stand in sharp contrast to Christian psychiatrists (Hahn 1985 and Gaines 1985, respectively); and non-Western physicians of Western medicine are shown to bring their culture to their medical knowledge and practice (e.g., Lock 1980 and Ohnuki-Tierney 1984 for the Japanese case). A diverse set of medical discourses mediates personal meanings and institutional struggles (M. Good 1985); individual practitioners draw upon distinctive models of the world, and these are reflected in their diagnostic work (Gaines 1979); and physicians' views of particular conditions—obesity, menopause, chronic illness—are steeped in cultural meanings and institutional double binds.

Thus, the portrayal of a monolithic "biomedicine" or a univocal medical "discourse" can be juxtaposed to studies of particular medical clinics, each housing a diversity of conflicting perspectives and voices, or of individual practitioners, idiosyncratic and personally motivated while constrained by the medicine they have learned, the problems they face, and the institutions in which they work. Efforts to reconcile these face a difficulty similar to that pointed to by Mulkay and Gilbert in their review of recent literature in the sociology of science. Studies of "science," they argue, often fail to specify the types of scientific discourse their arguments are based upon. Consequently, highly divergent characterizations of science—in themselves, each quite cogent—can be developed. They propose a methodological solution: "We have suggested that, at least initially, we should concentrate on understanding how scientists' discourse is organized to convey varying conceptions of scientific action and belief on different occasions and in different contexts" (Mulkay and Gilbert 1982:588–589). This is an important suggestion for a medical anthropology of either biomedicine or traditional healing systems, and we are yet to have a full ethnography of the types of medical discourse in a complex biomedical institution. But difficult problems remain, even when this approach is followed. Discourses often seem to appear without interlocutors, untainted by personal meanings or the world of disease and suffering. "Institutions" are said to construct discourses that mask interests, though we hear little of the mediators of this process. Thus precisely the problems that were the basis for the Wenner-Gren conference come to the fore: how should we combine alternate perspectives and frames of analysis in our cross-cultural studies of illness, care, or medical knowledge?

The research on which this chapter is based is grounded in a conviction that general analyses of "biomedicine" and "the biomedical model" serve us poorly either for understanding contemporary medicine or as a basis for comparisons with other forms of medical knowledge. Such analyses tend to produce glib characterizations, indicating more about the analyst and his or her social theory than that which is being analyzed. At this stage in the development of medical anthropology, little can be expected of studies of the nature of medical knowledge unless they are situated, contextualized, and ethnographically rich.

More specifically, the work described in this chapter is focused on how medical knowledge and the world of medicine is constituted from the perspective of those learning medicine. Although cognizant of the literature on medical education (e.g., Merton 1957; Becker et al. 1961; Fox and Lief 1963; Mumford 1970; Colombotos 1988), our research is not designed to address many of the traditional concerns about how medical students learn the roles of the mature physician. Instead, we are concentrating on the phenomenological dimensions of medical knowledge, on how the medical world, including the objects of the medical gaze, are built up, how the subjects of that gaze—the students and physicians—are reconstituted in the process, and how distinctive forms of reasoning about that world are learned. This is closely related to our arguments in previous publications about the social constitution of "illness realities" (Good and Good 1981) and about the importance of studying folk illness categories in relation to the construction of such realities. We make the epistemological assumption that mind is no "mirror of nature," to use a phrase from Richard Rorty, but that mind and a particular world are jointly constituted. This serves not as a mere philosophical backdrop for the work, but as its methodological base.

In this research, we focus on how the medical world is constituted by examining how it is literally constructed in the experience of the students. Allan Young (1981:380) has argued that there are five types of medical knowledge, each "connected to particular intentions and particular acts," and that actors "have more than one kind of knowledge about a particular event." Although not using these categories, our work is aimed at examining ethnographically the "process" of coming to know rather than simply the "structure" of medical knowledge (ibid.:179). Our work also draws from Michel Foucault's analysis of discourses "as practices that systematically form the objects of which they speak" (Foucault 1972:49). However, having begun with an interest in the historicized structure of medical discourses and a variety of practices with which they are associated, we have found it necessary to return to the subjects, to what Foucault (1970:xiii) called "scientific consciousness" in contrast to the archaeological order—to examine the extent to which medical knowledge is "personal knowledge," to explore the "personal meanings" associated with common discourses, and to examine the construction of medical knowledge as intersubjective reality in the context of highly organized interpersonal and institutional relationships. It should be added that a phenomenological analysis need not, indeed cannot, assume consensus in the constitution of the commonsense world of medicine. The nature of that world and its objects, though intersubjective, is often highly contested and is framed by competing interests and power relations. The experiential emergence of a dominant medical world and a pervasive medicalized perspective and the cultivation of medical knowledge take place within a setting sharing many characteristics of Erving Goffman's "total institution," and both the competing perspectives and the dominance of the medical are reproduced in this setting.

Not surprisingly, we have focused attention in this research on the construction of the body as the object of medical knowledge (cf. Csordas 1988, Scheper-Hughes and Lock 1987, Turner 1984), and on the reconstruction of the subject in relation to that object. The fuller study of which this is a small part will examine this knowledge in relation to the laboratory production of scientific knowledge, the social organization of the teaching enterprise at Harvard Medical School, and the clinical sites in which it is applied to the treatment of patients.

Our goal in this chapter is to provide an initial analysis of data from our research, exploring methods growing out of the position outlined here. We briefly indicate the setting and methods of our study, outline data from our experiences in histology and anatomy, then examine several themes that are emerging in our interviews with medical students. In the process, we rephrase some traditional critiques of the "assumptions" of biomedicine as questions about the nature of medical reasoning and how it is learned. It is our hope that our analysis will ultimately provide insight into a very peculiar healing system, one to which many of us are so accustomed to entrusting our mortality that we seldom wish to face up to its peculiarities. Our goal is to begin to rethink the analysis of a form of medical knowledge that typically serves medical anthropology as the basis for cross-cultural comparisons.

The Research Setting and Methodologies

In September 1984, twenty-four students entered a new program at Harvard Medical School. Dubbed "The New Pathway in General Medical Education," the program represented what Harvard president Derek Bok (1984:2) called "Harvard's most important innovation of the 1980's." Many at the medical school felt the evolving program represented the most significant reform in medical education in many decades. The New Pathway was designed to bring two new perspectives to bear on medical education: a new educational philosophy, focusing on tutorial-based active learning, a case method akin to that of the Harvard Business School, and new integrated curricular blocks; and a new vision of the physician for the twenty-first century—one who is constantly engaged in self-learning in a context of rapidly changing medical knowledge, who makes use of computer-based (rather than just memory-based) information sources, who recognizes the importance of the origins of many diseases in behavior and lifestyle, who learns to operate within the cost constraints of contemporary medicine, and who combines the best qualities of the skillful and caring physician.

Several mechanisms for evaluation of the new program were developed, focusing on gathering student feedback about their experiences and the much more sensitive issues of comparing knowledge levels and psychological characteristics of students in the New Pathway with those in the "Classic Curriculum." Although comparisons between the more traditional curriculum and the New Pathway were constant—indeed a critique of traditional forms of medical education was fundamental to the justification for the whole program—the project was not narrowly conceived as an experiment. Although it was described by the dean of the medical school as an experiment, the decision to develop a common curriculum based on the experimental model did not await a systematic outcome evaluation. Few believed such an evaluation could really be undertaken, and it was clear from the outset that the goal was to reform medical education for all Harvard medical students, not just a small cohort. In this context, it was recognized that a broader form of evaluation, combining a social history of the project, documentation of the process of social and educational reform, and a description of the experiences of students in the new and traditional curricula, was desirable. Our study is a part of that overall "evaluation," and this chapter represents a set of early reflections on our experiences in this project.

During the first year of the research, we recruited three groups of students from the class of 1990, representing the three Harvard Medical School curricula experiences, the traditional or "classic curriculum," the second round of the New Pathway, and the Health Sciences and Technology curriculum, which confers a joint Harvard-MIT degree. We interviewed these students several times throughout the year, attended occasional classes and teaching clinics provided for first year students, and interviewed faculty and administrators about the events that were unfolding. By the end of the first year of research, although we had learned a great deal about the various curricula at Harvard and some fascinating dimensions of the politics of medical reform, we felt our own perspectives on medical education, built up over eleven years of teaching in similar settings, often precluded our understanding of the perspective of those learning medicine. To develop a more anthropological perspective, we decided that one of us, Byron Good, would participate more fully in selected parts of the preclinical years as an auditor/ethnographer in the New Pathway curriculum. The goal of this aspect of the research was not to focus on observing medical students, but on trying to understand the process of learning medicine by trying to do it, by trying to learn anatomy and histology, immunology, or neurology. The research text for this chapter includes interview material with students from the class of 1990 and data drawn from participant observation.

Entry into the Body

"The Human Body," integrating anatomy, histology, and radiology, was designed to provide an introduction to the "basic principles governing the organization of the human body from the molecular to the organismic level" (*Tutor Guide* 1987) and organizes the first eight weeks of learning medicine.[1] A brief description of the first week will provide data for the analysis to follow.

At the core of the experience is a daily tutorial: a group of seven students and a faculty member gather to discuss a "case" and to work through dimensions of histology and anatomy needed to understand and "solve" the case. The case is presented as a simple text—a straightforward description of an individual and his or her medical condition, with separate pages with new information passed out on subsequent days as the case unfolds. Additional handouts outline learning objectives for the week. The first case, passed out on the first day of Week 1, was based on a newspaper account of the death of a Bulgarian intellectual who defected to Britain and became a BBC commentator. Ten hours after experiencing a sharp pain and itching in the back of his leg while riding a bus, he developed a fever and vomiting; he was hospitalized and two days later died, his condition complicated by irregular heart rhythms. The next two paragraphs passed out later in the week, described the pathologist's finding—a small metal pellet embedded in the dermis, connective tissue showing no signs of bacterial invasion—and the discovery in the pellet, by an expert on toxins at Scotland Yard, of traces of ricin, a lectin isolated from the castor bean with properties similar to diptheria toxin.

This simple case was designed to provoke entry into the body and an introductory examination of issues in histology and anatomy. The discussions, directed by the students with selective guidance from the tutor, began with three basic categories written on the blackboard: Data, Hypotheses, and Agenda. The bare data provided in the case were listed, hypotheses about the cause of death were generated in common parlance, and a discussion was begun about what one would need to know in order to understand the case. Students were aware this was simply an approach to learning about the human body, to learning histology and anatomy, therefore discussions also focused on areas in these sciences students wished to pursue and cover.

Within this rather simple format, a wide variety of issues were addressed. If something enters the leg and produces symptoms of vomiting and heart irregularities, what course would it have to travel through the body? What kinds of tissues would it pass through? What are the boundaries between such tissues; how does transport across such boundaries occur? For example, what types of cells constitute connective tissue? How would a toxin travel through connective tissue? What would be the response of the various cells in the connective tissue? What is the nature of the inflammatory response? What is swelling? What is a generic model of how fluid moves around in the body? How do toxins—or bacteria, or viruses—enter cells, move around inside cells, affect them? How does a toxin affect the body? Does one molecule kill one cell? Is death caused by the majority of cells being attacked? How many cells are in the body? How many toxin molecules would fit in a small pellet? What was the pathologist looking for? What would be left in the tissue after several days and after death? How did the pathologist know it was not bacterial? These questions, stimulated by the case, often began with commonsense knowledge of the body (what is fever or swelling like?) and moved quickly to restating the issues in terms of cell biology and macrostructural characteristics of the human body. Types of cells—simple squamous keratinizing epithelial cells, macrophages, fibroblasts, mast cells, eosinophils, lymphocytes, monocytes; the architecture of cells—the phospholipid bilayer membrane, rough and smooth endoplasmic reticulum, the Golgi apparatus; types of transport across cell membranes—passive diffusion across concentration gradients, endocytosis—all of these quickly became the language for discussing questions originally generated in ordinary language, such as "what is a toxin and what does it do?"

Tutorials provided the central organizing experiences for learning during this first week. Questions were identified and placed on the agenda, and students divided up topics to explore and bring findings back to the group. However, there were several other critical sites of learning. First, daily lectures brought the students in this curriculum together as a single group, arrayed before one of the major researchers or clinicians in a traditional medical ampitheatre. During this first week the first lecture, delivered by a histologist who was director of the "body block," was an introduction to cell biology, a kind of histological semiotics of biological systems. From organelle to cell to organs to organism, all biological systems maintain identity by establishing boundaries and providing mechanisms for communication and transport across and among systems. Illustrated with histological and anatomical examples, the lecture provided the basic conceptual structure for the block. This lecture was complemented by a senior faculty radiologist, who introduced the radiology sessions that were to accompany each major anatomical system studied. In addition, one of the medical school's leading clinicians lectured on clinical uses of "anatomical thinking"—on understanding the nature of bounded anatomical systems, the progression of pathology within such systems, the hazards of any pathology that breaches boundaries, and the use of such thinking in diagnosis, prognosis, treatment, and research.

Second, the histology lab was a central site for entry into the body, with the microscope providing entrée into the world of the cell. Students began a process of learning to recognize structure amidst the apparent confusion revealed when viewing tissue through the microscope at various levels of power. A lab book developed for the course, a set of slides, and supporting texts were provided for use both within specified lab hours, when histologists were present to work with students, and during afternoon or evening hours.

Third, gross anatomy lab, which began on the second day of classes, epitomized entry to the body. Five anatomy labs, maintained within closed doors, eight cadavers—wrapped and draped—per room, four students in white lab coats per cadaver, three instructors per room— these constituted the paradigmatic site for entry into the human body. During the first lab, the wraps of the cadavers were opened, leaving hands, feet and head bound by separate wraps, and the first incisions were made on the chest—from the jugular notch along the clavicle to the acromion (on the shoulder), and down the middle of the chest to the xiphisternal junction, then around to the side of the rib cage. The skin was then reflected or peeled back, leaving the breast and nipple in place, revealing superficial fascia, adipose tissue (fat), and the underlying deep fascia. Three major muscles—pectoralis major and minor and serratus anterior—were identified, cleaned, detached, and reflected.

Finally, although represented during the first week only in lecture and slides, radiology provided the final mode of entry into the body. Drawing on traditional x-ray, CT, and NMR images, radiologists met with small groups of students to view aspects of the anatomy under consideration, focusing both on learning to make sense of projectional images (traditional x-rays, sonograms) and sectional images (CT, MRI, NMR) and on engaging substantive issues in anatomy of joints, abdomen, mediastinum, or other representative parts of the body.

"OK, Now Let's Talk Some Science"

Several elementary analyses are suggested by these observations. First, medicine is introduced as science. During the first lecture of medical school, the head of the course spent fifteen minutes of introductory comments about the organization of the course, then commenced the course with: "Okay, now let's talk some science!" One of the women in the class told me, with some excitement, "For many of us [who were not science majors in college], this is our first experience of thinking of ourselves as scientists." Although efforts have been made to bring clinicians into teaching during the first two years and to introduce students to the clinics as well as increase exposure to the basic sciences during the clerkship years, the first two preclinical years (or "precynical years," as they are sometimes called), are predominantly in the hands of the basic scientists, often world-renowned laboratory scientists. Science is the point of entry into medicine, and however restricted the science courses are from the perspective of faculty or Ph.D. students in those disciplines, it is made profoundly clear that learning medicine during the first two years is above all learning the biomedical sciences.

Second, medical education begins by entry into the body. Viewed through the microscope, entered physically in the gross anatomy lab, viewed through the marvels of contemporary radiologic imaging, or presented by master scientists, the body is revealed in infinite detail. Students begin a process of gaining intimacy with the body—attempting to understand its gross organization and structure three-dimensionally, examining tissue from gross function to molecular structure. Students are as geographers moving from gross topography to the detail of microecology. The body is the object of attending and skilled manipulating, and the site of unending learning. Within the lifeworld of medicine, however, the body is newly constituted as a medical body, quite distinct from the bodies with which we interact in everyday life, and the intimacy with that body reflects a distinctive perspective, an organized set of perceptions and emotional responses that emerge with the emergence of the body as a site of medical knowledge.

Third, more explicitly in the new curriculum than the old, medicine is learned from the perspective of individual cases. The case is the frame for learning, that *through* which learning is undertaken, the ground rather than figure of the gestalt. Anything worth learning in medicine can be learned through the case, and the case is an individual, a single human sufferer, standing alone before the physician. The individual is the object of medicine—what else could be? The medical case can be easily constructed in a few paragraphs. Social data are present—but present as identifying features and significant indicators of potential pathology, dimensions of lifestyle, of risk factors. And the individual is presented as a problem, the site of a problem to be identified and solved. From the first tutorial, diagnosis is the assumed goal. Hypotheses and Agenda: the twin goals are to solve the puzzle and to learn medicine using the case as the means, learning driven by the intrigue of problem solving.

These observations are not intended as generalizations about the "biomedical model" or "biomedicine," entities which are constructs of the social sciences more than distinctive phenomena in the world. They are rather intended as summary notes on a few of many dimensions of medical education that seem strikingly clear during the first few weeks of Harvard Medical School, based on observation and entry into the process.

In the following pages, we focus attention on the experience of this process, the experience of learning medicine, as reflected in our conversations with students. We argue that American medical culture is characterized by an ideology that reifies the domains of "scientific facts" and "human values" through the juxtaposition of two key symbols, "competence" and "caring"; and that the training of students to be "competent" physicians entails a reconstruction of commonsense views of the patient, sickness, and the personal boundaries of the medical student. Students experience a culturally distinctive configuration of contradictions as they attempt to maintain qualities of "caring" while encountering the world of medical science.

Caring and Competence:
The Dual Discourse[2]

When we ask medical students during initial interviews to reflect on the meaning of being a good physician, two juxtaposed themes quickly emerge. These themes, condensed by two central symbols— "competence" and "caring"—are linked to a dual discourse characteristic of contemporary American medicine and contemporary medical students, regardless of curricula experiences. The reflections of a first year student are representative:

> I think there are two components, neither of which can be done without, that are equally important and make up a physician. One is a thorough understanding of a wide range of disease processes, symptoms, diagnoses— you simply cannot do without the basic science, the basic medicine background. It does no good to see a physician who can't make a diagnosis or can't elicit symptoms. So I think first of all is a fundamental understanding of medicine, the basic science. And the other part of making a good physician is the ability to practice the art of medicine, to listen to a patient, to elicit information, which is important to make your diagnosis. But also to show genuine compassion, and understanding, that's an indispensible part of medicine. That's what makes us different from a biochemist or physiologist. We are able to . . . lay on hands."

These themes, constantly salient, representing a cultural tension, develop through the education of the student. Physicians must be competent; they should also embody caring qualities. "Competence" is associated with the language of the basic sciences, with "value-free" facts and knowledge, skills, techniques, and "doing" or action (cf. M. Good 1985). "Caring" for these students is expressed in the language of values, of relationships, attitudes, compassion, and empathy, the nontechnical or as one student called it the "personal" aspects of medicine. It is also conveyed in terms such as "the laying on of hands." Competence is closely associated with the natural sciences, caring with the humanities. Competence is a quality of knowledge and skills, caring a quality of persons.

From the first days of medical school, students repeatedly express anxieties about competence, that learning the details of anatomy, pathophysiology, or pharmacology are essential to their becoming competent physicians, that one day they may stand before a patient and need to know a fact they are now struggling to remember. This anxiety pervades much of medical education and adds a quality of seriousness to all that is done.

It is the sense that what you learn now may make the difference in someone's life. The material begins to impress you over and over again. This is serious. You need to know it to treat people.

As students move through their first two years, these concerns often intensify.

These third year students you hear about have no experience, and they are entrusted with the care of a patient. And you hear all sorts of stories. When you look at the number of facts we've been handed this year, including "you should never do X when Y is present," you always feel it's inevitable that you'll screw up. And competence comes into the issue all the time. And it's part of the reason for being frustrated—the overwhelming volume of material.

These concerns are buttressed by "horror stories" that are casually told by clinical faculty to impress students with the importance of what they are learning. In one of the radiology labs a warm, supportive radiologist was reviewing CT scans of the mediastinum, indicating the relative locations of the heart, arteries, veins, esophagus, and trachea. He remarked to the students,

One day you will be doing catheterization, running tubes down into the veins and arteries. You need to know where they are relative to each other. I knew one case where a physician went through the esophagus to try to biopsy the trachea. Unfortunately he biopsied the aorta instead and the patient died. The blood rushed into the trachea and esophagus and the patient died before the doctor could stop the bleeding.

Even though the radiologist quickly went on to say this is not a common problem, Byron Good's response as observer was a kind of visceral feeling of the terror of undertaking such a procedure and the consequences of error. Such feelings are often present when students attempt to explain why they feel so driven to master the material presented.

Students' earliest interviews are marked by a concern to become caring practitioners, to practice medicine differently than they have experienced it in the past, or to live up to the model of some ideal physician they have known. However, as the pressure grows to learn the basic sciences necessary for competence, students increasingly express fears that they will not be able to balance these two goals, that they may be a "zero sum," that in their struggle to achieve competence they may lose those caring qualities that led them to study medicine. Some feel that too little time is given to teaching the caring dimensions of medicine. Many, however, feel that the science has to be learned, but that caring is an innate human quality, to be cultivated but not taught.

> In our tutorials the hard science is the hard science and it's still the most important stuff you have to learn. And if you don't learn that you're not going to be competent. And if you don't learn the other, well, you'll pick it up. It's not clear what is to be learned.

As students begin to acquire experience interviewing and physically examining patients, the meaning of "caring" becomes transformed and increasingly complex. At times, the abstraction of "helping people" is experienced as "invading" the other, as they are instructed to ask patients about intimate aspects of their lives, and as they cross personal and sexual boundaries in physical examinations. A second year student, reflecting on the process of learning the physical exam and history taking, remarked,

> Before going to medical school, the way I had envisioned caring about people and helping people, which I still think is my motivation for doing this, and I am still sure about that, was on a completely different level, much more abstract. . . . I'd never have to . . . learn how to do it. You're nice to someone and you listen, and that does a lot; and care about and respect others, and if something's wrong, you try to help. That's the level that I came in at, and I think a lot of others did too.

In spite of this growing complexity, the discourse on caring maintains its basic form. It is a language of relationships, of attitudes and emotions, and of innate qualities of persons; it is a nontechnical, commonsense language of interpersonal engagement, not a language of knowledge and facts.

This juxtaposition of competence and caring and their associated meanings emerges across many contexts, and is present throughout the history of Western medicine. It is built into American medicine as a cultural institution and the struggle between technology and humanism, between science and culture, as *Naturwissenschaft* and *Geisteswissenschaft* are seen as opposing forces in Western civilization. This dichotomy is expressed clearly in C. P. Snow's 1959 essay, "The Two Cultures and the Scientific Revolution," in which he characterizes scientific and literary elites as groups "who had almost ceased to communicate at all, who in intellectual, moral and psychological climate had so little in common that . . . one might have crossed an ocean."

Medicine as a Western cultural institution accepts this dichotomy as fundamental, then defines as essential to the role of physician qualities of both of these cultures. This image of the physician is maintained in popular culture, in the self-understandings of students long before they enter medical school, and in a long history of humanist (and social science) critiques of medical education. Throughout, competence is given primacy, as is bioscience as the presumed basis for medical practice, and the language of competence has come to be increasingly powerful in expressing the self-worth of the physician, in negotiating boundaries among specialties, and in providing the sole grounds for compensation for failures of medicine to provide benefit.

Central to medical education is the demand to educate competent physicians while maintaining the qualities of caring. Contradictions, both socially and culturally constituted, necessarily result. Several themes that emerge in the interviews illustrate this.

The Reconstruction of the Person as the Object of the Medical Gaze

One of the critical and multifaceted changes through which medical students pass en route to becoming competent physicians is the reconstruction of the person who is the object of the medical gaze. This is a subtext of much that goes on more explicitly in medical education. For example, in the "case method" learning of the New Pathway, no explicit attention is paid to how cases are constructed (with minimal social and personal characteristics and great physiological detail) and how sufferers are reconstructed as cases, but a process begins that finds fuller expression in clinical years.

The most dramatic expression of this process, however, occurs in the anatomy lab. As we interviewed students about their experiences in anatomy, some described how they began to experience people differently after spending weeks exploring the inside of the body of their cadaver, and how they began to experience themselves differently.

> It was second semester that we started anatomy and I remember going into peer group and saying, I'm changing. Something's happening here. After a couple months of that, I said, I feel like I'm growing, that there's a funny way I know I'm not the same person I was two months ago.

This student described the experience as being like an Outward Bound experience or like combat.

You take people, you take them completely out of context from their normal life, subject them to a whole new set of rules, and have them do a lot of things you never thought you could do. And then when you take that back into your life in general and realize you're capable of that is when you realize you've grown so much.

Several steps are important in the phenomenological reconstruction of the person, described here. The anatomy laboratory is demarcated as a separate order, having distinctive moral norms. Within this redefined context, the human body is given new meaning and a new manner of interacting with that body is appropriate. Intrusions from ordinary reality into this space are experienced as "violation."

I can remember a person who I think was an applicant, who was spending a day with one of the students kind of getting a feel for the experience. And she came in and just hung out in the anatomy lab. And I felt very violated in some funny way. I felt like she was an intruder . . . that without being properly introduced and given a context, I didn't want to be seen doing these coarse things in such a cavalier way by that person.

Similarly, carrying something out of this space would dramatically alter its meaning. It would be shocking, the student suggested,

to imagine taking something out of the lab like that and saying, look I have this liver or this finger. Everything would change as soon as you took off the white coat and walked outside. The whole context of that body part would be completely different. The seriousness of not understanding that boundary does seem significant.

Students describe a variety of changes in their perception that occur within this demarcated space. In normal reality, the body surfaces—the skin, the hands, the eyes, the face, the clothing—convey personhood. The interior of a person is his or her thoughts, experiences, personality. In the laboratory, the hands, the feet, the head remain bound, and the torso and limbs are the object of sustained attention. As the skin is drawn back, a different "interior" emerges.

Emotionally a leg has such a different meaning after you get the skin off. It doesn't mean at all what it meant before. And how the skin, which is our way of relating to other people—I mean, touching skin is . . . getting close to people—how that is such a tiny part of what's going on, it's like the peel of an orange, it's just one tiny little aspect. And as soon as you get that off, you're in this whole other world.

This "whole other world" becomes the paramount reality in the anatomy lab. It is a world with which the physician-to-be develops a tremendous intimacy. It is a biological world, a physical world, a complex three-dimensional space, a thing of compartments, tubes, an electrical system.

In anatomy, the body is revealed as having natural compartments. One of the most shocking moments in anatomy lab was the day students entered to find the body prepared for dissecting the genitalia, the body sawn in half above the waist, then bisected between the legs. Students described their shock not at close examination of the genitalia, nor simply at the body being taken apart, but rather at the dismemberment, and at dismemberment that crossed natural boundaries. Dissection follows planes of tissues. Here the plane that cut the body was straight and hard, cutting across natural layers of tissue in an unnatural fashion. The natural "compartments" that are investigated include muscle groups, compartments of organs (mediastinum, peritoneum), vasculature, and individual organs. These are gradually broken down and examined not only in relation to each other but in finer and finer detail.

Students, undoubtedly drawing on cultural images available, describe increasingly experiencing the body as "machinelike."

> I've had some real perception changes of people. We all have this sort of thing—I'm good at tennis, say, or something else—and therefore, I'm good. I started realizing more and more, I can't help but think of us as machines. And there's none of this individuality and goodness; it's just whether or not you synapse quickly.

This image of the machinelike qualities of the body includes perceptions of its having compartments and parts, of these being defined functionally, of human similarities and differences being essentially bodily, and of the sheer physicality of the human person. It is experienced in the anatomy lab not idealized as in the texts and atlases, but as gross and dirty: "Suddenly you envision your body as being full of this stuff that just works. And it's magic. When you study anatomy, it's dirty!" In addition, a growing set of complementary experiences bring home quite clearly the contingency of the body. In teaching cases, patients succumb to cancer, heart disease, and other conditions that medicine cannot control. In anatomy and in early experiences of autopsies, the contingency of the body—and the person—are experienced with varying levels of intensity.

Students are quite aware that they are learning an alternative way of seeing, that it is a way of seeing that they can "turn on and turn off," and that they are learning to "think anatomically" in a way that is central to the medical gaze. However, during anatomy, this way of seeing is not neatly contained in the lab or confined to the appropriate contexts for the medical perspective. While participating in anatomy as an observer,

Byron would occasionally be walking down the street and find himself a body amidst bodies, rather than a person amidst persons. Students report an uncomfortable inability to shut off this way of seeing, "to turn it off and . . . quit worrying about whether you are turning in or turning out," to experience touching persons in commonsense terms rather than anatomical terms.

Finally, early educational experiences teach implicitly that the appropriate response to the medicalized body is an active one: "Let's figure out how it works and let's fix it."

> The response to coming across an accident, or somebody falls down and breaks something or is bleeding . . . has more to do with the way you react to a cadaver, which is, what do I see here, what could I put back, how could I put it together, how can I stop the bleeding? . . . That kind of active response as opposed to just a purely emotional or other kind of responses is a crucial change that happens. . . . The hands-on experience with a dead person three times a week for three months is really the most important for that kind of thing I've had.

Our point here is not that anatomy is a "dehumanizing" experience, substituting technology for humanity, but simply that it is one significant contribution to the reconstruction of the person as an object of the medical gaze, an object identified as a case, a cadaver, or a patient. Anthropology makes it clear that the person is a cultural construct, a complex and culturally shaped way of experiencing self and other, a "common sense" that richly combines culture and ideology, interpersonal relations, and development. Cultural "work" is required to reconstitute the person who is the object of medical attention. This person is a special abstraction, requiring a reorganization of experience from commonsense reality, and this reconstruction of the person is essential to a student becoming a competent physician.

Learning the Language of Medicine: Reconstructing Common Sense

"Learning a foreign language" is a central metaphor for medical education. During orientation a biochemist remarked, "Learning medicine is like learning a language, and biochemistry has become the lingua franca of medicine." The metaphor is commonly referred to by students and faculty alike. On the surface, the meaning is clear. There is a huge vocabulary to be learned, a working vocabulary as large as most foreign languages, and competence in medicine depends on learning to speak and read the language. Here too, however, there is a subtext. Learning the language of medicine consists not of learning new words for the commonsense world, but the construction of a new world altogether. The world revealed is one of incredible detail. At every level, from molecular to cellular to the classification of diseases, it explodes into greater and greater detail. As visualization shifts from the electron microscope to levels of the light microscope to forms of radiography, new levels are revealed, each subsuming the previous. The language learned and the world revealed to the medical gaze are closely linked. It is a biochemical world, a world of cell biology and of physiological systems as well as of discrete diseases. As one student said,

> In a sense we are learning a whole new world. Some of it is just learning names, but learning names is, now you get into linguistics or semiotics of something, because learning new names for things is to learn new things about them. If you know the names of every tree you look at trees differently. Otherwise they're trees. As soon as you know all the names for them they just become something different. That's kind of what we're doing.

Several aspects of the medical world and the experiences associated with discovering this world may be identified. First, it is wonderfully reductionistic. The experience in anatomy and histology of observing the same tissue at increasing levels of magnification is striking. At each level, quite distinctive structures appear, each subsumed by the others. Tissue with distinctive functioning is revealed to consist of specialized cells, these too have highly specialized organelles, inner structures that are now understood as bounded environments for specialized biochemical processes, these revealed at the molecular level. Learning the language for distinguishing such structures suddenly opens a world and makes available a literature for understanding a physical condition from gross to molecular levels of organization.

Physiology elaborates this world in the language of mechanism and function.

> I don't know who introduced the term [mechanism], but I do know that you see it most when you're dealing with hormones, and you start to chart out this series of causal events, causal chains that happen after you introduce hormone X. From that, you're basically taking an observed event and tracing back the biochemical mechanisms which somehow caused this to happen. That's where it comes from. But it gives you the notion—and sometimes not outrageous notion—that you can find a mechanism for everything that happens.

This form of reasoning is developed in students in science classes long before medical school, is reinforced as the basis for thinking throughout the human biology courses, and is made experientially real in the "dog lab" in physiology (a critical experience for most medical students where they see physiological responses to various chemicals introduced into a living animal). It serves as the architecture for developing medical knowledge. When individual mechanisms are not known—and at the cutting edge of science the unknowns are many—they are presumed to be of a certain functional type, allowing for research to progress on details as the whole structure is being constructed. Systems—biochemical reactions in metabolism, liver function—are treated as isolable for experimental purposes, even though they never appear in such form. This allows for problems to be broken into small parts and for mechanisms to be identified and studied.

This form of reasoning has counterparts in clinical material to which students are introduced in the basic sciences and early teaching clinics. In learning the basic physiology and pathophysiology, it quickly seems the only reasonable way to think. In physiology and biochemistry, a new language of mechanisms and function is learned that allows disorders that we have come to have commonsense knowledge about—liver disease, kidney functioning, diabetes—to be described and understood in incredibly rich detail. Complaints are most voiced by students when the links between the science and the commonsense world of disease are not drawn, or when nearly exclusive attention is given to research topics at the edge of current knowledge. For such topics, the architecture of the knowledge becomes more visible.

> It is assumed by almost everybody that there is something out there that just has to be discovered. By that I mean, if you consider the way people talk about making a diagnosis—I remember Judah Folkman saying of a pediatrician at CHMC that he had never missed a diagnosis, and that was really impressive to everyone. If you think of what that means, it's that every case that came by there was really some objective thing that was wrong and that there was *a* correct label to stick on it. That's nice in theory but it just doesn't seem to work out that way, but it leaves you with the impression that it does. And then you get from the other side a whole host of categories of idiopathic, autoimmune. Is it a correct diagnosis to slap "idiopathic" down before any disease—it means you have no idea—is that a correct diagnosis? But you come away with the notion that even for these idiopathic things, that for everything there is a mechanism, and that as physicians your object is, right off the bat, to figure out what *the* thing is that's going wrong with this person.

This is true not only for assumptions about mechanisms but for the assumption that knowledge of isolated subsystems generalizes to functioning physiological systems (i.e., sick people).

> There is definitely a tension between clinicians and laboratory scientists. The clinicians would be the ones to tell you that more often than anybody

else—they say, "That's fine, it works in the lab, but it doesn't do squat here on the floor." You get that all the time. They're different worlds.

"Boundaries": The Reconstruction of the *Subject* of the Medical Gaze

The transformation of the person who is the sufferer and the sickness from commonsense reality to special realities has not only profound implications for the cognitive development of students and for the development of the medical gaze but also for the experiential development of the self of the physician. As students move toward identifying themselves as physicians, they find it necessary to redefine their personal boundaries in several ways. Many describe struggling to resist being "swallowed" up by medicine, losing their personal lives to their growing professional selves and "the medical machine" or the medical "whale closing its jaws on me." This results not only from the demands placed on students, not only on their drive to cover the mass of material because of their fears about competence, but also because many hope to live out a myth of being "impassioned" by the medicine they practice.

Q. What's the myth of passion? That's a tough one to live up to.

A. I think it's the combination of being so excited about what you're doing that you don't think about other things, and being able to impart that to your patients, to let them see that you're committed to them, that this is where you want to be and what you want to be doing.

This same student worried that she would choose a less demanding subspecialty, such as emergency medicine, and then "might feel as though I missed an opportunity to become impassioned about my work because it would have required twenty-four hours a day." As a result of these various demands, students express enormous concern about how to relate medicine to their private lives and how to reconstruct the boundaries of their personal selves.

Quite profound changes in how students think about and experience boundaries between themselves and patients are suggested in the interviews. As students gain clinical experiences, they begin to question what constitutes appropriate personal boundaries in relation to patients, what aspects of the private lives and bodies of patients they should seek or accept access to, and what aspects of themselves they should reveal to patients and to colleagues and faculty; these issues become paramount and coincide with early clinical experiences. Grappling with this process, a second year student reflected,

I never really thought I'd have to get so intimate to be able to help, I never thought that I'd be asking questions about sexual history or such detailed questions to help someone the best I could. For example, I saw a woman who had been vomiting for three weeks. I asked her all these questions about her vomiting. When I was writing up the case that night, I was thinking, this is absurd, [spending an hour] . . . going into detail about her vomiting! . . . I'd never imagined that I'd be doing that in a million years! That is something that is taught to you as important information that's going to help the patient. That's something I'm just coming to learn. I'm still not sure it's important to be able to help someone. The vomiting is an extreme example. But we are taught to ask these questions which are foreign.

The development of the professional self is in part a redefinition of what is "foreign," of what appears invasive. One student contrasted his first year's sense that touching other people during the physical exam was "invading another person—you feel like you are getting too close to a person in some ways" to his experience of patients' bodies in the second year.

I don't feel like another person's body is so foreign to me now. The concept of the other body is changing. At first, you are very aware that you are dealing with another person. Now I just don't think about that any more. You just do the routine. If there's a head at the end of the body, that's better for the interview! (Question: So you are thinking "this is another" what?) You are thinking about findings, whereas at first you think about touching another person. But now you are concentrating, because you know you are looking for certain things. . . . You are hyperaware of what you are doing.

Students find themselves struggling with the commonsense way in which one relates to others and the way in which they are being trained to relate to patients. The language of "foreign," "invading," and "penetrating" suggests the magnitude of the process through which the redefinition of personal boundaries occurs.

I still feel hesitant asking questions that are going to get down deep into what people think . . . because I still think I am invading information that, while it's important, it's personal. To a large extent, I think I am getting comfortable in dealing with people in a completely different way. It's no longer that I deal with people in trying to make friendships and trying to work out a relationship based on a progression of learning about each other. To change that relationship with people is hard—to attack people in a way that's not on that level.

Students, in addition, express concerns about opening themselves to the pain associated with the suffering of patients, about how they can remain available to that pain without being overwhelmed. Thus not only are the patient and the sickness reconstituted through medical education, but the person of the medical student and the normal boundaries of his or her relationships are also transformed in the process of becoming competent physicians.

Conclusion I:
A Substantive Reflection

The problem of overcoming the "disabling" qualities of medical education is often restated as the problem of how to maintain caring attitudes while developing the knowledge and skills of the competent physician. This was certainly true in the planning process for the new curriculum at Harvard, where "knowledge" and "skills" were the focus of the basic sciences, "attitudes" the focus of the "patient-doctor" curriculum. This restatement is embedded in and reproduces a series of dichotomies, organized around the dual discourse of competence and caring. The medical gaze is directed to a reconstituted person—a patient, case, or body—which is juxtaposed to a commonsense person who is suffering. A technical language is juxtaposed to everyday discourse, a specialized language of disease to the world of illness experience, and technical activities to the natural caring response. The subject of the medical gaze is also reconstructed within this framework: a physician with reorganized personal boundaries is juxtaposed to the normal individual relating to another human being who is suffering. The conviction that the physician is an individual who embodies both of these juxtaposed, often contradictory qualities is fundamental to Western medicine. Humanist critiques of medicine as overly technologized are essential to the history of Western medicine; such critiques play a significant role in maintaining the dual discourse of medicine as a cultural institution and the conviction of both the public and physicians that physicians should be able to mediate these contradictions. The social sciences, including medical anthropology, have contributed to this discourse.

The teaching of social sciences to medical students, however, typically engenders resentment. As they begin to redefine the object of the medical gaze in the language of science and the body, medical students express nostalgia for the commonsense view of human suffering, fearing that they will lose precisely those qualities they most hoped to bring to medicine. The critical social sciences have often called for science in place of art, for bringing a new conceptual language and accompanying knowledge and skills to problems of human suffering, rather than simply reproducing the view that caring attitudes and the commonsense perspective on the patient, illness, and the work of doctoring are adequate solutions for what ails medicine. Anthropology in medical schools thus occupies an ambiguous position; critic of the role of the natural sciences and the individualized and mechanistic forms of reasoning about disease and its treatment, critic of the social organization of medicine, and critic of the nostalgic view of the human sciences as the producers of caring.

Conclusion II:
A Theoretical Reflection

This chapter is primarily a descriptive one. It represents our first substantial effort to work through data that we have been gathering over the past eighteen months. However, a theoretical approach is embedded in the data, as we described at the beginning of this chapter. We have sought not simply to describe the structure of medical knowledge, but to analyze the emergence of the life world of medicine as the grounds of experienced reality for students during their first year of medical school. As our work proceeds, we are examining the continued development of that world as students move into the hospitals and clinics and as the strangeness of their original encounter with the medical world slips ever further from their consciousness.

From a theoretical point of view, several conceptual domains are essentially problematic in this approach to the study of medical knowledge. First, the *epistemological:* how are we to represent medical knowledge as socially constructed while recognizing the powerful advances of biological sciences? We have followed philosophers such as Nelson Goodman (1978), Hilary Putnam (1981), and Richard Rorty (1979), who argue against a correspondence theory of knowledge ("The trouble . . . is not that correspondences between words or concepts and other entities don't exist, but that *too many* correspondences exist" [Putnam 1981:72]), and who argue that our theories of knowledge are fundamentally about how worlds are constituted.

Second, the *phenomenological:* how are distinctive medical worlds constructed experientially so that they appear singularly convincing, natural, objective, the only way to imagine the world? What are the "discursive practices" through which such worlds are constructed? How is the "medical consciousness" constructed—during the time that dimensions of the biological sciences, new forms of practical activity, an elaborate language, and new forms of organizing the self in relation to others, are all learned, in the context of individual life histories—and how are we to represent our understanding of such knowledge? What are the most significant dimensions of particular medical worlds, as viewed phenomenologically? Can phenomenology be a tool of the critical social sciences? How? In general, we argue that detailed examination of the processes by which medical worlds are constructed, focusing on entry into that world as well as on those critical moments, the "primal scenes" of social process when the foundations of that world are shaken, offers special opportunity for critical reflection.

Third, the *political economy* question: how are we to produce "an interpretive anthropology fully accountable to its historical and political-economy implications"? George Marcus and Michael Fischer (1986:86) argue that the problem is primarily one of representation and textual construction, rather than of political conviction. How are we to represent adequately what we know about the nature of medical institutions, their social and economic organization, and the nature of power relations within them in the context of an interpretive and phenomenologically rich account of medical knowledge? How are we to demonstrate what we intuit to be a relationship between medical knowledge and the social organization of medicine? For example, how is social hierarchy reproduced and how is it embedded in the structure of medical knowledge? What is the impact of the recent corporatization and commoditization of American medical care on medical knowledge, and how is it represented in the recent curricular reform?

And finally, a *practical* question: how are we to reimagine medicine in a manner that neither reproduces conventional ideological knowledge nor represents an ungrounded fantasy, but which recognizes medicine's mediation of the world of biological sciences and that of human suffering?

Acknowledgments

This research was funded by a grant from the Kaiser Family Foundation to Harvard Medical School to support the development and evaluation of the New Pathway. Special thanks are due to Deans Daniel Tosteson, James Adelstein, and Daniel Federman, as well as to Professors Leon Eisenberg and Daniel Goodenough, for their support of this project. Added thanks are owed to Eric Jacobson and Karen Stephenson, who conducted many of the interviews in this study, and to students, faculty, and administrators who spent many hours with us.

Notes

1. The first week consisted of five hour-long "tutorials," 4½ hours of lecture, 4½ hours of histology lab, and 2½ hours of anatomy lab. In addition, students spent one afternoon in a "patient/doctor" course, which combines tutorials and clinical experiences, and spent other afternoons individually or in groups in the labs—often with instructors—or studying, and in a few cases taking elective courses.

2. Some paragraphs in the following pages are drawn from Good and Good 1989.

References

Armstrong, David
  1983   *Political Anatomy of the Body: Medical Knowledge in Britain in the Twentieth Century.* Cambridge: Cambridge University Press.
Arney, William Ray
  1982   *Power and the Profession of Obstetrics.* Chicago: University of Chicago Press.
Becker, Howard, Blanche Geer, Everett C. Hughes, and Anselm L. Strauss
  1961   *The Boys in White: Student Culture in Medical School.* Chicago: University of Chicago Press.
Bok, Derek
  1984   President's Report on Medical Education. *Harvard University Gazette* 79(33):2–12.
Cassell, Joan
  1987   On Control, Certitude, and the "Paranoia" of Surgeons. *Culture, Medicine and Psychiatry* 11:229–250.
Colombotos, John, ed.
  1988   Continuities in the Sociology of Medical Education. *Special Issue of the Journal of Health and Social Behavior* 29(4):271–400.
Csordas, Tom
  1990   Embodiment as a Paradigm for Anthropology. *Ethos* 18:5–47.
Fabrega, Horacio, and Daniel B. Silver
  1973   *Illness and Shamanistic Curing in Zinacantan.* Stanford: Stanford University Press.
Foucault, Michel
  1970   *The Order of Things. An Archaeology of the Human Sciences.* New York: Vintage Books.
  1972   *The Archaeology of Knowledge.* New York: Harper & Row.
Fox, Renee, and Harold I. Lief
  1963   Training for Detached Concern in Medical Students. In *The Psychological Basis of Medical Practice,* Harold I. Lief et al., eds. Berkeley and Los Angeles: University of California Press.
Freidson, Eliot
  1986   *Professional Powers.* Chicago: University of Chicago Press.
Gaines, Atwood
  1979   Definitions and Diagnoses: Cultural Implications of Psychiatric Help-Seeking and Psychiatrists' Definitions of the Situation in Psychiatric Emergencies. *Culture, Medicine and Psychiatry* 3:381–418.
  1985   The Once- and Twice-Born: Self and Practice among Psychiatrists and Christian Psychiatrists. In *Physicians of Western Medicine,* Rob-

ert Hahn and Atwood Gaines, eds., pp. 223–246. Dordrecht, Netherlands: D. Reidel Publishing Company.

Gaines, Atwood and Robert Hahn, eds.
1982   *Physicians of Western Medicine.* Special issue of Culture, Medicine and Psychiatry 6 (3):214–324.

Good, Byron and Mary-Jo DelVecchio Good
1981   The Semantics of Medical Discourse. In *Sciences and Cultures,* Everett Mendelsohn and Yehuda Elkana, eds., pp. 177–212. Sociology of the Sciences, vol. 5. Dordrecht, Netherlands: D. Reidel Publishing Company.

Good, Mary-Jo DelVecchio
1985   Discourses on Physician Competence. In *Physicians of Western Medicine,* Robert Hahn and Atwood Gaines, eds., pp. 247–267. Dordrecht, Netherlands: D. Reidel Publishing Company.

Good, Mary-Jo DelVecchio and Byron J. Good
1989   Disabling Practitioners: Hazards of Learning to be a Doctor in American Medical Education. *Orthopsychiatry* 59:303–309.

Goodman, Nelson
1978   *Ways of Worldmaking.* Indianapolis: Hackett Publishing Company.

Gordon, Deborah
1988   Tenacious Assumptions in Western Medicine. In *Biomedicine Examined,* Margaret Lock and D. R. Gordon, eds., pp. 19–56. Dordrecht, Netherlands: Kluwer Academic Publishers.

Hahn, Robert
1985   A World of Internal Medicine: Portrait of an Internist. In *Physicians of Western Medicine,* Robert Hahn and Atwood Gaines, eds., pp. 51–114. Dordrecht, Netherlands: D. Reidel Publishing Company.

Hahn, Robert, and Atwood Gaines, eds.
1985   *Physicians of Western Medicine.* Dordrecht, Netherlands: D. Reidel Publishing Company.

Lock, Margaret
1980   *East Asian Medicine in Urban Japan.* Berkeley, Los Angeles, London: University of California Press.

Marcus, George, and Michael Fischer
1986   *Anthropology as Cultural Critique.* Chicago: University of Chicago Press.

Merton, Robert, George G. Reader, and Patricia L. Kendall, eds.
1957   *The Student Physician.* Cambridge: Harvard University Press.

Mulkay, Michael, and G. Nigel Gilbert
1982   Joking Apart: Some Recommendations Concerning the Analysis of Scientific Culture. *Social Studies of Science* 12:585–613.

Mumford, Emily
1970   *Interns: From Student to Physician.* Cambridge: Harvard University Press.

Ohnuki-Tierney, Emiko
1984   *Illness and Culture in Contemporary Japan: An Anthropological View.* Cambridge: Cambridge University Press.

Putnam, Hilary
   1981   *Reason, Truth and History.* Cambridge: Cambridge University Press.
Rorty, Richard
   1979   *Philosophy and the Mirror of Nature.* Princeton: Princeton University Press.
Scheper-Hughes, Nancy, and Margaret Lock
   1987   The Mindful Body: A Prolegomenon to Future Work in Medical Anthropology. *Medical Anthropology Quarterly* 1:6–41.
Snow, C. P.
   1959   *The Two Cultures and the Scientific Revolution.* New York: Cambridge University Press.
Turner, Bryan
   1984   *The Body and Society.* Oxford: Basil Blackwell.
Young, Allan
   1980   The Discourse on Stress and the Reproduction of Conventional Knowledge. *Social Science and Medicine* 14B:133–146.
   1981   The Anthropologies of Illness and Sickness. *Annual Reviews of Anthropology* 11:257–285.

5

A Description of How Ideology Shapes Knowledge of a Mental Disorder (Posttraumatic Stress Disorder)

Allan Young

This chapter is about a mental disorder called posttraumatic stress disorder and a psychiatric unit called the Institute for the Treatment of Posttraumatic Stress Disorder (a pseudonym), a part of the U.S. Veterans Administration Medical System.

According to the current edition of the *Diagnostic and Statistical Manual of Mental Disorders* (*DSM-IIIR;* American Psychiatric Association 1987: 247–251), the clinical handbook of the American Psychiatric Association, every case of posttraumatic stress disorder (PTSD) originates in "an event outside the range of usual human experience that would be markedly distressing to almost everyone." These events are usually instances of extreme violence, of human or natural origin. Most of the patients at the Institute are Vietnam War veterans whose traumatic events are said to have occurred during their combat experiences.

DSM-IIIR connects PTSD with three kinds of symptoms. First, the traumatic event is persistently reexperienced. In some cases, the event is reexperienced in intrusive recollections or distressing dreams. In other cases, victims suddenly feel or act as if the events were actually recurring—for example, on awakening or while intoxicated. In still other cases, they experience intense psychological distress when exposed to occasions (e.g., anniversary dates) or circumstances that have symbolic links to the traumatic events. Second, victims try to avoid reexperiences by insulating themselves from stimuli associated with the traumatic events (e.g., thoughts, feelings, activities, situations) or by numbing their emotional responsiveness to all sorts of stimuli (often leading to feelings of estrangement from other people). Third, victims suffer persistent symptoms of autonomic arousal, evidenced in difficulty falling or staying asleep, irritability and outbursts of anger, difficulty concentrating, hypervigilance, exaggerated startle response, and physiologicial reactivity (e.g., sweating) to circumstances that resemble some aspect of the traumatic events. Finally, PTSD may occur in combination with other psychiatric disorders.

PTSD is unlike most of the other disorders described in *DSM-IIIR* in two respects: It is undiagnosable without evidence of the etiological trauma—symptoms alone are insufficient for distinguishing PTSD from other disorders, notably from depressive disorders and other anxiety disorders. Further, PTSD is unusual in that the content of the etiological events is embedded in the disorder's symptoms—for example, in dream imagery, reenactments, and intrusive recollections.

The Institute

The Institute consists of inpatient and outpatient units, and an education section responsible for developing programs to train PTSD therapists working in other institutions. The inpatient ward generally contains thirteen to sixteen patients and a staff of twenty-two, including a psychiatrist, a physician's assistant, psychiatric nurses, clinical psychologists, social workers, and rehabilitation counselors. The administrative hierarchy coincides more or less with the staff's professional qualifications, descending from the clinical director (a psychiatrist) at the top to therapists without advanced degrees (counselors and nurses) at the bottom.

Before being admitted to the inpatient treatment program, men undergo a period of diagnostic evaluation and assessment, designed to screen out men with severe personality disorders, psychoses, and factitious cases of PTSD. The program is divided into three phases: one week of orientation, eight weeks of individual and group psychotherapy and training in cognitive or "coping" skills, and a two-week reentry phase. Relatively few men complete the second phase in eight weeks; most patients are required to extend this phase by a month or even longer. About half of the men who enter the program leave before completing it, either for personal reasons or, more often, for violating the Institute's regulations, to which they are contractually bound. The use of alcohol and nonprescribed drugs during the course of treatment is strictly forbidden, and infraction of this rule is the most common reason for the discharge of patients.

PTSD is a "new" disorder, entering the official psychiatric nomenclature only in 1980. Medical writers trace PTSD's genealogy through a line of diagnostic classifications, going back from "gross stress disorder" (*DSM-I* 1952) through "combat neurosis" (World War II), "shell shock"

(World War I), and "neurocirculatory asthenia," "railway spine," and "soldier's heart" (American Civil War). The psychiatric histories of the Institute's patients do not coincide with this genealogy, however. The men have waited an average of twelve years between the onset of symptoms and the time they first received a PTSD or PTSD-like diagnosis. The most common interim (mis-)diagnoses are alcohol and substance abuse disorders, paranoid schizophrenia, depression, and major anxiety disorder. While the men waited for their current diagnoses, their symptoms grew more obtrusive and distressful, and their maladaptations to the symptoms, usually self-dosing with alcohol and drugs, became more disabling.

During the early 1980s, veterans organizations successfully lobbied Congress to have the Veterans Administration (VA) medical system provide specialized treatment for PTSD. The groups claimed that large numbers of Vietnam War veterans were suffering from PTSD and that the undiagnosed and untreated disorder was a significant cause of the veterans' high rates of mortality (connected with self-destructive behavior) and psychiatric morbidity. Congress responded by mandating the VA to establish a "national center" with responsibility for developing a treatment program that could then be adopted by other VA medical centers (Public Law 98-528).

The Institute was created in 1985 as a result of this mandate. It was given two primary tasks: (1) to provide specialized medical treatment for its patients, and (2) to accumulate and distribute clinical findings relevant to the diagnosis, assessment, and treatment of PTSD. In these ways, the Institute's directors were given a strong incentive to develop a *distinctive* treatment program, one that would clearly distinguish the Institute from other psychiatric units treating PTSD in the VA system and that would justify the Institute's relatively large staff. Given the undeveloped state of the psychiatric discourse on PTSD, the congressional mandate had the effect of linking the Institute's tasks: the Institute would accumulate knowledge of PTSD in the course of treating patients, and its therapeutic techniques and procedures would be continually modified as the staff learned from their newly acquired knowledge.

The drive toward producing a distinctive treatment program was given direction when, soon after the Institute opened, the original clinical director resigned and a psychiatrist with strong psychoanalytical convictions was appointed in his place.

The Importance of Talking

Although the Institute's treatment program evolved over time, three assumptions remained constant:

1. The psychodynamic core of PTSD is a repetition compulsion. The PTSD victim is psychologically compelled to continually re-enact the behavior that precipitated his trauma. His reenactment is a vain attempt to gain mastery over circumstances analogous to the ones that overwhelmed him on the occasion of his etiological event.

2. In order to recover, each patient must satisfactorily recall his etiological event and then disclose it, in detail, to his therapists and fellow patients in the course of psychotherapy sessions. This narrative is the Rosetta stone of his disorder. The postwar life of the typical patient is suffused by misfortune and failure: barroom brawls, domestic violence, unsuccessful marriages, erratic employment, impulsive relocations, and so on. A properly decoded narrative delineates the pattern beneath the chaos.

3. The patient's disorder erects obstacles (resistance) that make it difficult for him to reclaim his traumatic memories and, once they are recalled, make it difficult for him to see how his experiences and actions in the past are reflected in his symptomatic behavior in the present. Therapists, through their knowledge of the psychological conflict at the root of the patient's disorder, have privileged access to the meaning of the recalled events and, ipso facto, to the meaning of the patient's behavior in the here and now.

Therapeutic activity at the Institute consists mainly of talking between patients and therapists. Most of this talking takes place during group psychotherapy, individual psychotherapy, and group autobiography sessions, and in cognitive skills groups devoted to topics such as rational thinking, communicating, values clarification, and death and dying. Aside from a weekly film series and relaxation therapy, nearly all scheduled psychotherapy consists of talking. Even the films are followed by discussion periods led by therapists.

Talking is simultaneously a therapeutic modality and evidence of a patient's progress. From the therapists' point of view, the most important talking consists of patients' narratives of their traumatic experiences and symptomatic events that occurred later. Therapists believe that authentic narratives are evidence of the men's mental operations. Hence the act of narration is usually referred to as "processing an event" or simply "working."

In most psychiatric units in the VA system, drugs are an important form of treatment. At the Institute, however, they play an insignificant role, despite the fact that many patients arrive with long histories of taking prescribed medicines for psychiatric problems. In principle, the

Institute is a drug-free therapeutic milieu. Once on the ward, no patient is permitted to continue on antianxiety medicines; these drugs are said to limit the patients' ability to "process" and "work through" the psychological conflicts associated with their disorder. In the case of antidepressants (the most common category at the time of admission), men are either taken off the medicines or made to reduce intake to minimum tolerable dosages. This is also the policy for the few patients who have been taking antipsychotic medicines.

Changes Produced by the Treatment Program

Patients and therapists see the Institute as a place whose job is to transform defective selves into selves-on-the-mend. Nearly all of the staff and a majority of the patients think that the Institute is doing its job in most cases. Their shared perception is based on very problematic evidence, however.

Before a patient is allowed to move out of the treatment phase into the reentry phase, he is expected to meet a set of behavioral criteria set at the time of his intial diagnostic assessment. Men who arrive with severe sleep disturbances are expected to show improvement in their sleep patterns, men with problems controlling aggression are expected to give evidence of modulating their anger, and so on. *All* patients are expected to give three kinds of verbal evidence that they are on the road to recovery: coherent narratives of their traumatic events, correct intepretations of these events, and descriptions of their present behavior consistent with the repetition compulsion thesis.

In reality, patients show few clear-cut changes in their *nonverbal behavior* over the course of the treatment program. That is to say, most patients say that their behavior changed when they were admitted to the Institute. For example, men who say they were frequently involved in fights on the outside become nonviolent when they enter the unit, and they maintain these changes while they are at the Institute. The point I want to underline is that these changes do not *develop* over the course of the treatment program, but appear at or soon after admission. The staff say that these changes are attributable to the treatment program, but it is unclear, even doubtful, whether this conclusion is warranted. The changes are just as easily explained as the patients' adaptation to life in a highly structured social environment in which correct behavior is a precondition for continued treatment. In other words, one can hypothesize that, given equivalent incentives, the men would do equally well in any highly structured clinical setting devoted to the treatment of PTSD. (Anecdotal evidence from other VA PTSD units support this conclusion.)

In addition, many patients come to the Institute immediately after completing inpatient programs for alcohol and drug abuse. The Institute's assessment and evaluation section sees alcohol and drug use by PTSD victims as a maladaptive response to their primary symptoms (e.g., intrusive imagery), anxiety, and depression, and refer to this use as "self-dosing" (in contrast to dependency or addiction). In reality, the cause-and-effect relationship between alcohol and drug abuse and PTSD symptoms is more complicated, since episodes of violent behavior and quasi-dissociative episodes ("flashbacks") are commonly precipitated by intoxication. Thus some of the therapeutic changes observed at the Institute, especially the modulation of anger and aggression, may be rooted in circumstances, especially abstinence, that are not specific to the treatment program.

Therapists also credit the treatment program for the patients' good conduct on weekend passes and on occasions when the men are overtly frustrated by regulations and sanctions, for example, by confinement to the ward. Again, the men's behavior tends to change at the time of admission rather than over the course of the treatment program.

There *are* developmental changes during the treatment program, and they consist of what patients say to therapists about their thoughts and feelings—that is, changes in *verbal behavior.* Many patients report feeling progressively less angry, less depressed, more in control of their emotions, and more self-confident. Here again, it is unclear which is having the greater effect on the patients, the institutional environment or the treatment program. Patients report other changes also. For example, some men report decreases in nightmares and intrusive thoughts and images. But the significance of these reports is not easy to assess, since an equal number of patients report opposite effects—increased frequency of nightmares and intrusive images, bouts of dysphoric emotion, significant somatic complaints—and they, too, are described by therapists as giving evidence of improvement. Therapists reason that decreases in symptoms are an index of direct improvement, while increases are an index and side effect of "getting close" to traumatic events. In other words, a temporary exacerbation of symptoms foretells a permanent (postdeparture) diminution.

The most unequivocal evidence of (putatively) therapeutic change occurring over the course of treatment is the fact that most long-stay patients eventually give acceptable narratives and interpretations. From the therapsits' point of view, narratives and interpretations are surface manifestations of cognitive processing and the transformation of disordered psychic structures. As I have tried to show, there is little corroborative, nonverbal evidence to support their conclusion, even though it is conceivably true. (Follow-up data on discharged patients could test claims regarding efficacy. So far the data do not exist.)

The Knowledge Production Process

Given the evidence described in the preceding section, it would be premature to conclude that the Institute is mending selves. If the place is not producing what clinicians and patients think it is producing, exactly what is it doing? My answer is that (1) the treatment program's main output is a *knowledge product* and not psychiatric transformations; (2) this knowledge is produced while people talk about traumatic events and compulsive behavior; and (3) this knowledge is the basis for everyone's (mis)understanding of the patients' nonverbal behavior.

This process of producing knowledge at the Institute can be broken down into three stages:

Stage 1.   Therapists elicit etiological narratives from patients during group and individual psychotherapy. Therapists interpret narratives at this point and use the interpretations to explain to the patients their behavior on the ward.

Stage 2.   Each therapist provides the clinical director with a double account of what happened at stage 1: an account of the patient's narrative and his behavior and an account of the therapist's own perceptions, talk, emotions, and intentions while eliciting the narrative. This occurs during weekly clinical supervisions and at the "debriefings" that follow group psychotherapy sessions. Stage 2 mirrors stage 1 in the sense that the meaning of narratives is again appropriated through claims to privileged knowledge (patient → therapist → director).

Stage 3.   The knowledge product of stage 2 is transformed into propositions and paradigms and then inscribed in internal documents (programmatic statements, staff memoranda, etc.), a quarterly PTSD newsletter edited at the Institute, articles in scholarly journals, and papers presented at Veterans Administration conferences and at meetings of professional groups such as the Society for the Study of Posttraumatic Stress Disorder.

Resistance and the Production of Knowledge

This is how the knowledge production process is *supposed* to work at the Institute. In reality, there are people at the institute who resist the movement of meanings and knowledge from one stage to the next.

Before going further, let me say a few words about how I am using the term "resistance." The word has two relevant meanings. On the one hand, it refers to a sequence in which (*a*) someone refuses to collaborate in the production process, (*b*) the meaning of his behavior is appropriated from him, and (*c*) the reinterpreted act is absorbed into the production process. For example, a patient claims that he is unable to recall any traumatic experience (= refusal) and the therapist says the patient is repressing his memory of the event. The patient intends his words to mean that there was no event and so there is no memory of an event; the therapist interprets the words as meaning that not only did the event occur but it has a special significance and because of this it is inaccessible to the patient (= appropriation). The patient's claim is meant to take him out of the production process; the therapists's claim inserts him back into it.

The second meaning of "resistance" refers to behavior that impedes or blocks the production process and cannot be assimilated but must be overcome. Both forms of resistance are part of everyday life at the Institute. For the moment I want to concentrate on this second, unassimilable variety.

The most serious resistance in the Institute's production process occurs during stage 1, when either patients or therapists refuse to collaborate in producing narratives and decoding behavior. Patients resist through rejecting the therapists' interpretations of their traumatic events and current behavior. In the course of treatment, the patient's traumatic events are nearly always shown to involve morally forbidden acts, such as torturing prisoners or killing civilians and Americans. In order for these events to be properly "worked through" or "processed," patients need to give detailed accounts, including descriptions of their thoughts, feelings, and perceptions before, during, and after their "acts of commission." Patients resist by suppressing details, saying that the memories are too painful to recall or that therapists are incapable of understanding the events. ("You had to be there to know what I'm talking about.") The patient resists by shifting the account's locus of moral responsibility away from himself, by transforming himself from an agent to an object of aggression, from perpetrator to victim (of incompetent officers, corrupt politicians, duplicitous civilians, and so on). Patients also resist by rejecting the idea that they are replaying their traumatic events in their behavior on the ward; for example, patients argue that "reenactment" mislabels their morally justified response to the Institute's arbitrary rules and harsh punishments.

Therapists too have reasons to resist. Often they experience a strong identification with the sufferings of their patients, based in no small part on the veterans' moral claims: the patients were only boys when they were sent to Vietnam, nothing in their previous experiences had prepared them for what they encountered, they were cynically manipulated by men whom they have been taught to trust, they returned to an ungrateful and contemptuous public, they continue to be treated as pariahs and are even now discriminated against by potential employers. Second, therapists also believe that recalling traumatic memories is painful and exhausting work for the patients, and that it often produces gastrointestinal disorders, headaches, nightmares, distressful and intrusive images, anxiety, and depression. Therapists are naturally reluctant to inflict pain on their patients, especially when they have doubts about the efficacy of the treatment they are providing. Some therapists worry that they are exacerbating the patients' disorders by eliciting narratives. (I know of only one incident in which a therapist reacted with strong *negative* emotions to a patient's account of a wartime murder.) Other instances of therapists' (passive) resistance can be traced to their inadequate professional resources, specifically, not knowing how to go on or what to say next, how to manage patients' disruptive behavior, or how to make convincing claims about the treatment program's efficacy and their own professional competence.

An Institutional Ideology

This brings me to the subject of this chapter: the role of ideology in the production of knowledge. Because "ideology" is a notoriously polysemous concept, I want to make clear what the term is intended to mean in the following pages.

I am writing about an institutional ideology, and not a pervasive, societywide set of ideas. I call the ideology's beliefs and practices "ideological" because (1) they are used to convince people to do things they might otherwise *not* want to do, (2) they subvert or devalue rival ideas that might lead people to behave in other ways, and (3) they serve important interests, as identified by the Institute's directors, by either transforming or overwhelming resistances in the mandated production process. Put into other words, this ideology is a medium that ensures the Institute's knowledge producers are integrated into the detailed division of labor.

Not every institution has an ideology. In some institutions, power holders have effective ways of controlling people through surveillance, coercion, and rewards, and ideologies are not needed to convince people to behave correctly. In other institutions, ideology is superfluous because power is shared, technical knowledge is evenly distributed, and labor power, skills, motivation, technology, and modes of social organization are sufficient for meeting institutional goals and individual and collective wants.

The Institute fits neither of these patterns. On the one hand, its directors and senior staff lack effective means for coercing correct behavior. On the other hand, there are often sharp disparities between institutional goals and individual wants.

The key to understanding the Institute's ideology is its division of mental labor (separating patients from therapists at stage 1 and therapists from the clinical director at stage 2). Allow me to elaborate: Following Congress's mandate to the Veterans Administration, a plan for a national center was proposed by a clinical psychologist who had been active in the PTSD lobbying effort. His proposal was accepted and became the basis for the Institute. There is no standard table of organization for psychiatric units in the Veterans Administration system, and the proposal's eclectic mix of workers was shaped by a combination of factors: the official division of labor (which classifies psychiatric workers into psychiatry, psychology, nursing, social work, rehabilitation counseling, and occupational therapy services), the unit's orientation and dominant therapy (units that rely on drugs are generally less labor intensive than units that concentrate on psychotherapy), the unit's budget (one psychiatrist costs as much as several counselors), and the unit's ability to recruit workers in each category (lower-skilled workers are generally easier to recruit than workers with advanced degrees).

Because of the Institute's psychotherapeutic orientation, it is a distinctively labor-intensive operation, with a staff:patient ratio averaging about 3:2. This ratio is economically feasible because the unit recruits its staff mainly from the less intensively trained categories. Further, the Institute has difficulty filling its allocated psychiatric positions, partly because of its unusual psychoanalytic orientation (see below). It is funded for two psychiatrists: a clinical director and a head of inpatient services. However, except for a short period, the second position has remained unfilled and the clinical director has had to divide his time among the Institute's different units (inpatient, outpatient, diagnosis and evaluation, education), further diluting the presence of skilled and experienced workers.

To summarize: (1) a distinctive treatment program is a condition for the Institute's existence; (2) the Institute has adopted a program that places considerable psychological burdens on its staff; (3) therapists who are not intensively trained and experienced find it particularly difficult to shoulder these burdens and are likely to resist, both actively and passively, being integrated into the knowledge production process; and (4) forces outside the Institute ensure that a high proportion of its clinical staff is recruited from less skilled and less experienced categories of workers.

Discourse and Ideology

Scientific knowledge of PTSD is the product of scholarly discourse and institutional ideologies. The discourse on PTSD consists of a network of statements inscribed and circulated in scholarly works, the product of a physically dispersed circle of writers. Within this circle, writers compete and collaborate through the exchange of statements, for symbolic rewards ("reputation") and professional advantages.

Discourse and ideology on PTSD share the same technical language ("avoidance behavior," "self-dosing," etc.), the same terminus a quo encoded in *DSM-IIIR*'s authoritative description of PTSD, and the same stock of tacit knowledge and unexamined assumptions. Unlike discourse, however, ideologies are local systems of knowledge embedded within particular institutional hierarchies and production processes. Each PTSD ideology is autonomous. What these different ideologies have in common is their shared object (PTSD).

Ideology depends on discourse for this object. It is discourse that naturalizes PTSD, provides it with an existence prior to and independent of both discourse and ideology, and instructs therapists on how to materialize PTSD in the clinic by means of diagnostic criteria and diagnostic instruments (e.g., the PTSD subscale of the widely-used Minnesota Multiphasic Personality Index). At the same time, discourse also depends on ideology, which provides the institutional surfaces on which discourse's object, PTSD, acquires its materiality.

Discourse and ideology are, then, separate but intersecting systems of knowledge. This is not how the Institute's therapists and patients see things, however. In the early days of the Institute, the more experienced therapists tended to see what I call discourse and ideology as being parallel rather than intersecting systems. In their view, one system (science/discourse) correctly represented PTSD, while the other (the treatment program/ideology) distorted these same facts. As the Institute's ideology matured and began to develop authority and efficacy (described below), this view gradually faded. Today, it is replaced by the view that there is *no* ideology at the Institute, that the official beliefs and practices are nothing more than the penetration of science (discourse) into clinical practice. This current view (intersection without ideology), like the earlier one (ideology without intersection), is premised on the positivist idea, shared by the patients and nearly all of the staff, that science uncovers its objects and does not construct them.

Etiological and Therapeutic Codes

The Institute's ideology is organized around a written account of its distinctive object, PTSD. Embedded in this account is the idea that PTSD, in the form in which it is objectified on the ward, exists independently of what happens on the ward and is not, as patients occasionally argue, a product of the Institute's procedures and labels.

The core of this account is inscribed in a series of memoranda, distributed to everyone on the clinical staff. The account is referred to as either "the ten propositions" or "the model," and the staff are expected to show signs that they are in the process of understanding it. During clinical supervisions and debriefings where patients are discussed, nearly all conversation is oriented to the account. Since each member of the daytime staff has direct responsibility for at least one patient, everyone is periodically obligated, during supervisions and debriefings, to demonstrate how satisfactorily he or she understands the account.

The account is a gnomic text and quite obscure in places. It is represented in clinical talk in three codes, that is, shared oral commentaries and interpretations: an etiological code explaining how the past connects each patient to his symptoms, a therapeutic code explaining how each patient's consciousness connects him to his recovery, and an institutional code explaining how each patient's disorder connects him and his therapists to the Institute.

DISCOURSE ---➤ object ⬅--- IDEOLOGY (account and codes)

Each code has evolved over the course of the Institute's history. There is no space here to trace these changes, however, and I shall limit myself to describing the codes in their current form.

The *etiological code* is based on psychoanalytic concepts and reflects the professional orientation of the account's author, the Institute's clinical director, who traces his ideas back to Freud's distinction, in *Beyond the Pleasure Principle* (1920), between "actual neuroses" and "traumatic neuroses." The etiological code begins with the idea that all human behavior is the product of two drives, a libidinal drive expressed as tenderness and a longing for attachment, and an aggressive drive expressed as an urge to destroy the objects of its anger. Ordinarily, the drives are integrated to the extent that their different demands do not lead to deep-seated or enduring psychic conflicts. The individual accommodates both drives and also satisfies the superego, generally by sublimating aggressive urges into the service of libidinal goals.

The traumatic event that lies at the beginning of every case of PTSD changes all of this. At that point, the PTSD victim is forced to choose between contradictory aggressive and libidinal goals (e.g., exterminate life or preserve life). Unable to find a solution that is compatible with these urges and also consistent with the demands of the superego, he discharges his aggressive impulse in a destructive act of commission.

Sometimes a patient claims that his only traumatic memory is of an act of omission—for example, an act in which failure to do something resulted in a comrade's death. In this case, the code says it must be assumed that he is either unwilling to recount an act of commission or, if he is sincere, that he is reporting a screen memory—that is, a substitute account or an incomplete representation of his actual act of commission.

The patient's traumatic act resulted in splitting the self into two part-selves: an aggressor-self organized around his destructive impulses and a victim-self organized around his pathological feelings of tenderness for victims of aggression. The split was accompanied by the increasing peremptoriness of the now unintegrated destructive impulses, evidenced in the typical patient's postwar history of explosive violence. This condition persists on the ward, where therapists see patients through the medium of their verbal behavior as alternating between victim-self (e.g., expressing guilt, blaming authorities) and aggressor-self (e.g., making threats, being verbally abusive).

The *therapeutic code* carries forward into action two ideas that are embedded in the ideological account.

1. Each patient's pathology is traced to a reversible misalignment of intrapsychic forces (the aggressive and libidinal drives). This characteristic distinguishes PTSD from disorders that originate in mental decomposition (schizophrenia), physical degeneration (organic psychoses), or permanently abnormal intrapsychic structures (character disorders).

2. The key to the disorder is located in the patient's consciousness. PTSD originates in the patient's conscious choice to execute the intent to do harm. It persists because he continues to choose to behave this way, and this helps to explain why his behavior in the here and now mirrors his behavior on the traumatic occasion. The patient may be unaware of making these choices, but this is not inconsistent with the fact that the choices are also

products of his conscious mind—that is, awareness is only one state of consciousness.

The therapeutic code says that each patient must recall his traumatic event. Knowledge of the event enables him to discover the medium—that is, consciousness—through which the past is being reproduced in the present. Knowledge demystifies the sources of his symptomatic behavior and shows him that he is responding to internal, psychic strivings and not, as he has incorrectly believed, to provocations in his external environment. Once he knows that he was the author of his traumatic event, that he actively chose to be destructive and could have chosen to behave otherwise, he is enabled to reassert control over his behavior. And once he knows that he has this power over himself, he can start sublimating his aggressive urges.

At the same time that the account makes the patient's consciousness the locus of responsibility for his recovery (and therefore for his disorder), it also subverts consciousness's moral claims—for example, the claim that acts of commission are instances of evil and therefore outside of medicine's purview. Patients are told repeatedly that moral judgements about their wartime acts of commission, the events of their postwar lives, and their behavior on the ward are irrelevant and inappropriate, and that the difference between an instinctual longing for attachment and an instinctual urge to destroy is not the same thing as distinguishing between things good and bad. Patients who insist on making moral judgements concerning their acts of commission are told that they are splitting, talking through the mouth of the victim-self, and expressing pathological tenderness. In this way, the therapeutic code explains away an important limit to the therapists' competence and the Institute's authority.

The Institutional Code

This point brings us directly to the *institutional code,* which tells the account a third time. Recall that the etiological code connects the patient to his disorder, and the therapeutic code subordinates the patient to the authority of his therapist. The institutional code, as we shall see, brings both patient and therapist under the authority of the therapeutic regime.

According to the institutional code, people everywhere are moved by a powerful desire to somehow resolve the intrapsychic conflict that is engendered by the desire to inflict grievous harm. This class of problem-solving behaviors is known at the Institute as "stress responses." The stress responses of PTSD patients are distinctive because they are part of a repetition compulsion in which elements of traumatic experiences are reenacted. Reenactment takes place through the patient's analogical re-creation of certain features of the traumatic situation. (For example, one of the Institute's clinicians told the following narrative on several occasions, to visiting colleagues and at conferences. It is the story of a patient who claimed that he abandoned his comrades to their deaths. In the clinician's account, the patient reenacted the abandonment—his puta-tively traumatic event—during group psychotherapy. While patients would ordinarily sit in a circle facing inward, this patient habitually moved his chair to the corner of the room, where he turned it and himself to face away from the circle, symbolically abandoning the other patients.)

Stress responses are often somatized—expressed through physical symptoms or body parts that are symbolically connected to the patients' traumatic incidents (e.g., event = head wound, reenactment = chronic headache). Whatever form it takes, reenactment is an obstacle to recov-ery because it protects patients from confronting their etiological events and intrapsychic conflicts.

The patients' stress responses create conditions for two kinds of ex-changes: exchanges of aggression and exchanges of valuables and obliga-tions. For the moment, I want to concentrate on exchanges of aggression.

The institutional code says that the patients are habituated to behav-ing in intentionally provocative ways and they use this behavior to elicit aggressive responses from other people. In this way they create the conditions for exchanges of stress responses and use them to justify their own anger and aggression. This behavior continues at the Insti-tute, where patients elicit stress responses from their therapists. Be-cause stress responses impede the patients' ability to disclose traumatic events and recognize the repetition compulsion, the institutional code says that therapists must be vigilant for instances of this symptomatic behavior. For this reason, therapists spend a lot of time in group psycho-therapy sessions (stage 1) talking to their patients about their stress responses. (In practice, "stress response" is nearly synonymous with any behavior that (1) is overtly aggressive or disruptive or that therapists "feel" has aggressive intent or (2) stands in the way of getting additional details about the traumatic event and its reenactment.) A similar pro-cess occurs during clinical supervision (stage 2), where the clinical direc-tor listens to the therapists' narratives and talks to them about their own stress responses.

Recall that the patient's traumatic event is said to result in a split into part-selves and a tendency to act out unintegrated aggressive impulses. An effective treatment program cannot exist in the face of uncontrolled and disruptive acting out. If no limits were placed on acting out, patients could walk out of psychotherapy sessions whenever they felt themselves growing anxious or angry, and the therapeutic process would be cut off precisely when men are "getting close to their issues" (traumatic events). Uncontrolled acting out also makes the ward a physically unsafe place. The code says that when patients feel physically unsafe they also feel psychologically unsafe, lack of psychological safety is an obstacle to disclosure, and without disclosure there can be no recovery.

And so the Institute has created a system of "limits" or regulations to control acting-out behavior. Before coming on the ward, men are required to sign a "patient contract" in which they agree to conform with these limits. Limit breakers are brought to quasi-juridical proceedings, where obedience to the rules is enforced through a schedule of sanctions extending from restriction on the ward to involuntary discharge. Patients complain that many of these limits are arbitrary and rigidly applied and penalize men for behavior over which they have no reasonable control (e.g., the need to urinate during long group psychotherapy sessions). The institutional code acknowledges that limits are often arbitrary and that sanctions are sometimes excessive from an everyday perspective, but it justifies these conditions on therapeutic grounds, as a way of making symptomatic behavior into an "episode," throwing a frame around it, and forcing patients to see it as something discontinuous from other kinds of behavior.

According to the institutional code, at the same time that limits and sanctions are serving therapeutic goals in these ways, they are also threatening to set off destructive strings of stress responses. The code says that the patient's disorder has robbed him of the psychological resources he needs for overcoming obstacles to disclosure and recovery. It is because of this that he depends on the intervention of therapists. And there is the rub according to the institutional code, for it is dangerous for therapists to come into contact with the patients' anger, threats, and pathological tenderness. Therapists are in jeopardy of being drawn into the patient's pathology to the point where the "therapeutic alliance" between patient and healer is displaced by a pathological bond sustained through exchanges of stress responses. Once this happens, therapists are robbed of their healing powers.

Faced with the patient's anger and fear of his own anger, ability to inflict pain, and active intention to execute harm, the therapist is inclined to react with stress responses. On the one hand, he may identify with the sufferings of his patients, and transform himself into their ally against the clinical regime. On the other hand, he may react to the patients' anger with his own anger and lash out against the men, confirming their symptomatic view of life in general and the Institute in particular. In both events, the therapist is seduced by the pathological strivings of his patients' split-selves. The code identifies this behavior by the evocative phrase, "colluding with the patient in his pathology." Collusion means a double betrayal. The therapist betrays his patient, consigning him to a psychiatric purgatory to live out his life in a perpetual reexperience of his traumatic event. At the same time, he betrays his own colleagues, undermining their faith in the rules and reasons on which the clinical regime is based.

Exchanges and Obligations

In this way—through "stress responses," "limit setting," "collusion," and ideas about the exchange of acts of aggression—the institutional code picks out and medicalizes the resistances of patients and therapists to being integrated into the knowledge production process. As we shall see in this section, the code also creates conditions for the emergence of certain practices through which the same resistances can be either transformed, appropriated, or extirpated.

These practices in which patients and therapists exchange valuables and obligations are anchored in two recurring events: narrations of traumatic experiences and acknowledgments of stress responses. The patient contract says that patients must give narratives during group psychotherapy. Men enter the inpatient program individually (not in cohorts) and leave individually. Thus the membership of psychotherapy groups gradually changes over time, and a patient from whom one receives (hears) a narrative is not necessarily one of the men to whom one gives (discloses) a narrative. Narratives given during individual psychotherapy sessions are insufficient by themselves. The code says that narrators need groups, because the other patients give "feedback" that enables narrators to connect their everyday behavior to their traumatic events. Also, groups need narrators, because disclosures are tokens of trust and safety.

Patients distinguish authentic disclosures ("events") from counterfeits ("war stories"). Authentic narratives are expensive and therapists and patients often talk about the high cost of "sharing" (giving) them, in terms of the attendant physical pain (psychogenic headaches, etc.), anguish (impacted grief), depression and feelings of hopelessness, and fears about moral and legal culpability.

Authentic disclosures usually take place several weeks into the treatment program. According to patients, they are almost never spontaneous, since men need to plan ahead. A narrative must begin early enough in a session so that it can be completed before time is up, since therapists insist that group sessions begin and end precisely on schedule. Patients who start narratives toward the end of sessions are generally cut off by their therapists and told that they are "having a stress response," that is, avoiding their "issues" (conflicts) and acting aggressively by flaunting secrets (the opposite of "sharing"). Patients who fail to make disclosures after being in the treatment program more than two months are often criticized by men who have already narrated traumatic events, and accused of "being aggressive" and "not working" (malingering). Eventually these men are brought before panels of therapists where they are "strongly encouraged to work." Recalcitrants are discharged. The code says that allowing a patient to continue without disclosing his event is equivalent to "colluding with him in his aggression," and therapists see these discharges as instances of limit setting. (Former patients can ask to be readmitted thirty days after discharge.)

The acknowledgment of stress responses is the basis for another set of exchanges. During psychotherapy sessions, therapists emphasize that stress responses are not bad in a moral sense, even when they are instances of limit breaking and lead to the discharge of patients. The code says that stress responses are bad only in a clinical sense. The patient is told that feelings of guilt and shame are stress responses and expressions of the victim-self. His job is simply to acknowledge to the other members of the group that he actively chose to "execute the intent to do harm." He is told, "You must own your aggression." The act of owning stress responses objectifies them, pushes the motives behind them into awareness, and makes it possible to sublimate aggressive urges.

From a clinical point of view, giving narratives and giving acknowledgments are linked activities, since disclosures are expected to show patients the compulsive pattern underlying their everyday stress responses. Unlike narratives (which therapists rarely give to patients), however, acknowledgments are sometimes exchanged between patients and therapists. The possibility of such exchanges is encoded in the idea that patients are continually trying to elicit stress responses from other people, including therapists, in order to justify their own anger and aggression. Patients say that because therapists do have stress responses, they too must "own" their responses when these are brought to their attention. According to patients, this is a matter of equity. ("What's good for the goose is good for the gander.") Therapists sometimes acknowledge their stress responses, and patients generally respond with approval and occasionally even gratitude. But therapists make a point of rejecting the equity principle, since it would threaten the authority of the institutional code. According to the code, the therapist's acknowledgment is justified only because it helps bring his or her potentially collusive behavior under control.

Conclusion:
How Ideology Persuades

In time, all the Institute's therapists and most of its patients are persuaded to behave in ideologically correct ways despite the fact that they arrive with strong motives for behaving otherwise. Different people have different motives for changing their behavior, but most of these motives can be traced back to two sources: the authority commanded by its principal advocates (the Institute's clinical and adminstrative directors) and the real and perceived efficacy of its propositions and practices.

Ideology and Authority

The Institute's ideology is the official view of things and it is sanctioned by the administrative authority of the Institute's directors.

Therapists are bound to a clearly articulated standard. Mere conformity to ideologically correct nonverbal behavior is not sufficient, and staff are expected to behave as if they believe the ideology's propositions are true. Therapists who cannot meet this standard are sometimes described as having an "attitude problem." Difficulties in this connection are minimized by the fact that therapists are self-recruited and are offered positions only after they have been interviewed at the Institute. No one joins the staff without having a good idea of what he or she is getting into, and discontented therapists are free to leave or transfer without penalty.

Therapists are unionized civil-servant employees with well-entrenched employment rights, and institutional authority over them is usually exercised in diffuse ways. Its characteristic expression is the clinical director's comments made during debriefings and clinical supervisions. Because the Institute's administrative hierarchy coincides with its mental division of labor, therapists regard the clinical director's comments as simultaneously an official assessment and expert opinion of their competence and professionalism (signified by not colluding with patients). There have been three instances of staff members being forced to leave the Institute. A counselor was sacked for misrepresenting his credentials, and a physician was obliged to go because of professional misconduct in a previous position; only the third individual, a counselor involuntarily transferred for refusing to learn the therapeutic code relating to her clinical responsibilities, was separated on ideological grounds.

The Institute demands a great deal less from patients in this regard. It is assumed that many patients have an "attitude problem" as part of their pathologies. The men are simply required to comply with the regulations outlined in the "patient contract," and they are not expected to act as if they also shared the beliefs on which these regulations are based.

Ideology and Efficacy

Ideology throws a frame of meaning around the unbounded and incoherent misfortunes of the patients' postwar lives. By medicalizing the past, ideology offers men the possibility of exculpating themselves of moral responsibility for their present state and the possibility of a cure and end to the unbroken stream of misfortunes. Further, ideology gives the men sickness without psychosis—an attractive idea to someone who fears he is going crazy or who was once diagnosed as psychotic.

At the same time that ideology provides the patient with these cognitive satisfactions, it also gives him a communally sanctioned sense of self-efficacy, a feeling that he is gradually gaining control over his thoughts and emotions and is developing a new interactional style, a substitute for maladaptive oscillations between violent acting out and withdrawal (phobic behavior, psychological self-numbing, self-dosing with alcohol and drugs, nomadic lifestyle, etc.). Actually, what the men perceive as self-efficacy may reflect nothing more than the capacity of a benign total institution to routinize and shelter their disordered and vulnerable lives, and the capacity of their newly learned language ("the intent to do harm," "stress response," etc.) to objectify heretofore anonymous states of mind and emotion. Whether or not the men's ideas about the locus of control is correct, the fact is they believe the ideology is efficacious—that is, doing something desirable for them.

Earlier in this chapter, I described why therapists believe that changes that occur in the patient's behavior can be evidence of ideology's efficacy. Therapists have more reasons for attributing efficacy to ideology. Recall that the treatment program presents every therapist with two serious problems: knowing how to go on and knowing how to protect himself against his patients' anger and his own anger. Ideology is efficacious in this connection because it tells him what to do and say next, exculpates him of moral responsibility once he has done it (inflicted therapeutically necessary pain), and explains his therapeutic failures (e.g., patients who backslide) in ways that preserve his confidence in himself as a clinician and in the essential correctness of the therapeutic regime.

In addition to giving the therapist a sense of cognitive mastery over events, ideology gives him experiences in which he successfully manages his (overt) anger and (putative) aggression, through the codified exchange of "stress responses" and acknowledgments. Recall that stage 1 of the knowledge production process (where patients give accounts to therapists) is symmetrical with stage 2 (where therapists give accounts to the clinical director). At both stages, therapists associate the act of giving accounts with anger and aggression: patients are angry at their therapists because giving accounts is painful; therapists are angry at themselves and at the clinical director because giving accounts results in embarrassing and frustrating critiques.

In debriefings, supervisions, and weekly "support" groups, therapists give frequent testimonials regarding how "the model" (ideology) has enabled them to deal with these two sources of anger. But it would be a mistake to think of clinically constructed anger merely as a negativity, a force isolating therapists from patients. Therapists also talk about anger as if it were a bridge linking their experiences at the Institute with the patients', as when they refer to themselves in clinical supervision as "being the same as patients."

Through the mediation of ideology, the therapist's experience of anger is transformed into a highly prized professional attribute, "clinical insight." Anger (and its complement, fear), initially an obstacle to integrating the therapist into the knowledge production process, is not simply overcome; it is appropriated.

References

DSM-I
  1952   *Diagnostic and Statistical Manual of Mental Disorders.* Washington, D.C.: American Psychiatric Association.
DSM-IIIR
  1987   *Diagnostic and Statistical Manual of Mental Disorders. Third Edition.* Washington, D.C.: American Psychiatric Association.
Freud, Sigmund
  1920   *Beyond the Pleasure Principle.* London: Hogarth Press.

6

The Shape of Action

Practice in Public Psychiatry

Lorna Amarasingham Rhodes

In his *The Reflective Practitioner: How Professionals Think in Action,* Donald Schön remarks,

> In the varied topography of professional practice, there is a high, hard ground where practitioners can make effective use of research-based theory and technique, and there is a swampy lowland where situations are confusing "messes" incapable of technical solution. The difficulty is that the problems of the high ground . . . are often relatively unimportant to clients or to the larger society, while in the swamp are the problems of greatest human concern. (1983:42)

Medical anthropologists who immerse themselves in the "messy lowlands" of medicine find that they are in fact face to face with "problems of great human concern" in settings where neither the goals nor the means of practice are clear. "Theory and technique" (the models practitioners presumably follow) do not help very much in understanding the actual unfolding of events; knowledge (in this sense) appears to be a subset of action rather than the reverse. Furthermore, attending to what Deborah R. Gordon (1988) calls "situational understanding"[1] embroils us in methodological and theoretical difficulties: What kinds of situation? What do we mean by understanding? How are we to think of the relationship between "actor" and "system"?

My subject in this essay is a "swamp" of the first order, a small psychiatric emergency ward serving an inner-city population. Here the poverty and despair of the patients, the internal contradictions of psychiatry, and the ironies of public administration create a setting in which the situational nature of practice cannot be avoided. The unit (which I call here the "Acute Psychiatry Unit," or "APU") is part of a one-hundred-bed hospital. This hospital, or "community mental health center," was built ten years ago and serves patients who cannot pay for treatment. Some of these patients have been released from state hospitals in response to the policy of deinstitutionalization that was developed in the 1960s. Deinstitutionalization is based on the premise that patients can be spared the effects of incarceration in large asylums by being returned to their "communities." Some APU patients have never been in a state hospital, but are dependent on the mental health center for frequent periods of inpatient care. The center is faced with diminishing community resources and increasing demand from patients; thus, keeping patient stays short is an important goal of its operation. The emergency unit supports this goal by functioning within the hospital to "hold" patients for short periods while staff determine a disposition for them. The unit is very small (nine beds) and labor-intensive, with a total staff of about thirty psychiatrists, nurses, social workers, and aides. Residents and medical students from a nearby medical school are an important component of the staff.

What makes the APU a "swamp?" It is a setting of crosscutting and contradictory demands, in which no one mode of action adequately addresses the situation of the patients or the needs of the institution. The contradictions of practice on the unit reflect the paradoxes of deinstitutionalization itself. While the movement to get patients out of asylums was ostensibly based on the iatrogenic effects of incarceration (as documented by, e.g., Goffman 1961), there was also a hidden economic agenda: under new social welfare programs states can spend less to "maintain" patients in the community than in asylums (Scull 1979, 1984). The original mandate to keep hospitalization short and patients "in the community" has not been accompanied by the resources to carry it out. This puts the APU staff in a frustrating position; it is expected to discharge patients to "dispositions" that don't exist. Another paradoxical aspect of deinstitutionalization is its highlighting of the problems involved in psychiatric medication. Although there is evidence that medication does not necessarily allow patients to live independently (see, e.g., Warner 1985; Scull 1984), nevertheless the staff of the APU is influenced by the biomedical perspective and by the needs of the moment to routinely medicate the patients.

Other conflicts impinge on the staff. Each worker on the unit must balance the mandate to treat efficiently and maintain open beds with the fear that patients who are released too soon may harm themselves or others. In addition, the unit's workers differ among themselves in which aspect of the work is most important to them: for nurses and aides the day-to-day management of patients is primary, while for students and residents the opportunity to practice diagnosis and treatment often takes precedence (see Light 1980 and Mizrahi 1986 for examples of this conflict in other settings). Finally, all are aware that the problems of their patients are somehow connected to the social fabric within which they themselves must function. The patients' poverty, powerlessness, and extreme behavior obviously emerge out of social conditions, but the staff members are prevented by their position in the system and by their medical perspective from confronting this issue directly. They alternate uncomfortably between blaming the patients, blaming the "system," and blaming themselves for the intractable problems they encounter.

In this essay I explore two aspects of the work of the APU staff, drawing on the results of two years of fieldwork on the unit (see also Rhodes 1991).[2] First I discuss the link between practice on the unit and its historical context; contradictions in context were inextricably linked to contradictions in practice. Secondly, I explore some of the ways in which practice on the unit involved specific gestures that were passed on from one generation to the next through teaching by the more experienced staff members. These gestures allowed the staff to encompass (and also perpetuate) contradictions that would otherwise have been overwhelming.

The Emergency Unit as Pentimento

William Ray Arney and Bernard J. Bergen in *Medicine and the Management of Living* suggest a powerful image for understanding contemporary medicine. Medicine, they say, "looks like a pentimento. Pentimento is the term used to describe those old paintings in which one image has been painted over another, but the overlying image is so thin that the one under it still shows through" (1984:8; see also Hellman 1973). Medicine resembles a pentimento because "different images of the doctor and patient are intertangled, the new not absolutely clear, the old still discernible but no longer dominant." This metaphor is helpful because it suggests that we look for the historical depth of contemporary practice, counteracting a tendency (particularly in discussions of psychiatry) to emphasize current reforms.

The pentimento-like aspect of medicine can be seen in the contemporary management of birth, where old-style obstetrics (the draped, anesthetized woman "being delivered" by an impersonal, white-coated doctor) coexists with midwife-managed, family-centered birth in birthing rooms and homes. The "new" image overlaps the old; each holds sway within its own domain, yet they can occur side by side, perhaps on the same maternity floor. Arney and Bergen caution against the assumption that a "good" patient-centered orientation is "overthrowing" a "bad" doctor-centered one. They argue that patient-centered "management," in which the medical gaze penetrates into the individual's personality and social life, is a version of what Michel Foucault means when he speaks of "capillary power": social power exercized not through direct domination but through normalizing strategies that permeate the inti-. mate life of individuals.

The image of the pentimento may be too static, however, suggesting layers frozen in history. Perhaps it is more accurate to imagine these layers in a state of tension, shifting according to context, coexisting within practitioners as contradictory or alternative ways of thinking. Thus the same doctor might perform birthing-room and delivery-room obstetrics, shifting his or her perspective rapidly from one to the other; the same patient might hold in suspension the two images of "ideal birth," choosing at the end the one corresponding to the "brute facts" of her delivery.

Psychiatry is a particularly layered domain of medicine (see, e.g., Gaines 1979).[3] Diverse approaches to problems seem to remain in suspension, lending a complex and often confusing texture to the psychiatric ward. We can tease apart these layers (I suggest three here) and see that each calls forth corresponding forms of practice.

Confinement

Foucault (1977) suggests the confinement of unreason, the exclusion of the mad from society while constructing them as an object of knowledge, as the primary layer upon which our understanding of psychiatric institutions must rest. Certainly this layer is not hard to find in the APU. The construction of the mental health center was intended to remedy the faults of the old state hospital system, including the routinized and prisonlike conditions imposed on patients. Yet much in the unit's architecture and daily operation suggests that the primary function has not changed: patients are confined in a small and sealed-off area in which they are treated as potentially dangerous. The unit is dark and devoid of decoration; seclusion rooms are often used to isolate difficult patients. The staff describes the place as the "unconscious of psychiatry" where prisoners, the homeless, the violently psychotic, and the demented elderly are "held" until they can be sent elsewhere.

The Medical Gaze

To simplify I will describe the medical gaze in psychiatry as having two aspects. On the one hand, it is the classic gaze of medicine that penetrates the body, looking through CAT scans, autopsies, and drug studies for the brain abnormalities at the root of psychosis. On the other hand, it is the gaze of Freud, looking through the patient's speech to the psychic pathology producing it. Theoretically we can understand these two to have quite different implications, but on a ward where patients pass through within days or weeks they have similar implications. The "underlying" problem (behind the symptomatic, deranged behavior) is looked for upon admission; medication or, more rarely, psychological intervention aims to act upon it.

Since the APU staff recognizes that medication changes behavior without touching its "cause" and that psychotherapy (were it effective with patients this disturbed) cannot be undertaken in the time available, both forms of gaze are continually thwarted in practice. However, the unit is set up as though this were not so. The APU looks as though it belongs to the world of traditional medicine, and it carries out the acts of medicine—examining, diagnosing, prescribing and charting—but the "results" of medicine remain elusive. The patients return again and again, disheveled, rebellious, depressed, hungry, rarely better, often worse. The staff sometimes offers psychoanalytic interpretations of patients' behavior, but rarely do these make much sense of the patients' real situations.

The Systems Approach

Arney and Bergen suggest that the surface of medicine today—the most recent layer of the painting—consists of a systems or ecological approach to situations. This perspective, which took shape in the fifties (e.g., DuBos 1965),[4] looks beyond the body to both the external and the intrapsychic environments. It involves a refiguring and expansion of the medical gaze to include more of what surrounds the patient, including the physician in the pattern.

> As the notion of disease expands, so must the medical gaze. The physician must consider real, legitimate and relevant to the medical encounter aspects of life not captured by the informed gaze previously. . . . The physician must become . . . dedicated not to the treatment of disease but to the management of each patient. (Arney and Bergen 1984:78)

Much of the ideology of community psychiatry rests on this approach, in which all the patient's problems are considered relevant to medical management. Even though it is pinched by underfunding and limited by the quick turnover of patients, the APU participates in this new definition of the medical role. Its staff is supposed to uncover the truth of the patient's situation, make sense of it in relationship to the available norms and resources, and "fit" the patient back into an appropriate ecological niche. Part of the task is to get the patient to reveal himself—what is his real name? Is he a veteran? Is there a permanent address on file?—so that he can be sent where he belongs. Part of the task also is to sort out the disturbed relationships—abusive family, recently lost job, previous institutionalizations—that constitute the "systemic" cause of his problems. These tasks are layered onto the others—confining him if violent, or keeping his family from disturbing him; taking blood tests, administering medication, providing a diagnosis—belonging to the other two strata of the picture.

The practitioners' adroitness, then, cannot consist of a single skill such as "diagnosing" or even a set of skills that are all of the same type. The skills themselves, the appropriate actions, are distributed among these strata and can only make sense in their specific contexts. But these contexts implicate contradictory objects, or at least objects with conflicting needs—the patient, "society," the "community"—so that the practitioner is not really skilled until he or she can maneuver, reflectively, among them. Here are two examples, one spatial, the other strategic:

The hospital was built with the idea that it would extend into the community, replacing the isolated asylum with an open and inviting structure, "like a mall," as one staff member put it. This open structure would enable the staff to continue the kind of outreach work that had begun about a decade earlier (in the sixties) in small community mental health centers. A nurse who had worked in one of these centers described it nostalgically as "*real* crisis intervention. You could talk to people *right then* about a problem." The hospital did not fulfill its promise to continue this tradition. The building itself turned out to be forbidding and bare, and the open doors had to be shut off because of vandalism. It resembles an office tower; guards stand at the entrance and prevent outsiders from entering and patients from leaving. The emergency unit is dark and enclosed, and characterized by the staff as a "dungeon"; physically it is a place at least as confining and isolating as the old chronic hospitals. Yet the idea of penetrating the "outside" lives of patients is not lost; it permeates the charting process, the ideology of some practitioners, and the relationship between the institution and the community.

The space of the hospital itself speaks of the layered quality of practice; the boarded-up front door blocks off the same "community" the social worker must seek contact with. ("You have to get your hands dirty," she says, "or you cannot do this kind of work.") But notice, too, that this is not a straightforward layering, as though these historical residues stacked up in a progressive way. The old image of confinement supersedes the newer one of "outreach" at some places in the hospital's structure and recedes into the background at others. At a family conference the front door is almost forgotten; at the guards' desk, family conferences seem one of the remoter possibilities.

The attempt to link "sense" and context, to make the action fit the layer at hand, is a major topic of conversation among the staff of the unit. This example is taken from the morning meeting at which the disposition of patients was discussed.

> *Resident:* I wonder if we're messing [this patient] up with drugs. He had akathisia; he's stiff. Maybe his meds are causing his symptoms. If he's got private insurance we're gonna get rid of him. I met his mother yesterday; there's no precipitating factor that she knows of.
>
> *Psychiatrist:* I think the mother is a precipitating factor; her . . .
>
> *Resident:* Her whole behavior is strange.
>
> The psychiatrist talks (in a "teaching" gesture) about the patient's separation anxiety in relation to the mother's behavior.
>
> *Psychiatrist:* . . . You could make a case that the mother is behaving unreasonably and making him worse. If he's got insurance, work toward private hospitalization. With her, work with her denial; she may be unresponsive to any rational approach.
>
> *Resident:* Seclusion makes him worse.
>
> *Psychiatrist:* That's a good observation. Seclusion is bad for separation problems.
>
> *Resident:* But he's hard on the staff. But I'm gonna write not to seclude him and to reduce his meds.
>
> *Social worker:* What should we do when he kicks the doors, restraint or what?
>
> *Psychiatrist:* . . . We can make an effort to try other things before we put him in seclusion where he might freak out.

Here we see the staff exploring the options, the various kinds of practice, that would fit with the intricate situation created in the interface between patient and institution. They can dominate and repress (seclude) the patient in the interest of the whole system (both inside and outside the hospital). They can use the medical model (medicate), though they are uncomfortably aware that in psychiatry this move cannot get them past the symptom. They can bring to bear an analytic perspective, understanding the relation between the intrapsychic (the internalized mother) and the behavioral (separation anxiety). They can take an ecological approach, trying to balance elements of the situation (talk to the mother, working with what she says though knowing it is "denial"), extract financial information and use it to shift the problem somewhere else in the system and balance the needs of the staff and other patients against the patient's violence. It is as though the staff members are shining a rapidly moving light on all these possibilities, shifting from one to another, looking for a place to come to rest. Where they come to rest varies from situation to situation—for one patient rapid discharge is the answer, for another, more medication, and for a third, perhaps, a talk that will uncover a real name and address. But the point here is that the staff cannot stay put in one layer of the pentimento; they must learn (and this is a major aim of teaching) to move around among the layers according to whatever aspect of a situation is uppermost at any given moment.

Practice as Gesture

This brings me to my second point. Practice within the layered context of the clinic is inherently gestural. It is composed of a variety of kinds of gestures appropriate to different kinds of situations. These can only be learned properly *in* situations, which is why students must undergo "practicums" in order to learn their trade.

It is helpful here to think about the implications of Foucault's notion of the medical "gaze." As a noun, it is easily reified and made, I think, more thinglike than Foucault would seem to intend. In the *Birth of the Clinic,* Foucault suggests that practitioners "gaze"—that is, make a certain kind of gesture with their eyes. Thus, he says that the gaze

> could . . . grasp colours, variation, always receptive to the deviant . . . it was a gaze that was not content to observe what was self-evident; it must make it possible to outline chances and risks; it was calculating. (1975:89)

Later he describes the gaze as "an operation that makes visible . . . that totalizes by comparing . . . that recalls normal functioning," one that "scrutinizes the body and discovers at the autopsy a visible invisible" (1975:93). In other words, the gaze *does,* acts, moves; it is a gesture, not a thing.

We can extend this insight beyond biomedical practice and use it to understand how all practice is constituted. Perhaps a cross-cultural example, because it is of a less familiar kind of practice, can make this clear.

In Sri Lanka, ritual specialists who perform exorcisms must perfect a gesture that is relatively unfamiliar to us, a gesture we might call "becoming-another." In the course of ritual treatment they "become possessed by" or simply "become" the possessing demon. They enact, for the patient and sometimes with the patient, the gestures (forbidden, obscene, dangerous) known to be the special province of the demonic. The whole practice of exorcism depends upon the exorcist's ability to create and sometimes to transfer to the patient this repertoire of specifically (for Sri Lankans) demonic actions. Thus Bruce Kapferer describes how

> the exorcist in trance, or in the demon role, will crouch before the patient, fix the patient in his gaze, and furiously shake his body in time with the drum rhythm. The intention is not just to model the demonic before the victim but to effect a transfer of the demonic into the victim. (1983:197)

This "conversation of gestures" is not so much the "acting out" of a role recognized by specific gestural markers; rather the gestures themselves effect the transformation—*they* are at the center of the exorcist's practice.[5] Like the gestures of Western medicine, they must be learned in context and through action, with skill dependent upon sensitivity to the situation.

Practitioners in the APU, like the Sinhalese exorcist, must perfect certain gestures that are essential to their work. These gestures, because they participate in the contradictory nature of practice on the unit, are not reflected in the face shown by the hospital to the outside world. Thus written records, site visits for accreditors, case conferences, and other formal presentations rely on the ideology of community psychiatry and conceal the practical orientation of the unit in dealing with the problems related to this ideology.

Perhaps the most basic gesture on the unit is *disposing of.* On a small unit emphasizing emergency treatment the maintenance of open beds is an essential requirement. The staff experiences a more or less constant press of urgent cases coming in, and these must be balanced by patients going out. The staff must discharge patients efficiently to whatever places are possible—other facilities, boarding homes, shelters, family members, the street.

A major component of the staff's expertise consists in effective (rapid, efficient) disposition.[6] For instance, the unit's director says,

> From the beginning we aim toward separation. Other wards have an orientation for new patients. It would be absurd to "orient" someone to the APU. Do you get an orientation when you go to a hotel?

He means by this that the unit begins to plan for disposition as soon as the patient comes in the door. Just as one goes to a hotel for a brief stay and with a plan for one's departure, so patients are routed quickly through the unit. They do not need to become oriented to such a temporary environment.

Here is a conversation from a meeting in which the staff planned their strategy for the disposition of a psychotic patient.

> *Psychiatrist:* (to student in charge of the case): Find out his base-line, how far he is from his usual level of functioning.
>
> *Nurse:* Not far!
>
> *Another Nurse:* His brother and sister visited on Friday.
>
> *Psychiatrist:* Ah! Family! [to student] Try to contact the family. . . . Also, ask him if he can sign a voluntary. No, perhaps we should keep his certs [involuntary certification] in order to get him out.

Here the staff considers several angles on getting the patient out. Perhaps he can be almost this sick and still manage outside; perhaps he has a family who will take him in; perhaps he can remain involuntary, necessitating a move to another institution. The primary gesture is disposition; all else—legal considerations, family involvement, "diagnosis"— is subordinated to it.

> A demented old man is admitted to the unit only because he has no-where else to go. The staff cannot find a placement and he stays for months. The staff becomes preoccupied with an attempt to "find" a diag-nosis for him that will "fit" some niche where he could be placed. They try "alcohol-induced psychosis," they try "mental retardation," they try "or-ganic brain syndrome." Nothing works.

Here the gesture that appears to be "diagnosis" is really "disposing of": conversations about diagnosis subordinate the medical gaze (look-ing into the patient for the entity causing the problem) to a gaze outward (looking for the spot in the "community" where any particular diagnos-tic entity might find a home).

We can see in this last example that without an understanding of the primacy of gesture the notion of the pentimento is both too static and too loose. Too static, because it appears as though individual practitio-ners take up positions in particular layers of the picture, when actually the whole point of practice is in the movement among them. Too loose, because the picture doesn't tell us when any particular layer is most prominent. In these examples of the gesture of "disposing of" it is the situation, the context, which causes a particular gesture to become domi-nant. Thus, pressured by the presence of the old man, the staff try our different diagnoses, using the gaze in its older sense, but they keep coming back to "disposing of" as their primary goal.

The gesture of *taking in* is in contrast to disposing of. In these two examples the staff use it when disposition repeatedly fails, as it often does. Many of the unit's patients are young men who are chronically ill but cannot be legally retained; they are able to manage outside the hospital for periods of time, but return to the unit at intervals.

A young patient came back to the unit repeatedly. One psychiatrist became interested in helping him come for regular appointments rather than erratically. He said to the patient, "You need an alarm clock, a watch, a calendar, and a schedule. So you aren't drifting through the universe." He started writing down the dates of appointments and making a list, saying, "Do you think you're really gonna do this, or are we making it up?" The patient said, "The last time I made one I couldn't follow it." The psychiatrist added to the list: "Things for you not to do: do *not* visit your mother." The patient said, "What I need is some *friends.*"

Another young man came back to the hospital at frequent intervals; he could appear quite "healthy" after a few days off the streets but became psychotic again within days of discharge. The staff decided to present the hospital to him as a "home" to which he was welcome to return at will. Said the social worker, "In this capitalist society it's a pyramid, a whole lot are at the bottom. And a certain percent never get well. But they know where home base is, where to get nurtured." One day the patient said to her, "You're getting pretty full; throw me out of here.' She said, only half joking, "Oh no, we're gonna keep you indefinitely. This is home."

Taking in and disposing of are related to one another, but not in an easy way. In this context discharge mimics "production," with the perverse product the empty bed and efficiency the goal. Taking in, on the other hand, mimics the interpenetrating relationships of the family. The staff tries to teach patients how to "have a home," but this instruction must occur within a "scheduled" context.

The unit's permanent staff members teach the students to discriminate among situations so their responses to patients fit the immediate context.

A student is charged with sending away a drop-in patient who has just been released from jail and is staying at a shelter.

"I'm telling him to make an appointment [at a clinic] and he wants to make the call but he has no money. So I give him a quarter." The psychiatrist overseeing this tells the student to go and get the quarter back, saying sarcastically, "OK, why don't we make this a *bank.*"

The student has made the wrong kind of "taking in" gesture, one that jeopardizes the normal role of the unit. His ineptitude exposes the contradiction in the situation, saying both "go away" and "I'll help you." Later he clowns with the permanent staff members, exaggerating what he has done ("I should have offered him my apartment") to show that he has learned the lesson.

What we hear when we listen for the expression of gesture—"I gave him a quarter," "We turfed her to 5 West," "I told him he had a home," "Discharge him tomorrow"—is that the unit functions for its staff as what Rom Harre calls a "hazard"(1980:313). Harre means by this a social event, for example, an examination, which involves the risk of gaining either contempt or respect. The idea of hazard can be extended to places; the unit, then, was a place where the staff had to take risks, "hazard" their careers. Students on the unit imitated the style of their teachers; the successful students saw that competence lay in practicing the gestures specific to the unit's practice. Those who tried too hard to be "good" earned contempt, not because they were considered hypocritical, but because they could not move quickly to accommodate varying contexts. As one psychiatrist put it, "The closer you are to the patients, the harder it is to be good." On the other hand, people who could shift readily from one perspective to another earned respect; they were flexible and imaginative in using their repertoire of possible moves. The layered context of the pentimento provides many of these—tried and true ones, like listening to a patient's chest, and newer, startling ones, like "being confrontive" with a difficult patient. The practitioner chooses and refines; in this lies both the hazard and the art of practice.

Conclusion

I have suggested here two ways of looking at clinical practice, one the idea of overlapping and coexisting layers of meaningful action, the other the notion that action should be understood as gesture. Here I want to consider several implications of thinking about practice in these ways.

The first is that despite the noun-oriented tendency of our language, it is helpful, in listening to practitioners, to listen for verbs, for doing rather than thingifying. Many of the nouns used to describe practice (diagnosis, treatment, aftercare) imply that "things" are being created; indeed, these things are often the first content of practitioners' training. But training has to go beyond this to be effective, so that students can imitate doing. On the APU the permanent staff constantly reflected on their own doing, showing students *how* they practiced. Unfortunately attempts to pinpoint this for outsiders (e.g., "One of the things I like to show my students . . .") imply less contradiction and overlapping of gesture than really exists. As one aide said of a student who was struggling with her desire to be good, "The *place* teaches." It is the place, in all its complexity, which provides the ground for action. It cannot be abstracted and turned into a "map of all possible routes" (Bourdieu 1977:2).

Secondly, this view of practice makes "reform" quite problematic. Each attempt to refigure the clinic creates a new layer of practice—the systems approach tried to improve upon the impersonality of the medical gaze, which was itself (in part) a reformulative response to confinement. The old layers do not go away entirely, nor do the new ones ever achieve full coverage of all the possibilities. On the APU, where the staff were disillusioned with deinstitutionalization, some workers favored more and better somatic care (medical solutions) while others liked the idea of returning to "moral treatment" in isolated asylums. Andrew Scull points out this tendency to circularity and the recycling of old ideas in his analysis of mental health reform (1979, 1984); it is clear that few reformers (perhaps with the exception of Basaglia [Scheper-Hughes and Lovell, 1986]) have been able to disengage themselves from the cyclical and self-perpetuating aspects of the system. So much of medicine is organized around ideas of progress that we need to be aware of this tendency toward circularity. I think that in our attempts to understand practice we, as anthropologists, should try not to "buy" ideas about improvement or reform presented to us by institutions or practitioners; watching practitioners, we see them acting out contradictions on which a more realistic critique might be based.

When we try to analyze practice in terms of its historical context and current shape, we come to the problem of continuity which is raised, but far from resolved, in Foucault's work. Foucault suggests leaps and disjunctions between historical periods and implies that when an institution or idea (such as confinement) does carry through several epochs, it may mean something entirely different at different times (1975, 1977). At the same time one has the impression, in his work and simply from dwelling on his examples, that once something (such as an institution) has taken a certain shape (e.g., confinement/objectification) that shape is extraordinarily persistent. In thinking of the clinic as a pentimento with overlapping, sometimes contradictory gestures, we in fact see continuities that are obscured by the rhetoric of practice; for example, the prominence of seclusion/isolation and the *way* the gesture is made in the clinic surely hark back to the eighteenth century and earlier. On the other hand, there *are* breaks, disjunctions. The gaze that prescribes medication and the gaze that looks for placement in the community seem radically different; they coexist in the same person, but the person experiences them as contradictory.

This of course raises the further and even more problematic question of the relationship between individuals and the "system." Sherry Ortner

(1984) points out that this question plagues a practice perspective: to what extent do we, taking the perspective of actors, see them shaping the system that shapes their actions? The network of power relations operating in the clinic (and Foucault would describe these as interlinked and fluid rather than as fixed structures of domination) powerfully permeates the gestures of practice and shapes practitioners' and patients' senses of self. Thus the student scolded for giving money to a patient and the patient asked to make a schedule are being acted upon, impressed with the kind of capillary power that shapes subjectivity. However, the notion that subjectivity is shaped by power does not take us far enough in understanding how people working in institutions develop ways of understanding and manipulating their environment (see Berman 1982:34; Lemert and Gillan 1982:100–106). The capillary quality of power on the APU provides a field for the creativity of individuals. The APU staff find highly original ways to maneuver in their dense environment and to express themselves on their problematic work. They are creative with language, using metaphor, for example, to create shared images of their workplace. They are creative also with gesture. For instance, the psychiatrist who offered a clock and calendar to his patient later realized the futility of this gesture and said, "Maybe the problem is us rather than him . . . we are on scheduled feeding and [he] is on a demand feeding schedule." He changed his approach to the patient accordingly.

This inventiveness suggests that clinics, though mired in ironies reflective of those of the larger society, also compress practitioners into a small and active space where these ironies must be attended to, acted on, and elaborated. These "swamps" of professional practice may offer us access to problems of human concern that, if we can listen well enough, will reveal their intricate connections to our society and ourselves.

Notes

1. Gordon provides an interesting discussion of the development of expertise out of theoretical knowledge, emphasizing the contextualization of knowledge through practice (1988).

2. The material used in this chapter was gathered through participation, observation, and interviews with the staff of the emergency facility; I am deeply grateful for their help. I have changed the name of the unit and some other details in my examples. Quotes are taken directly from notes or tapes. For a more complete discussion of practice on the unit see Rhodes 1991.

3. The psychiatry department connected to the emergency unit was shifting away from a psychodynamic orientation and toward a more biological approach at the time of my work; however, the unit's patients were so sick, and their social situations so extreme, that this theoretical dispute was largely irrelevant in the

clinic. For accounts that suggest "layering" in other areas of medicine see Hahn 1985 and Hilfiker 1985.

4. Arney and Bergen suggest that the "systems-ecological-problem-oriented" approach can be found in medical texts, new forms of record keeping, screening programs, and new ways of apprehending the "individual." "The mission of medicine remains the same, but the scope of medicine's interests enlarges" (1984:93). Obviously, though they do not mention it, much of the recent agenda of medical anthropology falls within this approach.

5. These are not, of course, the only gestures of exorcism, which also sustains contradictory images of person and society.

6. This orientation toward discharge is described for other settings in medicine as well as psychiatry. See, e.g., Matthews 1980 and Mizrahi 1986.

References

Arney, William R. and Bernard J. Bergen
    1984   *Medicine and the Management of Living: Taming the Last Great Beast*. Chicago: University of Chicago Press.
Berman, Marshall
    1982   *All That Is Solid Melts Into Air: The Experience of Modernity*. New York: Simon and Schuster.
Bourdieu, Pierre
    1977   *Outline of a Theory of Practice* (trans. Richard Nice) Cambridge: Cambridge University Press.
DuBos, Rene
    1965   *Man Adapting*. New Haven: Yale University Press.
Foucault, Michel
    1975   *The Birth of the Clinic: An Archeology of Medical Perception*. New York: Vintage Books.
    1977   *Madness and Civilization: A History of Insanity in the Age of Reason*. London: Tavistock.
Gaines, Atwood D.
    1979   Definitions and Diagnoses: Cultural Implications of Psychiatric Help-Seeking and Psychiatrists' Definitions of the Situation in Psychiatric Emergencies. *Culture Medicine and Psychiatry* 3(4):351–415.
Goffman, Erving
    1961   *Asylums: Essays on the Social Situations of Mental Patients and Other Inmates*. New York: Doubleday.
Gordon, Deborah R.
    1988   Clinical Science and Clinical Expertise: Changing Boundaries between Art and Science in Medicine. In *Biomedicine Examined*, Margaret Lock and D. R. Gordon, eds., pp. 257–295. Dordrecht: Kluwer Academic Publishers.
Hahn, Robert
    1985   A World of Internal Medicine: Portrait of an Internist. In *Physicians of Western Medicine: Anthropological Approaches to Theory and*

Practice, Robert Hahn and Atwood Gaines, eds., pp. 51–111. Dordrecht: D. Reidel Publishing Company.

Harre, Rom
1980   *Social Being: A Theory for Social Psychology.* Totowa, N.J.: Littlefield, Adams and Company.

Hellman, Lillian
1973   *Pentimento: A Book of Portraits.* Boston: Little, Brown.

Hilfiker, David
1985   *Healing the Wounds: A Physician Looks at His Work.* London: Penguin Books.

Kapferer, Bruce
1983   *A Celebration of Demons: Exorcism and the Aesthetics of Healing in Sri Lanka.* Bloomington: Indiana University Press.

Lemert, Charles C., and Gillan, Garth
1982   *Michel Foucault: Social Theory and Transgression.* New York: Columbia University Press.

Matthews, Daryl B.
1980   *Disposable Patients: Situational Factors in Emergency Decisions.* Lexington, Mass.: Lexington Books.

Mizrahi, Terry
1986   *Getting Rid of Patients: Contradictions in the Socialization of Physicians.* New Brunswick, N.J.: Rutgers University Press.

Light, Donald
1980   *Becoming Psychiatrists: The Professional Transformation of Self.* New York: W. W. Norton.

Ortner, Sherry
1984   Theory in Anthropology since the Sixties. *Comparative Studies in Society and History.* 26(1):126–166.

Rhodes, Lorna A.
1991   *Emptying Beds: The Work of an Emergency Psychiatric Unit.* Berkeley, Los Angeles, Oxford: University of California Press.

Scheper-Hughes, Nancy, and Ann M. Lovell
1986   Breaking the Circuit of Social Control: Lessons in Public Psychiatry from Italy and Franco Basaglia. *Social Science and Medicine* 23(2):159–178.

Schön, Donald
1983   *The Reflective Practitioner: How Professionals Think in Action.* New York: Basic Books.

Scull, Andrew T.
1979   *Museums of Madness: The Social Organization of Insanity in Nineteenth-Century England.* London: Allen Lane.
1984   *Decarceration: Community Treatment and the Deviant: A Radical View.* 2nd ed. Cambridge: Polity Press.

Warner, Richard
1985   *Recovery from Schizophrenia: Psychiatry and Political Economy.* London: Basic Books.

Part Three

Contested Knowledge
and Modes
of Understanding

Introduction

Contested Knowledge and Modes of Understanding

Just as there are many forms of knowledge in the world, there are many kinds of "medical" knowledge. The authors in this section discuss the different modes of understanding and of dealing with illness in specific contexts in Nigeria, the United States, Papua New Guinea, and Italy.

The lay contribution to medical knowledge is the topic of the paper by Tola Olu Pearce. The chasm between lay and professional knowledge, characteristic of Western science, does not exist for the Yoruba of southwestern Nigeria. Here, the range of acceptable medical evidence includes dreams, visions, intuition, and feelings, as well as empirical signs. This allows room for nonprofessional contributions to medical knowledge and for choosing the type of knowledge to be used in particular situations. Pearce's emphasis on the primacy of intuition as a mode of apprehension, as well as on the importance of lay contributions to medical knowledge outside the clinic, recalls themes raised earlier by Kaufert and O'Neil and by Rapp and discussed later by Lock, Estroff, and Frankenberg. That is, beliefs about illness and the behaviors that follow as a consequence of these beliefs communicate and confirm important ideas about the nature of existence. Thus, forms of knowledge that are not widely shared are difficult to incorporate into the diagnostic and therapeutic practices of biomedicine, which screen out the social relations of sickness (see Young 1982). While Yoruba and Inuit modes of knowing arise in the context of resistance to the imported therapies and medicaments of the West, these other papers identify local knowledge and contested ways of seeing the world that exist within cultures and communities.

The problematic nature of medical knowledge and evidence is an issue raised also by both Horacio Fabrega and Gilbert Lewis. As physician-anthropologists, each experiences the contradictions of an applied anthropology that is not easy to reconcile with certain forms of medical practice. Fabrega describes the anguish experienced by a psychiatrist who testifies as a witness for the defense in a case of homicide. Patient-anthropologist/psychiatrist relationships of sharing and empathy, forged in the privacy of the clinical encounter, do not mesh well with the role of an expert witness who is an agent of the legal system. Key information that might contribute to healing (in this case, to prevent the suicide of the defendant) has no bearing on the impersonal and objective testimony required for litigation. The power of the state to impose limits and constrain the witness to follow a single path of action is shown to be problematic for the therapist and potentially damaging for the patient. The structural problems inherent in Anglo-American psychiatry, its links with deviance and marginality, and the regulation of professional behaviors by state agencies are issues raised here and in other chapters by Sue Estroff and Lorna Rhodes, who reach their conclusions by following a different route.

Gilbert Lewis questions the nature of medical evidence by asking whether the same standards should be used in evaluating the efficacy of medical treatment in all cultures, giving new life to the rationality debates (Horton 1973) that stemmed from an earlier anthropological encounter with African medicine. Taking as an example the treatment of leprosy in the West Sepik region of Papua New Guinea, Lewis notes that lay medical knowledge is accepted on trust from figures of authority, just as it is in the West; we each value our own forms of medicine and distrust others. The practical implications of this behavior arise when people fail to comply with a treatment regimen considered biomedically effective. Lewis asks whether anthropologists—whose methods and equipment do not lend themselves to objective validation—can find an appropriate workplace beside those who offer Western medical care and also among those who are the recipients of that care.

While Fabrega and Lewis explore the contradictions that arise for those who suffer from a kind of professional dual vision, Ronald Frankenberg reflects upon the issues that unite and divide anthropology and epidemiology. In a hopeful vein, he depicts a more productive joint future if the two disciplines could agree on a common language and some shared concepts. Taking as an example their different approaches to the concept of risk, he proposes two shifts in the epidemiological frame that would bring them closer: a reevaluation of the accepted units of analysis, and a view of sickness as "dramatic cultural narrative" to modify the narrower clinical view of disease as timeless or episodic. Such a space/time shift in epidemiological risk assessment, he suggests, would allow for the inclusion of moral, social, and political choice. Frankenberg's chapter is additional evidence of the "bridging" activities necessary when anthropologists and epidemiologists meet on the same terrain, a situation to which we were already alerted in the earlier chapters by Kaufert and O'Neil and Rapp. Here, epidemiology is asked to modify its framework. Usually it is the anthropological vision that retreats to accommodate an epidemiological method that provides little room for the historical, political, and economic factors that determine disease.

References

Horton, Robin, and Ruth Finnegan, eds.
    1973   *Modes of Thought.* London: Faber and Faber.
Young, Allan
    1982   The Anthropologies of Illness and Sickness. *Annual Review of Anthropology* 11:257–285.

7

Lay Medical Knowledge
in an African Context

Tola Olu Pearce

The central concern of this chapter is the development of a framework within which the creation of medical knowledge among lay people can be better understood. The data used come from various studies among the Yoruba of southwestern Nigeria, to which I have added an analysis of my own research conducted in two rural communities in the state of Ondo (jointly with Simi Afonja) and in Ile-Ife, a provincial town in the state of Oyo, between 1985 and 1987. I argue that the general framework presented here is applicable to laypeople everywhere. Only the specifics—that is, the concrete ideas, meanings, and relationships available to the individual—differ according to cultural and historical circumstances. However, the degree to which health professionals in any given society draw on or reject lay knowledge varies cross-culturally. My focus, then, is on everyday medical knowledge generated by the public at large, as opposed to the theoretical knowledge of medical practitioners, or the written ideas of intellectuals (Abercrombie 1980). As Peter Berger and Thomas Luckmann (1966) have indicated, our perception of reality is socially constructed as persons go about solving the problems of everyday life. Individuals and groups thus accumulate a repertoire of information relevant to their various domains of activity, and knowledge about health matters remains an important dimension of information for survival. In Nigeria, the medical sector is recognized as pluralistic more readily than appears to be the case in many Western societies. In this context, lay people freely use and integrate aspects of competing knowledge bases in their attempt to handle health matters. I am particularly interested in what appears to be a wave of redefinition and creativity among the Yoruba with respect to knowledge within the popular medical sector at the present time. How much of these ongoing activities will become normalized or even help to transform the behavior of the various types of medical practitioners remains to be seen. Nonetheless, an attempt is made here to comprehend the way medical "facts" are generated among the public, and how these facts are related to and in part products of other aspects of Yoruba culture.

My argument is that people draw on many different aspects of their environment and their daily lives to construct medical "truths." For the purposes of analysis, I view the framework within which this knowledge is generated as three tiered, consisting of macro-, intermediate-, and micro-level factors. When confronted with a health problem, individuals and groups make use of and integrate societal/cultural factors (macro) with features drawn from the medical sector itself (intermediate) as well as the physical and psychological dimensions of their own experience (micro) to represent reality to themselves and to others. Thus, the creation of knowledge is complex, involving processes both intrinsic and extrinsic to the individual.

The Role of Macro-Level Factors

Medical knowledge, whether pertaining to health promotion, disease prevention, diagnosis, or treatment, is significantly influenced by general social factors. Medical knowledge and practice, like other social activities, are products of specific historical and social contexts, and thus vary according to time and place. As Stephen Toulmin (1976:41) has argued, there is always a context within which what is to be accepted as medical understanding is agreed upon. It is important therefore to note some of the sociohistorical factors that have influenced the social construction of medical knowledge in Nigeria.

Several authors, including John Janzen (1978) and Steven Feierman (1985) have discussed the ways in which the structure of the family in Africa and the responsibilities of family members affect medical activity and, by implication, medical knowledge. Within the extended family, the structure of "therapy managing groups" allows input from a wide circle of relatives in connection with diagnosis, treatment, and choice of providers. A recent study conducted in Ilesa (Adedoja 1986) among two hundred residents revealed that although increased physical mobility and formal education have shrunk the size and function of the therapy managing group, people still consult certain family members over serious illnesses. It is still the case, however, that such groups are involved in decisions about choice of health care provider, performance of rituals, preparation of medications, and assistance in paying for therapy, and in visiting the patient. Traditionally, apart from one's parents, the *baale* (head) of the extended family compound and three or more elders were the decision makers. In terms of lay development of medical knowledge, this arrangement gave maximum opportunity for the joint construction of "facts," although Feierman reminds us that authority within such groups need not be distributed equally. Nevertheless, the control exercised by the group affects opportunities for the development of knowledge. What is noticeable today is that differential social mobility within the family and exposure to new experiences or belief systems (especially religious ones) have affected the ideas that members of the family bring to these deliberations. For example, in one family I studied in 1986, an elderly man with recurring leg cramps that failed to respond to orthodox Western treatment received a wide range of suggestions from family members. These included treatment by herbs, prayers, the burning of candles, and private covenants with God. Interestingly, it is believed that all methods can be used simultaneously.

The economic context within which people must operate has an important influence on the way they go about taking care of their health or generating information about their problems. The present economic recession in Nigeria has had a differential impact on the various medical systems. The dependency of Western medicine on imported drugs and technology has resulted in a sharp rise in the cost of treatment and a shortage of materials (including teaching materials). There is thus a growing opinion that biomedicine is too expensive and is also deteriorating. This has led to a renewed interest in faith-healing and indigenous medicine.

Moreover, both preventive and curative aspects of medicine are implicated. In many households self-medication prevails. Although Western drugs may be bought from the chemist or drug hawker, many people use home remedies developed within their own families. Of the two hundred respondents in the Ilesa sample, 40 percent reported that they regularly used local medications developed by family members or friends for preventive care. Most of these consisted of various herbal mixtures (*agbo*) consumed daily or weekly to keep the body healthy. Insofar as the government has reversed its former policy of free medical services, we can expect more interest in local home remedies for curative care as well. The families in this study reported a wide array of recipes for common ailments such as fevers, colds, sore throats, stomachaches, and so forth.

A third issue related to the economic situation but transcending it concerns the general uncertainty and unpredictability of life in many Third World nations, and in Nigeria in particular. This is a problem keenly felt at all levels of society. A distinct feature of present-day life in

Nigeria is a sense of chaos and uncertainty. As noted elsewhere (Pearce 1987), the history of the slave trade, colonialism, neocolonialism, and poor leadership have all taken their toll on the possibility for economic and social stability and predictability in Nigeria. This situation readily leads to anxiety, followed no doubt by attempts to control the situation. I suggest that this condition of uncertainty is fertile ground for the development of new forms of everyday medical knowledge.

The Use of
Intermediate-Level Factors

The composition of a pluralistic medical sector particular to any given society will influence lay construction of medical facts. In southwestern Nigeria, the population can choose from a number of medical traditions in order to interpret their health problems. These include biomedicine, indigenous medicine, and Islamic and faith healing (the latter in old and new versions). Matthews Ojo (1988) has referred to these two versions of faith healing as the pentecostal and charismatic, respectively.

From data that I collected in 1986, both in the township of Ile-Ife and in rural areas of the state of Ondo, there are strong indications that a systematic use of the various available frameworks is not what occurs. This is not to deny that regular patterns of action (such as visiting specific providers) can be uncovered. However, the deliberations that precede these activities need not be systematic. Nor do the final actions tell us how different types of evidence are marshalled to clarify the problem. It is also possible to head for the hospital while harboring strong suspicions that the illness has preternatural causes. For instance, a thirty-six-year-old male informant related to me how his older brother was taken to the hospital after the latter experienced dizziness and collapsed, even though *aye* (the evil machinations of others) was suspected. Paralysis was diagnosed at the hospital, and his relatives decided to remove him to the care of a diviner. Later, a prophet was sought when the patient did not respond. My informant expressed the view that it is important to visit the hospital first, even if other services have to be tried.

Afonja (1986) has also reported that the prevalence of a belief in metaphysical (preternatural and supernatural) causes in addition to natural causes did not hinder visits to medical centers in the rural communities. Western medical practitioners are generally sought out, after home remedies have been tried. Afonja concluded that "the data on hierarchy of resort in infants', childrens' and adults' illnesses do not corroborate beliefs and perceptions of illness and health" (1986:110). In addition, she discovered that Western medicine is assessed as good for providing an initial diagnosis. This perhaps explains why some find it expedient to visit the hospital first.

Finally, information that I collected on thirty-four patients in the same communities in 1987 showed that people consistently combine different traditions, even for preventive/promotional care when there is no immediate health crisis. Thirty-three persons (97 percent) combined a number of such activities. An average of 3.8 activities (prayers, taking vitamins or traditional herbs) were carried out daily, with prayers mentioned by 85 percent as the most important. Keeping peaceful relations with significant others featured in 82 percent of combinations. Likewise, 50 percent mentioned the use of indigenous home remedies and charms.

Thus the different frameworks can be seen as loosely connected in people's minds. As Robin Horton (1982) has now conceded, African systems of thought are indeed quite open (Janzen 1981; Anyanwu 1981). The numerous choices are accommodated. Writing specifically on the Yoruba, Akinsola Akiwowo (1986) holds the view that different types of beliefs are not generally seen in terms of conflict, contradiction, or confrontation. Niyi Oladeji (1987) has also highlighted the emphasis on pragmatism among the Yoruba, whereby different dimensions of a total repertoire can be used at different times to solve various problems. A repeated idea among the Ile-Ife informants was that all cures (including the doctor's) come from God/the Supreme Being. All healing knowledge comes from that ultimate source. All bona fide providers are merely instruments or conduits of His force. Thus, it is not wise to reject alternative sources of dealing with a problem.

Following from this is the belief that each group of providers has its own strengths and weaknesses. Certain types of illnesses are seen as best treated by certain types of providers. Broadly speaking, Western medicine is believed to be good for surgical problems, accident cases, and a variety of aches and pains. Problems of the mind, such as sleeplessness, bad dreams, and mental disorders, should be left to indigenous practitioners or prophets. It has already been noted that Western medicine is often viewed as the most efficacious for symptom diagnosis, that is, for stating what a physical problem is. Other scholars have also commented on the lay idea of a division of labor among practitioners (Ademuwagun 1979). This development simply points to the fact that the public is attempting to generate information about the efficacy of the competing approaches. The implication is that even if Western medicine were totally covered by health insurance, certain problems would still be treated elsewhere.

One can argue that what is developing is general knowledge based on experience, which allows clients to use the various services more efficiently given their view of providers as "specialists" in different types/

groups of illnesses. In other words, from the clients' point of view, being able to retrieve information (stored with providers) is an important dimension of medical knowledge. Insofar as the populace increasingly acts on this knowledge, they influence the development of each type of medicine by the demands they make on the providers.

In addition, new therapeutic activities are being undertaken among lay persons. A variety of new (charismatic) faith-healing groups are presently springing up throughout southern Nigeria. These are distinct from the older Pentecostal (e.g., Aladura) sects studied by John Peel (1968) and others. However, in forging new healing modalities, they too can be seen as combining old (indigenous) and new (Western) beliefs.

Ojo (1988) has shown that these Charismatic groups arose in the early 1970s within some institutions of higher learning. The University of Ibadan and later Obafemi Awolowo University (then the University of Ife) were important centers of activity. Today in Ile-Ife, the university campus is still a major hub for the activities and the further development of these groups. Observations and interviews with some group members reveal interesting patterns of behavior. In this university location, several small gatherings known as "fellowships" meet for prayer meetings and faith healing. Members regard themselves as Born Again Christians, but each attends the official church of his or her choice. These fellowships attempt to deemphasize the special healing role of elders or prophets, a pronounced aspect of the older Aladura sects. The spiritual capability of each individual is highlighted. More importantly, the force of the *group* is seen as a significant element in the healing process. It should be noted that the idea of health and healing as a group affair is deeply rooted in the African traditional setting (Pearce 1986). Further, I would suggest that such fellowships have retained an indigenous belief in the "life force."

K. Anyanwu has argued that in Africa there is a deep-seated belief that everything has its own share of life force. This is believed to have an important impact on knowledge generation. This "life force" is thought to have existed since the beginning of the world. It is active. "Man, animals and plants share from this life-force and it can be communicated to things" (Anyanwu 1981:89). Forms of communication are therefore expected between plants, humans, and spiritual beings. Life force guarantees life in everything, and it can be readily identified. When removed, the object dies, as when breath and speech are gone. The spiritual force that the new fellowship groups focus upon is also seen as a gift from God that needs to be developed to its fullest potential. For each individual, spiritual talents differ and are useful to the group. It is believed that the totality of the force generated by a group in prayer is important for healing. God's healing power works through humans and the materials (water, white cloth, oil, food) they use. One female member expressed the view that "there is power in group prayer." Members are strongly encouraged to bring all problems to prayer meetings. Thus, the therapeutic potential of the group is being exploited, and the group becomes an instrument for healing. In addition to the practical advice and assistance that group members give each other, the various talents—dreams, visions, speaking in tongues, interpreting tongues—are brought to bear on the members' various problems.

Although it is believed that cure can occur through prayer/faith alone, members may also visit the hospital or clinic. Indeed, such visits are often encouraged and supplemented with private or group prayers. Psalms have become an important dimension of these prayer sessions. One female informant, for instance, has developed for her own use the reading of Psalms 3, 20, and 35 in the treatment of her children when they become restless and have difficulty sleeping. For many members of the group, Bible-reading sessions known as devotional studies have also become imperative as the last activity of the day before bed. Rosalind Hackett's recent research (1987) on the new religious groups in eastern Nigeria indicates that as a result of the rapid exchange of literature and the movement of individuals among the groups, a common religious subculture is developing. These exchanges will no doubt also result in common healing techniques in terms of symbols, materials, and beliefs. The medical knowledge developed from such group activities is based partly on the old ideas of "caring, consoling and comforting," which Ivan Illich (1975) feels are endangered by technological medicine. In Africa, however, health and religion have remained intertwined, and the language of religion in health appears to be maintaining its position even though the framework of religion may be changing from indigenous forms to new configurations of Christianity. Thus, medication is said to alleviate illness through the "grace of God" and health is seen as a blessing or an important reward for living according to the dictates of the Christian religion.

Individual and Micro-Level Factors

At the micro-level of the individual and his or her body, it is important to acknowledge how subjective experience is culturally produced. According to Berger and Luckmann (1966), people internalize aspects of a culture, rework them, and often create new ideas/information. In the creation of knowledge, what is accepted as evidence of the truth is crucial, but variable, in different cultures. For instance, there is a wide gap between the synthesis of religious, moralistic, empirical, and folkloric evidence that laymen often develop in the West and what is accepted as scientific evidence by physicians in clinical encounters. Among the Yoruba, however, a gap between the beliefs of indigenous practitioners (or prophets) and the general public does not exist. The range of acceptable evidence for both groups is wide and includes dreams, visions, intuition, and feelings, as well as empirical items. Such a situation allows greater leeway for lay persons to construct medical knowledge and practice.

For African communities the process of knowing in general is no different from the acquisition of medical knowledge. From Anyanwu's discussion one can see that this process is based on a number of assumptions: the ultimate nature of reality is that of relationships between life forces; reality cannot be separated from personal (both individual and collective) experience; immediate experience is important in knowing; and humans experience as a totality (body, mind, and spirit). This belief in the continuous interaction between humans and other forms of life force is at the root of J. Omosade Awolalu's (1972) thesis that the Yoruba see humans as "being-in-relation." The emphasis is on the web of life (networks) with individuals as connecting points in the matrix. This leads to the view of humans as open to external/nonhuman communication. It then becomes clear why dreams, religious experience, symbolic items, and the like are significant in generating medical "facts." For instance, dream interpretation is very popular for obtaining evidence about causes, future episodes and methods for the treatment of illness. Several authors have expressed the view that the Yoruba see dreams as the effort of supernatural beings to communicate with humans (Peel 1968; Simpson 1980). In a recent study of twenty-seven persons (ten spiritual leaders, nine dream interpeters and eight members of the general public), Mark Payne (1985) concluded that dreaming is seen as a meaningful activity via which knowledge is imparted to the dreamer. Dreams are not believed to be created by human psychic processes, but are "communications from an intelligence from without" (1985:94). Thus, a female hospital attendant believed that a "dream is something that God sends to give you meaning" (1985:96). Among my informants, the following statement of an elderly male expresses a commonly held view: "I believe that if I dream about the illness of a person or myself, about the cause, symptoms or treatment, it will *definitely* happen." Concerning the knowledge believed to be imparted through dreams, various examples were given. In one case, during a prolonged bout of illness, a middle-aged, educated male dreamed of a headless snake that was lodged in his stomach. Its headlessness was interpreted to mean that the illness would not be fatal. Over the years, the snake dream persisted but gradually more and more parts of the snake were missing. This was seen as a weakening of the "forces" causing the illness. When such forces significantly weaken in any illness "it is then possible to use Western medicine" along with the usual prayers for maximum efficacy. In another example, a dream was used to decide on the appropriate method of treatment. A forty-six-year-old female disagreed with her husband's wish to treat a sick child at home, since she had had a dream in which both she and a doctor pulled the drowning child out of a river. Thus, the child was taken to the hospital after indigenous treatment and an appropriate sacrifice had been conducted. Both the husband and his relatives refused to visit the child throughout its hospitalization. The child recovered after surgery. The mother insisted that since the dream had indicated that a doctor was involved in saving the child's life, she decided to disobey family members.

These dreams usually contain symbolic items, events, or colors that are often intuitively interpreted by the dreamer, although many people go to professional dream interpreters or church leaders (Payne 1985). For instance, the snake mentioned above was taken to represent Satan or demonic forces, the river, a symbol of serious danger. Relatively new items are also being incorporated into the symbolic system. Thus, coffins have become important. The presence of one in a dream signifies the death of the sick one, although a broken coffin is believed to foretell recovery. Likewise others items such as lit (white) candles, "heavenly hosts," or angels are also believed to signify recovery. The human body itself remains a powerful symbol. It symbolizes channels of communication. For some it is essentially the place through which healing power can be transmitted to the sick. It is also the place where good and bad (demonic) forces struggle for ascendance. Certain things symbolize power and are very important—the "name" of Jesus, the Bible, the blood of Jesus, for instance. As Peter Lloyd (1974) has noted, the concept of power (*agbara*) is important to the Yoruba. Apart from physical strength and command over persons, there is the spiritual connotation in which an individual is assessed as having access to sources of spiritual power and thus protection.

As in many societies, much symbolism is associated with colors. However, it would appear that subtle changes are occurring here. Since, as noted earlier, the Yoruba traditionally refrained from seeing things in terms of the intrinsic incompatibility (conflicts and contradictions) of phenomena, an item was rarely assessed in isolation as either totally good or absolutely evil. The role of the item, or its relationship with the other items, affected its status at a given point in time. With this perspective, colors such as black and white were not viewed in absolute terms. I believe this is an important, but undeveloped, dimension of Anthony Buckley's discussion on colors in Yoruba approach to health and disease. Black, for example, represented the hidden, secrecy and the mysterious, and it is at night that frightening things descending from the spirit world are believed to take place within the community. Nonetheless, it is only within a black medium (the mother's body) that a healthy conception can occur as the sperm (white) and menstrual blood (red) unite. Again, a good layer of black topsoil is necessary to cover unfertile red soil (laterite) (Buckley 1976). Thus, black could have a positive role to play in the scheme of things. Among the Christian groups, however, it would seem that black is exclusively associated with evil, the devil, and mischief. As one female typist noted, "Black means terrible things [will happen]." When she dreams of being approached by persons in black, it means that *aye* is the cause of the problem. It is quite common to hear people refer to the wicked as people with black innards. At the same time, there is an increasing association of white with purity, peace, and beneficial things. Some of the Aladura groups wear white robes for worship. In dreams, white candles and clothing are said to be signs that an illness will be arrested.

The belief in visions is similar to that of dreams. Among the Aladura sects, visioners are thought to be a special group of people who possess an "inner" eye that enables them to see visions. They are therefore more spiritually powerful than those who do not (Olayiwola 1986). Through such visions it is believed that any piece of information relevant to the client's problem can be imparted. This especially includes what an individual or his significant others must do to regain health.

As a result of the dreams, visions, and knowledge imparted by others, or because of individual creativity, home remedies are commonly developed for self-medication. They are considered efficacious if the symptoms disappear or if the expected outcome is achieved. The use of such medication for preventive care was mentioned earlier in this chapter. In Ile-Ife, a specific example given by an informant was the development of a worm expellent by his mother. It is prepared by boiling, for four hours, certain leaves and roots (known to his mother) with an onion in water skimmed off *ogi* (uncooked pap). Only one shot should be taken before breakfast. The mixture is prohibited to children under ten years, as it is considered far too strong. Other examples relate to fertility regulation and to the array of home-based medications and beliefs handed down from parent to child.

Finally, I wish to elaborate a little on the role of emotions and feelings discussed elsewhere (Pearce 1986). I am persuaded that among the Yoruba, and perhaps more widespread than is currently recognized, feelings and emotions have contributed greatly to an assessment of what is taken as "reality." Anyanwu has insisted that for the African, "imagination, intuitive experience and feelings are also modes of knowing" (1981:89). They are not discarded or belittled for rationalistic modes. In illness, emotions such as fear, shame, anxiety, guilt, hope, trust, confidence, feelings of being in the right, and so forth are meshed with reasoning. These feelings affect the review of received tradition, the ordering of incoming information, and the assessment of possible lines of action by all persons. Both the afflicted person and significant others are affected. I wish to stress here that all persons use emotions to create facts. I am not arguing that the African uses emotions while the non-African does not. I am merely noting that Africans have consistently recognized the place of emotions in human activities and welfare, and that the important role of the emotions in behavior and thinking should be more widely recognized.

The assumption that one is physically well is also dependent on how the body feels. Although the Yoruba have a number of different concepts denoting various dimensions of health (e.g., *ilera, san,* and *alafia*), stress is laid on the possession of a strong and active body. The concept of *ilera* (*lile*—strong, *ara*—body) focuses on a functional approach to health (Ademuwagun 1978). *San* signifies wellness/restoration. With san is the connotation of attaining the ideal. San can be used interchangeably with *sunwon,* which comprises *sun*—move toward—and *iwon*—measurement/standard. Thus, a person who is well approximates the ideal. The Yoruba underline the ability to carry out one's work and do what one set out to do. Not surprisingly, therefore, the following responses were given to the question, "How do you know when you are in good health?" (*alafia*—general well-being).

> I will be strong. I will feel light. I will be able to do such things as eating what I like, play, work and sleep.

> I will be strong, able to go to my shop to sell. Will be able to do household activities. Do my personal hygiene.

> Ability to lift all parts of my body and do my work. Health to me is painlessness and ability to do my work.

Given the Yoruba emphasis on network and group participation, the focus on one's work obligations is not unexpected. The stress on strength and activity will influence the types of symptoms recognized as important (Mechanic 1968) and their presentation both to other laypersons and health providers. As noted above, the emotions these symptoms generate will have an impact on how medical reality is viewed.

Summary and Conclusion

It is now widely recognized that there are many ways of constructing knowledge and this includes medical knowledge. Revisions of the orthodox view of scientific knowledge admit the role of intuitive and tacit processes in knowledge generation (Mulkay 1979; Polyani 1946). In this paper I have reviewed the ways in which persons construct and modify medical knowledge, particularly outside of the clinic and away from encounters with practitioners. The experience of Yoruba in urban and rural communities formed the background for the present discussion.

It was argued that macro-, intermediate-, and micro-level forces interact in the construction of medical knowledge and affect the behavior of groups and individuals. At the macro level, the increased social insecurities felt by Nigerians over the past ten years have had their effects. In the 1970s there were high expectations for economic development and social stability. Insofar as these are far from being realized, groups and families attempt to ease the situation and fall back on their own devices. In the area of health it can be said that certain developments serve to reduce the tensions and frustrations encountered in everyday life, and others produce new medical remedies for self-treatment. Thus the proliferation of old and new faith-healing sects or groups suggests the search for answers, and the attempt by lay people to gain some control over what happens to their lives. The change from the oil boom years to the present situation has been traumatic. Within the past few years, old and new health problems have surfaced. Thus, nutrition-related illnesses such as kwashiorkor and cancrum oris (inflammation of the oral mucosa) are on the increase in many places (Pearce 1987b). There have been renewed outbreaks of old diseases such as yellow fever and typhoid fever. The health problems of the developed world have also made appreciable inroads (e.g., diabetes, accidents, and hypertension). And yet the official medical system (biomedicine) is run down and underfunded. From a just-completed survey of the utilization of health services in the state of Oyo conducted by UNICEF, the average household spends 11 percent of its income on obtaining care from government and private institutions. Those who make less than 150 naira (approximately $38) per month spend 23 percent on health care. As the federal government withdraws funds, the consumer bears the cost (Obasa 1987). The consumer is thus tempted to look elsewhere for care. The economic pressures on the entire medical sector encourage initiative on the part of lay persons to develop their own solutions. Thus even within the Charismatic groups there is an increased emphasis on developing an individual's healing/spiritual talents or skills. Church leaders are no longer seen as the only or the main source of special healing powers. An unintended consequence of this could be the development of more confidence that lay people can find workable solutions to health problems. It has been argued (Opefeyitimi 1987) that the traditional Yoruba approach to prayer formerly stressed the importance of status and word-perfect recitals. Certain persons by virtue of their position were allowed to pray for the collectivity, and had to perform the rituals and say the prayers without mistakes. Perhaps the development of the current less structured approach, which gives more prominence to innovative activity and the joint efforts of lay people, has the potential for unleashing (or even regaining) ideas about lay competence in health matters.

At the intermediate level, the presence of various types of medical systems influence people's behavior. Here we find both the serial and simultaneous use of competing systems. Aspects of faith healing and biomedicine can be used by one individual, while biomedicine and indigenous approaches are combined by another. The lay person makes the choice. Although biomedicine is still the most prestigious system, its present level of functioning and the growing pride in aspects of indigenous culture have narrowed the gap between it and other forms of care in the eyes of many. Indeed, one increasingly hears of the use of biomedicine to alleviate menacing symptoms or for surgery, while other systems are used to understand or neutralize the "cause" of the problem. In addition, new therapeutic systems are entering the picture. An acupuncture center has been set up in Lagos, for instance, and more recently reflexology has arrived on the Lagos scene.

In looking at the individual (or groups/families) who decides what to do and what to accept from providers, I have emphasized the role of emotions and feelings in the generation of knowledge. Again, there is an interplay at three levels. What a person finally decides is affected by her or his feelings toward macro, intermediate, and micro factors. Sociopolitical events influence individual views and reactions. These are, in part, affected by the individual's own socioeconomic standing. Deep-seated feelings exist also about each of the competing medical systems. For instance, there are indications that while the educated believe in the supernatural dimensions of health and illness, the present generation of diviners, as bearers of such knowledge, are viewed with suspicion (Pearce 1987). Finally, emotions are instrumental in assessing what is happening to the body, what to accept from others as facts, and what line of action to take. Feelings remain fundamental in the restructuring of information, the development of new symbols, and the understanding of new and often disturbing social relations. The lay community, therefore, continually evaluates what the different types of providers do and say. One thing is certain: among the Yoruba it is believed that the emphasis of Western medical professionals on the physical aspects of life limits the scope of medical knowledge that can be developed. It is assumed that healing goes far beyond the development and application of scientific principles and high technology.

Acknowledgments

I wish to thank Dr. Simi Afonja for giving me unrestricted access to her report on the 1986 phase of the project in two rural communities. I would also like to thank Mr. A. Adetoro and Mr. A. Ojo for assisting with parts of the data collection in the ongoing studies.

References

Adedoja, Elizabeth
  1986   Therapy Managers Within the Family: A case Study of Ilesa, Oyo
            State. Bachelor's thesis, Department of Sociology and Anthropol-
            ogy, Obafemi Awolowo University, Ile-Ife.
Ademuwagun, Zacchaeus
  1978   Alafia: The Yoruba Concept of Health. *International Journal of
            Health Education* 21(2):89–91.
  1979   The Challenge of the Co-existence of Orthodox and Traditional
            Medicine in Nigeria. In *African Therapeutic Systems,* Zacchaeus
            Ademuwagun, John Ayoade, Ira Harrison, and Dennis Warren,
            eds., pp. 165–170. Waltham, Mass.: Crossroads Press.
Afonja, Simi
  1986   The Impact of Primary Health Care on Household Seeking Behav-
            ior in Two Rural Communities. Unpublished report submitted to
            the International Food and Nutrition Programme, United Nations
            University.
Akiwowo, Akinsola
  1986   Ibayeje and Itunayese: A Study in Dialectics. Paper presented at
            the Faculty of Social Sciences Forum, Obafemi Awolowo Univer-
            sity, Ile-Ife.
Anyanwu, K.
  1981   The African World-View and Theory of Knowledge. In *African
            Philosophy,* E. Ruch and K. Anyanwu, eds., pp. 77–99. Rome:
            Catholic Book Agency.
Awolalu, J. Omosade
  1972   The African Traditional View of Man. *Orita* 6(2):101–118.
Berger, Peter, and Thomas Luckmann
  1966   *The Social Construction of Reality.* New York: Doubleday and
            Company.
Buckley, Anthony
  1976   The Secret—An Idea in Yoruba Medicinal Thought. In *Social An-
            thropology and Medicine,* J. B. London, ed., pp. 396–421. London:
            Academic Press.
Feierman, Steven
  1985   Struggles for Control: The Social Roots of Health and Healing in
            Modern Africa. *The African Studies Review* 28(2/3):73–147.

Hackett, Rosalind
    1987   Current American Religions' Influences in Africa. Seminar talk given to the Ife Humanities Society, Obafemi Awolowo University, Ile-Ife.
Illich, Ivan
    1975   *Medical Nemesis*. London: Marion Boyar.
Janzen, John
    1978   *The Quest for Therapy in Lower Zaire*. Berkeley, Los Angeles, London: University of California Press.
    1981   The Need for a Taxonomy of Health in the Study of African Therapeutics. *Social Science and Medicine* 15B:3185–3194.
Lloyd, Peter
    1974   *Power and Independence: Urban Africans' Perception of Social Inequality*. London and Boston: Routledge and Kegan Paul.
Mechanic, David
    1968   *Medical Sociology*. New York: The Free Press.
Mulkay, Michael
    1979   *Science and the Sociology of Knowledge*. London: George Allen and Unwin.
Obasa, Roland
    1987   Poor Families Now Spend More on Healthcare—UNICEF Study. *Guardian* (16 October):3.
Ojo, Matthews
    1988   The Contextual Significance of the Charismatic Movements in Independent Nigeria. *Africa* 58(2):175–192.
Oladeji, Niyi
    1987   Language Signposts in Yoruba Pragmatic Ethics. Paper presented at Conference on Ethics in African Societies, Obafemi Awolowo University, Ilfe-Ife.
Olayiwola, David
    1986   The Aladura Movement in Ijesaland, 1930–1980. Ph.D. diss., Department of Religious Studies, University of Ife (Now Obafemi Awolowo University).
Opefeyitimi, Ayo
    1987   The Ethics of African Prayers. Paper presented at National Conference on Ethics and African Societies, Obafemi Awolowo University, Ile-Ife.
Payne, Mark
    1985   Itumo Ala: A Socio-cultural Approach to the Interpretation of Dreams Among the Yoruba. M.Sc. thesis, Department of Sociology and Anthropology, Obafemi Awolowo University, Ile-Ife.
Pearce, Tola
    1986   Professional Interests and the Creation of Medical Knowledge in Nigeria. In *The Professionalisation of African Medicine,* Murray Last and G. Chavunduka, eds., pp. 237–258. Manchester: Manchester University Press.

1987   The Assessment of Diviners and Their Knowledge among Civil Servants in South Western Nigeria. Paper presented at the 10th International Conference on Social Science and Medicine, Barcelona, Spain.

1992   Health Inequalities in Africa. In *The Political Economy of Health in Africa,* Toyin Falola and Dennis Ityavyar, eds., pp. 184–216. Athens, Ohio: Ohio University Center for International Studies.

Peel, John

1968   Aladura: *A Religious Movement Among the Yoruba.* London: Oxford University Press for the International African Institute.

Polanyi, Michael

1946   *Science, Faith and Society.* Chicago: University of Chicago Press.

Simpson, George

1980   *Yoruba Religion and Medicine in Ibadan.* Ibadan: Ibadan University Press.

Toulmin, Stephen

1976   On the Nature of the Physician's Understanding. *Journal of Medicine and Philosophy* 1(1):32–52.

8

Biomedical Psychiatry as an Object for a Critical Medical Anthropology

Horacio Fabrega, Jr.

Introduction

Distinctive ontological and epistemological problems characterize psychiatry compared to the rest of medicine (Fabrega 1974*a*, 1975, 1980). General medical theory argues for the reality and centrality of disease factors (that is, organic changes) and research involving psychiatry's traditional disease entities, such as schizophrenia and melancholia, attests to the importance of such factors. However, thus far it has not proven possible to specify precisely which disease mechanisms accurately account for specific illness configurations. In addition, there exist "disorders" (the official term used to signify medical entities in psychiatry) for which no disease candidates appear immediately forthcoming. This is illustrated in conditions of illness variously termed hysteria, neurosis, and/or adjustment disorders. As a biomedical discipline, then, psychiatry is somewhat compromised in not having its ontological roots well articulated and validated.

A further epistemological matter concerns the fact that the criteria for knowing and defining psychiatric illness are anchored in social behavior. To be sure, the language of psychopathology is highly secularized and appears to rest on a positivistic framework. A chronicle of its evolution reveals how analysts have been able to identify and refine basic categories of human cognition and emotion and stipulate their role as indicators of diagnosis (Berrios 1982, 1984, 1985). The fact that this is a Western cultural style of emotion and cognition needs to be emphasized (Fabrega 1989*a*, 1989*b*). Despite their abstract nature, however, indicators of illness cannot be said to refer to impersonal and technical attributes of a body, but to potentially highly personal components of the self since they implicate beliefs, intentions, and modes of thinking and feeling. Whereas disease accounting in general medicine and surgery is a commentary *about* the physical body and *indirectly about the self,* disease accounting in psychiatry is a direct commentary *on* the self and *of* the self (Fabrega 1989*a*, 1989*b*). Furthermore, to the extent that psychological experience and social behavior together compose the self, and putative psychiatric disease mechanisms directly alter such a composite in a compelling way, to diagnose psychiatric disease is of necessity to qualify the self medically. Psychiatric diagnosis, then, necessarily entails a medicalization of social and psychological behavior in a way medical and surgical illnesses do not. Furthermore, insofar as conventions of diagnosis rest on social and personal norms and diagnostic indicators on deviations from them, psychiatric diagnosis entails social and psychological (i.e., self) deviance marking. Lastly, since intrinsic to the idea of illness is its disvalue and the need to act to correct it, we can fully appreciate how psychiatric diagnosis and treatment is controlling if not actually coercive and potentially stigmatizing.

Social Conflicts in the Practice of Biomedical Psychiatry

In other publications I have emphasized that special social and cultural problems characterize the rationale and practice of contemporary biomedical psychiatry (Fabrega 1989*c*). Drawing on the work of critics of psychiatry, I have indicated that this has to do with psychiatry's involvement in matters that create controversy and polarize a community, matters that involve the nature and way of conceptualizing/dealing with the mentally ill, the criminally insane, and more generally, the socially maladjusted and deviant (Baruch and Treacher 1978; Donnelly 1983; Donzelot 1979; Foucault 1965; Grob 1983; Ingleby 1980, 1983; Kovel 1980; Rothman 1971; Scull 1979; Sedgwick 1982). These problems have a historical basis in the care of the mentally ill, specifically, and have a parallel in the deliberations of other social institutions aimed at caring for and controlling the maladjusted, the able-bodied poor, the criminally insane, and the deviant more generally. The totality of these issues has led critical observers to underscore the role of psychiatry in what Nicholas Kittrie has termed the "therapeutic state" (Kittrie 1971).

The social problems of psychiatry are outcomes of and reflected in its special focus on the self. The problems are energized by the mode of operation of modern, complex industrialized societies wherein bodies and minds are said to be subject to surveillance, regulation, and control, all under the guise of the pursuit of health (Foucault 1965, 1979; Scull 1979). A sharpening and intensification of these problems have been conditioned by the growth and evolution of modern medicine and biological science, which have refined the technical knowledge of disease. An outcome of this evolution for medicine generally has been a subtle and more powerful form of bodily control through the establishment of an ever more abstract technical language of disease that allows diagnosis and treatment to move away from the self and its social connections. Although psychiatry adheres to the tenets of this science, and the logic of its scientific efforts as well as the momentum of its advances seem to propel it toward the achievement of a similar goal, this has not been possible. Moreover, there are grounds for questioning whether an impersonal language of psychiatric disease could ever emerge, given the natural and logical link that exists between mental illness, the self, and its social products.

An irony in all of this, of course, is that the objects of modern medical surgical as well as psychiatric science—the illnesses of social actors and citizens—have in earlier epochs and other societies always been regarded as social entities and as commentaries on the self. Ethnomedicine informs us that the "natural" languages of illness offer rich portrayals of how selves can be altered and what implications such alterations have; and such portrayals partake of basic social and political concerns of a people and reflect and feed back on moral assessments of the self. In short, modern medicine attempts to render disease as the impersonal essence of an object that ethnomedicine shows is rooted in social, moral, and existential concerns. Moreover, just as the phenomena of illness in preindustrial societies partakes of the social, religious, and moral as well as medical (and is demarcated in terms of deviations in behavior that are disvalued), so also does the phenomena of psychiatric illness embrace matters of concern to other social institutions. Thus, the evolution of modern medicine and surgery have served to move them away from directly implicating the self socially and politically, and psychiatry seems to want to follow suit, but is not fully successful. Biomedical psychiatry thus affords a potentially rich topic for an ethnomedical inquiry.

Social Conflicts of Psychiatry as Mirrored in its Clinical/ Individualistic Versus Corporate/ Institutional Functions

The medical practitioner's role is deeply embedded in the history of humankind. Given the social, religious, and political roots of illness historically the practitioner became identified with the social, legal or quasi-legal, and psychological realities of the client. The healer's theory of illness and his or her expertise and knowledge unquestionably created a distance between participants in medical transactions, but that healing required a highly personalized involvement with the afflicted is hardly to be doubted.

Personalized involvements with patients are much less a feature of contemporary biomedicine. One important factor accounting for this is the increasing centrality given to highly abstract and impersonal biological/organic factors in the definition and explanation of illness, and the correlative emphasis on a technological and engineering approach to medical treatment. Although rhetoric is directed at the importance of trust and sharing in the doctor-patient relationship, the exigencies of focusing on disease and the classical liberalist ethos of the contemporary society and medicine render the achievement of this objective difficult, as the increasing dissatisfaction of consumers suggests. The basic ingredients of the ontology of biomedicine are outgrowths of the formation of the European states, the growth of industry and science, and the process of secularization more generally.

As indicated earlier, psychiatry is unique among medical disciplines because its object is still the whole person in all of his or her complexity. In this emphasis, and in its accompanying mode of operation, psychiatry is concerned with bettering the individual's plight and in helping that individual achieve a fuller and more satisfying life. Psychiatry also embodies what one may term a corporate and institutional function. As a medical discipline with its own professional association and as a component of society's medical institutions, it plays a role in medical policy matters. In the political economy and structure of modern society, moreover, corporate psychiatry becomes involved in the deliberations of other corporations and institutions having patent social control functions. Here, its knowledge and pursuits affect and reflect how that society operates. In carrying out its institutional/corporate functions and in medicalizing the behaviors of actors, it can overlook the individual's needs, exculpate or depoliticize their actions, and stigmatize them or otherwise label them in ways that undermine their social credibility as well as responsibilities as citizens. Conversely, persons labeled psychiatrically ill can appear to have their individual (and at times deviant) actions medicalized and thereby rescinded or seemingly excused, and in this sense it is the society and its remaining institutions that are burdened. In either instance, to the extent that an individual's needs are overlooked or full citizenship questioned and suspended, the individual's long-term credibility is injured regardless of any medical and/or social advantages that may accrue in the short run as a consequence of medicalization.

It follows from the above that the clinical/individualistic and corporate/institutional directives of psychiatry can be opposed and can become a potential source of conflict and controversy. To address a person in the individualistic mode is to seek that person's well-being as a social and psychological creature. Here, psychiatry is engaged in the time-honored and altruistic pursuit of the medical practitioner/shaman and, given the definition of psychiatric illness as in opposition to medical/surgical illness, it embraces the person in his or her full humanity. Conversely, to address people in the institutional mode is to potentially thwart, bring discredit, or weaken their full citizenship through psychiatric labeling and eventual exculpation and control if not coercion. The individualistic/institutional conflict of psychiatry is writ large on society, occasioning "societal distress" in the form of criticism and attack; the conflict can also impact on the individual, or patient, occasioning distress; lastly, the conflict can also be focused in the activities of the practicing psychiatrist, occasioning distress by promoting goals and pursuits that are opposed and in competition.

Individualistic/Institutional Conflicts and the Insanity Defense
General Introduction

Clinical evaluation invariably requires of the psychiatrist unique involvement in the life situation of the patient. While maintaining a degree of objectivity and neutrality, the need to understand, and the orientation to help, naturally generate empathy, a form of concern and caring. Thus, although a professional and hence contractual relationship entailing formal universalistic features is established, the psychiatrist-patient relationship is also a sharing human relationship, and emotional features linked to its humanistic side invariably come to color it.

Directives related to alliances and attachments forged in the intimacy and privacy of clinical encounters are blurred and made more complex when the psychiatrist conducts evaluations in the capacity of an expert witness. Indeed, the problems latent in the individualistic directive surface in a dramatic way when psychiatrists move out of the clinical arena and come to play a role in the institutional sector. As an expert witness, outside evaluator, and agent of the legal system, the psychiatrist is wanted for his or her "testimony." In this instance, emotional understandings and alliances forged in the intimate exchanges of the clinical setting are inconsistent with the requirements of objective reporting, and may in fact be problematic, given that the psychiatrist's insights reflected in a truthful testimony may be damaging to the patient as defendant or plaintiff.

Case Material

Dr. A was retained by the defense counsel and asked to serve as an expert witness in a criminal case involving the possible application of the insanity defense. A late-middle-aged man had shot and killed his wife. They had been married for over thirty-five years. Dr. A's directive was to enter into the mental world of the defendant in an attempt to understand what led to or motivated the shooting and to seek to determine what role, if any, mental illness or "insanity" might have played. It is clear that self-interest unconsciously, if not consciously, will come to play a role in how one individual will formulate and "present" to a psychiatrist-witness the events and experiences involving the commission of a sharply condemned social act. For this reason, as well as for the obvious need to obtain ample information, Dr. A indicated from the outset that he would need to interview the three adult children of the "defendant" as well as significant others who knew the defendant, his wife, and the kind of marriage that had prevailed.

The relevant facts of this case can be summarized briefly: The defendant and his wife had experienced significant conflicts recently and she had indicated her desire for a divorce, something that hurt, angered, and otherwise threatened the defendant. The defendant had felt alienated from his wife and children, who were allied together. Alcohol use and a deepening depression on the part of the defendant had prominently characterized events during the weeks and especially days before the shooting. The defendant, it was eventually agreed upon by both teams of defense and prosecuting psychiatrists, was psychiatrically ill prior to the shooting. Symptoms of depression and delusions as well as hallucinations involving themes of abandonment and sexual infidelity were reported. Dr. A judged that psychotic manifestations of a Major Depression had compromised the cognitive and emotional functioning of the defendant to the extent of rendering the shooting a product of the illness. One of the prosecuting psychiatrists' testimony was consistent with this formulation, whereas, the second defense psychiatrist stipulated that anger at rejection was the main reason for the shooting and that psychiatric illness had not played a determinative role, although the reality of psychiatric illness was not contravened.

The rendering of Dr. A's opinion and his readiness to provide court testimony at a future date marked the limits and boundaries of his formal involvement in the case. Defense counsel kept Dr. A apprised of relevant facts pertaining to the progress of the case. In addition, the defendant and his family on several occasions phoned Dr. A seeking advice and opinion related to psychiatric care and matters related to an interpretation of the shooting, despite being apprised of his functioning in an institutional/corporate capacity and not in a clinical/individualistic one.

Following Dr. A's initial formulation, he communicated his "expert" opinion to defense counsel. Dr. A also communicated his clinical concerns to counsel, family members, and significant others: he judged the defendant currently to be psychiatrically ill and to pose a very serious suicidal risk. Dr. A strongly advised against the seeking of bail in the weeks after the shooting. When this was nonetheless sought and obtained and upon learning of this, he insisted on the need for psychiatric treatment and careful follow-up in the community. Within a few days following the posting of bail the defendant made a suicide attempt and was hospitalized. Dr. A spoke with the hospital psychiatrist and communicated his findings. Following discharge the defendant while awaiting trial underwent outpatient treatment, but on occasion called Dr. A for advice and support.

The conflicts and antagonisms between the defendant and his children, which had antedated the shooting, persisted and intensified during the months following it. The pressing of charges by the children had property settlement implications, and this complicated matters. The evaluation of Dr. A was seen as an attempt to excuse the defendant and this contributed to family conflicts, although in the earlier evaluation interviews with family members Dr. A made an effort to acknowledge their feelings of loss and took a neutral position. The "family" that remained following the shooting was clearly in a state of disruption and crisis and could be said to be in need of "family intervention" therapy. However, even were this an appropriate need, there was no clinician available to carry it out. Dr. A resided at some distance from family members and the defendant. Furthermore, he was precluded from getting "clinically involved" because of his role as "expert" for defense counsel. The local psychiatrists involved in treating the defendant were not aware of the full clinical situation, since they had not seen the defendant when he was most medically compromised. Moreover, the defendant was not able to relate openly to them, judging them as distant. The local psychiatrists were residents of the community where the killing took place and were exposed to its publicity. This may have worked against the development of an optimal therapeutic approach to the patient and to family conflicts. In sum, the adversarial quality of the upcoming trial, exigencies of property/economic settlements, the degree of mutual distrust, anger, and alienation between family members and defendant, and a natural reliance on the upcoming trial for a definitive or "factual" explanation of the shooting rendered an optimal "clinical" resolution of family conflicts difficult, if not impossible.

After completing his report and communicating his clinical concerns to the family, local psychiatrist, and defense counsel, Dr. A became, in effect, a distant observer of the drama that resulted from the shooting. Following discussions between defendant and children through family members and attorneys, something resembling a family rapprochement appeared to have been achieved in an agreement to plead a lesser crime (than first degree homicide) that would require the serving of a short prison sentence. Following this agreement, the defendant appeared to feel tricked by his children into admitting guilt and serving a sentence. The defendant, now incarcerated, was found dead in his cell several days later. A post mortem examination disclosed that suicide (through over-dose) was the cause of death.

The underlying psychiatric disorder, repercussions of the shooting, and conflicts linked to interaction between the defendant and his children in and around the shooting, trial, and property settlements were important factors in the suicide. The clinical insights of the expert psychiatrist were never fully implemented. Thus, exigencies devolving from his institutional/corporate role militated against the realization of directives borne in the clinical/individualistic dialogue.

Case Analysis

The key parameters of the problem posed by the case involve (*a*) directives to heal which bear on the psychiatrist as a result of the highly personalized exchanges between a patient/defendant and a doctor: what can be termed the clinical/individualistic exigency; and (*b*) directives for a focused and detached involvement geared to producing an abstract, impersonal, and objective testimony for purposes of litigation: what can be termed the institutional/corporate exigency. Exigency (*a*) generates concern for the plight of a troubled individual and significant others, urges further involvement, and seeks to diminish the personal suffering of those affected through resolution of individual and family conflicts, whereas exigency (*b*) generates concern for cold facts, urges limited (controlled, bounded) engagement, and seeks to bring aid to legal agencies empowered to reach a prudent adjudication. A clear conflict exists. It is reasonable to argue that had it been possible to realize exigency (*a*), the defendant might be alive today, and in a state of improved relations with his children (insofar as Dr. A's knowledge of the dynamics of the case provided him with insights that if pursued therapeutically might have healed the family crisis). However, given the constraints stipulated by the requirements of exigency (*b*), this could not take place, and merely communicating the clinical facts to involved family and medical and legal personnel was not sufficient to prevent a persistence (if not escalation) of the dispute, which culminated in suicide. It is, of course, likely that the crisis occasioned by the shooting was an insurmountable barrier to any kind of family integration or resolution of family crisis.

In summary, I would like to draw attention to several factors that condition and shape the problem for psychiatrists in the legal arena, and which serve to highlight the cultural and comparative distinctiveness of psychiatric practice in a contemporary industrialized society.

1. A shooting or killing is first and foremost an affair of the state and from its standpoint appears to have either a legal or medical basis and a medical or sociopsychological cause.

2. There exists one official theory of mental illness/disease and psychiatrists are privy to it (though they may apply it differently in a given case).

3. The psychiatrist represents but one institution in a settlement of a dispute that in the society requires the participation of several autonomous institutions, each of which views the actor and his or her action from a different theoretical framework.

4. To arrive at a prudent assessment of criminal responsibility the psychiatrist should ideally obtain a rich variety and depth of anamnestic and clinical data.

5. Following from this, the psychiatrist is forced to look at the alleged criminal behavior or action simultaneously from the standpoint of the actor's personal and social situation (e.g., what was he or she responding to and intending?), from a scientific-academic-clinical framework (e.g., did psychiatric illness play a role in generating the action-behavior?), and to some extent from a motivational framework (if psychiatric illness played a role in generating the criminal action/behavior, did it motivate an action/behavior that was morally flawed or wrong?).

6. To understand the action/behavior appropriately as in (5) the psychiatrist comes to understand the social and familial conflicts underlying the action/behavior, is drawn into the life situation of the actor and significant others involved in the conflict and on whom the criminal behavior impacts, and is thus provided with an opportunity to heal/treat the problem at hand.

7. In providing "expert testimony," the psychiatrist attempts to achieve objectivity and neutrality, which draws him or her away from (6) and this, in turn, is counter or detrimental to a prudent resolution of the conflicts and problems that generated the criminal action or which are impacted by it; and finally,

8. The state as an agency of control and as a dominating partner of official psychiatry imposes limits and constraints on psychiatrists

and counsel, forcing them to define a complex and multifaceted problem in a unitary way.

Individualistic/Institutional Conflicts and Corporate Services

A conflict that shares the properties of those discussed above with reference to the insanity defense is often found in the setting of psychiatric corporate services. Members of the psychiatric profession not infrequently function as a group of evaluation and service "experts" and for corporations from the industrial world. For example, just as corporations wish to provide medical benefits to their employees (no doubt, ultimately, to maximize productivity), they often are in need of "expert services" with regard to the mental health and general problems of employees. A variety of problems plague industry, including those of substance use and abuse, marital and other familial problems, and other frank psychiatric illnesses, which in some instances are consciously denied by or unknown to the employees themselves. Such dialogues between the industrial client and the professional service provider frequently result in requests for psychiatric evaluations in which are sometimes concentrated a host of conflicts devolving from the individualistic/corporate functions. The actors requesting evaluation are often unwilling "clients" who fear its consequences, and (sometimes unwilling) clinical psychiatrists employed by a private agency or academic department who are forced to negotiate a potentially difficult clinical encounter. The following account illustrates some of the conflicts that impact on the psychiatrist and his client when both pursue clinical/individualistic rather than institutional/corporate functions and dialogues.

Case Material

Mr. A, a twenty-six-year-old, single executive trainee was referred for psychiatric evaluation by personnel assistance representatives of a corporation. He lived alone in a moderately large city. He was close to his parents, who lived several hundred miles distant. Mr. A had difficulties in performing at work. These difficulties, which were judged to have a psychologic basis, had occasioned frictions between Mr. A and his superiors, and the latter had communicated this to employee assistance personnel who initiated the request for expert evaluation. The corporation had an agreement with a nearby mental health center to refer clients there about whom employers and supervisors were concerned regarding possible difficulties in the realm of mental health. The personnel assistance representative had "urged" this evaluation on Mr. A, who presented for evaluation feeling somewhat coerced and victimized. He judged the evaluation to be part of an effort to remove him from work.

Mr. A was seen by a psychiatrist (Dr. B) and introduced himself by accusing the psychiatrist, indicating that he (the psychiatrist) was Mr. A's executioner. When asked to elaborate, Mr. A indicated that his superiors were against him and were unfairly seeking to remove him from his job; he judged that the task of the psychiatrist was to certify a psychiatric condition for purposes of termination of employment. The psychiatrist explained that he was in fact acting as an agent of the center, which in turn was performing a function for the corporation, but that he also had a clinical responsibility to help and advise Mr. A as a result of learning of his circumstances and needs. The psychiatrist explained that as a professional healer, he could use his medical knowledge to diagnose any medical condition that might be present, provide treatment if necessary, and suggest courses of action that would provide Mr. A with more informed alternatives regarding his relationship with his supervisors at the corporation and in his future life more generally.

After several meetings, during which a history and mental status information were obtained from Mr. A (no information or communication transpired between psychiatrist and corporate personnel), it became clear to the examining psychiatrist that Mr. A was compromised from a neuropsychiatric standpoint. A recent head injury had produced cognitive symptoms involving some impairment of memory, concentration, motivation, and general morale. These neuropsychiatric deficits had compromised Mr. A's work performance and his superiors had become concerned. All of this had deeply depressed Mr. A. To the psychiatrist, Mr. A appeared to cope with these problems partly by minimizing—if not denying—any personal cognitive deficits, partly by projecting blame onto his supervisors, partly by using the ideology of victimization, and partly by developing feelings of indignation and despondency. Mr. A clearly met criteria for Adjustment Disorder with mixed emotional features and received a tentative diagnosis of Organic Brain Syndrome.

Discussions between Mr. A and superiors regarding substandard performance and the need for help had not been harmonious and Mr. A had felt victimized and persecuted. After several meetings, the psychiatrist recommended getting formal neurological and neuropsychological testing to clarify whether any impairments in functioning might be present, something which Mr. A agreed to with difficulty. Throughout the four or five meetings with Mr. A, the psychiatrist upheld a confidential relationship with him. The psychiatrist learned of Mr. A's ambitions and goals during college, of his unfortunate recent (six to nine months previously) car accident, and of recent disappointments as a result of his compromised work performance.

Although the psychiatrist attempted to build a therapeutic alliance with Mr. A, this was not entirely successful. Mr. A was critical, rejecting, guarded, and frankly evasive. Although acknowledging the psychiatrist's interest and concern for him, he also felt distrustful and of course feared the results of a neuropsychiatric evaluation and its consequences. Mr. A presented himself to Dr. B in emotional control, showed no overt despair, depression, or hopelessness, and reported no suicidal ideation when directly probed. There was no history of mood disorder or suicidal behavior in the family. Mr. A was unwilling to seek a medical disability and through his denial of disability sought a medical vindication. The circumstances of Mr. A's difficulties, as perceived by Dr. B, were such that they compelled a careful neuropsychiatric work-up as well as much support, tact, and understanding regarding Mr. A's plight.

Unbeknown to Dr. B, Mr. A was in fact very much in despair and preoccupied with the question of his future. He felt quite hopeless and had entertained thoughts of suicide. Mr. A had recently purchased a gun. A neighbor of Mr. A at times functioned as a friend and confidant and the question of suicide had been discussed with him. Denials as well as threats of suicide and "gallows humor" about his circumstances had punctuated conversation between them. Mr. A's neighbor was very concerned about this and had been in communication with Mr. A's family. In addition, once, following a missed appointment, Mr. A's family had called Dr. B regarding A's whereabouts, and during the conversation indicated they and Mr. A were worried about Dr. B's evaluation and feared work dismissal. Mr. A had also seen a private therapist and the latter was aware of some of Mr. A's personal anguish and despair, and had been in communication with Mr. A's family. It is important to emphasize that none of these parties made an effort to communicate to Dr. B the depth of Mr. A's despair, his lack of self-control, and his threats of and preoccupations with suicide. All of them judged such a communication to Dr. B as inappropriate and harmful since it would "establish" Mr. A's distraught state of mind, which in turn would contribute to a negative psychiatric evaluation and his dismissal.

Two perspectives on Mr. A's condition thus existed: Dr. B saw an angry, distrustful, and deeply worried young man in need of neuropsychiatric evaluation who appeared to accept his course of action. On the other hand, Mr. A's confidants saw a despairing, hopeless, and tormented person who had alluded to suicide. As a result they were deeply worried about Mr. A, but the circumstances surrounding the evaluation worked against a clear course of action (e.g., informing Dr. B, seeking involuntary hospitalization).

On the day he was to be evaluated neuropsychologically, Mr. A shot and killed himself in his apartment.

Case Analysis

In this instance, both the psychiatrist and the patient were victims of the individualistic/corporate conflict outlined earlier. The psychiatrist attempted to fulfill his "healing" role of helping Mr. A. He was able to discern some of Mr. A's neuropsychiatric deficits but was not privy to its devastating symbolic consequences for him currently (e.g., with respect to job, and in the long term regarding his future employability). In pursuing the individualistic mode, the psychiatrist attempted to communicate his clinical concern about Mr. A's work-related difficulties, and sought to obtain a medical evaluation, which was needed for prudent diagnosis and treatment. Dr. B attempted to provide support, counseling, and advice to Mr. A. The psychiatrist, however, was also entrapped in the institutional/corporate mode insofar as he was employed by a service facility that had a consultative arrangement with the firm that employed Mr. A, and representatives of the latter were rightly dissatisfied with Mr. A's performance, given his neuropsychiatric deficits. Because of his institutional/corporate identity, Dr. B was perceived ambivalently by Mr. A. The latter had developed some trust and positive expectations from Dr. B's stated clinical objectives, but also feared the impact of his findings. This conflict militated against Mr. A's full disclosure of his despair and also against disclosures from Mr. A's family, friends and therapists. They all probably reasoned that full disclosure might involve a full appreciation of Mr. A's deficits, his despair, and his suicidal thoughts, which would mean, in addition to possible involuntary hospitalization, a clinical evaluation that would be disadvantageous to Mr. A's job security.

In sum, the dilemma embodied in the individualistic/clinical versus the institutional/corporate functions of the psychiatrist proved deleterious to the optimal realization of Dr. B's resources and tragic for Mr. A, his family, friends, and therapist. As in the previous example, an omnipresent actor in this case was the modern industrialized "therapeutic" state. Its agencies in the form of corporations had the power to inflict damage through an intimidation and control of the behaviors of participants in ways that proved detrimental. Many of the generalizations drawn above regarding the insanity defense apply here as well.

Comment

Interesting ironies involving corporations, the state, the individual, and deviance are contained in these two cases. The social opprobrium attached to homicide and the idea of an insanity defense in contemporary society no doubt contributed to the unfolding of the first case. Complex psychological factors linked to this opprobrium contributed to the anguish experienced by its fateful victim and influenced the process and course of his ordeal. In effect, his plea, had he been able to articulate it, was a request for medicalization as a trade off for his existence. To him, it was a punishing state that failed to provide therapy. On the other hand, the ease with which the agencies of control entered and segregated the personal space of the second victim influenced the process and course of his ordeal. His plea, by way of contrast, was to avoid medicalization, but at the price of his life. For him, ironically, it was the therapeutic state that proved punishing.

These case studies illustrate a dilemma inherent in the practice of contemporary psychiatry. The dilemma is conditioned by the contradictory sets of roles, obligations, expectations, and directives it instills in its practitioners, consumers, or clients as well as those allied people who conduct business with it. This dilemma, may be held to act as a factor that produces many casualties or victims. Those individuals who were caught in the dilemma and who resolved the anguish it produced by terminating their lives are obvious victims. Their relatives, friends, and agents are also casualties and victims. Finally, the other central protagonists, the psychiatrists, must also be regarded as casualties or victims; their genuine efforts to help and heal not only proved ineffective but contributed to an aggravation of the crises that produced the tragic outcome (e.g., by alienating the family in the first instance, by augmenting pressures in the second). In effect, the resources available to the psychiatrists as healers could not be used since full access to clients and basic information were blocked; potentially helpful actions were constrained by directives inherent in their corporate/institutional roles.

A dominating factor in the outcome of the two cases is the strength and impersonality (or in Michel Foucault's sense, brutality) of the power inherent in modern "disciplinary" institutions and their bureaucracies, as well as in agencies of the contemporary state (Foucault 1965, 1979). Inseparable from this is the legal coercion, which can be backed by physical coercion. Both cases result from the attempts of psychiatrists to pursue overlapping tasks, and they raise questions about policy that are difficult to resolve. Moreover, both cases lend themselves to a critical, perhaps Marxian, analysis insofar as acquisitive capitalistic motives were operative in the deliberations of the parties that opposed the fateful victims and in the ultimate justification of the psychiatrists actions: all parties could be said to have been "class" actors. However, these factors will not be pursued further.

I want instead to draw attention to the special aspects of psychiatric practice as played out in contemporary society. The cases illustrate the force and power inherent in social institutions, with their capacities to annihilate individuals possessed of full civil liberties, ample economic means, and tangible social resources (not simply dependent or marginal ones) under the guise of medical care. This form of "medical" care is a relatively new phenomenon. What needs emphasis is how the ideology and rationale of surveillance and disciplinary control, which operates through state-influenced institutions and corporations (including corporate biomedical psychiatry), comes to bear on personal crises involving psychiatric illness, how it influences the work of the psychiatrist, and the way in which such crises are played out socially. All of this gives a distinctive cast to medical practice viewed in a comparative ethnomedical framework.

In preindustrial societies, conflicts produced by medical, personal, and social conditions, analogous to those plaguing our fateful victims, often lead an individual to act in ways that are maladaptive and consequential to his or her family and allies. The discords and quarrels that result set in motion mediational and adjudicatory efforts by kin, elders, experts, shamans, or physicians, depending on the nature of the society (Fabrega 1974*a*). The resulting process has spiritual, legal, political, and medical overtones. Such social dramas are often open, face to face, complex, and involve as participants representatives of aggrieved and opposed parties. In other words, all parties in a dispute or crisis are linked socially in intricate and overlapping ways. Many different "realities" of events no doubt exist, some of which may never be directly revealed to selected participants but are nonetheless known, especially to the mediators. In principle, an open exchange and full disclosure is possible and is usually realized. However, there is no theory or ideology that stipulates that phenomena of the type described above are either medical, and hence allegedly morally neutral, or sociopsychological, and hence morally binding. Moreover, nothing parallels the impersonal and bureaucratic power or sanctions at the command of the corporations and institutions of social control, be they of the state or powerful vested interests within it. In effect, in such preindustrial societies an institutionalized and binding "medical" view of illness-related phenomena does not exist; nor is there the power to coerce and impose a single overriding view that thwarts the efforts of those caught in the social crises and who were sought out for help.

Social Conflicts of Psychiatry in Historical Perspective

The predicament of contemporary biomedical psychiatry is conditioned by overlap in the medical and social functions of psychiatrists who in diagnosing illness, medicalize the self and its products (deviance), thereby attempting (but failing) to neutralize its social and political aspects. The overlap in institutional functions is of course all the more striking when compared to societies in which the idea of a medical (or legal) system can be applied only with difficulty, as in the preindustrial societies studied by anthropologists and in earlier epochs of European history. In this light a review of writings of social historians of medicine will prove illuminating.

Keith Thomas (1971) has described the variety of medical and quasi-medical practitioners that prevailed in early premodern England, many of whom fulfilled medical and nonmedical functions. In addition to diagnosing and treating illness, they offered advice regarding the weather, love and marriage, the whereabouts of lost or stolen property, the suitability of economic ventures, and the identity of witches who perpetrated medical or social evils. Many of them also invoked religious sanctions and some were identified as theological persons of social standing. The theory of illness prevalent at the time accommodated natural and preternatural agencies of causation, illness being ethnophysiologically explained in terms of magic, sorcery, humoral notions, and theological premises. Michael MacDonald (1981) has also made clear that an illness entity, whether viewed now as psychological or medical in nature, very often partook of religious and physiological parameters, and was often seen as linked to important social-familial happenings.

The account by D. P. Walker (1981) of demonic possession and witchcraft in the late sixteenth and early seventeenth centuries of England and Europe also illustrates the overlap of clinical medical functions of physicians with social and religious ones. The overlap was made possible by contemporary theories of illness that applied to deviant behaviors that were similar to psychiatric illness. As Daniel Walker documents, even at this rather late date, when a medical practitioner was beginning to be seen as a "professional" with well-defined roles and duties, physicians were frequently called upon to consult in cases of witchcraft and demonic possession. In the former instance it was often to establish whether an individual displayed physical evidence that reflected status as a witch, although on occasion physicians were asked to comment on the "sanity" of the person (e.g., were delusions present?), which then rendered the witches' "confessions" problematic. In the case of demonic possession, physicians' consultations were sought in an attempt by civil and religious authorities to reach a "differential diagnosis" between illness-related or demonic actions. In all of these instances, then, we have evidence of how easily medical practitioners' actions and opinions entered into the deliberations of representatives of diverse institutions of the society. The scenarios depicted by these materials show the competing interests of the clinical/individual and the corporate/institutional in the practice of psychiatry.

One major theme in the development of the individual/institutional conflict that is a feature of the history of biomedical psychiatry, then, is the increasingly public role that the medical profession came to play in the society of early modern England. The themes of demonology and witchcraft were a dominant social, political, and religious concern and "proto-psychiatrists" played prominent roles in helping to resolve them. The developing corporate identity of the profession of medicine had in fact been a feature of English medical practice since late medieval times, and even in this early period the profession was involved in social policy matters as well as in settling issues related to malpractice (Gottfried 1986; Park 1985). In brief, dilemmas of psychiatric practice that today can be ascribed to the individual/institutional conflict have their roots in the corporate framework of medical practice evident from very early times, a framework the influence of which is not altogether absent even in non-Western peasant societies (Fabrega and Silver 1973).

Another theme in the development of the individual/institutional conflict that is evident in contemporary biomedical psychiatry involves matters linked to the insanity defense. The social and legal problems that the mentally ill offender poses to the biomedical psychiatrist well antedate the establishment of psychiatry as a branch of medicine, or even the distinction between organic/somatic versus mental/emotional illnesses. The matter is well documented by theoreticians who trace the evolution of legal thinking in the history of common law (Foucault 1978; Kaye 1967; Platt and Diamond 1965; Smith 1981; Walker, 1967; Walker and McCabe 1973). Walker (1967) emphasizes that in order for a rule of precedent regarding the adjudication of an offense to be represented in a legal code, the need for it must be perceived and the problem for which the rule constitutes a solution must be prominent in order for it to give rise to concern, discussion, and formulation. Although "the mentally disturbed offender raises questions which have troubled theologians, moral philosophers and lawyers throughout the Christian era" (Walker 1967:6), criminal law was slow to develop in England following the first record of insane offenders.

Two related factors explain the reluctance to accept psychiatric illness as a mitigating factor in the adjudication of crime: on the one hand, the opprobrium, horror, and odiousness attached to serious crime and, on the other, the basic difficulty of demarcating illness/insanity from criminal intent and guilt. Homicide, like other crimes, constitutes a social act whose rationale is explicable in terms of motives and intentions that have a readily apparent meaning to social actors. Thus, the act has an obvious symbolic (i.e., psychological and cultural) and situational (i.e., linked to current social contexts) basis. To stipulate that illness is a mitigating factor in homicide requires a view of the person as capable of actions that are not willful or motivated in terms of ordinary and rational human concerns, and a complementary view of illness as possessing a reality or ontology that also places it beyond personal willfulness and responsibility. In essence, mental illness as a defense of homicide requires something of a suspension of our attribution of personhood, if the latter is equated with (willful) symbolic behavior.

Legal historians are of the opinion that even in pre-Norman England psychiatric illness was a consideration in the way serious offenses were dealt with through existing legal institutions. It is more certain that since the establishment of jury trials (sometime during the thirteenth century) the presence of insanity in an offender was explicitly taken into account, and mercy shown the defendant first in the form of an appeal to the King and later as an integral part of the unfolding and resolution of the trial by jury. The matter of the criteria that counsel and jurists struggled with and slowly evolved in attempting to deal prudently with the question of criminal insanity in England, and indeed the controversies and intricacies involved in such criteria, are not important for our purposes. Suffice it to say that it entailed a broadening of the understanding of insanity and psychosis generally. More importantly, it was not until 1731 that psychiatric-related testimony was used in a criminal trial and 1798 that an accused was able to call a medical witness during the trial itself. It was in the nineteenth century that direct attention was first given to the content and nature of an insane person's delusions and the extent to which they may have motivated, justified, or exculpated serious offenses like homicide.

What requires emphasis is the natural conservatism of the legal institution and its consequent reluctance to accept that psychiatric illness could weaken, if not rescind, the matter of moral and legal culpability for a crime such as homicide which is instinctively viewed as abhorrent and revolting. That legal institutions, as formal embodiments of a societies' values and norms, especially moral ones, should demonstrate conservatism in the matter of criminal insanity should not be surprising. One has only to take notice of the controversy surrounding the insanity defense in the United States, in a society whose system of medicine embodies refined knowledge about the organic substrate and psychodynamic/symbolic ramifications of psychiatric illness. In that controversy and in the reactions to acquitted persons we see the deeply embedded "natural" inclination to punish and condemn an offender, and the reluctance to contemplate mitigating circumstances that might produce tolerance if not exculpation. In this controversy, we witness the medicalization of deviance—the way badness can be transformed into sickness.

The perpetrator of homicide who seeks understanding and mitigation for his deviance confronts a "punishing state." The nineteenth-century penal reforms, involving a change from torture and the spectacle of the scaffold to "generalized" and what Foucault ironically terms "gentle" forms of punishment, are a testimony to the strong aversion to homicide. Both the brutal atrocities to the offender's body and the controlled, sanitized, abstract, and impersonal but personally annihilating handling of it by the machinery of the modern penitentiary, indicate the degree of social aggression embodied in the political economy of punishment. Such forms of retribution reflect the personal abhorrence that individuals have of homicide.

It is in the light of these underlying factors that one should understand the slow acceptance of psychiatric knowledge about mental illness on the part of legal institutions and the concomitant need to treat such knowledge as abstract, technical, and objective, an approach that is disconnected from considerations of the health/well-being of the defendant which would raise the question of possible condonation. Concern for treatment and care of the defendant can of course be secondary consequences of a decision that insanity was a mitigating factor, but such individualistic concerns cannot be allowed to intrude into the impersonal, institutional handling of the affair. In the courtroom, where the functioning of a society's constitutions are on display, order, control and the "bureaucratic manner" hold sway, and it is in terms of these requirements and institutional standards that scientific knowledge pertaining to insanity intrudes, but not in a form borne from the individualistic mode.

What is being claimed here is that powerful emotions and highly moralistic concerns lie concealed beneath the surface of the institutional mode of explaining and justifying a criminal act as stemming from insanity. The professional's ("expert witness") testimony and role are geared to this impersonal objective style of deliberation. The style eschews and minimizes and guards against identifying with concerns related to the health and well-being of the defendant, who after all has committed a homicide. The features of the courtroom drama, the slow and halting manner in which it has evolved, and the history of earlier atrocities and brutalities perpetuated in the pursuit of punishment, all attest to the powerful controls and constraints that impact on the expert witness.

Acceptance of the insanity defense has thus been slow to evolve and it is arguable whether acceptance actually exists in contemporary society. An insanity defense in the case of homicide is in effect the end point in a continuum of social circumstances that the state, its representatives, and citizenry might consider in granting exculpation. In short, it is perhaps the hardest form of deviance for the agencies of social control to neutralize through medicalization. However, as sociologists and other critics of psychiatry have documented, such agencies have been less reluctant to medicalize other forms of deviance and human failings. (Perhaps this is the case precisely because they have acceded or accommodated to the demands posed by homicide [Conrad and Schneider 1980; Ingleby 1980, 1983].) Indeed, a contemporary crisis is felt by many to exist by virtue of the existence of directives that increasingly allow the individual not to honor his responsibility by paying for his misdeeds. Kittrie (1971), for example, documents the inroads that the therapeutic state and its agencies of control have made in the domain of human social accountability, a situation that Peter Conrad and Joseph Schneider have termed a movement from badness to sickness.

Recent Criticisms of Psychiatry as Expressions of its Social Conflicts

A body of literature has evolved within recent decades which sharply criticizes the role of medicine, especially psychiatry, in contemporary society. A fundamental tenet in the "critical psychiatry" literature involves the inappropriateness of using the positivistic paradigm of the natural sciences (i.e., its concern with causality and the behavior of physical objects) to explain phenomena of a social and political nature, wherein the notions of meaning, symbols, and interpretation properly apply. In using the positivistic approach, deviant behavior—and by extension, mental illness—is said to be "neutralized" through medicalization, its social and political significance thereby nullified. In performing this role, psychiatry is said to quiet and conceal the social protest of the deviant and the indicator that points to socially noxious contexts that generate the (deviant) behavior or "illness" in question. By reducing human problems of the social, economic, and political structure of the society to symptoms of illness to be treated with drugs and other physical measures, the potential of reaching a more humane amelioration of the "social pathology" that gave rise to the deviant behavior is said to be aborted. In these and related ways, psychiatry is said to regulate and control deviance in the service of the establishment: namely, the state and its representatives.

This critique of psychiatry is paralleled by a critique of its rise as a profession in the nineteenth century. In this instance, attention is given to the social and economic changes that led to the creation of asylums. The allegedly self-serving motivations of asylum superintendents are said to have played a role in this movement. Despite a lack of expertise and success in dealing with insanity, they nonetheless managed to appropriate the basic tenets of the moral treatment reformers. Joining these tenets with prevailing organicist ones, they evoked and stabilized the medical model of insanity, thereby placing themselves in central positions in the management of lunacy and reform in asylums. Later they extended their directives outside the asylum into the society at large, ultimately locating their tenets in many other social and welfare institutions concerned with surveillance and control, culminating in the creation of the modern therapeutic state. In this scenario, terms such as psychiatric imperialism and professional entrepreneurship are used to characterize the alleged self-serving interests of psychiatry (Strong 1979; Zola 1972, 1975).

An ethnomedical perspective of psychiatric theory and practice somewhat qualifies this critical side of its theories and practices. A review of ethnomedical knowledge shows that illness, the basic datum of medical concern, not only involves social behavior but also deviance: the illness consists of (is logically entailed by) deviations in personal and group norms. Moreover, a proper understanding of how the illness is perceived and resolved necessarily involves an understanding of native cultural beliefs, values, and actions that have a social and political character. Through a form of medicalization (i.e., the prevalence of human suffering, the seeking of relief, and the attempt to undo the social disorder that produced the illness), preindustrial societies deal with structural problems that have social and political overtones. Moreover, in these societies, medical practitioners clearly carry out adjudicatory and mediatory functions in their communities. In some societies (e.g., the Ashanti) one finds explicit rules that provide for an exculpation of individual action through an appeal to notions of illness (i.e., criminal actions judged an outcome of insanity or medical illness) (Hoebel 1954). It would thus appear that the so-called social control actions of physicians, and especially psychiatrists, are found in a number of different types of societies, not only in early modern Europe, and that members of all types of societies show a natural inclination to medicalize deviant behavior.

References

Baruch, Geoff, and Andrew Teacher
1978   *Psychiatry Observed.* London: Routledge and Kegan Paul.
Berrios, German E.
1982   Disorientation States and Psychiatry. *Comprehensive Psychiatry* 23:479–491.
1984   Descriptive Psychopathology: Conceptual and Historical Aspects. *Psychological Medicine* 14:303–313.
1985   The Psychopathology of Affectivity: Conceptual and Historical Aspects. *Psychological Medicine* 15:745–758.
Conrad, Peter, and Joseph W. Schneider
1980   *Deviance and Medicalization.* St. Louis, Missouri: Mosby.
Donnelly, Michael
1983   *Managing the Mind: A Study of Medical Psychology in Early Nineteenth-Century Britain.* New York: Tavistock Publications.

Donzelot, Jacques
1979   *The Policing of Families.* New York: Pantheon.
Fabrega, Horacio
1974   *Disease and Social Behavior: An Interdisciplinary Perspective.* Cambridge, Mass.: M.I.T. Press.
1975   The Position of Psychiatry in the Understanding of Human Disease. *Archives of General Psychiatry* 32:1500–1512.
1980   The Position of Psychiatric Illness in Biomedical Theory: A Cultural Analysis. *Journal of Medicine and Philosophy* 5(2):145–168.
1989*a*   The Self and Schizophrenia. *Schizophrenia Bulletin* 15(2):277–290.
1989*b*   The Significance of an Anthropological Approach to Schizophrenia. *Psychiatry* 52(1):45–65.
1989*c*   An Ethnomedical Perspective of Anglo-American Psychiatry. *American Journal of Psychiatry* 146:588–596.
Fabrega, Horacio, and Daniel B. Silver
1973   *Illness and Shamanistic Curing in Zinacantan.* Stanford, California: Stanford University Press.
Foucault, Michel
1965   *Madness and Civilization.* New York: Pantheon.
1978   About the Concept of the "Dangerous Individual" in the 19th Century Legal Psychiatry. *International Journal of Law and Psychiatry* 1:1–18.
1979   *Discipline and Punishment: The Birth of the Prison.* Alan Sheridan, trans. New York: Random House.
Gottfried, Robert Steven
1986   *Doctors and Medicine in Medieval England.* Princeton, New Jersey: Princeton University Press.
Grob, Gerald N.
1983   *Mental Illness and American Society to 1875.* Princeton, New Jersey: Princeton University Press.
Hoebel, Edward Adamson
1954   *The Law of Primitive Man; A Study in Comparative Legal Dynamics.* Cambridge: Harvard University Press.
Ingleby, David
1980   Understanding Mental Illness. In *Critical Psychiatry: The Politics of Mental Health,* David Ingleby, ed., pp. 23–71. New York: Pantheon.
1983   Mental Health and Social Order. In *Social Control and the State,* S. Cohen and A. Scull, eds. New York: St. Martin's Press, Inc.
Kaye, Joseph M.
1967   The Early History of Murder and Manslaughter. *The Law Quarterly Review* 83:365–395 and 569–601.
Kittrie, Nicholas N.
1971   *The Right to be Different.* Baltimore: Johns Hopkins Press.
Kovel, Joel
1980   The American Mental Health Industry. In *Critical Psychiatry: The Politics of Mental Health,* David Ingleby, ed., pp. 72–101. New York: Pantheon.

MacDonald, Michael
1981   *Mystical Bedlam: Madness, Anxiety and Healing in Seventeenth Century England.* Cambridge: Cambridge University Press.
Park, Katharine
1985   *Doctors and Medicine in Early Renaissance Florence.* Princeton, New Jersey: Princeton University Press.
Platt, Anthony M., and Bernard L. Diamond
1965   The Origins and Development of the Wild Beast Concept of Mental Illness and Its Relation to the Theories of Criminal Responsibility. *Journal of the History of Behavioral Sciences* 1:355–367.
Rothman, David J.
1971   *The Discovery of the Asylum.* Boston: Little Brown.
1986   Early Manifestations and First Contact Incidence of Schizophrenia in Different Cultures. *Psychological Medicine* 16:909–928.
Scull, Andrew T.
1979   *Museums of Madness.* New York: Allen Lane and St. Martin's Press.
Sedgwick, Peter
1982   *Psycho Politics.* London: Pluto Press.
Smith, Roger
1981   *Trial by Medicine.* Edinburgh: Edinburgh University Press.
Strong, Patrick Martin
1979   Sociological Imperialism and the Profession of Medicine. *Social Science and Medicine* 13A:119–215.
Thomas, Keith V.
1971   *Religion and the Decline of Magic.* New York: Penguin University Books.
Walker, Daniel Pickering
1981   *Unclean Spirits: Possession and Exorcism in France and England in the Late Sixteenth and Early Seventeenth Centuries.* Philadelphia, Pennsylvania: University of Pennsylvania Press.
Walker, Nigel
1967   *Crime and Insanity in England. Volume One: The Historical Perspective.* Edinburgh: University Press.
Walker, Nigel, and Sarah McCabe
1973   *Crime and Insanity in England. Volume Two: New Solutions and New Problems.* Edinburgh: University Press.
Zola, Irving Kenneth
1972   Medicine as an Institution of Social Control. *Social Revolution* 20:487–504.
1975   In the Name of Health and Illness: On Some Sociopolitical Consequences of Medical Influence. *Social Science and Medicine* 13A:83–87.

9

Double Standards
of Treatment Evaluation

Gibert Lewis

*Corals are of two sorts: one, a clear bright shining
red; the other, a purple dark red. The bright is
good to quicken phansie, and is against phanta-
sies, or nocturnal spirits, which fly from these
bright corals, as a dog from a staff, but they gather
where the dark coral is. A spectre or ghost is the
starry body of a dead man: now these ethereal or
starry bodies cannot endure to be where the bright
corals are, but the dark-coloured allures them; the
operation therefore is natural, not magical, or superstitious, as some may think. Bright coral re-
strains tempests of thunder and lightning, and de-
fends us from the cruelty of savage monsters, that
are bred by the heavens contrary to the course of
nature; for sometimes the stars pour out a seed, of
which a monster is begotten; now these monsters
cannot be where corals are.*

The voice might be Prospero's. But Paracelsus wrote it. I found it
quoted in an anonymously written book, *Sketches of Imposture, Deception, and Credulity* (1837:347). Amulets were worn not only to cure but
also to prevent diseases. Medical practice has long been a place for the

play and struggle between reason and imagination, experience, magic and trickery.

Issues of Judgment

Western medicine (biomedicine), when it is being scientific, looks for facts and evidence. Anthropologists now like to take a sophisticated and self-critical (sometimes self-obsessed) line on whether they can achieve objectivity in observation or in their writings. The arguments reflect those over objectivity in science in general, and in the social sciences in particular. The questions lead far back in philosophy. But in medical anthropology the practical issue is quite often, I think, a question of observations being adequate and pertinent more than fine points about objectivity. For instance, if anthropologists attribute the efficacy of alternative treatments to physiological or psychological effects, or to the pharmacological effects of herbs, medical people are bound to want some relevant evidence.

This may raise the question of double standards in our judgments of different forms of medical treatment, especially those of other societies. We note cultural differences; we meet the relativity of points of view. Why should we apply our critical standards to their treatments? We expect certain standards of safety and effectiveness in treatment we might receive ourselves—should we ask for the same to be applied to the practice of alternative medicine? Or do we have double standards— one lot for them, another for ourselves? Perhaps the answers seem obvious.

Closed or Open

Who should judge? The criteria a medical person uses to judge the efficacy of treatment may involve matters of pathology or biochemistry that other people do not ordinarily know about. The Western medical system is specialized and seems rather closed. Parts of medicine may be open to the anthropologist, but to do what there? No doubt some medical scientists read anthropologists and wonder whether they recognize the limits of their naivety. Is work in this field so different from work in economic anthropology or in the anthropology of religion or law? When Max Gluckman focused on the issue of "closed systems and open minds" (1964), the writing of anthropologists using ideas from economics, psychology, and psychoanalysis came in for scrutiny. Is the difference, then, one of kind or just degree; that some subjects are more specialized, more complicated, take longer to learn; or is it something to do with making mistakes when people might decide about what to do on the basis of your advice? (If your opinion makes no difference, who, except you and your colleagues, will care?)

Our Standards—Their Standards

One level of the question involves comparing the views of the anthropologists and the doctors. Another level has "us" as Westerners (with a system of medicine we like to call scientific or biomedical) and "them" as foreigners (with exotic medical ideas and practices). Their criteria of illness and ways of judging success in treatment may differ from ours. Are we to say they are wrong?

The biomedical analysis of illness is undeniably selective and partial. It has chosen criteria of relevance. It is after facts, regularities of nature; these regularities would be ones that hold for human beings in general, in a loose sense, for all, or universally. That would be the reason for using it as a standard or reference. But biomedicine, like biological sciences, changes, finds errors and new things, corrects previous ideas. The intrinsic complexity of the problems makes progress hard. People are vulnerable to error about illness. Biomedicine may be scientific ideally; that does not mean to say that it is complete and perfect now.

It is clear that people may have quite different ideas about illness. *The relativity of opinions* is a matter of observation. Our criteria may not be suitable for assessing their views about treatment, its progress, or the processes of illness. The strong or normative relativist (e.g., Winch 1970) might argue that it is inappropriate to subject alternative views (alternative social and linguistic constructions) of reality to scientific criteria because those criteria only make sense to someone who is already conversant with that kind of scientific activity and accepts its methods. There are philosophers' arguments to say that truth is different on the other side of the Pyrenees; and there are Thomas Kuhn's observations on paradigms that change (1962). Anyone who is sensitive to cultural relativity must surely see that we should use standards appropriate to the context, and not assume that only our own are true. Double standards? More than just double? Is that the answer a skeptical relativist should make?

The history of medical treatment is loaded with examples of faith and credulity,[1] some of which pose problems for these theories. Does the treatment work? Many still ask that question. A long line of famous believers and famous skeptics have offered answers—some by calling on authority, others on faith, or experience, or reason, or logic, or psychology, or physiology. I would soon tie myself in knots if I tried to argue about the logic and philosophy of issues of truth, science, and belief. The issues may be detectable in questions of treatment, but treatment seems a more practical matter. "Pure" issues of theory get messed up by ordinary life, and the abstract and intellectual is brought low by material things and by trivial daily considerations—as you will hear in my examples, for some tediously I fear. I know high theory is finer and more exciting, but the point about pertinence lies partly with the trivia and the unabstract, undignified mess.

Credulity and Explanation

We may be cautious and critical about others but not enough about ourselves. When distress or need makes us hope for something, the wish to believe or a suggestion may have some effect (perhaps good or bad), or it may just be self-deception. Double standards go unrecognized in our own actions. For instance, the large doses of vitamin C taken to ward off the flu, or countless hours wasted organizing ulcer diets, or tons of anticoagulants eaten and millions of hours of technicians' time spent measuring the clotting times produced by anticoagulant therapy after myocardial infarct—examples of abandoned therapies in which we have believed—join the history of bleeding and purging, and the debates between the Rationalists and the Empiricists. It is easy to forget them. Western medicine also has contained a variety of effort, error, and folly. With anticoagulants, reason and theory triumphed over evidence for some years; hope too must have played a part, as perhaps did vanity or unwillingness to admit error. Think of the reverses of dogma and advice about breastfeeding or the treatment of diarrhea.[2]

It is hard to strike a *fair balance between trust and distrust;* we have to take many things on trust because it is impossible, in practice, to question everything and put it to the test. Much of what we learn comes on the strength of authority from those we see, or once saw, as our elders and betters. The transmission of culture—of custom—encourages us to accept what we are taught at home. Most believe in their own medicine and distrust foreign versions. But some, quite the opposite, believe there is greater power in what is strange. It is difficult to come to a clear opinion about the value of medical treatment.

Explanations of Effect

And it is easy to sound smug when criticizing others. Suppose as anthropologists we attribute efficacy to some treatment we see in another society. On what grounds do we do so? One answer (certainly an important one) is "Well, the people say it made them better." But is there a link between what they did and their feeling better? Some might say, doubtfully, "Perhaps it was the herbs," or else we might refer to suggestion, or placebo effect, or psychosomatic efficacy, or symbolic efficacy. We use the words and invoke the ideas, but it is rare that we can show any evidence, or say exactly what it was that changed for the better, or when. Did the disease just end in its usual way, and get better by itself? Half the time, or more, we do not know precisely what was wrong with them, in biomedical terms, in the first place; or even if anything *was* wrong. The explanations are suggestions, or a nod in the direction of parallels that seem to offer a possible "scientific" explanation. We may leave an impression that we think much in their illness is imaginary or emotional. Are the people so suggestible? W. B. Cannon's essay on "voodoo" death (1942) gave some authority for that view. Anthropologists were quite ready to accept it, but there has been some discussion since (Eastwell 1982, Lewis 1977, Lex 1974, Read and Williams 1984), and it is quite speculative.

We are too ready to credit the mysterious powers of psychological and psychosomatic forces when the cases come from distant places and are about Aborigines or Africans. The readiness goes with a certain romanticism about exotic people and a set of attitudes or beliefs attributing emotional lability or oddness to other people, especially those called primitive, simple, or oriental. The following is an illustration of the problem:

> Attitudes and behaviours of the nurses at the Yuendumu hospital [on a government settlement for Aborigines in Central Australia] between 1969 and 1971 varied greatly. Some were very willing to co-operate with a medicine man and to enlist his aid, particularly if a patient requested that he be consulted. For example, there was some doubt about whether a very sick man in his thirties (Jungala . . .) was suffering from a blow on the head or from a psychosomatic disorder produced by the knowledge that he had been "boned" and "sung" following his wife's recent death. A medicine man was asked to come to the hospital to treat Jungala. . . . On 1.6.70 Jungala, Nungarai's husband, died in Alice Springs Hospital from a cerebral abscess after a sickness of a week's duration, during most of which time he was on the settlement. . . . It was rumoured that he had been "boned" and "sung." Everyone on the settlement, including the nursing staff, felt that his illness might have been the result of this rather than the after-effect of a blow on the head received during a drunken brawl in Alice Springs. (Middleton and Francis 1976:135, 41)

The Indian Rope Trick Problems

One difficulty is the anecdotal evidence of cases (as with the Indian Rope Trick); another is how to provide appropriate or adequate evidence in such circumstances. Investigators for the Society for Psychical

Research faced similar difficulties. How do you test for ghosts? In the case of the Indian Rope Trick, it is worth making sure the trick has really been done before spending time trying to explain how it was done. But often people are only too quick to explain how it might work; they find doubts boring, and resent skeptical requests for more detailed descriptions of exactly what happened, how often, and who witnessed what. That sort of response is quite common, and it is similar whether we are dealing with shamanic healing, paranormal or psychic phenomena, or new cures for cancer. As in the case of scientists who fudge facts, or in deliberate fraud, it is often not the deceivers who deserve study so much as the deceived, their victims (Ziman 1983). Reviewing investigations of Uri Geller's abilities, Stuart Sutherland (1981) comments that the physicists who studied them were rather simple-minded about people, the psychologists were more skeptical, but the professional magicians, disliking the dishonest use of their own tricks, were downright scathing. The report of an amazing new drug for cancer (for instance, a report that something called Norgamem would shrink tumors of the head and neck, which got into the *Lancet*) hits the headlines; hopes surge, although the experimental details are not quite clear, and those who then seek to check sound like doubters who wish to snuff out the hope—perhaps mean, jealous doctors. The short-lived claim is never really followed up in the press; the negative report will never have the public impact of the first press announcement (Brugarolas and Gosalvez 1980, Wingerson 1980).

It is rare to find examples of anthropologists who record the frequency of therapeutic failures, do follow ups, or find out how many people do not bother to come back next time to the shaman. A particular strength of Arthur Kleinman's analysis of the healing process (1980:311–374) is that he sought out and provides that sort of information on those attending a Taiwanese *tang-ki*. It is more like the investigation that would be made of a new treatment or a new drug in a Western medical setting. It is difficult enough to assess the efficacy of treatment in a highly controlled hospital setting, but the difficulties outside an institution are far greater.

If an anthropologist wants to explain how a treatment works or how magic works by attributing physiological or psychological effects to it, he or she invites the interest of doctors and their requests for evidence for thinking so. Why should the anthropologist expect them to change their critical standards and criteria? If they have to, the changes will probably make the anthropologist's answers seem weak or second rate, and diminish credence. An anthropologist's simple assertion, however confident, that a treatment works psychologically, psychosomatically, or by suggestion, or through symbolic efficacy, rings hollow. They look for findings to support it because the anthropologist has staked a claim in a field where people look for facts and want to use objective criteria. If those are the explanations we wish to put forward, we must provide the facts ourselves (which may require learning new methods and new skills), or else employ those who can to carry out the appropriate investigations.

Rare cases and rare medical events are difficult to investigate. In Western medicine the collection of patients in large hospitals, and the dissemination and exchange of published information (Shryock 1948; Ziman 1976) helped reduce some of the problems of rarity. But with some of the most striking of the cases anthropologists report (for example, suspected "voodoo" death, or dramatic rituals for healing) it is unreasonable to expect full investigations at such times in such places. The attempt itself would alter the circumstances. The investigative techniques and equipment would probably disturb people and disrupt the event. In this domain, as in every other, some of the problems cannot be answered unless appropriate methods for tackling them are devised. That is different from saying that such phenomena are intrinsically unsuitable or inimical to scientific investigation, which sounds more like the evasive defence of the spirit medium who says the spirit will not manifest itself in the presence of a sceptic.

More Subtle and Observable Forms

I was impressed, when thinking about the topic of "voodoo" death, by some remarks of David Mechanic (1966:14–15) on "more observable forms" of the link between reaction pattern and physiological response. He pointed out that physicians have commented on the importance of the patient's "will to live," although it has been difficult to quantify this phenomenon or to present clear evidence in support of its importance. If we are to integrate anecdotes about death following sorcery and proferred explanations of the physiological mechanisms that might be involved with orthodox medical conceptual schemes, "we require a better understanding of such phenomena as they occur in more subtle but more observable forms." One way is with experimental models, and he referred to some of these. But experimental settings are contrived, and the artificiality may reduce their value for understanding human behavior in real life. So he also described a study of hope and despair in the parents of children with leukemia (Friedman et al. 1963a, b).

The urinary output of certain corticosteroids provides a measure of the physiological effects of distress; the parents' output of these steroids was measured throughout the illness of the child. According to steroid output, in most parents the highest point of "distress" occurred well before the death of the child, the most common situation being when the child was put on the critical list for the first time. "Other parents, however, who maintained hope despite evidence to the contrary, and who showed little marked acceleration in 17-hydroxycorticosteroid levels at crucial points during the illness, seemed to experience a marked acceleration after the child died. The study illustrates both the tremendous variability in response to difficult circumstances, and the probable link between coping reactions and physiological responses under stress." In effect, this was a study "in a more subtle and observable form" of the physiological effects of hope and despair during serious illness.

The chemistry of laboratory tests, the numbers needed for statistical significance, the equipment, the invasive and/or specialized procedures for investigating pathology—these are not our province. Is there something that we can contribute as anthropologists? There is, I think, often something. Think of Sutherland's observation about the physicists who were naive about people but jumped in to try to explain Geller's powers, the skeptical psychologists, and the scathing magicians. We have to find the aspects of the problem we can tackle, and how best to approach them given our means and limitations. What is the purpose of our observations, or are we wasting someone's time?

The Investigation of Other Reactions

So far I have assumed a position in which either (1) they (the other/exotic people) believe in some treatment and the observer is skeptical, or (2) the anthropologist believes something about an exotic treatment and the medical scientists are skeptical of what he or she says. I will now reverse the position by asking you to consider a situation in which both the anthropologists and the medical scientists believe in a treatment but they (the other/exotic people) are skeptical. Fair's fair. We don't believe them; all right, they don't believe us. In other words, it is a problem of compliance: why don't they follow this good advice and treatment being offered?

I shall describe an example of the difficulty of establishing what the people in a situation are doing. They say different things about themselves and about each other. The difficulty of establishing the facts is part of the truth about the situation. As in the film *Rashomon,* we want to get the story clear; we want to know the facts before deciding what the problem is and what we must explain. And when we know these facts about how the people concerned mistake each other's wishes and actions, we find that part of the larger question of compliance has been answered. The local people have, of course, reasons for their actions concerning treatment for a serious disease. Some of these can be explored also in common ailments. The serious one, first, is leprosy, and the common one is skin complaints such as sores and fungal diseases.

The skin complaints are meant to provide simpler, more observable forms of the same problems. We find the people involved are evaluating the treatment, finding out who has effective power to decide or to control them, judging their style, manners, and authority, and also judging each other and themselves.

Leprosy

Leprosy is spreading rather fast in the West Sepik Province (Papua New Guinea) where I did fieldwork. Villagers do not seem to have had it before pacification and external contact. In the village in which I lived (with a population between 370 and 420) there was one leper in 1968, about thirty-three diagnosed by 1975, and about fifty-five said to have been infected by 1985. Patrols were sent to identify new cases and educate people about the disease and its dangers. The local health center, which started as a mission hospital staffed with a doctor and nurses, built a ward/house set aside for the segregated treatment of lepers (as government health policy then required). The health center is now run by mission nurses but without a doctor, and has a leprosy mission nurse in charge of the services for leprosy and tuberculosis. The segregation policy has ended. I have briefly sketched elsewhere (Lewis 1987) how the segregation policy for treating lepers blighted the life of P., the first man in this village with lepromatous leprosy (which is the most contagious form). He was sent to prison, then sent far away for treatment because he persisted in absconding from the hospital. He was newly married in 1968, and over the following years, his wife has had no children. She has been shot by him with an arrow and stabbed by him for adultery during his absences, and these affairs have led to family misery, fights, fines, or prison for other people, too.

Compliance: What Is the Truth?
According to Whom?
Rashomon Perspectives

The Nurse   Let me jump to 1985. The leprosy mission sister said that P. was not taking his medicine. He should be on three drugs because of the high risk of bacterial resistance, given his long history of intermittent treatment. He didn't come to see her for his checkups. When he did come, she said, he was perfectly friendly; they got on well, and joked together. But he was unreliable and she didn't believe he took his drugs. He hadn't come for months.

The nurse is Canadian—from Toronto. She has been four years at the health center in charge of leprosy work. She is trained for it, and does biopsy, staining, and searching for the bacilli herself. She is, as a leprosy mission nurse, part of a Christian mission—an unmarried woman with a quick, barbed wit, and strict. At our first meeting she is helpful with information about the village in which I have worked. They are, she tells me, a bad lot: ungrateful, unreliable, negligent. They are always going off to hunt in the bush and abandoning the village for weeks, even months. They cause a lot of trouble and get into fights. There is all the past mess about the aid post with the chasing out of one of the aid post orderlies, and also fighting with the next village over the materials and the use of the aid post. They haven't done anything to improve their foul water supplies; their latrines are disgusting; they don't bother to come to the mother and child health clinics when the nurses make the effort to go to the village. She doubts whether anyone is taking the leprosy treatment as they should; at least, they are certainly not coming for follow-up appointments, nor have they come to get further supplies of Dapsone (the drug used) at the right times. P. (with his lepromatous leprosy) is a real hazard to others in the village. What can she do? He won't listen. They won't listen. She defers to my status as doctor and shows me interesting cases for an opinion, but she can see that I don't know much about leprosy compared to her. The APOs are meant to supervise treatment in the village, but, she says, they don't do it properly. She finds they aren't cooperative; they get *belhot* (angry) if she criticizes them, they don't accept her as their boss because she is a woman. Could I make it clear to the people in the village that they must take their treatment? I think she expects me to give them a stern talking-to, and to show some effective authority.

The APO (Aid Post Orderly)   I couldn't really do that, but I did talk to people. The APO in this village is someone of considerable reputation in the subdistrict; he was once health education orderly for the area. When he had that job, he did a lot of patrolling, explaining about leprosy and finding cases.[3] The aid post work he has now is not arduous the way he does it. He has known P. (the lepromatous man) for years, since P.'s childhood, and he first spotted and diagnosed his leprosy. Years ago, he had to report him to the *kiap* (government patrol officer) when he absconded and would not take treatment. I found that out by looking at P.'s hospital record card. Speaking about P., the APO says he has talked and talked to him in the past. He can't get him to take the treatment now. Telling him about spread to others has no effect. P. has been taking the drugs for so many years and can't see the point of going on with them. He no longer cares about getting sores and injuries. It's true that people with leprosy should come to him as APO to get their fresh supplies of Dapsone, but not many do. He's fed up with telling people to do so. He lists the people who have come regularly, and those who have completed their course of treatment. Most others have taken only part of the course; they have pills mouldering in their houses. He leaves it up to them now. The sister (leprosy mission sister) gives them appointments every three or four months, but they don't come. They are *bikhet* (uncooperative, obstinate, they do as they like). I asked what happened if they didn't attend. Nothing, it's not like before, they can't call the *kiap* and get him to send a policeman to fetch them. He (the APO) used to go round, when he was doing the health education and leprosy work, to find people who were defaulting on treatment, or absconding. But the leprosy control people can't do it all the time. Now really the only thing the sister can do is to ask the village councillor (*kaunsil*) or his chief assistant (*komiti*) to try and persuade someone to come. That doesn't work.

A Young Man in the Village   I followed up his point about those who had completed treatment later, especially when a number of the people I questioned said they had been told to stop because they had finished; that did not fit with the impression I got from the sister. Meanwhile other people commented on P. and his treatment (only because I asked). Surai,[4] a cheerful young man, a *mauswara* (= "mouthwater"— glib talker), agrees P. is fed up with taking his pills. So, he asks grinning away, why doesn't he die and clear out of this village? Or why don't we get up a fight with the next village, and get them to kill P. in it? Perhaps he said that to tease me for my tedious speeches about taking pills properly. Three weeks later, when he had a passing fever, I saw him and went back to the subject. He said most people took the medicine for leprosy for a while, then threw it away, but told the sister they were taking it; or else didn't go back. The older people felt they needn't bother because they would die anyway and clear off that way. I asked who really felt like that and he cited P.'s aged mother, who had in fact had leprosy too, and had died for other reasons. But, I said, that cannot be true of Delen (someone else, younger, with lepromatous leprosy). He spoke now more seriously, and said that people like Delen think they have eaten some medicine, they can't feel anything wrong, it must be enough, so they stop; or they look at their skin, think the lesions are not significant, why bother about them? Infected sores are worse.

Patients   How do you find out the truth? Delen is a calm, easy-going, dependable man in his mid-forties. I know him quite well. I broached the topic of his treatment. He said he takes his pills as he was told to; he puts his hand into his *bilum* (stringbag) and brings out the tin of Dapsone to show me. I had been there for five weeks; I just happened to ask him that morning. He says that he takes the pills and that he has more in his house. His manner is unbothered. I can't see why I should disbelieve him; I have no grounds to say he's lying. It would simply be offensive. There are laboratory urine tests for telling whether someone is taking Dapsone (impersonal objectivity there), but no real question or possibility then of me using them. I could ask his family. His son didn't care, and didn't know. One of his daughters said he didn't take them; his wife said he did. Whom should I believe?

I didn't see P. for nearly two months after my return in 1985. He lives in the hamlet most distant from the main village, and he has shifted his house to one that lies further on the outskirts. For most of this time, he has been quite far away from the village at a bush site, Saikel, the original ancient site of his clan.[5] Most of the whole village was away hunting to prepare for some celebrations during this period. I also went off to stay with hunting parties in the distant bush and was out of the village for two weeks, so I didn't see him until a day on which most of the village gathered for a boy's puberty rites. P. and his brothers arrived late, by which time there was a crowd already gathered in the *warkao* (dayhouse, place for gathering). P. came in very discreetly and sat at the back of the *warkao* on a *garamut* (slit gong). He didn't say anything, though he looked at me and observed that I noted him. He didn't smile or indicate a greeting. I was in the middle of talking to someone. P. didn't contribute to the chat going on around him, but sat at the back, listening and looking. For this reason I had the impression of some tension about his venture into public, and also some anxiety about my response. I imagine that he must view whites, and me, as a threat or risk.

I did not speak to him for half an hour—partly because I was involved in another conversation, partly because of the crowd and animation, and partly through a wish to see whether he would make a move. He saw me stare at him from time to time. He couldn't have supposed I didn't recognize him. Then, after half an hour, I got up and pushed through the crowd to speak to him—a very public move, given the crowd. I sat down beside him on the garamut. He smiled. I asked how he was. He said he was well, and that he had been staying at Saikel. "Can you do everything you want to?" "Yes, I can hold a bow and arrow, I can shoot." "Can you do gardening?" "Yes." "How about your hands and feet?" (He was wearing plastic sandals to protect his damaged feet). He showed me his hands and feet, and said they are all right. I asked how he could go up and down steep slopes with those sandals (I couldn't). He said he takes them off on steep slopes. Abruptly, unfairly, I asked about his medicine. He said he is taking it; he has four bottles for four months' supply. He takes the pills every evening before sleep. He gets them, he said, from the sister. He and she get on well. Yes, they joke together.

Since my visit in 1975, he had stayed in the village, he said, and he did not want to have to leave it again. We talked a bit about the past when I had been there; he cheered up especially recalling the dispute about Saikel, and how old W. nearly got speared. I told him he ought to make sure he saw the sister regularly about his treatment so that she was clear that he was taking it.

He has depigmented scars on one elbow, from burns, I think. His hands are obviously affected, with right little and ring fingers deformed and clawed—contractures. His appearance shows his disease more obviously than before—thickening of his eyebrow ridges, no eyebrows, fleshy ear lobes. His eyes look all right. His toes are damaged, with the loss of part of one. I didn't try to examine him—this was what I could observe as we talked. His manner is quiet, smiling, outwardly submissive.

The Villagers' View

One more vignette before I come to some analysis. I am sitting by a garden in the bush called Namelim with Tilpetau, a man in his early thirties. His wife had died some weeks before in the hospital at Vanimo on the coast; she had been sent there from the local health center. Her death is a calamity for him, and their two children. Tilpetau is looking through his *bilum;* he takes something out and wordlessly holds it up for me, as if challenging me to guess, just as he did before with his wife's family planning card. This one is also a crumpled card. It states that he is on Dapsone 100 mg a day, and it has a note to say "for sandals and gris [ointment]." What is the card for, I ask? It is because of the holes in his feet, he says, and shows me. It is hard to see them on the soles of his feet: about four tiny punched-out holes, around 3 mm in diameter. They hurt on strong pressure. Yes, he knows it is a *sik lepro* card, they gave him medicine to eat every day because a lot of people in the village have *sik lepro,* but he doesn't have it. The medicine he has is "for something else" (*beiya menamdem*), it is for his feet. He ate it for a while, he still has a lot left, but he hasn't been eating it since he went to Vanimo with his wife. He had only started it at the time his wife was ill at the health center. What he was taking, he said, is not the same as the "big medicine" they take for *sik lepro* because that kind they eat on Mondays and Thursdays. Yes, he knows they say he has leprosy, but he does not believe them; what he has is not serious. The only serious cases in the village now are P. and Delen. He points out to me that he doesn't have any skin marks, not the kind that involve loss of feeling; and he hasn't swollen up anywhere. He just has these holes on his feet. He wants to get the plastic sandals. So do a number of men in the village, but I shall come back to that in a moment.

He likes to be enigmatic, to come up on one silently from behind. I had noticed that before, but even so I was struck by the way he didn't reveal at first how much he knew about leprosy: the other (two-day) treatment schedule he had observed at the health center (multiple drug treatment to stave off resistance to Dapsone), or his conclusions about types and severity of the disease. He, and many other people, make a clear distinction between the kind of illness P. and Delen have and the other kind of *sik lepro* that most of those affected have—this is the tuberculoid type that shows as painless marks on the skin. As an eighteen-year-old boy said to me, people don't think leprosy is serious. It is not a bad disease in the sense that you could die from it. Leprosy is *wuyinda* (good, mild in quality), the signs are just marks, they don't harm or incapacitate you. People do not believe what the health education people tell them. If they apply what those people tell them or show them in pictures of the disease, to themselves, there is no match. It is not anything like as bad as they make out. The skin lesions they see in the village look much like other skin troubles with which they have been long familiar—*gapati watelila* and *gadu'et wanu'en,* which are benign fungal infections. They are used to putting up with the unpleasant fungal disease called *grili* in Tokpisin. Leprosy doesn't even itch or hurt or smell or scale off. Scabies, infected sores, abscesses, and wounds are worse. The swelling kind of leprosy, the kind P. amd Delen have, is different. People might die from it.

The "swelling kind" of leprosy is lepromatous leprosy, but the people in the villages have expanded the category with some quite different serious illnesses, ones accompanied by painless swelling of limbs, face or body, which they suppose are cases of *sik lepro* (I have discussed this shift and expansion of the category or diagnosis elsewhere, in Lewis 1987).[6] We regard leprosy as a serious disease and we expect them to, but they don't. Health authorities are understandably worried by the indifference. The people have plenty of other skin conditions that to them are more obvious, more painful, or more unpleasant. We set leprosy apart, and discuss leprosy treatment in isolation as a special problem, but leprosy does not look to them worse than other skin conditions. Comparison with these other skin conditions may help to clarify some of the reactions of the people in the villages. The explanation is not the uncooperativeness and apathy that it seems to be to the leprosy mission sister.

Misconceptions on Both Sides

But before I discuss the treatment of skin conditions in general, I must draw attention to misconceptions specifically about leprosy. One side I have mentioned: that is, the villagers' disbelief that the people diagnosed with leprosy really have a serious disease. The other side is the sister, the nurses more generally, and people like me. We are inclined too quickly to think the villagers are not taking treatment—that the main fault lies with them. When I followed up the answers from villagers who said they had been told to stop their treatment, I found they were right. The cards kept by the sister showed that in 1978 and 1983 many of them had been told to discontinue treatment. There were only a few records of any follow-up noted, which made it impossible to judge from these cards what appointments, if any, had been missed. The cards also recorded the results of biopsies. Some people on the leprosy list had negative biopsy reports, although they had been put on treatment.[7] Clinical suspicion of the disease had been enough, even though the skin signs and palpable nerves are signs which may be mistaken. There was less defaulting on treatment going on than she supposed. There were some people on the cards for leprosy with no conclusive evidence of the disease.

I had even more doubts about the plantar ulcers. In leprosy, loss of feeling in the feet from the effects of the disease on nerves can lead to bad ulcers and damage of the feet. This can be crippling, so people are prescribed plastic sandals to prevent further destructive complications. P. already showed some of these destructive changes, but there were a number of other men recorded as having plantar ulcers on the cards. The ulcers were the only signs apart from a possibly thickened ulnar nerve given to support the diagnosis in one or two cases. But I knew the men. Like Tilpetau's "holes" in his feet (he used the Gnau word *burap*), they were nothing like plantar ulcers from leprosy. The tiny punched-out holes were edged by horny skin. They hurt when the man stepped on a hard root or a stone. The "holes" were plantar warts in my opinion, not plantar ulcers from leprosy. The sandals were certainly a great attraction, and the men concerned were keen to get them. The sister has issued them only to P. and one other man (miles away from the village in the hunting bush I came across his one sandal print on a dry river bed; it was like a version of Man Friday's print there); she wasn't going to issue more to anyone until the person proved by regular attendance that he was taking his treatment properly. I explained my doubts to her, and I think she began to share them.

The diagnostic questions are obviously technical medical matters, but the point of bringing them up is show that the health authorities have misconceptions about the extent of defection and apathy in treatment, and that when villagers express some doubts about the seriousness of what they have got, even when they express doubts about whether they have real leprosy, I think they are sometimes right. Misconceptions? Double standards? It is very easy to suppose the cards must tell the truth, and that the authorities must know. It is also very easy to criticize, as I do, from the sidelines. I would say that notes and follow-up are thin. Why don't they do more patrols in the villages, find out what is really happening, set clear treatment goals, and do something if they don't achieve them? But I'm concerned with only one village; they have scores of villages to deal with. Have I tried to go round and check up on thirty villages in my life? What am I asking them to do each month, year in, year out? Double standards again—me in theory and me in practice.

Their Reasons:
For and Against Treatment

Active vs. Passive in Treatment

Leprosy stands out as the example of a disease in which diagnosis and treatment has been imposed or brought to them. The wish to treat came from the providers (the health service people), not the recipients who were passive or simply tolerant. They were unaware of the diagnosis, are unconvinced of its seriousness. If the recipients really believed in its dangers and in the benefits of treatment, they would act differently. They did so over *grili.*

Fungal Diseases

Fungal diseases are common. The most disfiguring of them, *grili,* tinea imbricata or scaly ringworm, may be a life-long affliction. They have had to put up with it because, although they tried various leaves, barks, and plant juices, none really worked. The scales are disfiguring and itchy, and some people complain of the smell. They observe that body contact is the mode of spread. At one time, years ago, I got some griseofulvin tablets to treat a few people for it. The tablets were too expensive for the Public Health Services to offer; instead they provided a green staining preparation of Whitfield's ointment, which burns quite painfully when first put on and requires regular application over weeks for effective results. Many people quickly turned up when they saw the striking effects of griseofulvin. I didn't have enough, and I explained the cost. They even offered to help pay for it, although they had hardly any money. I was a fool to have started. The treatment costs too much, and the infection is quite likely to recur when treatment stops. But the burst of active interest showed their eagerness for treatment when they see something works. The tablets changed gray, scaly patches into brown, shining skin within a few weeks. The tablets for leprosy, on the other hand, made no apparent difference to the pale, painless, seemingly harmless macules on their skin. And they were supposed to go on taking them for months—and years, it turned out. What was the point? There was no visible goal or achievement to show that the treatment was a success.

Time Delay and Perception of Effect

With leprosy, compliance was a matter of persuasion or, sometimes in the past, something close to enforcement when there were sanctions and the police might be called out. But those sanctions have gone. Any long-term treatment puts its own merits in doubt because of the wait and the lack of obvious results. The time allowed from cause (the treatment) to effect (improvement) is short, and the longer it takes the less likely the people are to recognize an effect. They have not understood the slow working of some forms of treatment—they want the quick relief of aspirin, bandages, liniment, and cough medicine. The need for repeated treatment reduces belief in its value. There is scant chance that someone in the village will have a full course of treatment if it involves many repetitions of the same thing (whether injections, dressings or pills), especially if it is left to the sick person to make the moves.

Availability, Effort, and Dependency

I often saw people with neglected scabies and sores, although they had an aid post in the village. The topic sounds trivial, but explanation for the neglect may throw a little light on their attitudes to treatment more generally. Practical considerations and matters of belief are both relevant. Most people say that the bandages and the injections of penicillin make infected sores and cuts better. Flies settle on open sores; dressings keep them off. They must have supplies of dressings, or access to them, which is not always simple. If they have no dressings, then people may cover sores with a rag. But traditional leaf bandages and bark dressings are scarcely ever to be seen now. The new dressings have displaced the old, but the people can not make the new kind, and they do not control their supply, either. They are less self-sufficient than before. Availability, distance, cost, and distribution may be overriding determinants of whether someone receives the treatment he or she might like to have.

Arguments from Past Experience

A common reason given for neglect is that the sores will shortly get better. So, until then, they will put up with them. This is an argument from past experience, to set against the annoyance from flies, and the effort of going to the aid post. Some point out that if they do go, they may find the aid post shut. It is not worth the chance of a wasted journey for only a small sore. They are used to having to put up with sores; the aid post has been there for a few years but it has only been sporadically open. What they are prepared to tolerate now reflects past experience, which was worse. Moreover, people now do not have big, chronic tropical ulcers as they did in the past.

Learned Tolerance

When they do get a sore dressed, they rarely keep the dressing on for more than a day or two. It soon gets dirty. Many people pull it off next day because they say it is uncomfortable or itchy—as infected sores are—or they don't like the smell. Some say it will get worse if they leave the covering on because that has been their experience before. If people take dressings off quickly and do not come back for repeated dressings, the treatment will not make much difference. At the hunting camps where people had been for two weeks or more, there were a lot of flies, and some festering cuts or sores to treat. It was one of the rare circumstances in which I saw traditional methods for sores being used in 1985. A man had made a mixture of yellow sap, crushed vine creeper, and lime to put on the children's sores. Some were foul; I dressed them, but the dressings didn't last twenty-four hours. Children play without worrying about the flies—they limp because an infected sore hurts, but they go on playing. They are used to putting up with the flies, the scabs, and the pain; they have different expectations, a different level of tolerance. They don't have much choice.

Idiosyncratic Belief and Innovation

One youth said his grandfather said if flies got at the sores ("ate them"), they would dry up quicker. He insisted that he wasn't teasing me, and that Walbasu, his grandfather, preferred to leave a cut or sore to heal by itself. The only exception would be a clean cut; then he would use penicillin powder (*marasin beiya su'esem*—medicine for injections) sprinkled directly on the cut. I know Walbasu well—a formidable old man, fit and tough. He is the man who made the sap mixture. I remember dressing an infected bite he got from a young crocodile he thought he had killed. It was a big bite on his calf. He kept my dressing on for three days, but didn't ask for any after that. I put one more on; it lasted two days. But the wound cleared up well. In 1985 he cut himself badly with a bushknife on the foot; he quickly got that cut dressed. He is old-fashioned, and will leave little sores or cuts alone, or sprinkle lime on them. But I asked him about flies and he doesn't think flies help sores dry up. He, like others, says flies make sores go bad and stink, and they put maggots in them. They have always known that. They did not need white people to tell them that.[8]

I would like to pursue three things here: (1) the difficulty of establishing what people really believe (Was it a statement or a question about his grandfather's belief? What did he really believe?); (2) their ideas on infection and germs (What do they think germs are?); and (3) the use of penicillin powder (an innovation). Let me take the penicillin powder first.

Adaptive Innovation: Penicillin

Everyone now knows that the white powder for injection (procaine penicillin), which is meant to be dissolved for injections at the aid post, can be sprinkled directly onto an infected cut or sore to clear it up quickly. Adults and children pick up half used vials when the APO is not looking. They keep them "bilong was tasol"—"just in case" they need it. A number of younger men have small supplies of purloined lint dressings, or plaster and penicillin powder in case they or someone in their family might need it when they are in the bush or when the aid post is closed. The APO knows they shouldn't put the penicillin powder directly on sores. He knows about resistance and hypersensitivity. He says he has told them repeatedly not to take the used vials, but they do because they know how effectively the powder makes sores dry up. He describes someone he once saw have an acute hypersensitivity reaction after an injection. He says all this with his brother-in-law's twelve-year-old son sitting on a bench beside us in the aid post, wearing nothing, clutching two half-used penicillin vials in his hand. He had just stolen them for his father. The APO takes them from him when I draw attention to them a second time. This use of penicillin is an innovative misuse of the powder; they observe that it works well. Someone somewhere must have experimented first. Probably they learned it from neighbors, or when away at work on the coast. It also seems suitable because it is like their old use of silt, or termite dust, to dry up cuts quickly, and like the similar sprinkling of lime or *kaona* lime on cuts.

Belief in Germs

With something common like sores, they know what to expect; they can see the benefit. Their own observations support their belief in the value of penicillin. When we justify the need for treatment of leprosy, we do it by referring to the dangers of future damage to the infected person, and of spread to others. It is notoriously difficult to convince people that you have stopped something worse from happening in the future. Leprosy was new to the villagers and they had no experience of its development. They were told they might spread the disease to their children and family. It spread by "germs." Germs are not visible; we talk about them and expect them to believe in them. An idea of germs (*jiem* in Tokpisin) has taken strong root in relation to some illnesses, although not *sik lepro*, except what they define as the bad sort with swelling, which they have expanded into a new and broader category. The ideas they now hold concern infection and contagion—that an illness can pass or jump from one person to another—and about agents of illness in the form of spirits, dirt, worms, and *jiem*.

Assimilation of "Germs"—A New Term, Old Ideas

The idea of germs has been readily assimilated, I think, because it resembles ideas the villagers already held. Patrol officers, missionaries, nurses, and health patrol personnel have all strongly advised and ordered them to dig latrines, change their water supplies, and dispose of corpses, placentas, and rubbish in new ways, and have repeatedly observed that flies and germs spread disease. Before the whites came, they had rules about washing, hygiene, and food, strong rules about the disposal of excrement and rubbish, fear of dirt on food, disgust at feces on paths and at roundworms (*dilgep*, roundworm, is the main term of abuse), and they also have a certain fear of worms. A dead village rat or mouse is treated as if contaminated: it is picked up with a stick or leaf and held at arm's length because it eats feces and refuse. Blowflies lay eggs on rotting things; the eggs turn into maggots. They knew that well. People recall the flies around corpses on funeral platforms. Blowflies, maggots, feces, roundworms, worms on paths—these were loosely associated by feelings of disgust and repulsion. When they were told about hookworm and germs, these sounded like the same sort of thing.

The parallel is explicit drawn. In 1985, a "singsing" (Tokpisin term for a big dance ritual or ceremony) was going on in a neighboring village. It lasted a few weeks. The Gnau name of the singsing, *Gadugep Balwawogep*, means "Fish Landcrabs." When they explained what it was, they said, "It's for a man who is sick to cure him." They listed the villages that "knew" (that is, performed) the singsing, and linked it with the ground and with worms (*yibergep*), which are found in the ground and in wet mud and which cause belly pain. They immediately added that worms are like germs (*mawopa jiem*), like hookworm; they get at you in the mud, through the ground. The singsing dance is performed with tall, light masks, the local form of the Fish Singsing (Marshall 1938; McGregor 1975) found around Lumi. Where I stayed they did not perform it, and spoke of it as a singsing for a bad spirit. The ground and mud were associated especially with land crabs, which eject a little pile of wet mud from their holes at night. Worms had the *jiem* or agent role in this, and were ambiguously associated with the spirit of the singsing.

The idea of invisible infection corresponds also to ideas they have always had about the way spirits jump from one sick person to another, turning their attention from one person to another if they pass too close by. I am not sure if anyone bothered to distinguish between the idea of *jiem* as material agents of disease—like dirt, worms, maggot eggs, or the germs and bacteria referred to in talks on hygiene—from the idea of *jiem* as an invisible spirit agent, like the spirits *malet* and *belyipig*. Spirits can manifest in material forms as stones, images, or as animals, so why should *jiem* not be the same? The idea could be readily accommodated to earlier ideas. The spread of disease by touch is obvious to them in the spread of *grili* (from mother to baby where the baby's body touches hers), as well as in the spread of scabies and in the everyday observation of dirt contaminating food. The imagery for invisible spirit transmission exists in wind, smell, and sound. All indicate presence without visibility.

They may understand "germs" in medical or material terms or in spiritual terms, and the ambiguity helps in the accommodation of new terms and new ideas. People can talk to each other about the same thing while giving it different significance; it can allow them to shift according to the situation. But problems arise when people are concerned about defining clearly what they are doing and what it means. My last case illustrates how this problem struck some village notables. The nub of the problem was whether the singsing they were doing was a medical or a religious act. If it was religious, it was heathen and wrong for a Christian to take part. But if the purpose was to heal an illness, did that make it medical and excuse him? Distinguishing medicine from religion would not have occurred before the introduction of Christianity and European ideas about kinds of work and specialized responsibilities.

Conflicts of Belief

The man for whom the singsing was in progress in 1985 was the mission station pastor, thus a committed Christian prayer leader, and his

home village was the same as that of the APO in the village where I
lived. The APO told me the story (in Tokpisin). It presented problems
for him. He, too, was a Christian and someone who owed his training to
the C.M.M.L. (Christian Brethren) Mission, especially to the first missionary doctor there. When Pastor Woperel became ill, the APO said,
they could not find out what was wrong with him. He went to the
hospitals in Wewak and Lae for investigations. The doctors there could
determine nothing, yet he felt ill. He kept dreaming of fish and the
spirits of the dead who said he must do the singsing. So, against his will,
he said yes. His dreams indicated that he would have diarrhea for three
days after the singsing started, and this would remove the sickness from
him in the watery stools. His main trouble had been pains in his belly,
and the feeling his feet were going to take off and he would fly. This, said
the APO, was what made the doctors at Lae concentrate on his earlier
motorbike accident and on blows to his head, even though he had not
felt that he had hurt his head at the time. So, against his will they did the
singsing, and soon after it started, he did have diarrhea and then he felt
better. He has danced in the singsing since then, and he stays well.

The APO says that some of the people in his village, strong converts,
said it was wrong to do the singsing, a sin God would see. Some of them
left the village for the duration of the event (either in protest or to
escape God's wrath or the mission's—it was not clear which). The APO
can see that the singsing made him better. It is possible that bad spirits of
the village made him ill, and also the doctors at Lae could find nothing.
Perhaps the accident could have harmed his brain. Then, speaking for
himself, the APO wonders what is right; he himself is a Christian, God
sees everything and everywhere, and the singsing is bad (*pekato,* a sin,
was the word he used). Yet Woperel (the pastor) is a strong Christian; he
had prayed. Why hadn't God healed him? Why had he then got better
with the singsing? I thought he was genuinely perplexed by the moral
issues and the question of the nature of the illness. But I was also aware
of his ambiguous position toward me, a doctor, and someone who knew
the missionary doctor who had trained him, and a bit about his past. Was
it calculated a little by what he thought I might tell the mission people?

Ten days later I was going through the village where the singsing was.
The Summer Institute of Linguistics' linguist-cum-Bible translator who
has been working for sixteen years on Au, the language spoken in that
area, had just come up the hillside to see Woperel. I found the pastor
and the linguist sitting on the ground in the porch of the pastor's house.
They were talking in Au. I understood nothing, but afterwards the
linguist told me he had gone to see Woperel, having himself been away
for many months, because he heard that Woperel was deeply upset,
conscience stricken, about allowing the singsing to be done for his ill-

ness. Woperel had said he had allowed it only because of the heavy insistence of his relatives, and after all the investigations, and much prayer. He told the linguist that he was annoyed the singsing was going on so long, that he had repeatedly urged them to end it. He had prayed until he was exhausted. Then his relatives from another village turned up to dance and he could not refuse them. While the singsing is going on, Woperel says, he feels that he cannot act or take part in any Christian services. He prays but he feels in the wrong.

From the linguist I learn that his illness has consisted of dizziness, ringing in the ears, and feeling light-headed. It has been diagnosed as Ménière's syndrome. He has also had migraine with visual aura. He is on some pills for his symptoms from the doctor at Lae. Woperel said they didn't help, but that the singsing did.

On that day, Woperel looked well, and was neatly dressed in white shirt, clean shorts, boots and socks, and a wristwatch. He was courteous when I turned up, and interrupted his conversation. I didn't know him. I left after ten minutes, having arranged to meet the linguist later.

However, Woperel seemed different when he came later to the village where I was living. He came with some women from his village for the ceremonies to celebrate the birth of someone's first child. *Garamut* slit-gong messages to call them the night before had gone unanswered, so a relative went to fetch them at dawn next morning. As they walked in, they were greeted by Walbasu, a rugged old heathen wreathed in smiles, with loud ribald remarks on the reasons for their failure to answer the *garamut* the night before.

Woperel has on a blue floppy hat, his wristwatch, a shirt, shorts, boots, and thick socks. He sits down to chat. They offer him the mash of yams, coconut, and taro. No, he can't eat that; tubers come from the ground. Then there was a lot of chat about all the things he cannot eat because of the singsing, and a lot of reiteration and knowing agreement from his listeners: all food that has association with the ground, ground-living birds and animals, and fish—even tinned fish. He speaks about these food avoidances as a committed believer. He told me he used to have belly cramps and pains after food and feel pins and needles running about his skin, his guts twisting and turning. You could hear them making noises like sago grubs inside the trunk of a palm. He felt unsteady on his legs, but things didn't seem to turn round outside him (i.e., it did not sound like marked vertigo). He had had a small, high ringing sound in his ears. Both the ringing sound and dizziness had gone since the singsing. He intends to keep the food avoidances for some time, and then try tiny amounts of the foods, waiting in case any of his symptoms come back. (His experimental attitude to trying out foods that he has been avoiding is a common one.)

What strikes me now is his cheerful and sincere conviction that the singsing helped. In this setting, I would never have guessed at his perplexity, or his pangs of conscience. In different situations, beliefs and the relevance and intensity of different beliefs vary. Single, unswerving commitment to only one set of beliefs—the idea that truth is single and exclusive—is characteristic of monotheist religious expectations; local patterns did not seem to me at all like that.

Gnau religious beliefs and terms of knowledge are pluralistic and not ordered into a unified or smooth unitary system. New things might be added or tried out. Conflicts of principle or practice were not apparent to them in the way they might be to a monotheist believer. The addition of something new to an existing range of alternatives need not require in principle (although it might in practice) other adjustments of the preexisting system. It is consistent with a pluralistic attitude that local people should not feel that they must renounce all that they had before if they adopt new beliefs and practices. Monotheists, who argue that their religion alone is true, are more likely to wish to reject on principle other beliefs and practices that are not in accord.

It is easy to give too much attention to theory in the analysis of religion and medical behavior. Medicine and religion both involve matters of belief and practice. Ordinarily, people are more concerned with efficacy and practical considerations than with explanatory consistency or logic. But where the two, medicine and religion, are fused or confused, the emphasis may fall differently. And practice then may put belief in question or in doubt, as it did for the pastor and the APO.

What is the truth? Why does one believe that something is the right thing to do? Why does one think that X is the right treatment? In many cases it is because that is what everyone says, or because someone else who is supposed to know says so. One may have had no opportunity or means to test it for oneself. We are used to having specialized authorities and guarantees for the source or status of facts. What these say, we believe.

In a West Sepik village I was sometimes struck by the way that what everyone said was the truth, or might become the truth. It was hard to tell in advance, for example, the day on which a ceremony would happen or a hunt take place, or when a party would set out on a particular visit. One or two people might say, "Oh yes, the day after tomorrow," yet the event would not happen then. But if many people said, "Yes, the day after tomorrow," then it would happen. In the case of false gossip, the victim should deny it vigorously, loudly, and publicly, before too many people repeated it and it gained currency and credence. People may repeat something as if it is a fact when they had only heard a rumor (for example, "My brother is coming to stay," "I'm going to be the next doctor at the hospital," "I want an airstrip built," "X has died," "Y has run away to marry"). Will I accept it or contradict them? The distinction between question and statement is blurred. Some of these assertions are really surreptitious experiments or tests to see if by trying them out they can pass and move on to stronger status as the truth. How much does the truth, or fact, turn out to be or to depend on what everyone accepts or says (as in history)? I recall some people saying to each other, but in my presence (and for me to hear), that the genealogies I was taking would be shown to the dead they were naming for me. I remember others asking the dead to answer them on the tape recorder.

This position in regard to truth came home to me in a conversation with Teimen, grandson of the rugged old man Walbasu about what he really believed and what his grandfather really believed. The conversation wandered from sores and flies to medicines, food taboos, and treatments for the spirits Gnau believe in. He said his grandfather, his father, and all the older men still believe in the spirits. He himself believes in God and what he has learned at school. I asked why he believed that. Because the Bible said so. He had heard it many times. From the Catholic Mission Father, at *missa* (in church). He thinks a bit more, and says it is true because of Jesus and the miracles. He uses the word *mirakel*. I ask what they are. The resurrection, and when things turn into something else. So I asked whether he thought their own miracles were true, like those in the Bible. No, was his answer, they are just empty (*gipi'im*) stories. But what about the Bird of Paradise or the Pig myths, I asked, in which animals or birds turn into people, or people into things; are these not the same as miracles? He said no, and began to tell me the story of the Resurrection. But why do you say you believe in the Bible but not in the spirits of your own stories—both are about what happened long ago? He thought a moment and said, "Well, the difference is that lots of people many times have told the Bible story. Many different people tell it. Only a few people, only here, tell our stories." I asked if he was saying that to me because I am white and missionaries are white. He said no, that is what he really thinks—*wuna'at wog galba,* his "thinking center right inside." Perhaps his argument and justification for belief is not so far from the analyses of Peter Winch (1970) or Thomas Kuhn (1962); you can go on believing many things without ever having to put them to any test. But that is not always the case with medical treatment.

The two sets of standards that I had in mind at the start of this paper were those of anthropology and medicine because medical anthropology inevitably brings them together and their meeting poses a challenge, especially when it comes to the assessment of treatment. The usual connotation of "having double standards" is duplicity or hypocrisy. Occasionally there may be a whiff of hypocrisy about the anthropologist who finds other people's treatments so satisfactory for them but leaves readers to wonder whether he or she would really wish an illness to depend on them. The anthropologist may add a proviso about other people's expectations, but still I feel like asking, "Do you mean that you would choose to be treated like that? And if not, why not?" The answer no doubt would bring up expectations and standards of evaluation. People's opinions and the information on which they are based are extremely varied. Ideally, medical criteria depend on certain kinds of evidence. Anthropologists, in practice, assert or imply quite commonly that other treatments they have observed might be judged effective also by these medical criteria. I argued in the first part of the paper that they should provide appropriate evidence if they want to make these assertions and be taken seriously (by doctors). Examples of error and self-delusion in medicine abound, and illustrate how difficult it is to meet scientific standards of evidence. That still applies to doctors too, and the very difficulty itself exposes the room left open for faith to fill. Therapeutic optimism can be a boon to the ill as well as a trap for the credulous. On the side of credulity there is also an overreadiness to offer explanations of the treatment and how it works before knowing whether it does work—the Indian rope trick problem. On the side of faith, the anthropologist can ask and hear directly what experience of benefit the sufferer felt.[9]

I tried to find out about compliance in the drug treatment of leprosy. From the mixture of information and mistaken views about other people's actions and intentions, a picture of apparent noncompliance grows into an explanation of part of it. I also wanted to stress by the simple approach of questioning different people that what is simple and obvious may also be relevant. Answers do not only lie in new ideas or abstruse theories. The observations on the treatment of sores were meant as an illustration of this. The problem of method is to find a pertinent way to answer a question. Study of something common or trivial may help in answering questions about the exceptional case; and study of what is common is more feasible. In many things, we look to others and their experience for advice. As children we were taught to accept instruction from older authorities. The magisterial article on medicine in the 1911 edition of the *Encyclopedia Britannica* states that "the habit of acceptance of authority, waning but far from extirpated, dictated to the clinical observer what he should see" (Allbutt 1911:55). In fact, Allbutt considered that the degradation of medicine between Galen and William Harvey consisted in part in the blind following of the authority of Galen, that its new development was not due to the discovery of the experimental method alone, but "social and political causes also are concerned in the advance even of the exact sciences" (Allbutt 1911:55). Illness makes people more dependent on others than usual. It is not surprising then that people should be so ready to follow advice and believe in the authority and experience of others when they face illness and its uncertainties. Herodotus thought the wisest of the institutions of Babylon, next to their arrangement of marriage, was this:

> They have no physician, but when a man is ill, they lay him in the public square, and the passers-by go up to him, and if they have ever had his disease themselves or have known anyone who has suffered from it, they give him advice, recommending him to do whatever they found good in their own case, or in the case known to them, and no one is allowed to pass the sick man in silence without asking what his ailment is.

But people have to choose what to do. We may be cautious and critical of others, but not enough about ourselves. There are good reasons, as well as bad ones, for being skeptical.

Notes

1. There are many examples of faith and credulity to choose from: from alchemy to Jung; from astrology to prognosis; the miracles in the Bible which showed the hand of God; the search for arcane knowledge, the Egyptian mysteries, Gurdjieff, transcendental meditation; Mesmer and magnetism, hypnotism, psychoanalysis; suggestion and placebos; shamanic healing, telepathy, homeopathy, Christian Science, psychic surgery, Castaneda, Uri Geller, J. B. Rhine, Jacob Isserls's treatment, and acupuncture. There were collections of miracles, of prodigies and monsters, and of Cabalist and occult writings, as well as collectors, the Fathers of the Church, the Hermetical writers; the curious and analytic, Sir Thomas Browne (Pseudodoxia Epidemica), Sir Francis Bacon, Sir Isaac Newton; and the skeptical—Montaigne, Pierre Bayle (thoughts on the comet of 1680), Fontanelle (questions on oracles), Spinoza (on miracles), Hume (on miracles), Voltaire (on miracles)—much magic, some science, and the vulnerable interaction of reason and feelings, hopes and experience. A mixture of sincerity and fraud.

2. After some of the switches, the proclaimed authorities might well have wished to hide. How hotly they argued about breastfeeding—on demand or to strict schedule, by bottle or breast—or about diets. Things might simply reverse when some therapeutic dogma was exposed as false—to treat diarrhea with fluids (give them or withhold them), with antibiotics, with electrolyte solution, or with rice water (Mehta and Subramaniam 1986). A history of medical bigotry stretches far back: discreditable opposition to the innovations of Ignaez-Philippe Semmelweiss, Edward Jenner, and so on. We may still meet skeptical excesses or the bigotry of closed minds, as well as rash zeal and dewey-eyed romantic

enthusiasm, cranks, frauds, and victims. Yet there is now a method of judgement, workable for some sorts of treatment if people think it worth the trouble—namely, the double-blind controlled trial of treatment.

3. He retired from his job so as to stand for election to the House of Assembly, failed by a little to get in, then after a bit decided to come back as an APO. He took the job, although he comes from a neighboring village that speaks a different language, but he has direct clan ties here, and he has married a second wife from this village, a woman much younger than himself. His first wife and grown-up children are at his own village; his second wife and children are usually here. He spends time in both villages.

4. I have used fictitious names for people throughout.

5. There was a dispute over the use of this ancient site seventeen years ago, nearly resulting in an intervillage fight with spears. It happened soon after my first arrival, and I was present. Someone tried to throw a spear, and was stopped; a young man began the trembling of the onset of trance to fight. The young man was P., who had run away from the hospital when he heard the dispute was brewing. Since the resolution of that dispute, his father and his brothers keep clear their strong attachment to the land at Saikel, and sometimes speak of breaking away from the village to go and remake Saikel their home, their village.

6. The singling out of *sik lepro* struck me. In 1968, there was a fad among the girls and small children for a certain way of clapping their hands so that they made a little echoing clapsound. When they had nothing better to do, they would often clap like that. It irritated some of the older men as they sat chatting. I remember one of them saying: "If you keep on doing that, you'll get *sik lepro.*" I heard it said a few times while the hand-clapping fad lasted. The name *sik lepro* did crop up, even in the conversation of those who did not speak Pidgin— sometimes deformed in pronunciation as *sik maipro.* It also cropped up as the suspected diagnosis in a few serious illnesses when someone had a painless swelling. One suspected case of *sik lepro* was, in my opinion, that of someone with heart failure, and another that of a child with acute rheumatic fever. I asked them why they called these *sik lepro.* The answer was, "Because they have swelled up." Indeed, after the death and burial of one (a ten-year-old boy), an unusual and elaborate washing ceremony took place with special water because, they said, they were frightened that the *sik lepro* of the dead boy might jump into some woman or another child in his hamlet. Later I was to hear of the death of a man I had known on my first visit. His belly and legs had swollen. He felt weak. He tried to walk down to the mission hospital, but the path along the ridge leading to it passed through the nearest neighboring village. When he came to this village, the people there would not let him pass through because they said his illness would infect them. They said he had *sik lepro.* He was turned back. He died shortly after at home, his belly grossly swollen. The body was buried with special haste for fear of the illness jumping to someone else. They told me about the events when I came back. People from his hamlet had gone in anger after his death to complain to the other village for turning him back; there was a fight, and some of them got jailed for fighting. In retrospect, people in the

village said he had died of *sik lepro*. The strange swelling was what counted in order to make a diagnosis of *sik lepro*. They also grasped its seriousness and the risk of catching it from someone else. They had learned that there were special horrors to leprosy. They were not convinced of them by the skin blemishes of early leprosy, but they granted them to what they took for the bad *sik lepro* where there was swelling.

7. Dapsone, the drug used for treating leprosy, occasionally provokes serious reactions. One woman (who had a positive biopsy for leprosy) absconded from hospital during a severe reaction to the drug. She died in the village soon afterwards. Another young woman's death may have been from an allergic reaction caused by the drug, although retrospective diagnosis from descriptions is not reliable. Dapsone must be used with care.

8. Teimen was not exactly lying, he was imagining. I told him that I had asked his grandfather and other older men about flies on sores and they denied that flies would help dry them. Teimen said he had worked out what his grandfather must think from watching what he did and listening to the way he talked.

9. Materials on which sorcery is worked provide a different sort of example of contamination and effect.

References

Allbutt, Thomas C.
1911   Medicine. In *Encyclopedia Britannica* 18:41–64. Cambridge: Cambridge University Press.
Anonymous
1837   *Sketches of Imposture, Deception and Credulity.* London: Thomas Tegg and Son.
Brugarolas, A., and M. Gosalvez
1980   Treatment of Cancer by an Inducer of Reverse Transformation. *Lancet* 1:68.
Cannon, Walter
1942   Voodoo Death. *American Anthropologist* 44:169–181.
Eastwell, H.
1982   Voodoo Death and the Mechanism for the Dispatch of the Dying in Eastern Arnhem Land. *American Anthropologist* 84:5–18.
Friedman, W. B. et al.
1963*a*   Behavioral Observations on Parents Anticipating the Death of a Child. *Pediatrics* 32:610–625.
1963*b*   Urinary 17-Hydroxycortisocosteroid Levels in Parents of Children with Neoplastic Disease. *Psychosomatic Medicine* 25:364–376.
Gluckman, Max, ed.
1964   *Closed Systems and Open Minds.* Edinburgh: Oliver and Boyd.
Kleinman, Arthur
1980   *Patients and Healers in the Context of Culture.* Berkeley, Los Angeles, Oxford: University of California Press.

Kuhn, Thomas
1962   *The Structure of Scientific Revolutions.* Chicago: University of Chicago Press.
Lewis, Gilbert
1977   Fear of Sorcery and the Problem of Death by Suggestion. In *The Anthropology of the Body,* J. Blacking, ed., pp. 111–143. London: Academic Press.
1987   A Lesson from Leviticus. *Man,* n.s., 22:593–612.
Lex, Barbara
1974   Voodoo Death: New Thoughts on an Old Explanation. *American Anthropologist* 76:818–823.
Marshall, Arthur Jack
1938   *Men and Birds of Paradise.* London: W. Heinemann, Ltd.
McGregor, Don
1975   *The Fish and the Cross.* Hamilton, New Zealand: Privately Printed.
Mechanic, David
1966   Response Factors in Illness. *Social Psychiatry* 1:11–20.
Mehta, M., and S. Subramaniam
1986   Comparison of Rice Water, Rice Electrolyte Solution, and Glucose Electrolyte Solution in the Management of Infantile Diarrhoea. *Lancet* 1:843–845.
Middleton, Margaret, and Sarah Francis
1976   *Yuendumu and Its Children.* Canberra: Australian Government Publishing Service.
Reid, Jan, and Nancy Williams
1984   On Voodoo Death. *American Anthropologist* 86:121–132.
Shryock, Richard H.
1948   *The Development of Modern Medicine.* London: Gollancz.
Sutherland, Stuart
1981   Tricks, Traps and the Will to Believe. *Times Literary Supplement* (January 2): 12.
Winch, Peter
1970   Understanding a Primitive Society. In *Rationality,* Bryan Wilson, ed. pp. 78–111. Oxford: Blackwell.
Wingerson, L.
1980   The Rise and Fall of a Cure for Cancer. *World Medicine* (September 20): 35–36.
Ziman, John
1976   *The Force of Knowledge.* Cambridge: Cambridge University Press.
1983   Fudging the Facts. *Times Literary Supplement* (September 9):955.

10

Risk

Anthropological and Epidemiological
Narratives of Prevention

Ronald Frankenberg

Introduction

Many critiques both by and about medical anthropology tend to focus
on the interactive experience of doctors and patients, or at best, sufferers and healers. Such encounters are seen in a notional *now,* in which
incumbents of both sets of roles look to a future that will constitute a
new and healthier present for the patient's body and the relegation of
both disease and interaction to their shared past. From the standpoint of
these episodic encounters it has been variously claimed that medical
professionals neglect the social experience of the patients and the social
construction of disease, that cultural and social anthropologists are in-
sufficiently aware of the clinical realities of the framework that constrains them, and that biological anthropologists exaggerate the natural
at the expense of the cultural (Browner, Ortiz de Montellano, and Rubel
1988).

By contrast, relatively few studies (notably Janes, Stall, and Gifford
1986, and in passing, Young 1980, Helman 1987) examine the supposedly nonproblematic professional and intellectual relationship between
those physicians and anthropologists who direct their activity, not toward present suffering or need, but to the avoidance of future suffering
(often unconsciously and perhaps dangerously conflated with the future
need for professional medical care). I refer to epidemiologists and those
anthropologists who work alongside them, usually as junior partners. As
James Trostle (1986:35) remarks,

Although contemporary research linking society and culture to health thus has venerable roots, the relationship between epidemiology and anthropology remains largely unexplored: the joint history of these disciplines might generously be characterized as a history of benign neglect.

The Conceptualization of the Body in Narrative

In this paper I want to focus once more on the relationship between anthropological and epidemiological approaches to a social science of health care.[1] To do so I shall begin to theorize about diverse (but not necessarily mutually exclusive) narrative conceptualizations of the body, and seek to clarify their implications for the views of risk taken respectively by biologists (*corporeal*), "biomedical" physicians (*somatic*), and social scientists (*incarnate*). This approach leaves aside, for the time being, the elaboration of the useful distinctions made by Nancy Scheper-Hughes and Margaret Lock (1987) concerning the individual body, the social body, and the body politic, and it views Arthur Kleinman and Joan Kleinman's (1985) concept of somatization as a special (and possibly controversial) case of the somatic. By adopting these distinctions I hope to draw attention to the customary social science conflation of the biological and the medical concealed within the term *biomedicine,* which seems to embody an ideological assumption and a rhetorical claim that need to be explored rather than uncritically accepted. The biological, or more properly the natural, (as others, in the spirit of Emile Durkheim, Claude Lévi-Strauss, and Marcel Mauss, have noted; e.g., Comaroff 1982; Gaines and Hahn 1986:6; Gordon 1988), seems to reach the social and cultural analyst of health already mediated by the medical. In the terms set out in the table below, the corporeal is perceived in terms of the somatic before the sociologist/anthropologist realizes it is incarnate.

Narrative style:	=	*Biological*	*Medical*	*Social*
Concept:	=	*corporeal*	*somatic*	*incarnate*
ext./int.:	=	built in	from inside	from outside
unit:	=	species	individual	group or category
symbolism:	=	animal	personal	social
time:	=	past	present	future
duration:	=	epochs or instants	era	life course

Medicine, Epidemiology, and the Situated Individual

Such an enterprise seems to be particularly important at the present time when, I suspect, interest in the potential of genetic engineering therapies in general, and in cancers and retroviruses in particular, is contributing to a shift of the medical gaze away from the focus on the body, its surface, and its tissue contents, and toward the biochemistry and physics of the cell nucleus (Dutton 1988: chap. 6 and especially quotation from Ethan Singer on p. 217; Nichols 1988). Although this might be seen as a natural and cumulative development from long-standing concerns with chemical physiology and pathology, I would argue that we are witnessing a qualitative change in focus, a paradigm shift (Kuhn 1962) beginning with the Krebs Cycle in the late forties and culminating in the clinical techniques flowing from the discovery of DNA and RNA in the fifties (Baldwin 1962). A parallel but less dramatic and still incomplete shift has taken place in epidemiology from a concern with the aggregation of individual attributes through shared behaviors to a focus on the "life styles" of risk groups (Dunn and Janes 1986:8–13.) The socially and culturally situated and self-situating person excluded already from technological medicine is now being abandoned by curative medicine and perhaps also by preventive medicine.

Social scientists in preventive medicine initially posed the questions, "How can we prevent future *individual* Fore from contracting Kuru (Lindenbaum 1979) or future *individual* women in London from becoming victims of crippling mental illness (Brown and Harris 1978)?" A further question poses itself: "Will both epidemiological and anthropological orientations inexorably drive their protagonists to supplement these questions about individual fate with others about the organization of Fore and London, which ask how can the society of Highland New Guinea or Britain be changed now to reorganize the future of suffering?" Mary Douglas suggests that this may be a sadly rare outcome when she remarks that the concept of risk pool makes possible, but not inevitable, a switch from asking the specific question, "How much risk is acceptable to you?" to the more general question, "What kind of society do you want?" (Douglas 1986:13–14).

Social Process Epidemiology: The Chianti Experience

These problems demand particular attention in light of the problems accentuated within epidemiology by the existence of AIDS. Manuel

Carballo's (1987) discussion of an action-oriented research incorporating both disciplines, which could be called social process epidemiology, suggests that such an approach is essential to limit, let alone
prevent, the future spread of AIDS. My own experience in helping to
plan research and health promotion intervention into cardiovascular
disease, motorcycle accidents, unwanted pregnancy among young people, and loss of autonomy among the aged in Chianti, Toscana, Northern Italy, reinforces this view. In this case the health education and
information section of a Local Health Unit (*Unita Sanitaria Locale*—
USL) asked its constituent *Comuni* to identify the health problems
they considered most pressing, and with the help of a World Health
Organization consultant, Maurice Backett, they arrived at the four
problems just mentioned. I obtained a grant from a British state
agency to monitor the progress of the USL's research and also to
study the cultural performance of sickness and the grass roots impact
of the then (1982) recently instituted *Riforma Sanitaria* (Frankenberg
1984). This Chianti research was both medically and politically in-
spired and, given the identity of the consultant, the problems were
unsurprisingly cast in terms of identifying and measuring the relative
importance of risk factors (a kind of shorthand expression for the
probable future need for care (Backett, Davies, and Petros-Barvazian
1984:1 and passim; see also below). These risk factors, if not entirely
social in nature, were seen as avoidable if individuals could be provided with an appropriately changed social and cultural framework.
The emphasis was to be on collective culture rather than on individual, "rational choice" lifestyle. Yet in the case of cardiovascular disease the outcome of culturally constrained (even determined) eating,
drinking, and exercise behavior was seen by physicians, social scientists, and sufferers alike as directly biological and thus internal to the
body, giving rise to specific nameable diseases and causes of death.
Patients were not seen as wearing their hearts on their social sleeves.
Motorcycle accidents, on the other hand, *were* seen as a social form of
injury and death, coming from outside the body so to speak, where, in
Cartesian fashion, we locate both mind and its social and cultural environment. The specific problems of the young and old are even more
interesting for the assumptions they involve, since it seemed to be
taken for granted in Italy (notwithstanding Lancaster and Hamburg
1986), as in Britain and the United States, that early teen pregnancy
was naturally problematic, rather than merely culturally and socially
so. In addition, the transition from debility to disability in old age was
considered more likely to be caused by defects of the body natural
than of the body social or political.

Time in Anthropology and Epidemiology

Frederick Dunn and Craig Janes (1986:11–12) have drawn attention to the use of concepts of time by epidemiologists relating to the period of the onset and the natural history of disease, the study of cohorts, and the parallels between this use and the use of temporal concepts by conventional cultural and applied anthropologists. Recent interest in narrative time by some anthropologists (Geertz 1988; Clifford and Marcus 1986; Frankenberg 1988) suggested to me that the contradictions between coevality and the tense of writing, and the presence of sickness and the future need for care, might be understood by examining the diverse meanings and uses of the concepts of risk and of the body in the differing narratives and narrative styles of epidemiologists and anthropologists. It is especially pertinent to ask how these might be related to the diversely recounted stories of the past, present, and future of those who, as a result of the efforts of both sets of practitioners, were destined to become the nonpatients, or even the unexpectedly still living, of the future.

While this is a discouragingly difficult, and to me a novel exercise, I was encouraged by the familiar experience that I had not invented a problem *de novo* but had merely arrived by a slightly different route, and was posing in a slightly different way, issues with which colleagues elsewhere were also beginning to grapple (Williams 1984; Brody 1987; Kleinman 1988), and which were of concern to many scholars in other disciplines.

Robert Hahn (1985) has correctly pointed out that the distinction between illness and sickness was initially made "to describe the contrast between the perspectives, or world views, of patient and physician and to place these perspectives in a sociocultural context." He goes on to complain, with justification in the self-critical view of the present writer, that "recent formulations still bear the impress of this biomedical ideology, including a mind-body dualism, an ascription of primacy to the biological over the psychological and the social, and a radical contrast between the 'knowledge' of biomedical practitioners and the 'belief' of patients everywhere and of traditional non-Western healers." Hahn suggests that we remedy these defects by restoring to pathology "its original sense as the science and treatment of pathos i.e. suffering." While I sympathize with the underlying premise of this approach, the concept of suffering returns us once more to the individual and her or his corporeal and or psychic experience. It thus misses the point of the concept of sickness, defined as a more or less legitimated cultural performance. Such a cultural performance is inevitably framed by, and embedded in, the social for both sufferer and those allowed or obliged by their professional standing to assuage present or prevent future suffering. For example, a focus on individual corporeal suffering fails to draw attention to the fact that while nation states or evil or incompetent systems that cause suffering to the masses may be seen as organized groups, the masses themselves are seen as mere aggregates of individuals or, at their most socialized, families.

Malign Conspiracy or Shared Discourse

When I argued that anthropologists fell almost unconsciously into the thought processes of physicians (Frankenberg 1986a, 1986b, 1986c, 1988), I was taken as expressing hostility to the latter (Kleinman 1986), and even as suggesting a professional conspiracy. Instead, I had intended a reproach to the lack of consciousness of many anthropologists rather than the lack of competence of physicians as individual curers of numerous but still individual patients. I argued that this lack of consciousness arose from a common experience, rare among other Western intellectuals, of interaction in real time with the human subjects (patients) of their studies. As Johannes Fabian (1983) has pointed out (in contrast to Feuchtwang 1973), anthropologists typically share quite fully in the ongoing life of the people they study; they become their coevals. However, by returning to their own countries and institutions, anthropologists distance themselves in time and space from the peoples that they studied. They be can seen as stealing their subjects' presents/presence, taking it out of the context of its past and future and as re-presenting/representing it as that of an unchanging other; they make the presence of the other, in both relative and absolute terms, allochronic. This is not true of all anthropologists (see Foster et al. 1979). Most anthropologists, however, have placed their subjects' present in a time other than their own and by doing so appear to place it outside time altogether. I have suggested that the practice of medicine is in some ways similar and that the term "taking the patient's history" could be regarded as more true than it is usually considered to be; patients' lived experiences in real time are translated into timeless disease and episodic sickness (Young 1980, 1982; Taussig 1980). For most physicians, asthma and AIDS, syphilis and measles, once established as syndromes, soon cease to have a social history in linear time and exist only, if in a time frame at all, in the cycles of supposedly natural time. On the other hand, physicians also use a model of curable, acute infection penetrating body boundaries from outside, by means of microorganism, bad habits, or both, in order to accommodate and control their patients' disorder(s). This model requires that individual cases have the Aristotelian qualities of beginning, middle, and end—that is, time and date of onset, course of illness, and date of cure and discharge or "negative patient outcome." I have called this the *tragic* temporal contradiction of current, curative medicine because I do *not* see it as a wicked deviation, let alone as a conspiracy, but as the *only* way in which practitioners can currently operate. Both the timelessness of disease and the episodic nature of acute sickness are usually enacted within the confines of the time-structured clinic (hospital, outpatient clinic, physician's office, doctor's surgery, healer's consulting room).

Dialects of Clinical Narrative: Diversity of Medical Models

The clinic, however, is not a site reserved only for the curative physician. It is a space, in both reality and discourse, which is shared by patients and their kin, by nurses, auxiliaries, and technicians (Strauss et al. 1985), and by many other healers—sometimes amateurs, sometimes professionals. Many of these, like the more "orthodox" epidemiologists, are also involved in a quest for health as well as, or instead of, the avoidance or cure of specific diseases.

Even for those who see sickness as dramatic cultural narrative, with onstage dramatis personae and backstage and unseen performers in subplots of preexisting and subsequent disease and illness, there is still the danger of seeing the discourse of biomedicine as a language without significant dialects. The relationship between the natural and the social (and indeed the biological and the medical) may be different not only for those who participate in different roles and time worlds but also for physicians of different specializations. The same actors may also perceive different relationships in different locations: hospital, home or office. The relation of narrative to story or narrating to narrative may also, like the social conditions of its production, be different (see below for definitions of these terms). Albert Kushlick, in a personal communication and in his evidence to the Jay Committee (see Kushlick et al. 1976), defined ten-minute, eight-hour, sixteen-hour, and twenty-four-hour care-givers according to the period of time each spent with the patient. He suggested that this influenced the different perceptions of chronic diseases by physicians, nurses, relatives (usually female), and patients respectively. Anselm Strauss, Shizuko Fagerhaugh, Barbara Suczek, and Carolyn Weiner (1985) similarly draw attention to the physician's knowledge of a wide body of cases, which stands in complementary opposition to the patient's deeper longitudinal appreciation of one case in one body (see Sacks 1986 for an insightful account of simultaneous existence in both modes.)

Sufferers or Merely Patients

Furthermore, it has to be recognized (Hahn 1985) that Arthur Kleinman, Allan Young (1982), and I at least have in common that we have all used illness to mean the narrative style of the prepatient sufferer rather than that of the sufferer *tout court*. Anthropologists as well as practitioners and clients who consciously choose alternative medicines are able only with difficulty to escape from what they see as inappropriate, but conventionally and socially legitimated, time and narrative styles. Thus in Britain and the United States, sufferers present themselves to alternative healers in the already learned role of patients who suspect they have specific diseases. Homeopaths, for example, see those who consult them as being at once physically and mentally out of balance, and as having a particular chemically named disposition and therefore requiring a particular remedy. Their reaction to this cultural clash between the patients' feeling of having a disease and the healers' totally different etiological theories may initially be the maintenance of a discretionary silence. (The advertising material for MacRepertory, a homeopathic diagnosis software, makes much of the fact that the patient cannot see what the homeopath is entering.) However, the moment of fruitful disclosure may never arrive, since the movement of symptoms outward, which the homeopath sees as as a sign of success, may be seen by the patient as the emergence of another disease and lead to defection (back) to an allopath or alternative alternative healer. Seekers after health who adopt particular dietary or health practices may well construe health (as do some epidemiologists in practice if not always like Maurice Backett and his colleagues in theory) as the avoidance of becoming a patient. This is a different approach to that of either their alternative or physician mentors.

The higher status of physicians may lead nurses to see what the former do as real medicine and curing and to devalue their own legitimate activities by seeking to imitate them. In one of the pioneer anthropological studies of the psychiatric hospital, William Caudill (1958) pointed to this aspect of the behavior of general nurses who criticized and rejected the therapeutic methods of psychiatric residents. They insisted that the primary job of physicians was to prescribe medicaments and that the job of nurses was to administer them (a view that dies hard—see discussion in Estroff 1981, chap. 5). They were more than skeptical about the professional value of talk as therapy, whether from patient or health worker's point of view. In treating male "psychopaths," Maxwell Jones carried the stereotype of nurses as beautiful *and* professional ministering angels to a kind of logical conclusion. He sought to overcome the problem by recruiting young women innocent of professional training as social therapists and separating the roles. Nurses ministered professionally to the patients' physical needs while the therapists were told merely to be attractive and to hold "natural" conversations with the patients. Those whose behavior with patients was considered perhaps too natural were dismissed. Similar behavior with health workers frequently led to marriage (Rapoport and Rapoport 1960).

In a similar fashion, in Zambia, even in the urban areas that Joyce Leeson and I studied in the late sixties (Frankenberg and Leeson 1976), not all sufferers were able to define themselves as patients (of Western medicine) in a way that seemed adequate to their doctors. They sometimes brought ridicule upon themselves by bringing seemingly inappropriate forms of suffering or potential suffering to the attention of medical practitioners. Their "illegitimate" demands for medicine to bring good fortune in love and to avoid accidental injury curiously anticipate, as we shall see, the "legitimate" social medicalization of such problems that I was later to encounter amongst the epidemiologists in Chianti. The obverse of this, when patients had learned to think in terms of disease as seen by biomedicine, was that the traditional healers adopted an interactive narrative style normally considered appropriate to "biomedical" disease. In this they were sometimes led by careless anthropologists (see Kapferer 1988), or they themselves inadvertently led anthropologists, to conceptualize spirit possession cults, for example, as being categories of disease. Bruce Kapferer himself (1983), Gananaath Obeyesekere (1981), and Victor Turner (1968) more cautiously, sensitively and, in my view, correctly, take care to avoid such anachronistic anatopisms (out of time *and* out of place).

The Narrative Styles of Epidemiology

Epidemiologists, who are most often physicians—except in the United States—and who work within a model of medical common sense, shared as we have seen by their patients, are involved in similar kinds of conceptual difficulty. They must not only define nonsufferers as prepatients but if successful will interrupt the progression of nonsufferer to sufferer, prepatient to patient or even, inadvertently, sufferer to patient. Examples of the last progression would be persons with AIDS reacting to the threat of compulsory serotesting or, in colonial Africa, potential TB or leprosy patients resisting the Sanitary Police. Furthermore, as I have suggested above, it is not always clear whether intervention is directed toward preventing disease or preventing people becoming patients or perhaps clients of social welfare services. In Italian society it appears acceptable that cardiovascular disease and also the other misfortunes should be seen in medical terms. It is possible to conceive of forms of social organization where early pregnancy and motorcycle accidents could be viewed as the responsibility of more overt policing agencies. However, people in Bavaria or the United States (especially California) who argue that the law and the police should be involved in preventing the spread of AIDS on the grounds of social good still oppose gun control to reduce homicide. Even while supporting the War Against Drugs, they do not advocate laws to control the intake of food and tobacco to curb the continuing "epidemics" of lung cancer and ischemic heart disease.

Narratives, Illth, and Time

Narrative can be seen as having three distinct meanings (Genette 1980; 1988): the *narrative* proper, a discourse that undertakes to tell of an event or a series of events; the *story,* a succession of events that are the subject of this discourse; and the *narrating,* the act of enunciating the narrative. What we call the analysis of narrative in medical anthropology, for example, is the analysis of the three relationships: narrative to story, narrative to narrating, and story to narrating (cf. Burke cited in Frankenberg 1986a:620). Here, the bias toward a dyadic patient/doctor biomedical curative model, which Hahn correctly perceives in us all, privileges the story as existing in nature and therefore as being real. The story is seen as being accurately reflected in, and revealed by, the medical narrative and is thus finally and totally encompassed in the narrative of disease. The epidemiologist, on the other hand, postulates contrasting narratives about the future and invites the (pre-non-?) patient to choose the one which the latter believes will most closely approximate the story that is hoped for but yet to happen.

In the earlier papers (Frankenberg 1986a, 1986b, 1988) I have noted the diversities in the narrative representations of the biomedical story by, for example, surgeons and physicians, psychotherapists, psychiatrists, and neurologists, as well as by nurses and other health workers. Such narratives may, however, *appear* unitary when seen in contrast to those of patients and their lay advisers, as well as to those of other healers. Concepts of disease, illness, and sickness are shorthand metonymic attempts to encompass their complexity; Anselm Strauss and his colleagues' "trajectory" and my "cultural performance" are metaphorical attempts to demonstrate the interaction and dramatic processual outcome of these narratives.

Risk and Measurement
in Epidemiology

The accounts of risk written by epidemiologists are as diverse as anthropological accounts of culture or clinical accounts of disease. Nevertheless, Backett and his colleagues, who enjoy the imprimatur of WHO, are not atypical in the way that they attempt to classify, define measure, and use risk. They also have the virtue of being more than usually aware of the cultural origins and the social consequences of their ideas, their rootedness in moral and ethical choices and of the diverse audiences for whom they are severally appropriate.

They classify the concept of risk in three ways:

1. Absolute risk associated with each risk factor, which is the risk to the whole population being considered and enables evaluations of interventions. It is used in alerting the health care system as a whole, as well as families and communities within it.

2. Relative risk: the ratio of incidence of those with a risk factor to those without. This is used for referral, the setting of individual priorities and for the development of policy related to them.

3. Attributable risk, which concerns

   a) the frequency of the unwanted outcome when the risk factor is present,

   b) the frequency of the outcome when the risk factor is absent, and

   c) the frequency of occurrence of the risk factor in the community. Attributable risk is important for setting social priorities and for the development of policy related to them (Backett, Davies, and Petros-Barvazian 1984:16, and passim).

Backett and his colleagues write,

> Because most people are concerned more with the threat of illness than with health, the notion of risk has become part of our thinking about the prevention of disease—the chances of health being thought of mainly as low risk of illness. We do not speak of our "vulnerability to health" and epidemiologists rarely study the characteristics of the healthy—though this is likely to become a more rewarding exercise as subtler indices of health are developed. (Ibid.)

We are here being usefully instructed in the culture, the actively invoked conventional wisdom (Douglas 1986:67), in which epidemiologists share and from which they draw their identity, the culture of "bio-logically" based medicine. As we have already seen, participants in this culture generally work with a classical narrative model of *disease* that is individual, episodic, and emplotted. Epidemiologists need to break from this model in two ways in order to promote health *in society,* just as alternative healers must in one way in order to promote the health *of individuals.* Both do so within the confines of an overarching culture against which they are rebelling, but which at the same time constrains them to a concern with disease and with individual patients. The "sub-tler indices of health" in the passage quoted above perhaps suggest a partial surrender to the biological and individual and, therefore, away from the cultural and social. In fact, the current use of risk in epi-demiology inextricably interweaves the individual, the social, and the cultural. As in the case of clinical curative medicine's larceny of the patients' history and present discussed above, this at once presents intel-lectual difficulties and beneficial advantages. First, it convinces the physi-cian or other health worker of her or his own legitimacy when faced with the problem of chronic or recurring sickness. The notion of risk provides the metanarrative, "I have done my best. I have pointed out the risks to the patients; now it is up to them." Second, different aspects of risk in general can be defined and presented in various (mathematical) frame-works and it can be suggested which ones are appropriate in which circumstances for persons with differing positions in the subculture of preventive healing. Thus it is argued that clinical (i.e., biologically mea-surable) risk factors like anemia and hypertension are appropriate in the education of health workers, while social, economic, and demographic factors need to be taught to policy makers. Objective, nonmodifiable, and easily recognizable factors such as age, parity, and previous history are relevant for health educators as the most identifying markers of (and for) people at risk. These last factors overlap with those appropriate for localized community policy and if not always immutable are immutably corporeal. They are signals to policy makers to be on guard rather than factors to be individually overcome by potential patients (Backett, Davies, and Petros-Barvazian 1984:25–29). Third, and perhaps most importantly from our point of view, such beneficial intertwining of per-sonal and social also makes possible a narrative in which the choices of the individual or of the group, while they obviously cannot change the ultimate terminus ad quem imposed by mortality, can change the time table and the routes by which final resting places are achieved.

Epidemiologists thus use risk-factor signals to indicate at which points it is possible or necessary to change tracks, avoiding thereby the framing of sickness in either too long or too short a time scale. They do not confuse epoch and era with life course—the characteristic error of those

who seek to map an anthropology onto a natural evolutionary frame
work (see Gramsci 1971:419–472).

Tales from the Tuscan Hills

In the work with which I am associated in Chianti, we aim either to
tell potential "patients," or especially to create conditions in which
they can discover for themselves, that if they do not exercise and if
they eat too much animal fat, or smoke, or drink alcohol to excess,
they will get cardiovascular disease, and therefore either arrive at the
terminus earlier than they might wish, or require care from the curative
employees of the health unit sponsoring the research. Incarnate body
habits of specific social groups will act on the corporeal to influence the
potential soma. These undesired but not unforeseen outcomes may
imply both individual moral blame for a person's own future suffering
and individual responsibility for higher future social taxation. Similar
considerations apply to present or future failure to take care in relation
to road accidents or "accidental pregnancy." Finally, the project is
directed toward the avoidance of failure by the elderly or their relatives
to maintain a situation where the former can remain relatively autonomous. (Or autonomous in relation to their relatives? A complicated
dialectic of reciprocities is involved. Focusing on the elderly as the
patients obviously involves a widely shared value judgment but perhaps, in practice if not in rhetoric, a rare moral choice.)

All these narratives about the future of individuals and their bodies in
their various aspects contain suggestions about future stories and are
amenable to individual (novel-like) or social (epic-like) styles of narrating. Risks may be presented as individual choices about the biological
corpus or the medical soma (similar to those faced by heroes and heroines
of novels who also apply rational choice theory to lifestyle decisions) as
they are in the contemporary U.S. public health thinking. Alternatively
they may be seen as constrained by external forces implicit in the body
social or the body politic and thus merely incarnate, carried forward by
relatively fate-controlled individuals as in classical myth and drama and in
the equally classical epidemiological thinking of Rudolf Virchow (Taylor
and Rieger 1984) and his currently misprized successors.

As I suggested at the outset, the distinctions of narrative style and
bodily form require more effort to discern in the case of cardiovascular
disease than in the other cases because the prevention of disease and
the prevention of the need for medical care are there most easily
conflated and because the moral decisions are more hidden and subtle.
Given that early pregnancy is a greater social "evil" than it is a natural
one, the evil could be exorcised by changing the social practices of

society at large (as may prove to be necessary for the survival of AIDS-affected societies) rather than changing the biological and social activities of young people (Lancaster and Hamburg 1986). By contrast, making cardiovascular disease socially acceptable is not an option (except presumably for tobacco manufacturers) in quite the same way. In the case of motorcycle deaths amongst young men, drunk-driving deaths, and deaths from intravenous drug use, social acceptability may be complicated by culturally and subculturally determined differential perceptions and meanings. It must also be recognized (as Douglas 1986 discusses at some length) that there are many levels of culturally defined moral responsibility involved and that the definition processes may be situated in institutions (Douglas 1987) as well as in individuals or in society as a whole.

The Chianti project, like other epidemiological exercises even when they are less committed to intervention, takes a moral and ethical stance in which the narrative constructs alternative future stories: "If you do not reorganize your culture to give more respect to the old or to educate the young more effectively, you will continue to bear the unnecessary burdens of residential care for the former and of supporting the unwanted offspring of the latter." It is perfectly possible to conceive of and even to find societies that not only failed to prevent semidependent old people from dying prematurely (as in England in the winter of 1986) rather than helping them to survive in residential care, but also societies that actually killed such people by direct commission rather than indirect omission. Similarly babies born to single mothers may be allowed to die through social neglect (with or without first being dubbed illegitimate) or they may be allowed to die through exposure or even deliberately killed. The World Health Organization, as well as Backett and his colleagues writing under their auspices, speak of an "ethical imperative" that health care should be equitably distributed even at the cost of positive discrimination. This, of course, is a moral, not a logical, assumption, with recognized limitations in the practice even among those who work for WHO. Some contemporary societies may not subscribe to it all and for some that do, it may be a rhetorical future aspiration rather than a current reality. Qualification and exceptions may occur for gays or prostitute women, blacks or Hispanics, Kurds or Shiites, or often in Europe, immigrants in general (Berger and Mohr 1975). Similarly, medieval societies were often ready to sacrifice those who already had the plague for those who were not (yet) infected, just as some writers are now prepared to countenance the sacrifice of the HIV seropositive in order, they claim, to protect the lives of the (as yet) HIV seronegative (Collier 1987).

Quantity and Quality
in Epidemiology and Anthropology

Paradoxically it is the qualitatively and morally determined delimitation of risk by the epidemiologist that leads ultimately to its definition in quantitative terms: "The more accurate the measure of risk, the more clearly need for help is understood." The general public nevertheless ignores clearly marked and recognizable quantitative differences in risk. This leads anthropologists to define risk more qualitatively in terms of culture. It is not that the public suffers from a systematic and entrenched neglect of culture by social science in general as Douglas (1986:2) suggests, but its opposite—the taking not merely of culture but of cultures for granted.

As Backett and his colleagues recognize, the risk approach in epidemiology is not only a way of making health interventions more effective but also of justifying medical intervention. This is as true in relation to diseases, episodic incidents, where it might seem to the unsophisticated lay person and the unparanoid physician to need no justification, as it is in relation to such phenomena as instantaneous accidents. Above all the measurement, rather than mere description, of risk factors and their relative importance enables:

1. provision of a mechanism (significant metaphor) for surveillance (significant metonym) of population and services to see whether problems are being prevented and whether interventions are beneficial or otherwise;
2. prediction of level of care required by individuals or communities at different levels of risk; and
3. provision of anticipatory care and allocation of resources to individuals and communities at different levels of risk.

Finally, the epidemiological risk approach (in the spirit of Virchow; see Taylor and Rieger 1984) increases popular knowledge and presents it in a way in which it can be assimilated and used (adapted and paraphrased from Backett, Davies, and Petros-Barvasian 1984:4). This is in contrast to most curative medicine.

The dialogue about risk and justice tends to be conducted in two languages: traditional English rhetoric on behalf of regulation, and mathematical language on behalf of principles of free choice. This is reminiscent of a medieval court in which the native plaintiffs made their vernacular requests and were answered in dog Latin. The parallel case is in medical practice where the doctor speaks one language to colleagues and another to the patient. Is this an inevitable result of professionalization and does it carry an element of coercion? (Douglas 1986:13)

The Politics (and Nonpolitics) of Generality

The last points illustrate an uneasy and only partially questioned assumption, which Backett and his colleagues recognize but lack space and opportunity to explore. It is that the directly interventionist style of epidemiology, which seeks to combine research with health promotion at both societal and at individual levels, translates future patienthood into the present without the presence of disease or the usual intermediate stages of suffering and seeking help. At the same time it assumes responsibility not only for preventing any kind of activity that might lead to disease, but also to other undesired eventualities, like road accidents, the need for residential care, or school-age pregnancies, which curative medicine might reasonably have regarded, were it not for epidemiologists, as beyond its concerns. The wheel has come full circle from the medically despised love and general success potions of the south central African *ng'anga* to the contraceptive and sex-education discussions and discourse on stress of progressive primary health care physicians. Health For All by the year 2000 is, perhaps, not so much a call to abolish death as a call to medicalize, and thereby depoliticize, everything. Politicization survives in possibly fruitful ambiguity in WHO literature as the recognition of the potential of *intersectoral* contributions to the health of communities.

Politics, in Virchow's words, indeed becomes here medicine on a grand scale, although less grand member nation-states can make use of the clinical style of narrating to read in their own apparently apolitical interpretations, when Backett and his colleagues write for WHO,

> Other contributions to the health of the population derive, of course, from genetic, environmental, socioeconomic and educational factors as well as from social and family support systems. Measures of risk by linking these factors to outcomes however crudely—may direct attention to the need for changes in resource allocation, social services or life style for both community and individual. This could be done by allotting a measure of the "blame" (or a proportion of the total risk) to risk factors such as poor social support, illiteracy, poverty and malnutrition—that is to "causes" outside the formal health care system. (Backett, Davies, and Petros-Barvasian 1984:5)

Obviously a public health paper in a WHO series does not present such activities as having revolutionary potential, although they clearly played a part in revolutions as diverse as that of the Chinese, which sometimes presented the process in lived-narrative form as telling the bitter past in contrast to the happy present and in order to inspire work for a better future; and the rise to power in the Philippines of Cory Aquino supported by the Catholic Church and its own health institutions (Rifkin 1985). The revolutionary (and sometimes counterrevolutionary) nature of health activities is pointed to by writers on the recent struggles of Nicaragua and earlier struggles in Algeria (Donahue 1986; Fanon 1978; see also Morgan 1989). Reducing the risk of disease from ignorance increases the relative risk of reform or revolution of the body politic through knowledge. It also highlights the state of the individual somatic body affected by events in the recent personal past, as well as the legacies of nature on the species corporeal and of history incarnate on the nation. If, as is often the case in disadvantaged societies or groups, the epidemiological measurement of future risk coincides with present discontents and at the same time renders more precisely popular perceptions of causation in the recent past, it may be more than acceptable—it may be explosive.

The Nonpolitics (or Politics) of Specificity

One way in which precision is achieved in epidemiology is by pointing to closely defined outcomes. Emphasis is laid, for example, not just on child deaths but child deaths from gastroenteritis. Clearly established paths from risk to consequence (or to increased risk) are demonstrated by dose-response relationships, by repeatability, and by consistency. Finally, "natural" (because *bio*medical) plausibility for the observer/intervener must match cultural [and political] plausibility for the "patients." In administrative terms this is interpreted as a liberal determination "not to reject some of the traditional wisdom 'embodied' in folklore." The wisdom embodied not so much in folklore but in the maintenance of cultural identity may however itself be a risk factor to corporeal survival, even when recognized and tolerated as such by those who practice it. Examples of such recognition are the deliberate (but rationally understood and even calculated) taking of risks by rock climbers, motorcycle gang members, Prussian and cowboy duelists, headhunters, and the like. Taking recognized risks with the body incarnate, even at the price of the body corporeal, is often the principal way in which cultural groups, and the legitimation of power and independent identities within them, are initiated, reinforced, and maintained. Rational choice is always culturally constrained, if not culturally determined. Groups like Fore brain-eaters, Sudanese infibulators, needle-sharing IV drug users, and those men who still, or in the recent past, define their identity by their practice of unprotected (anal) intercourse, symbolize their identity unaware of the risks in these symbolic and actual breaches of body boundaries. No cultural forms are sacrosanct or even impervious to change. It is romanticism of a high order to ignore the "natural" danger or worse still to view such individually, socially, and culturally meaningful acts outside their context. Once prized behaviors are shown to be dangerous they may be abandoned or substituted by less risky or even protective, materially superficial if still symbolically penetrative, incarnate body techniques.

Conclusions

A risk approach to epidemiology is, in practice, often capable of bridging the natural/social, corporeal/incarnate gap in such a way as to avoid the interposition of the medical somatic. The evolutionary epoch, the social era, and the genetic instant are made intelligible to and modifiable in the individual, partly cultural, lifecourse. Such an approach also enables a medical intervention, or an intervention by health workers who have partially escaped from orthodox medical curative training, to be sensitive to opportunities for social as well as for natural preventive measures. Backett and his colleagues correctly observe,

> Medical care in the past has concentrated on associations where the pathological processes could be interrupted. This preoccupation has led to the neglect of the more tenuous links in the causal chain which, like poverty, are difficult but "non-medical" challenges. (Backett, Davies, and Petros-Barvasian 1984:13)

As Douglas (1986:60) notes, "The well-advertised risk generally turns out to be connected with legitimating moral principles." Moral, social, and political choices are always involved in discussing risks to the individual body—corporeal, somatic, or incarnate. Scheper-Hughes and Lock (1987) also argue that the (mindful) individual and the social and political body are, in the last analysis, an inseparable whole. The risk approach in epidemiology thus poses for its practitioners two initial choices: which outcomes to focus upon and which risk factors ought to be given priority. Like all choices these are surrounded by culturally defined moral problems in which power relations always have a central position.

In making the first choice, Backett and his colleagues suggest that considerable weight is to be given to community priorities, preferences, and concerns (*but in whose view?*); common problems are to be given higher priority than rare ones (*but common to whom?*); more serious undesired outcomes are to be given higher priority than less serious outcomes (*life threatening, perhaps; but to whose life: mother or child, old or young, elite or mass?*); easily preventable conditions are to be given priority over those less easily preventable (*but at whose cost to whom?*); and finally, those disorders with an upwardly moving frequency trend (*amongst what groups?*) are to be given priority rather than those that are static and declining.

In the second choice, as we have already seen, Backett and his colleagues address the problem in the context of another set of essentially sociological questions. Which risk factors should be emphasized for which individuals or category (health workers, policy makers, health educators, families, mothers, or individuals) and at what social level (individual, family, local community, or society?). It may have been inappropriate in the context in which they were writing to raise the problem of the political risk to health workers themselves. In Central America such choices have certainly cost many their lives and even in countries where social conflict is marked by premature death from chronic disability rather than sudden violent death, senior health educators making the right choice from the point of view of epidemiology but the wrong one in the eyes of government have found their own careers and that of the agencies they headed cut short.

I began this chapter by suggesting that in a changing disease and medical environment, some epidemiologists will be tempted, having identified risk groups, to remain with them and to lead themselves astray by neglecting to advance to concepts of risk factor and behavior. Similarly, anthropologists have been tempted to take cultures as their units of analysis imposing an artifactual egalitarian homogeneity (and often an atemporal ahistoricity or a collusively populist and timeless romantic historicism) on cultures as diverse as the Navajo, the Nuer, the inhabitants of Bali, and various biomedicines. I have here tried to build upon but not to abandon attempts to solve the units of analysis dilemma by drawing selectively on Scheper-Hughes and Lock's three bodies, Young's discourses of production, and Strauss and his colleagues' trajectories. The analysis of narratives within the complexity of a culture or a social organization helps to reveal process. The many narratives told by or discernible in the body, in sickness and in health, in nature and in culture, have an enlightening and interpretive importance far beyond the legitimate concerns of mere medical anthropology or the reductionist concerns of so called body language. I hope that I have begun to show this through consideration of the narrative styles of one section of the epidemiological clan of the tribe of Western medicine.

Note

1. My earlier attempts to formulate these ideas will be found in Frankenberg 1986a, 1986b, 1986c, 1988, and especially 1992. Discussions with Shirley
Lindenbaum, Margaret Lock, Judith Marks, and Thomas Ob have been particularly helpful.

References

Backett, E. Maurice, A. Michael Davies, and Angèle Petros-Barvazian.
1984   *The Risk Approach in Health Care.* Public Health Paper no. 76.
        Geneva: World Health Organization.
Baldwin, Ernest
1962   *The Nature of Biochemistry.* Cambridge: Cambridge University
        Press.
Bell, Colin, and Helen Roberts, eds.
1984   *Social Researching: Politics, Problems, Practice.* London: Rout-
        ledge and Kegan Paul.
Berger, John, and Jean Mohr
1975   *A Seventh Man.* London: Penguin Books.
Brody, Howard
1987   *Stories of Sickness.* New Haven, Conn.: Yale University Press.
Brown, George, and Tirril Harris
1978   *Social Origins of Depression: A Study of Psychiatric Disorder in
        Women.* London: Tavistock Publications.
Browner, C. H., Bernard R. Ortiz De Montellano, and Arthur Rubel
1988   A Methodology for Cross-Cultural Ethnomedical Research. With
        comments. *Current Anthropology* 29(5) 681–702.
Carballo, Manuel
1987   Address to 10th Social Science and Medicine Conference, Sitges,
        Barcelona.
Caudill, William
1958   *The Psychiatric Hospital as a Small Society.* Cambridge, Mass.: Har-
        vard University Press.
Clifford, James, and George E. Marcus, eds.
1986   *Writing Culture: The Poetics and Politics of Ethnography.* Berkeley,
        Los Angeles, London: University of California Press.
Collier, Caroline
1987   *The Twentieth Century Plague.* Tring, England: Lion Paperbacks.
Comaroff, Jean
1982   Medicine, Symbol and Ideology. In *The Problem of Medical Knowl-
        edge: Examining the Social Construction of Medicine,* Peter Wright
        and Andrew Treacher, eds., pp. 49–68. Edinburgh: Edinburgh Uni-
        versity Press.

Donahue, John M.
1985   *The Nicaraguan Revolution in Health.* South Hadley, Mass.: Bergin and Harvey.
Douglas, Mary
1986   *Risk Acceptability According to the Social Sciences.* London: Routledge and Kegan Paul.
1987   *How Institutions Think.* London: Routledge and Kegan Paul (Syracuse, N.Y.: Syracuse University Press, 1986).
Dunn, Frederick L., and Craig R. Janes
1986   Introduction: Medical Anthropology and Epidemiology. In *Anthropology and Epidemiology,* Craig R. Janes, Ron Stall, and Sandra M. Gifford, eds., pp. 3–34. Dordrecht, Netherlands: D. Reidel.
Dutton, Diana B.
1988   *Worse then the Disease: Pitfalls of Medical Progress.* Cambridge, England and New York: Cambridge University Press.
Estroff, Sue
1981   *Making it Crazy.* Berkeley, Los Angeles, London: University of California Press.
Fabian, Johannes
1983   *Time and the Other: How Anthropology Makes its Object.* New York: Columbia University Press.
Fanon, Frantz
1978   Medicine and Colonialism. In *The Cultural Crisis of Modern Medicine,* John Ehrenreich, ed., pp. 229–251. New York: Monthly Review Press.
Feuchtwang, Stephan
1973   The Colonial Formation of British Social Anthropology. In *Anthropology and the Colonial Encounter,* Talal Asad, ed., pp. 71–100. London: Ithaca Press.
Foster, George M., Thayer Scudder, Elizabeth Colson, and Robert V. Kemper, eds.
1979   *Long-Term Field Research in Social Anthropology.* London: Academic Press.
Frankenberg, Ronald
1984   Incidence or Incidents: Political and Methodological Underpinnings of a Health Research Process in a Small Italian Town. In *Social Researching: Politics, Problems, Practice,* Colin Bell and Helen Roberts, eds., pp. 88–103. London: Routledge and Kegan Paul.
1986a   Sickness as Cultural Performance: Drama, Trajectory and Pilgrimage; Root Metaphors and the Making Social of Disease. *International Journal of Health Services* 16(4):603–626.
1986b   Time for the Subject? Time of the Subject? Time in the Subjects: Medical Anthropology and Clinical Medicine Disentangled. Paper presented at the American Anthropological Association annual meeting, Centre for Medical Social Anthropology, University of Keele, Staffordshire, England.

1986c   Comment in Arthur Kleinman, *Current Anthropology* 27(5):499–509.
1988   Your Time or Mine? An Anthropological View of the Tragic Temporal Contradictions of Biomedical Practice. *International Journal of Health Services* 18(1):11–34.
In press Radical Approaches to Risk and Culture in British Community Epidemiology: Targets, Relative Risk and "Candidates" and the Impact of HIV/AIDS. *Social Science and Medicine*.
Frankenberg, Ronald, ed.
1988   Gramsci, Marxism and Phenomenology: Essays for the Development of Critical Medical Anthropology. *Medical Anthropology Quarterly*, n.s., 2(4).
Frankenberg, Ronald, and Joyce Leeson
1976   Disease, Illness and Sickness: Aspects of the Choice of Healer in a Lusaka Suburb. In *Social Anthropology and Medicine*, Joseph Loudon, ed., pp. 223–258. London and New York: Academic Press.
Gaines, Atwood D., and Robert A. Hahn
1986   Among the Physicians: Encounter, Exchange and Transformation. In *Physicians of Western Medicine: Anthropological Approaches to Theory and Practice*, Robert A. Hahn and Atwood D. Gaines, eds., pp. 3–22. Dordrecht, Netherlands: D. Reidel.
Geertz, Clifford
1988   *Works and Lives: The Anthropologist as Author.* Palo Alto, Calif.: University Press.
Genette, Gerard
1980   *Narrative Discourse.* Ithaca, N.Y.: Cornell University Press.
1988   *Narrative Discourse Revisited.* Ithaca, N.Y. Cornell University Press.
Gordon, Deborah
1988   Tenacious Assumptions in Western Medicine. In *Biomedicine Examined,* Margaret Lock and Deborah Gordon, eds., pp. 19–56. Dordrecht, Netherlands: Kluwer Academic Publishers.
Gramsci, Antonio
1971   *Selections from the Prison Notebooks.* London: Lawrence and Wishart.
Hahn, Robert A.
1985   Rethinking "Illness" and "Disease." *Contributions to Asian Studies* 18:1–22.
Helman, Cecil
1987   Heart Disease and the Cultural Construction of Time: The Type A Behaviour Pattern as a Western Culture-Bound Syndrome. *Social Science and Medicine* 25(9):969–979.
Janes, Craig R., Ron Stall, and Sandra M. Gifford, eds.
1986   *Anthropology and Epidemiology.* Dordrecht, Netherlands: D. Reidel.

Kapferer, Bruce
1983   *A Celebration of Demons: Exorcism and the Aesthetics of Healing in Sri Lanka.* Bloomington: Indiana University Press.
1988   Commentary—Gramsci's Body and a Critical Medical Anthropology. *Medical Anthropology Quarterly* ns. 2(4):426–432.

Kleinman, Arthur
1986   Social Origins of Distress and Disease: Depression, Neurasthenia and Pain in Modern China. Review. *Current Anthropology* 27(5): 499–509.
1988   *The Illness Narratives: Suffering, Healing and the Human Condition.* Basic Books, New York.

Kleinman, Arthur, and Byron Good, eds.
1985   *Culture and Depression.* Berkeley, Los Angeles, London: University of California Press.

Kleinman, Arthur, and Joan Kleinman
1985   Somatization: The Interconnections in Chinese Society among Culture, Depressive Experiences and the Meaning of Pain. In *Culture and Depression,* Arthur Kleinman and Byron Good, eds., pp. 429–490. Berkeley, Los Angeles, London: University of California Press.

Kuhn, Thomas S.
1962   *The Structure of Scientific Revolutions.* Chicago: University of Chicago Press.

Kushlick, Albert, D. Felce, J. Palmer, and J. Smith
1976   *Evidence of the Committee of Inquiry into Mental Handicap Nursing and Care (The Jay Committee).* HCERT Research Report 129. Winchester: Wessex Regional Health Authority.

Lancaster, Jane B., and Beatrix A. Hamburg, eds.
1986   *School Age Pregnancy and Parenthood: Biosocial Dimensions.* New York: Aldine de Gruyter.

Lindenbaum, Shirley
1979   *Kuru Socery.* New York: Mayfield.

Lock, Margaret, and Deborah Gordon, eds.
1988   *Biomedicine Examined.* Dordrecht, Netherlands: Kluwer Academic Publishers.

Loudon, Joseph, ed.
1976   *Social Anthropology and Medicine.* Association of Social Anthropologists Monograph 13. New York: Academic Press.

Morgan, Lynn M., ed.
1989   The Political Economy of Primary Health Care in Costa Rica, Guatemala, Nicaragua, and El Salvador. *Medical Anthropology Quarterly,* n.s., 3(3).

Nichols, Eve K.
1988   *Human Gene Therapy.* Cambridge, Mass.: Institute of Medicine/National Academy of Sciences, Harvard University Press.

Obeyesekere, Gananath
1981   *Medusa's Hair.* Chicago: University of Chicago Press.
Rapoport, Robert, and Rhona Rapoport
1960   *Community as Doctor.* London: Tavistock.
Rifkin, Susan B.
1985   *Health Planning and Community Participation: Case Studies in South-East Asia.* Beckenham, Kent, England: Croomhelm.
Sacks, Oliver
1986   *A Leg to Stand On.* London: Picador.
Scheper-Hughes, Nancy, and Margaret Lock
1987   The Mindful Body: A Prolegomenon to Future Work in Medical Anthropology. *Medical Anthropology Quarterly* n.s. 1(1):16–41.
Strauss, Anselm, Shizuko Fagerhaugh, Barbara Suczek, and Carolyn Weiner
1985   *Social Organization of Medical Work.* London and Chicago: University of Chicago Press.
Taussig, Michael
1980   Reification and the Consciousness of the Patient. *Social Science and Medicine* 14B:3–13.
Taylor, Rex, and Annelie Rieger
1984   Rudolf Virchow on the Typhus Epidemic in Upper Silesia. *Sociology of Health and Illness* 6(2):201–217.
Trostle, James
1986   Early Work in Anthropology and Epidemiology from Social Medicine to the Germ Theory, 1840 to 1920. In *Anthropology and Epidemiology,* Craig R. Janes, Ron Stall, and Sandra M. Gifford, eds., pp. 35–58. Dordrecht, Netherlands: Reidel.
Turner, Victor
1968   *The Drums of Affliction.* London: Hutchinson for the International African Institute.
Williams, Gareth
1984   The Genesis of Chronic Illness: Narrative Reconstruction. *Sociology of Health and Illness* 6(2):185–200.
Wright, Peter, and Andrew Treacher, eds.
1982   *The Problem of Medical Knowledge: Examining the Social Construction of Medicine.* Edinburgh: University of Edinburgh Press.
Young, Allan
1980   The Discourse on Stress and the Reproduction of Conventional Knowledge. *Social Science and Medicine* 14B:133–146.
1982   The Anthropologies of Illness and Sickness. *Annual Review of Anthropology* 11:257–285.

Part Four

Constructing the
Illness Experience

Introduction

Constructing the Illness Experience

The experience of illness and the creation of medical categories are closely related processes. In Chapter 11, Sue Estroff explores the experience of disability and chronicity among persons with persistent psychiatric disorders, tracing the path by which persons who "have" an illness become persons who "are" an illness. Chronicity, she suggests, consists of a fusion of identity with diagnosis. Moreover, social welfare and health policies that codify cultural ideas about identity, illness, and productive activity aid in constricting social roles to a core of patienthood. Her analysis of the contradictions in the mental health sector arrives at the conclusion that in providing treatment, the dependency of patients is perpetuated, not ended—reminding us of Lorna Rhodes's more disillusioned statement that it is the de facto function of the health sector to employ mental health professionals, not to reduce dependency.

The second chapter in this section provides a further demonstration of the "creative" as well as the curative powers of Western medicine. In his investigation of Chagas disease, Roberto Briceño-León describes a condition caused by a parasite passed to humans by an insect that resides in the thatched roofs, cracks, and holes of poor domestic dwellings in Venezuela. Chagas disease, however, is a biomedical syndrome not recognized during most of its course by its sufferers (since it is at first asymptomatic, and cardiac complications are slow to take effect). Thus a broad attack on the spread of Chagas disease is said to depend ultimately on the recognition of disorder in indigenous reckoning.

Resisting a narrow focus on the disease, however, the research team adopted an applied approach. Houses were modified using local materials and local labor in a trial that also identified the social and psychological factors that led certain villagers to participate in the scheme. The findings provided the basis for demonstrating to public health authorities that changes in local health behavior and in the operation of the ministry of health would be more effective than medical intervention in controlling the disease.

The argument that institutional activities should not focus on the disease as a unit of analysis echoes Frankenberg's call for a wider analytic frame in epidemiological intervention. The irony here lies in the fact that a fully effective program for eradicating Chagas disease rests to some degree on the acceptance of a biomedical category as well as the "medicalization" of beliefs and behaviors currently viewed as unrelated by those who suffer from the condition.

As these two chapters illustrate, research into the experience of illness provides additional clues about the processes by which certain voices and institutional forms come to exercise their influence. As the study of Chagas disease also shows, however, interventions that alter the behaviors and circumstances that contribute to poor health may succeed in some contexts without first changing people's beliefs about disease causation.

11

Identity, Disability, and Schizophrenia

The Problem of Chronicity

Sue E. Estroff

Introduction

Marketing An Anthropology of Chronicity and Disability

A great deal of ink has been spilled debating the roles of sociocultural factors as conspirators that cause disease and affliction (Dunham 1968). Far less attention has focused on prognosis, outcome, accommodation, course, and response. These are the other ends of the illness event or sickness process, and are also a means for investigating the influence of sociocultural stuff on illness. Questions about who gets sick with what and why are worthy, but well worn. Who does *not get well,* and *why,* and *what happens to and about them* are topics less well understood and of at least equal importance for medical anthropology.

I take our tasks as medical anthropologists as another rationale for the study of chronicity. In one sense, we are up to what anthropologists have always been up to. But beyond this, there is almost always another project and another audience for our work. This second project involves making useful inquiry into suffering, healing, illness, and injury. Many of us work in settings and with subjects where the value of our findings is never presumed, but always to be demonstrated to the other audience. The challenge to contribute, to assist in the healing process (even if mainly via insight or interpretation), is strong. The pragmatic clinical audience and the pained, expectant subjects of study invite more than brilliant description. The call, often silent but nonetheless compelling, is for applicability, for implications, for "So what?" to be answered squarely and plainly.

Individuals who do not get well, and whose afflictions persist and baffle, represent substantial challenges to their kin and communities, and to biomedicine and other systems of healing.

Another reason for attending to chronic illness and disability is more theoretical in nature and is the alluring *possibility* of trying to "account for culture." Variations in prognosis for persons with biomedically similar debilitating conditions in the same settings, and in different sociocultural contexts, provide the opportunity for viable comparative research. Such promise has driven multicultural studies like the International Pilot Study of Schizophrenia Follow-Up (WHO 1979; Leff et al. 1992). Haunted by methodological goblins, the IPSS Follow-Up nonetheless represents one of very few investigations of differential outcome (of a debatably similar affliction), not simply prevalence and incidence, across national and cultural boundaries. The study of persons with unresolved illnesses and enduring, uncustomary dysfunction arising from *similar enough* conditions provides an illuminating beginning for both culture-specific and comparative outcome research, despite all the problems.

Study of those who remain infirmed and responses to them appeals also for methodological reasons. Logistically, one need not be present for the unpredictable onset and resolution of an episode of acute illness or injury. There is more time to locate and study with and about informants as the live process unfolds, relying less on retrospective reconstruction of an illness event. The longer time frame also permits careful observation of accommodation and assignation of meaning among kin and community (Kleinman 1988). Persistent, debilitating sickness perhaps poses a cumulatively more extensive burden on kin and community, which may be more readily observed and more reliably documented than a brief illness or injury (cf. Kaufert and Kaufert 1984).

While this advertisement could continue, I make final note of the growing concern in all quarters about the increasing number, if not visibility, of disabled persons in the West (Strauss and Corbin 1988; Institute of Medicine 1990; Stone 1984; Albrecht and Levy 1984). Sheer magnitude of the phenomenon recommends it for attention. Monroe Berkowitz (1986:192) estimates that there were 8.3 million severely disabled adults in the U.S. in 1983. There is evidence that similar trends exist in nearly all of western Europe, and that there are increasing numbers of disabled social welfare recipients and public and private expenditures in their behalf (Stone 1984:8). Nora Croce (1987) suggests the problems are not confined to the developed world, estimating that 90 percent of the 500 million persons with disabilities globally live in the developing world. Despite disputes over definitions and methods for counting, it seems clear enough that chronic illness and disablement are sociomedical subjects of some size and currency (Conrad 1987; Gerhardt 1990).

Over the past decade, "disability studies" has emerged as a discrete multidisciplinary enterprise, with the requisite professional society (The Society for Disability Studies), several new journals (e.g., *The Journal for Disability Policy Studies*), and a number of influential publications (e.g., Kleinman 1988; Zola 1982; Gerhardt 1990). Historically, there have been three broad types of disability work: (1) large-scale, econometric, demographic, or expenditure-focused analyses of the epidemiology of disabling conditions (e.g., Wolfe and Haveman 1990; Chirikos 1989); (2) ethnographic, narrative-biographical, and life history accounts of disabled persons (e.g., Kaufman 1988; Edgerton 1967; Ablon 1984; Kuckelman and Hamera 1986); and (3) analyses of national policies and clinical services for disabled persons (e.g., Strauss and Glaser 1975; Institute of Medicine 1990). The narrative, ethnographic area is enormously active at present, attracting anthropologists, qualitatively inclined sociologists, and clinicians with various perspectives. Perhaps most interesting is the relatively recent arrival of persons with disabilities and their relatives to the scholarly and literary enterprise (e.g., Hatfield 1986; Campbell 1991). An unprecedented interaction between subjects and scholars promises a lively field for the next decade.

The Course and Synopsis of This Chapter

In this chapter, I convey an intermediate formulation of chronicity, emphasizing analytic and methodological challenges posed by individuals whose impaired functioning and experience of suffering persist over time, often a lifetime. Specifically, I focus on the sociocultural construction and experience of disability and chronicity among persons who have schizophrenia and other severe, persistent psychiatric disorders. How does an individual who experiences psychosis—an internal, subjective, usually time-limited, altered sense of self, other, and environment— become "a schizophrenic," "a chronic," "a disabled person," with clinical, social, and political designations and identities? How does the researcher identify, document, and assess multiple, complex processes that occur over a lengthy time span, often out of awareness and out of public view, with informants who are thought to be unable to report accurately?

In response to the goals of this volume, the components of the approach include: (1) symbolic and sociocultural processes: "I am" illnesses and transformations of self and identity; (2) a political economy of disability: dependence and carrying capacities; and (3) biological and epidemiological dimensions: chronic disease or defeated person? In the following pages, each approach is introduced and discussed, accompanied by supporting data from a variety of disciplines and sources. Where pertinent, methodological concerns and strategies pertaining to data, data gathering, and analysis are examined.

The proposed analysis is applied to Western, industrialized settings and is not intended, at this stage, to account for chronicity in other cultural contexts. Though currently accumulating at a fantastic pace, data are scarce enough regarding disabled persons in other cultural settings, and my focus at this juncture is on the complex U.S. sociocultural systems I have studied.

Recently, I returned to the field to begin a follow-up study of the clients and staff who were the informants for an earlier investigation (Estroff 1985). Though continuing, the current research provides some data and stimulates conceptual rethinking for the present formulation. I was delighted to find seven of the twenty-four clients who were located markedly improved; some were nearly unrecognizable. An equal number had deteriorated seriously and were leading miserable lives, excruciating to chronicle. The ten in the "about the same" category had made gains in some areas and experienced losses in others. Two of the twenty-four have full-time jobs and no longer receive disability income (Supplemental Security Income [SSI]), and two work part-time and continue to receive SSI. None of the remainder (twenty) is employed and all receive SSI. One has lived in an institutional setting—a county nursing home—for all of the intervening decade. The others reside in apartments or rooms in the community, receiving varying degrees of psychiatric care and other rehabilitative services. This substantial diversity *and* commonality in current circumstance replicates patterns apparent among the group ten years ago. Yet I could not then have predicted who would decline or improve, and am certain to be occupied for some time accounting for these various trajectories and pathways.

A note on terminology is needed as I have, unhappily, chosen to discuss two subject areas fraught with profusion and confusion of terms. The terminological morass involved in the literature on personhood is substantial. For purposes of convenience only, I use *self* to refer to the inner, personal, private, "I," experienced and known subjectivity; and *identity* to refer to the public, social, other-perceived and informed, "me," role-related aspects. Differences among the terms pathology, impairment (functional and residual), and disability are more widely agreed upon, and I follow convention here. I use *chronicity* to refer to the persistence in time of limitations and suffering *and* to the resulting disabilities as they are socially and culturally defined and lived.

Briefly, my interpretation is that chronicity consists of a fusion of identity with diagnosis, a transformation of self to self and with others. We observe a constriction of social roles and identities to a core of patienthood and disablement, and an engulfment, loss, and often unauthorized but nonetheless demoralizing change of self from a person who *has* an illness to someone who *is* an illness or diagnosis. "I am fundamentally denied," protests a woman with multiple sclerosis (Corbin and Strauss 1987:249). With subtlety and with silent, penetrating force, a life history becomes a course of sickness and vice versa. We trace the development of a person who experiences an event (a psychotic episode, psychiatric treatment) into a type or category of negatively valued, dysfunctional, and chronically ill, disabled person. This transformation occurs over time, through private experience and public response, through simultaneous political, cultural, and healing (clinical) processes, among kin and with strangers (Glass 1987; Kovel 1987). Phillips (1990) makes a similar argument about physically disabled persons, suggesting that "physiological damage spreads, albeit metaphorically, to the total personality and life circumstances of the disabled individual." Our subject is then recounting the loss of the subject that occurs when disease designations and experience overwhelm individuals who do not "get well."

I argue further that social welfare and health policies codify cultural ideas about identity, illness, and productive activity. These are then expressed in mental health care systems that—in the U.S. in particular—facilitate, indeed operate a political economy of disability construction among severely mentally ill persons (see also Mollica 1987). Among the factors contributing to chronicity are (1) the growing number of and demand for jobs by mental health professionals (Witkin et al. 1987);(2) (fueled by) ardent public and political advocacy and espousal of medical models of mental illness among family members (Wasow 1982; McLean 1990); and (3) income maintenance resources that are illness-tested and bound to deservedness through disability (Stone 1979; Yelin 1989). Attention to these factors is necessarily selective rather than inclusive.

At the sociocultural core of chronicity in the U.S. are two interrelated, deceptively simple questions or suspicions. These apply to individuals as well as to social responses to them. The questions are: *can't* or *won't, inability* or *refusal, dysfunction* or *defiance?* Can't the person with schizophrenia get better/function/participate in producing activities? Or *won't* they? (Murphy et al. 1988; Yelin 1986, 1989). Are they *crazy* or *lazy?* (Foucault 1965:56). Is biomedical psychiatry and its large fan club, U.S. society (and the more numerous psychologists and social workers), *able* to provide more and better treatment and resources, or *won't* we? Are we *unable* or *unwilling* to respond to these persons in rehabilitative and restorative ways? Are our responses therapeutic or punitive? Or more accurately, why are they a mixture of both?

The "can't versus won't" controversy underlies—and, I suggest, explains—much of the apparent ambivalence in the West about persons who are chronically ill and disabled (Stein 1979). We cannot reward role refusal, but must assist inability borne of innocent, impaired functioning. We cannot invite or tolerate large scale, protracted defiance of functional requirements, but we should not punish and neglect those who are *actually* unable to contribute at expected levels. These complementary and reciprocal skepticisms applied to individuals, expressed in healing response and in public sentiment, fuel much of the political and clinical debate surrounding chronicity and disability in the West. A moving poem written by a psychiatric patient to staff illustrates this succinctly: "I have fallen from grace in your eyes. How *uncooperative* of me not to be well" (emphasis added).

Underlying and related to the dysfunction or defiance question is a more profound Western cultural problem regarding the ontological status of diseases. Are they *real*—that is, visible, verifiable, manifest in human biological material? *Real* diseases cause *actual* inability, the cultural-biomedical code asserts (Gordon 1988). Apparent dysfunction in the absence of *real* disease raises doubts all around and invokes repeated searches for offending organic matter. Thus the obsessive quest for and sometime construction of biomedical (real) mechanisms and explanations to account for unremitting suffering, pain, and disablement (see Fabrega 1987).

To illustrate, kin advocates for mentally ill persons picture on one of their national campaign posters a human brain. The slogan reads, "The brain is part of the body. It TOO can become ill. Schizophrenia, Depressive Disorders are *no-fault* brain illnesses." Legitimate incapacity arises only from real disease; if there is no real disease, incapacity may be interpreted as unwillingness or defiance in disguise. Mental disorders are especially well-qualified candidates for suspicions of disguised defiance or cloaked refusal, stalled still in the undecided-on disease lane (Erikson 1957; Ingleby 1982). Diagnosis then becomes a form of *dispute resolution* about deservedness for the suffering, malfunctional individual between the person and kin and between the individual and a larger social audience (Stone 1979). When diagnosis alone is ineffective, political advocacy by kin and afflicted individuals seeks to affirm deservedness and need through a variety of idioms of affliction.

Having telegraphed the thrust of the orientation taken here, we now consider more carefully the three components.

Symbolic and Sociocultural Processes: "I am" Illness and Transformations of Self and Identity

The following narration by Lara Jefferson conveys the conflicted process of joining her self with her mental illness, and the change in her sense of self:

Here I sit, even though I *was* one time a so-called intelligent *member of society.* . . . Unless I learn to think differently, I *shall* shortly *be incurably insane.* . . . *Something* has happened to me—I do not know what. All that *was my former self* has crumbled and fallen together and a *creature* has emerged of whom *I know nothing. She* is a *stranger* to *me.* . . . *Her* name is insanity. As long as there is a *shred of me left,* I dare not do other than try to find some balance between the *conflicting forces* driving me. . . . Madness. *It* has always been waiting before me . . . *it* did overtake me. . . . *It* caught *me* and swept *me. I* cannot escape *it*—*I* cannot face *it*— how can *I* endure *it.* . . . I can recall with humor the old sensation I had on finding that a *crazy woman* had moved into *my body.* . . . She is *not real*— she is *not I*—I never saw her before *I dreamed her.* . . . There is only a shadow remaining of the *person I used to be.* My whole *former life* has fallen away so completely. . . . If the *person I used to be* could not prevent the birth of the *person I have become.* . . . I looked at the *others*—and felt an odd feeling of *kinship.* . . as long as this *crazy woman I have become* wants to rave. . . . *I* know not how to deal with *her* because *she is a maniac.* Because *she is I*—and because I still have myself on my hands, even if *I am a maniac, I* must deal with *me* somehow. (1974:11–25, emphasis added)

At first, she rejects "it" (madness) and the stranger in her body. Gradually, "it" becomes "I." The pronouns change from third to first person, the verbs from past to present tense. Her former self crumbles; she feels kinship with the other patients. She *had* a former life and *was* another person until madness overtakes and becomes "me." The dreamed-up, crazy woman in her body becomes more real, less alien. This is the process, elegantly conveyed, that I wish to discuss here: the transformation of self that occurs in "I am" illness.

Sociocultural Notions of Self and Sickness

Cultural conceptions of person, self, and identity enjoy renewed attention recently, though the roots of these discussions run deeply into anthropological inquiry (Robbins 1973; Carrithers, Collins, and Lukes

1985; Shweder and Bourne 1984; La Fontaine 1985; Jacobson-Widding 1983). The relationship of these concepts to disease and illness has received somewhat less press from medical anthropologists, though there are significant exceptions (e.g., Fabrega and Manning 1972; Bateson 1972; Edgerton and Sabagh 1962).

Medical sociologists concerned with deviance and physical and mental disability, and social psychologists interested in identity formation, have produced a more extensive and explicit body of descriptive, experimental, and theoretical literature about the self, identity, and illness (see for example Charmaz 1987; Denzin 1987; Goffman 1963; Gara et al. 1987; Shrauger and Schoeneman 1979; Swann 1987; Lofland 1969; Rosenberg and Kaplan 1982). Western psychiatrists and psychologists have generated a similarly enormous corpus of propositions or ethnotheories about normal and abnormal selves, apparently oblivious to the ethnocentric nature of their enterprise (e.g., Kohut and Wolf 1978).

It is not, I think, accidental that Erving Goffman, Norman Denzin, Kai Erikson, John Lofland, and others (e.g., Snow and Anderson 1987) formulate and incorporate theories of self and identity as they examine alcoholism, homelessness, deviance of various types, and serious mental illness—all chronic conditions. There is ample reason to suspect that these analyses convey culturally authentic interpretations of long-term illness and the process of chronicity. I take this material as largely ethnographic, and as such persuasive about Western experiences with and understandings of disability and identity. Second, the prominence of the notion of self in Western ethnotheories of psychiatric disorder in general, and of schizophrenia in particular, is similarly convincing and suggestive of culture-specific validity. The *Diagnostic and Statistical Manual* of the American Psychiatric Association (DSM IIIR) is quite explicit in this regard. In this official description of symptoms of schizophrenia we read, "The sense of self that gives the normal person a feeling of individuality, uniqueness, and self-direction is frequently disturbed. This is sometimes referred to as loss of ego boundaries and is frequently manifested by extreme perplexity about one's own identity" (APA 1987). With this in mind, we examine briefly some of the anthropological contributions.

Gregory Bateson (1972) challenges the usefulness of a Western notion of self as a "delimited agent" in understanding the alcoholic. He writes that the self "network" is "not bounded by the skin but includes all external pathways along which information can travel" (1972:319)— for example, the blind man's cane. Bateson's concept of self is "only a small part of a much larger trial-and-error system which does the thinking, acting, and deciding" (1972:331). Robert Edgerton and Georges Sabagh (1962) work with a Western notion of self as socially constructed and individually experienced. Turning Goffman on his ear, they suggest that mentally retarded persons in institutions have "a surprisingly good opportunity for the maintenance or development of an acceptable—that is—nonretarded-self concept" (1962:271).

In a very important paper, germane to the subject of this one, Horacio Fabrega and Peter Manning (1972) acknowledge cultural variations in the experience of illness, and address explicitly the impact on self and identity of illness, especially that which is chronic. They also employ a Western sociological-psychological notion of self. Describing schizophrenia as a distinctive type of unremitting illness, they assert, "It is not possible to dissociate the self from the disease. . . . The manifestations, as it were, *become* the self or person" (1972:110, my emphasis). Further "in mental illness, it can be said that *the self is the illness,*" and mental illness is described as "self-bound" (1972:113, emphasis added). This position exemplifies both the widely held view of the special relationship between self and mental illness, and the fusion of self and psychiatric sickness identified by other Western social scientists, particularly those of the symbolic interactionist and labeling schools (Goffman 1961; Rosenberg 1984; Scheff 1984).

John M. Townsend (1976) challenges Goffman's widely accepted contention that mental patients convert or change their self-concepts or private selves in institutions. Cleverly, he demonstrates the lack of empirical support for the introjection of a mentally ill self. In his own research in Germany and the U.S., a majority of patient informants denied that they were mentally ill, declining to self-label. Rather, Townsend contends, the research confirms only that mental *patients* accept their public and social *status* as *patients,* not that they have changed their self-evaluations and self-concepts. This is a serious criticism, and raises concerns that are methodological as well as substantive. Whether people who have psychiatric disorders self-label and to whom this is revealed—whether they alter their sense of self, inside and outside of institutions or treatment settings, and the means for recognizing their experience and definition of self, remain problematic.

In the preceding, we encounter Western, binary notions of bounded inner and outer selves and personal and social identities, and distinctions between public role or status and private experience (Fabrega 1989). In addition, the controversy among students of the self and identity about constancy versus continual adaptation of identity and self-definition raises its unresolved head (see Ewing 1990). Hopelessly entangled in methodological debate (about experimental versus naturalistically collected data), the scholarly discourse is also accompanied by a confusingly long list of terms for layers, parts, and compartments of the person.

To summarize and continue, what can be made of the self-sickness and illness-identity dynamic? In Western cultural settings, sickness is seen to alter the self in an almost casual way. One might say, "I don't feel like myself" to indicate illness, usually vague or undiagnosed and minor in scope. Others comment similarly, "You haven't seemed yourself," or, "You look more like yourself" to acknowledge illness or recovery. While perhaps less literal than the interpretation advocated here, these statements and ideas illustrate that in a symbolic way, *we are not ourselves* when ill and dysfunctional (Brody 1987; Herzlich and Pierret 1987). The loss of customary function associated with illness is marked as temporary, and *not me*. We find this self unfamiliar, and prefer not to claim it. Within this cultural and symbolic nest of meaning, a more profound and exaggerated process occurs when the affliction is severe and long-lasting (Estroff 1989).

Data that are explicit regarding the relationship of personhood to infirmity in other cultural settings are not abundant, and found most frequently in the work of psychological anthropologists and cross-cultural psychologists (e.g., Kapferer 1979; Marsella 1980). Acknowledging that ideas of self and illness vary profoundly from place to place, we may still extend the analysis for purposes of focusing and deepening the discussion. Richard Robbins (1973) and John Blacking (1983) have suggested that the Western concept of self may be seen to be equivalent to the idea of soul in other cultural contexts. Taking this perspective for the present, I construe two propositions:

1. *Loss or absence of the self/soul results in illness* (Landy 1983; Kohut and Wolf 1978); and,

2. *Illness results in alteration and/or loss of self/soul* (Charmaz 1983, 1987; Glass 1987; Kovel 1987).

We focus on the second here.

"I am" Illnesses: Some Preliminary Considerations

Schizophrenia belongs to a Western category of enduring affliction that I call "I am" Illnesses. Epilepsy, diabetes, alcoholism, and hemophilia are also such illnesses, distinguished by the linguistic joining of identity with diagnosis. Individuals may say, "I *am* a schizophrenic," "I am an alcoholic," "I *am* an epileptic," and so forth. Others may refer to these persons similarly. "She *is* a diabetic," "He *is* a spastic." There is more than grammatical accident at work here, more than the technical possibility of adding the *ic* suffix to a diagnostic term. Other chronic diseases such as multiple sclerosis and cerebral palsy do not conform to this linguistic convention, and in common usage are referred to in possessive terms—for example, "I *have* arthritis," "I *have* cystic fibrosis." Table 1 lists some chronic "I am" and "I have" illnesses.

I cannot adequately scrutinize here all the distinguishing characteristics between these two types of conditions, but I wish to make the point that severity of dysfunction and persistence in time, common to these conditions, are not sufficient to place an illness into the "I am" versus "I have" category. AIDS, for example, is an "I have" illness, which may be attributable to an already politically active original target population—successful in their campaign to depathologize their sexual preferences—but nonetheless socially labeled with the "I am" condition of homosexuality. AIDS also became a public concern during a period of intense advocacy for person-first language by the disabled community (perhaps most evident in the Americans WITH Disabilities Act of 1990).

It appears that compared to "I have" conditions, "I am" illnesses are more mysterious and more stigmatized, entail more disruptive, disapproved expression, and are more likely to be centered in the brain or to involve cognitive function. They are also more offensive to moral convention regarding individual restraint and responsibility. The "I am" illnesses tend to include those where attributions of blame for the condition rest with the individual—for example, drinking to excess (alcoholism), driving a car recklessly (paraplegia, quadriplegia). Leaving aside this inviting and important discussion, some synthesis is in order.

Essentially, the argument is that Western notions of the nature of schizophrenia (and perhaps other chronic, debilitating conditions) combine with Western notions of the self and identity to produce "I am" Illnesses, a fusion of self with sickness, of diagnosis with identity—in *consequence*, chronicity. Schizophrenia and other psychoses are so closely associated with notions of the self that there may be extraordinary susceptibility to such engulfment of the person. Heinz Kohut and Ernest Wolf (1978:415), for example, refer to the psychoses as "primary disturbances of the self," proposing that schizophrenia occurs when "the nuclear self may have remained non-cohesive"—when "serious damage to the self is either permanent or protracted, and if no defensive structures cover the defect." Joel Kovel (1987:335) goes even further: "Schizophrenia cannot be disjoined from the person, for it is the person's whole being). . . . The center of schizophrenia is annihilation: the person becoming schizophrenic remains materially present and conscious, but ceases to be." We have also R. D. Laing's "divided self," Harry Stack Sullivan's "not me," and Michael Gara, Seymour Rosenberg, and Bertram Cohen's (1987) "negated and unelaborated identity" as explanations of schizophrenia. These ethnotheories lay the groundwork for the joining.

Table 1. *"I Am" and "I Have" Illnesses*

Chronic "I Am"	Chronic "I Have"
Alcoholic	Multiple Sclerosis
Hemophiliac	Osteoporosis
Diabetic	Cystic Fibrosis
Epileptic	Lupus
Manic	Arthritis
Retarded	Cancer
Schizophrenic	Hypertension
Spastic	Heart Diseases
Blind	Emphysema
Deaf	Bysinosis
Addict	Cerebral Palsy
Paraplegic	Black Lung
Quadraplegic	
Anorexic	

Simultaneously, cultural conceptions of the self and identity highlight the formative force of others, individual experience, and the passage of time. Thomas Luckmann (1983:71) sums up these ideas writing:

> Personal identity as a *temporal* structure may be described as an ongoing synthesis of body-bound, inner time, experienced as duration, of intersubjective time, experienced as synchronization of face-to-face, social interaction, and biographical time, experienced as the major spans of meaning in the construction and reconstruction of an entire course of life.

Chronicity and disability exist in a special relationship to time, only in part by definition. Three dimensions of this interaction are of relevance here. First, when pain or dysfunction persist in the face of attempts to heal and recover, customary explanations may be replaced by other *categories* of response and understanding (Kleinman 1988). Lack of recovery requires a shift in healing tactics and/or explanations for the affliction. Second (and consequently), suspicions may increase regarding the role of will or individual unwillingness to become well, especially in the West where biomedicine does not accept defeat gracefully (Kaufman 1988). Finally, profound alterations of self and identity are more likely because the prolonged presence of symptoms and impairments erodes denial of dysfunction. As time passes and as daily evidence accumulates, hope fades about the reappearing limb, the regained sight, the disappearance of voices and confused thinking. It is less and less possible to separate one's self from the stubborn presence of the impairment and resulting altered level of functioning.

Chronicity and disability are thus constructed by: the temporal persistence of self and other-perceived dysfunction; continual contact with powerful others who diagnose and treat; gradual but forceful redefinition of identity by kin and close associates who observe, are affected by, or share debility; and accompanying loss of roles and identities that are other than illness-related.

In the West, adults with unresolved, serious illnesses, especially schizophrenia, frequently fail to attain or retain the expected roles of student, employee, spouse, and parent. Thus, the opportunity to experience self and receive self-influencing indications from others that are other-than-illness-related constrict over time. What remains are the roles and situations of patient, malfunctioning or diseased relative, and disabled person. Peggy Thoits (1983) suggests that having multiple social identities contributes to increased psychological well-being, as failure in one arena may be compensated for by competence in another. *The progressive role constriction accompanying chronic illnesses contributes to simultaneous loss of valued, competent-role experiences and an increase in devalued, incompetent roles and experiences.* The most significant sources of confirmation of self and indications of identity become mental health professionals, relatives, and fellow diagnosees. As will become apparent in the next section, at least two of these groups have various personal and political-economic reasons for espousing and maintaining diseased, disabled conceptions about the individual (see Swann and Predmore 1985).

Investigating whether and how these processes occur remains problematical. Empirical assessment of identity and self-concept is a very difficult business (Weinreich 1983). The additional task of identifying a relationship between self and sickness complicates matters considerably. Several researchers have found that visibly psychotic persons decline to self-label when asked in a variety of ways if they are mentally ill (Warner et al. 1989). Self-labeling also may be temporary, changing during the span of just one psychiatric hospitalization (Doherty 1975; Kennard 1974; O'Mahoney 1982; Townsend and Rakfeldt 1985). Direct "I am" statements about schizophrenia are, admittedly, rare in my own research experience. Few informants are as explicit as Lara Jefferson. When pushed, most of those I reinterviewed recently could name their diagnoses, but in structured interviews several gave "false" in response to the statement on a role engulfment scale, "In my opinion, I am mentally ill." That particular scale proved so distressing to them, it was omitted after five interviews. However, in conversational interviews, and in the course of casual discourse, many more illness-identity statements were made, with much less emotional reaction.

In a much larger, ongoing investigation, we found that while over 45 percent of the sample agreed during the initial interview that the problem the doctor told them they had was a mental illness, only 27 percent answered "true" to the "I am mentally ill" statement in the next interview. At the third interview, we asked again if their problem was a mental illness, and the affirmative answers went back to the 40 percent level. I therefore suspect strongly that relative strangers who interview patients with direct questions, scales, and structured protocols at one point in time are unlikely to receive accurate responses to queries about illness and identity. The subject is so painful, and the information so private, that much of the data to date is questionable in my view (Estroff et al. 1991).

Illness-identity statements that occur in both casual and elicited conversation may provide important clues to how individuals represent themselves to others and self in relation to illness. David Snow and Leon Anderson (1987) advocate a similar approach, focusing on a particular type of "identity work" referred to as "identity talk." In their ethnographic study of homeless men, three patterns of identity talk emerged: (1) distancing, (2) embracing, and (3) fictive story telling. In our work, we identify normalizing statements (similar to distancing—e.g., everyone has emotional problems), illness-identity statements (similar to embracing—e.g., I have a small version of schizophrenia), and various self-illness descriptions that often elaborate on symptoms such as paranoia or hearing voices, but may not include labeling statements.

There are at least two additional dimensions of this relationship to consider in speech and other means of self representation: (1) degree of subjectness or objectness, and (2) sentiment.

Each person locates their illness in relation to self along a continuum of subjectness; that is, how closely linked to one's self or separated as distinct from one's self the illness is considered. This dimension includes actual location of the affliction, for example, whether an illness is seen to reside internally, bodily, constantly resident or intermittently intruding from the outside, or externally. Location does not necessarily determine degree of subjectivity, as when a tumor is located internally but seen as an intrusive not-me object, far removed from self. But in general, location and subjectivity co-vary in a coherent fashion. Externality is frequently associated with more pronounced objectness of the illness, internality often accompanying illness experienced as subjectness. What we seek in analysis of illness-identity statements is to what extent an illness is considered part of the self, part of "I," part of one's privately known, experienced, claimed self. We investigate the "itness" of the

illness, and whether the individual believes he or she *has* or *is* a diagno- *speech*
sis. Terms of reference and verbs associated with illness are especially
important data. If an individual speaks of "my illness" or says "I am
crazy," for example, the degree of subjectivity is high. Alternately, referring to an injury or condition as "it" or with verbs of possession (e.g.,
have) indicates more conceptual distance from self, and we would locate
that person toward the illness-as-object end of the continuum.

Speech is not the only means by which individuals apprehend illness
and so at the two-year interview, we ask persons in our study to draw a *visual*
picture of their bodies and to show us where they locate their illness or *rep*
problems. Most place the problem internally in the head, torso, or
groin—explaining that their minds, hearts, or sexuality has been affected. Several fix the illness or problem outside their bodies, between
themselves and others, or in the world at large.

The dimension of sentiment includes the feelings experienced and
expressed by the person about the illness, symptoms, and consequences.
We do not assume that such emotions are uniformly negative, even with
the most serious and debilitating conditions. This affective component
of the relationship between self and sickness is sometimes referred to
(somewhat imprecisely) in the clinical literature as adjustment or adaptation to an impairment or loss of function. It is imprecise because there is
a presumption that one should develop accepting if not positive senti-
ments about chronic conditions. In contrast, we take the position that
the relationship of sentiment to prognosis is an empirical question, and
seek first to simply establish what the emotions are.

Illness-identity representations no doubt vary by audience and
purpose—for example, the idiom of self-help and advocacy among psychiatric patients. Preferred terms of self reference such as "consumer," "psychiatrically labeled," and "former inmate" emphasize social status and
experience with treatment, explicitly refuting or ignoring having an illness
or diagnosis (see Campbell 1991). At the same time, "I am" statements
often precede public testimony and self stories at self-help meetings, and
at gatherings of professionals or policy makers. In these settings, the
designations may serve primarily to identify the person within a limited
universe of possibilities—that is, patient or professional, consumer or
provider. Paradoxically, public and political advocacy for resources and
power widens the audience to whom the person is labeled. To the extent
that influence is attained, it is by being linked to a disabled identity, and by
self-labeling; otherwise one has no credentials.

In summary, illness-identity representations of various kinds represent a promising means of exploring the relationships between individuals and illnesses that persist and disable. Several other appealing methods have also been proposed recently.

Morton Beiser and his colleagues (1987) have developed a Social Response Questionnaire to measure sick self-labeling, and test it among psychiatric patients and individuals with Crohn's disease (a chronic gastrointestinal condition). In this study, the psychiatric patients label themselves, and do so more negatively than did the people with Crohn's. Steven Lally (1989) worked for many months on a long-stay psychiatric unit and developed a true-false measure of patient identity engulfment. Results from the scale correlate closely with his clinical assessments, semistructured interviews, and the duration and severity of patients' psychiatric disorders: patients with longer hospital histories and more severe symptoms are more engulfed.

Thomas McGlashan (1987) investigates whether integration or sealing over of the psychotic experience is associated with long-term outcome. Integrative recovery style involves seeing the event as an emotional or nervous breakdown, seeking help, acknowledging some positive aspects of the psychotic experience, owning or incorporating the psychosis as an aspect of self, and retaining a sense of continuity of person before and after the event. Sealing over entails much the opposite response. The psychosis is alien, frightening, damaging, uninstructive, medical in nature, external in origin, and discontinuous with the person before and after the event. Using a scale and clinician raters, McGlashan finds that integration was associated with positive functioning at follow-up for persons with affective disorders, but neither recovery style is associated with outcome for persons with schizophrenic disorders. The latter *tends* toward sealing over styles. The lack of association between integration or sealing over and outcome for persons with schizophrenia may reflect the need for a longer time frame to incorporate such an affliction, or may indicate that recovery did not occur in this subgroup. Equally plausible is that the scales were not relevant to the process of having schizophrenia, or that the research subjects did not reveal their adaptations to the investigators.

Thoits (1985:244) argues that "persistent, or recurrent emotional deviance in the course of identity enactment or identity change will cause individuals to attribute psychological disturbance to themselves, which in turn will motivate help seeking." However, her position is explicitly theoretical and applied to voluntary help seeking, data about which she uses to bolster the argument. Bruce Link (1982) measured expectations of rejection among persons with varied duration and severity of psychiatric symptoms, and varied participation in treatment. He did not address self-labeling directly, but found higher expectations of rejection and withdrawal from social relations and work among those in treatment— that is, other or formally labeled.

I conclude, not surprisingly, that a long-term, ethnographic approach that incorporates valid quantitative measures is a preferred means for assessing and observing these processes. Careful inferences can be made and indirect indicators of the illness-identity relationships are numerous. Illness-identity statements made by others to the ill person also deserve attention. For example, clinicians and relatives may make "you have" or "you are" statements that are important to observe and record, along with the individual's account of how these others refer to them and their illnesses. Further, the composition of the person's social network is especially important, and often overlooked as a source of information. If most associates are others with psychiatric disorders, beleaguered and grieving kin, or mental health professionals, there is reason to infer that the illness-centered basis of these relationships will influence self experience and identity. In view of the significant role assigned to "others" in constructing and reconstructing the self, this indicator may be especially important. The number and type of social roles occupied and enacted by the person are also telling, as the role constriction proposition suggests. In short, I endorse study of what Allan Young (1982) has called the "social relations of sickness," along with the biographical and narrative approaches in receipt of much enthusiasm at the moment.

A Political Economy of Disability: Dependence and Carrying Capacities

In the preceding section, I outlined processes of identity definition and change and self experience that in part constitute and contribute to chronicity. In this section, I characterize the political, economic context within which this occurs, identifying operative cultural factors and processes. Having schizophrenia per se is not sufficient to result in chronicity. One has to be in the right cultural, sociopolitical, and health care system (see Marmor and Gill 1989 for an interesting analysis). First, there are some basic assumptions and concepts:

Needs and Resources

Figure 1 illustrates the idea that disabled persons have material and social needs exceeding the resources that they either generate or control or to which they have customary access. The American cultural ideal is that adults should have and produce more resources than needs, have or earn more money than is spent. Few adhere strictly to this rule, but there are commonsense understandings about acceptable deviations. Most adult persons whose functioning is restricted over time, especially in producing activities, inevitably break this fundamental rule (Nagi and

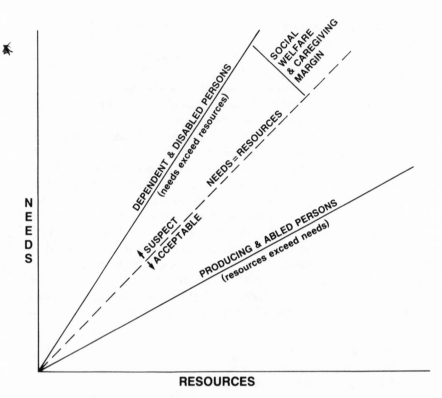

N
E
E
D
S

RESOURCES

Figure 1.   This figure illustrates a Western cultural rule about acceptable versus suspect need. The ideal producing person generates or has more resources than needs, while a disabled or dependent person's needs exceed their resources. The social welfare or caregiving margin varies across situations and societies, based on the amount and type of needs/resources discrepancy, and the reasons for the discrepancy.

Hadley 1972). Their material, functional, and often social and emotional needs are both exceptional and usually exceed their capacity to provide for them. (One of the various, recently invented, benign terms of reference is in fact "people with special needs.")

The combination of exceptional needs and reduced ability to produce goods and services does not bode well for the person with schizophrenia, or any disabling condition. As Kovel notes, "For all its wealth and power, capitalist society turns out to be one of the worst settings possible in which to be schizophrenic . . . [because historically] the labor of psychotics could not be a source of surplus value in the emergent capitalist economy" (1987:341–342). Those with schizophrenia fail to engage in commodity-reproducing behaviors, and are neither good workers nor good consumers. Eventually, "as their condition worsens to the point where they are unable to produce in the workplace—after all, the only real source of value under capitalism—a vicious cycle of mutual [society and the disabled individual] nonrecognition takes over" (1987:342). So, the dependent disabled person faces a toxic concoction of suspicion, incomprehension, and misapprehension from the invisible "others" who are society.

That the needs of persons with chronic, disabling illnesses frequently strain and often exceed the resources of Western nuclear and extended kin is well established (Noh and Turner 1987). Joseph Westermeyer and Ronald Wintrob (1979:757) suggest this is the case in Laos as well, noting that a common complaint

> was that the *baa* subject refused or was unable to work; this occurred in 27 cases. [Later direct questioning revealed that 34 of the 35 subjects were unproductive or underproductive.] Since the per capita gross national income was $70 in U.S. currency, this behavior had major implications for the family and community in terms of survival.

Similarly, Lawrence Fisher (1985:243–244) describes the strain on kin and resulting destitution among mentally ill persons in Barbados where "family" is an important organizing ideology:

> Two of these people (Officer and Ol' Sally) are on hostile terms with members of their own families. Both are believed to be principally responsible for their own sorry circumstances, and neither enjoys any degree of "representation" from family. . . . [They are] cut off from family support. . . . All four of the identifiably "mad" live alone, two in ramshackle chattel houses, two under even worse conditions.

In her cross-cultural survey of families of mentally ill persons, Harriet Lefley (1985:72) concludes that "large supportive networks mitigate family burdens by providing multiple resources for caregiving, attention, [and] economic sharing . . . providing occupations for the mentally ill . . . thereby assuring a productive social role."

If individual, adult needs exceed individual, adult resources, then either the needs go unmet (as seen above), or the resources must derive from a *broader* than usual base and from *different* sources than are expected.

Health Care Systems, Dependence, and Carrying Capacities

Social groups, in response to these exceptional needs, and in order to survive, make arrangements to regulate and control the amount and type of dependence among their members (Estroff 1984). By dependence, I mean primarily functional incapacity that results in an individual's material and social needs far exceeding resources that they can produce, generate, or access. Health care systems have as one crucial function the reduction, if not elimination, of dysfunction (and death) that leads to this unexpected and uncustomary dependence. This may be a task of healing universally. Building upon this notion, I argue that social groups have what may be termed heuristically carrying capacities with regard to the number of dependent persons and the amount of their needs that are acceptable to and sustainable by the producing, abled members of the group.

The concept of carrying capacities may be applied to both biological-epidemiological and sociopolitical processes. Biological-epidemiological carrying capacity refers to a hypothetical, absolute limit, very rarely reached, beyond which life cannot continue because the number and needs of dependent or disabled persons exceed the capacity of producers to maintain them. "Threateningly" needful persons may be abandoned or killed, or the group itself may perish. This sort of limit is approached or breached when disaster strikes, as in a famine, fire, or flood when not everyone can be saved. The concept applies also when prolonged drought enfeebles more persons than can be supported by abled persons and the nutrition-providing environment. Nancy Scheper-Hughes (1987) suggests a similar dynamic operates among Brazilian women who cannot feed all their offspring and so nourish selectively. Biological-epidemiological carrying capacity articulates the *can't*—the *actual inability* of groups to sustain their members.

Sociopolitical carrying capacity, in contrast, is about *won't,* and about *willingness* to support or sustain members of groups whose needs exceed their own resources. *Perceived* magnitude of need and numbers influences definitions of and responses to dependent/disabled people. This notion of carrying capacity suggests that social groups develop, with cultural influence, and articulate, via sociopolitical process, a limit of will in allocating attention and resources to dysfunctional, needful persons. For example, in the West, while we proclaim that resources to care for homeless, impoverished, disabled, and ailing persons are scarce or limited, what is expressed is a sociopolitical decision, a limitation and scarcity of public *will* to allocate abundant resources. We *could,* but often *won't,* pay more taxes, or we *would* if access to resources were universal and not restricted to suspiciously needful persons (Navarro 1987).

In the view proposed here, it is an essential function of health care systems, practices, and beliefs (or policies) to keep the biological and sociopolitical carrying capacities of any group from being approached too closely or breached, in perception and in actuality. To the extent that producing/abled persons operate health care systems, and respond to those who are impaired and dysfunctional, their *social* tasks are to restore functioning in order to reduce the burden of needs; to contain and decrease (or better yet prevent) the number of dependent persons and the magnitude of their unexpected needs. When responses to impaired and dysfunctional persons fail to reduce or eliminate their needs and dependence, but instead sustain, stabilize, or increase them, both types of carrying capacity can become more proximate than is preferred. At these junctures, we may query the efficacy of the system and healing techniques and apparatus, or we may consider alternative motives and functions of health care systems. At these junctures, definitions of and responses to needful persons are altered to restore a culturally comfortable ratio.

Figure 2 is a graphic representation of the idea of sociopolitical carrying capacity, illustrating proposed interrelations between producing/abled persons and dependent/disabled persons, mediated by health care systems, and influenced by cultural beliefs (policies) about health, illness, and disability. This threshold shifts continually, and is influenced profoundly by factors not on the figure, especially demography of the population, labor force conditions and producing arrangements, and availability of resources. But, for the purposes of argument, the essentials are here.

Now, there is every indication that the number of actual and designated disabled persons is increasing in the West. Numerous explanations have been offered ranging from "compensationitis" (Nagi and Hadley 1972) to the ravages of industrialization, capitalism, and medicalization (Navarro 1976; see Stone 1984 for an excellent review). I focus on schizophrenia and the mental health care system in the U.S. as a case in point to illustrate one of the processes involved in becoming designated disabled, and the various ways in which sociopolitical carrying capacity comes into play.

Professionalization and Politicization of Mental Health Care: Who Is Dependent on Whom?

Both the number of mental health professionals and their level of professionalization have increased significantly in the past decades. Table 2 shows that an overall increase of over 17 percent between 1976 and 1984 is concentrated among professionals, whose numbers increased over 100 percent. There was actually a decline in the number of persons employed with less than a bachelor's degree. While the number of psy-

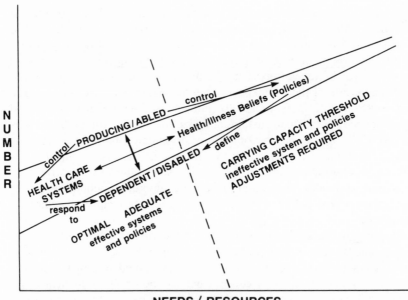

NEEDS / RESOURCES

*Figure 2.   This figure suggests that one function of health care systems is to
control the number of dependent or disabled persons, by cure or rehabilitation, so
that the carrying capacity of producing persons is not exceeded. When the number
and needs of disabled persons exceed the ability or will of the producing population to care for them (provide the resources they need but do not produce), we
may conclude that the health care systems or policies are ineffective. The diagram
illustrates a continuum from optimal care and resulting acceptable ratio of dependent to producing persons, to a hypothetical threshold that, when reached, requires redefinition of those who deserve assistance, increased cure and rehabilitation, or both.*

chiatrists has increased markedly (Mechanic 1987), growth is greater
among psychologists, social workers, and nurses (Witkin et al. 1987).

Meanwhile, professional and nonprofessional public mental health
workers increasingly have become unionized. Two hundred thousand
are represented by the mammoth AFSCME (American Federation of
State, County, and Municipal Employees), and others by 1199 (National
Union of Hospital and Health Care Employees) and the affiliated Team-
sters (who represent state hospital psychiatrists in Ohio; Marcia Jones,
personal communication, 1989; Mechanic and Aiken 1987). My experience of intensive consultation with the leadership of a large state mental
health authority over eight years establishes unequivocally the power of
these organizations to shape public mental health policy and treatment.
In the largest states, such as Ohio and Pennsylvania, unions object vocif-

Table 2.   Number of FTE Staff in Mental Health Organizations:
U.S. 1976–1984

	1976	1984	% Change
All staff*	375, 984	440,925	+17.2
Prof pt care staff	100,886	202,474	+100.7
Less than B.A.	140,379	110,769	−21.1
patient care staff			

Source: Witkin et al. 1987: table 2.10, p. 40.
(% Change computed as $\frac{1984}{1976}$)

* Includes administrative, clerical, and maintenance staff.

erously to the closing of state psychiatric hospitals, and openly demand
no loss of jobs in exchange for political support of governors who ap-
point mental health commissioners.

At times, an odd coalition forms between employees who wish to
protect jobs and relatives of persons with serious mental illnesses who
distrust the efficacy of community treatment and who insist on hospital
medical treatment for the brain illnesses affecting their kin. In response
to a suspected hospital closing in Ohio, AFSCME members invoked the
idiom of patients' rights, picketed the civil libertarian lawyer mental
health commissioner, and mobilized opposition among family members
by relating horror stories to the press of patients abused or neglected in
community settings. In states where there are no or fewer unions, often
generations of a majority of community members have been employed
in large state psychiatric hospitals, and elected representatives protect
their constituents' jobs. Often, kin advocates lobby for changes in commitment laws that make forced hospitalization easier to accomplish,
requiring more beds and more professionals.

Not surprisingly, state psychiatric hospital costs have soared as patient
populations have declined and professional staff have increased. Mechanic (1987:205) estimates that costs per patient in state psychiatric
hospitals tripled between 1970 and 1982. In Pennsylvania, costs per
patient are at present approximately $61,000 per year (Martha Knisley,
personal communication, 1989) Most states now find themselves spending nearly two-thirds of their mental health budgets on inpatient care,
when three-fourths of the persons using public services are in community settings (Mechanic and Aiken 1987).

From this perspective, Kovel's earlier assertion about the failure of
people with schizophrenia to produce economically is mistaken—they
produce jobs for thousands of mental health professionals and workers.
Clearly, the politics and economics of jobs for mental health personnel

play significant roles in directing the type, amount, and location of treatment for persons with schizophrenia and other serious mental illness. I have focused on the public mental health system because the vast majority of care for such persons is provided in these settings. An analysis of the first 600 persons screened for our current study revealed that 85 percent of the people with diagnoses of schizophrenia were found in the state hospitals.

Richard Warner has argued that recovery rates from schizophrenia are directly influenced by the level of employment in a society.

> Where the surplus population is large [i.e., unemployment is high], the conditions established for the psychotic patient tend to be least conducive to his or her recovery. Where the labor of the marginally productive is in demand [i.e., unemployment is low], there shall we find most highly developed community treatment programs and the most humane hospital conditions (Warner 1985:99).

Warner may be correct, but he has missed an alternative explanation and the other side of the argument: Recovery rates may also be influenced by the number and type of mental health professionals who are employed, and who want to keep those jobs because others are not available or pay less. The more professionals, the greater the need for and identification of patients—in essence, a created, increasing demand for psychiatric care. The fewer alternative jobs available for professionals *and* patients, the greater the incentives to maintain institutions and confine patients, thereby assuring that each group "cares" for the other.

Who indeed is dependent on whom? Literally hundreds of thousands of producing/abled persons depend upon dependent persons for their jobs. In the public mental health sector, these individuals have organized politically and demanded to retain employment providing a form of treatment (inpatient) that has been shown repeatedly to be more debilitating and costly and less effective than comprehensive community care. The suggestion here is that a predominant de facto function of the public mental health sector may be to employ mental health workers, not to reduce dependency or dysfunction among people with schizophrenia—or to do so only if employees do not lose jobs in the process.

The process of professionalization is aided and abetted indirectly by kin advocates, who seek with passion to frame both political and professional discourse about schizophrenia in the idiom of biomedicine and chronic disease (see Hatfield, Spaniol, and Zipple 1987; McLean 1990). The current term of preference for many is "neurobiological disorder," even instead of mental illness. Such emphatic medicalization of mental illness serves to relieve relatives of blame for causing schizophrenia and establishes the qualifications of their offspring, siblings, and spouses for illness-tested federal resources. (Bateson is much hated for proposing the double-bind theory, which implicates mothers in particular as sources of disturbed and disturbing communication that results in schizophrenia.) Though proclaiming the magnitude of need and chronicity or incurability causes these advocates considerable anguish and grief, it secures attention and otherwise unavailable resources, such as federal health insurance and disability income. The resonant voices of the kin advocates' despair and resignation are not unheard by the individual with the affliction.

So, for very different reasons, professionals and kin advocates protect *unintentionally* their personal and economic interests by affirming the severity and chronicity of schizophrenia. Via political processes they influence the definitions of disability and allocation of resources, and via simultaneous cultural process inform their relatives or clients of their disabled identity. The net effect is to increase both the ranks of designated dependent/disabled persons and the ranks of producing/abled persons whose employment derives from their continued disability.

I am in no way suggesting that kin or professionals seek deliberately to debilitate persons with schizophrenia. I am describing how sociopolitical carrying capacities may be approached, and how sociopolitical forces may eclipse the healing functions of health care systems. The problem is that people with schizophrenia are not unionized and have less political power than kin advocates. When adjustments occur because of perceived carrying capacity pressure, the redefinitions of disability and withdrawal of resources, the suspicions of malingering and punishments for having needs, are first directed at and experienced by them. Thus, we have thousands of homeless persons with psychiatric disorders, and increasing employment of mental health professionals. When the Social Security Administration abruptly removed thousands of disabled persons from the rolls in 1980, treatment personnel experienced few losses, but many recipients lost homes and sanity, both precarious enough before the withdrawal of support. The professionalizing, medicalizing system continues to dominate as resources are expended to hire more professionals to "treat" homeless people, and low-cost housing remains in desperately short supply (Hopper and Hamburg 1984).

Biological and Epidemiological Processes: Chronic Disease or Defeated Person?

We are beset currently with what seem to be largely polite and superficial biopsychosocial syntheses born of resignation among us, rather than resolution of profound tensions with biomedical thought and authority

(Armstrong 1987). Guilty of "punting" on this front myself, I mean to reroute some of the argument. The controversy about whether schizophrenia (or major mental illness in general) is a *real* (biological) disease or not is a wearisome argument. A more satisfying discussion concerns how to account for observable variations *and* similarities in debility in the presence of both similar enough and vastly differing pathology and impairment.

Biomedical thinking proposes that some disease processes are of prolonged, if not infinite, duration. The disease process itself is chronic unless interrupted or controlled by effective intervention. Physical and functional deterioration are inevitable. Yet the presumed direct correspondence between pathogen and subsequent dysfunction is not confirmed empirically by many persons with persistent conditions, especially schizophrenia (McGlashan 1988; Harding et al. 1987*a*, 1987*b*, 1988). Retreating to tautology is one response to this dilemma, arguing that misdiagnosis, not variability in outcome or recovery, is the problem (that is, if you get better, you did not really have schizophrenia). However, the weight of the evidence about differing responses to equivalent biological conditions is substantial (Kasl 1983), and represents an effective means of challenging such biomedical totalitarianism.

In the West at least, chronicity and disability are responded to, expressed, and experienced with substantial similarity across diagnostic designations and with marked variation within diagnostic designations. To illustrate several of these points:

Bob was one of the most disturbed and dysfunctional clients with whom I studied in 1975–1977. He was continually unkempt, infamous for aggressive panhandling, unapproachably suspicious, and living in shabby surroundings on meager local welfare funds. When reencountered in 1987, he was dressed immaculately, sociable and friendly, and unwilling even to let me buy him a cup of coffee. Bob is happily settled into a large public housing complex and eager to discuss politics, philosophy, and the details of amateur radio transmittal. At the same time, he continues to require legal intervention to force him to take psychotropic medications, and receives federal disability income because he is not employed. The quality of Bob's daily life is vastly improved by any measure—he suffers less. Likewise, his social conduct is more acceptable. This is in contrast to June, who carries the same diagnosis, and who has deteriorated in nearly every way in the intervening decade. She stays in her apartment, chain-smoking cigarettes, watching television, drinking beer, and worrying about her boyfriend's infidelity, contorted physically by tardive dyskinesia (a usually irreversible side-effect of neuroleptic medications that causes uncontrolled muscle spasms, often in the face or tongue). June, ten years earlier, had worked as a secretary, carried on an active social life, and was by my estimate then one of the more functional clients. June suffers poignantly and almost palpably. She told me, "I am completely hopeless. . . . If I had known what my life was going to be like, I would have tried harder to commit suicide when I was 16." More reflectively, she says, "I'd have had a more successful life if I didn't have schizophrenia."

Bob demonstrated his felt stigmatized status, despite his marked improvement, in two ways. His current, reclaimed avocation is amateur radio operation. One afternoon, as we sat at a downtown lunch counter, he was conversing via portable transmitter with a motorist on a nearby highway. This was a lively exchange and uneventful, until Bob inquired of his invisible acquaintance about his age and occupation. Up to that point the discussion had focused on radio equipment. When personal information—that is, who are you?—entered the discourse, Bob had to "cover" as the predictable reciprocal questions were posed. Aware that Bob was in a university town, the other man signaled what would pass, because he asked if Bob were "a student, in school, or working." Bob gave his age accurately, after an embarrassed pause, and said, "I'm a student. I was working for a while and then I was in school, and now I'm going back to school." The other way that Bob covered and signaled his felt stigma was to introduce me over the radio, and by association, confirm his creditable status. He referred to me as his "*friend* who is a professor from North Carolina, who is *visiting* me." A few minutes before he had declined a formal follow-up interview, so he was well aware of one of my other roles and motives in being with him.

June experiences and demonstrates her disabled status differently, but with similar bases. Like Bob, she subsists on federal disability income and receives rent subsidy for her apartment. She agonizes constantly over losing either of these, explicit in her concerns about getting and having a job that is menial or boring that might jeopardize continued receipt. She is caught up with indecision and fear. June claims that she cannot get interesting jobs because she has been identified by treatment staff to employers. At the same time she is reluctant to, and in fact does not, seek employment on her own. June discussed this dilemma repeatedly during phone calls and subsequent visits, often negatively comparing herself to me and her life to mine, which was wrenching to both of us.

Long-term outcome data from various Western and non-Western settings (Zubin, Magaziner, and Steinhauer 1983; Watt, Katz, and Shepherd 1983; Murphy and Raman 1971; Leff et al. 1992; Waxler 1979) suggest that the course of schizophrenia, and the lives of individuals who experience persistent psychosis, do not deteriorate inevitably, nor are they hopelessly grim. The cases just presented illustrate wide variation in functioning *and* similarity in experience between two individuals with the same psychiatric diagnosis. However, psychotic symptoms were among the least often mentioned and least observable sources of distress or dysfunction for Bob and June, and among the rest of the group as well. Biomedical factors alone illuminate little and predict less about Bob's and June's lives. If the disease process is itself chronic, how can we account for such diversity in functioning and such convergence in experience?

Conclusions:
An Optimistic Prognosis?

In the preceding, I have outlined a sociocultural understanding of the process of chronicity. I have identified sociocultural processes of identity transformation, political-economic forces of professionalization, and illness-tested resource allocation as distinct but simultaneous, separable but interactive, cumulative and formative but not determinative forces resulting in chronicity and disability. Kaja Finkler (1980) has suggested provocatively that therapeutic efficacy may be conceived of as the extent to which healing response symbolically terminates the sick role. I have argued that in the U.S. at least, response to persons with long-term impaired functioning, especially that associated with schizophrenia, results in precisely the opposite: the stabilization, exacerbation, and perpetuation of the sick role and thereby the sickness.

I have had to omit discussion of many nuances unique to schizophrenia: for example, the role of tardive dyskinesia in embodying and physicalizing permanently signs of mental illness, and the interesting response among mental health professionals to the use of alcohol and recreational drugs by people with schizophrenia. A second, stigmatized, diagnostically driven identity (alcoholic or addict) is in the process of being offered and applied to this population (Schneier and Siris 1987).

In conclusion and in summary, the essential elements of chronic illness and disability are outlined below:

An Outline of Chronicity

I. Temporal Dimension

   Chronic Illnesses:

   A. *Persist* through time; can last a lifetime;

   B. Often begin or present obscurely; may be present at birth or develop unnoticed later;

   C. Generally become identified, visible, or *apparent* in *early adulthood;*

   D. *Shorten the lifespan* by one or more decades;

E.   And, delay, interrupt, and otherwise *interfere* with *expected* stages of psychosocial *development*.

II. Sociocultural Dimension

Chronic Illnesses:

A.   Contribute to *diminished participation* in expected social *roles;*

B.   And, contribute to *diminished participation* in *producing activities,* providing material support to oneself and one's kin and community, or participation in the labor force.

C.   Individual *needs exceed* individual *resources* in areas of subsistence, reciprocity of social obligation, interpersonal relations, and daily function;

D.   Behaviors, forms, signs, and *expressions* of the illnesses are *aesthetically unpleasing, stigmatized* conditions.

III. Cultural Symbolic Dimension

A.   The prominence, persistence, and *ambiguity* of *origins* and *mechanisms* of impairment require the assignment of various *moral, cosmological,* and *cultural meanings* to the illness and evaluations of the individual.

B.   Afflicted individuals experience exclusion, derision, shame, and other derivations of *stigmatization.*

C.   The *persistence of suffering* over time and despite treatment contributes to *sadness,* negative evaluations of self, and loss of status.

D.   Continued contact with healers and clinicians, the intrusive nature of treatment, and visibility of expression of the affliction result in *less privacy* of person than is customary.

E.   Diminished capacity to function in expected roles leads to *suspicion* about *refusal* or *inability* to participate.

F.   Location of *responsibility* for the illness and response to the afflicted is *ambiguous, controversial,* and *shifting.*

G.   *Kin* experience *derivative* stigma and *suffering,* and above-average material *burdens.*

H.   Kin *seek explanations,* cures, restoration of function, and *assistance* among community, extended kin, and caregivers.

I.   Over time, individuals are defined and *experience themselves as a member of a category,* derived from the illness or diagnostic designation.

J.   The *impairment* or affliction becomes an *entity,* within and as part of the sufferer's self; sociopolitical and clinical *designa-*

tions for the impairment become *equivalent* to *self, and insepa-rable* from self, and *eclipse* other attributes, roles, and identities of the sufferer.

IV. Biological-Clinical Dimension

A. Biological *origins* and *mechanisms* are often ambiguous or *unknown* in the present.

B. Biological mechanisms and processes of affliction are of *infinite duration,* following a fluctuating but *deteriorating* course.

C. There are *competing* and *numerous theories* about origins, mechanisms, treatment, and response that persist among kin, community, clinicians, healers, and researchers.

D. *Continual treatment,* management, and special response are required to control or reduce suffering, dysfunction, or symptoms.

E. *Treatment* and healing responses may result in or create *additional dysfunction,* signs, and suffering while original symptoms persist.

V. Political Economic Dimension

A. Because individual needs often exceed individual and nuclear kin resources, a *broad social response is required;* material and interpersonal resources are required from society, community, or extended kin.

B. Diminished but distinct *expectations* or standards for *participation* in social life develop and are expressed or *codified* via *political* and *social* mechanisms, based on biomedical evidence and associated cultural meanings.

C. Health and illness *beliefs* and health *policies* express and shape *social willingness* to support, respond to, accept, or exclude these individuals.

D. *Allocation* of additional resources occurs via *political processes* mediated by healers, kin, caregivers, and competitors for resources.

E. *Social and material costs* for response, support, and inclusion of the individual are *significant,* resulting in pressure to continually define and assess the person, and to assign *responsibility* for care.

F. Social responses often result in *institutional arrangements* and *confinement* for extended periods of time; access to institutions is sociopolitically controlled.

G. In the West, *advocacy* and *illness interest groups* form and function to solicit, maintain, and increase resources available to afflicted persons.

H. *Poverty of material resources* at the individual level result from diminished participation in producing, and in spite of social and healing response.

David Landy (1983), in his critical reappraisal of medical anthropology, has repeated the call for a working "set of culture free categories" in order to do comparative research on health, illness, and healing. Gananath Obeyesekere (one of the discussants at the conference where the papers in the present volume were first discussed) warned that medical anthropologists' subversive stance toward biomedicine may be undermined, ironically, by an almost unnoticed infiltration of biomedical language, concepts, and agendas. His cautionary query is whether by paying such attention to the presumptions and practices of biomedicine we neglect or lose sight of our own cultural and conceptual projects. Does the object of protest become the focus of inquiry? While I do not think that any category is culture free or that we can resist absolutely the interpenetration of biomedical knowledge with our own, these are challenges well worth serious reflection.

I have proposed several concepts and questions that may be investigated in reference to persistent dysfunction in various settings that seek explicitly cultural, not medical, referents. These are:

1. Interrelations between self/soul and sickness, illness and identity/status; sickness as a cause or result of loss of self/soul; terminologies of illness and identity;

2. Arrangements to regulate and control unexpected dependence; the needs and resources problem; notions of inability or refusal to produce and diagnosis as a form of dispute resolution; and carrying capacities and the mediating role of health care systems;

3. Focus on variation in response to and experience of similar enough persistent impairments within and across cultural boundaries as a challenge to biomedical determinism.

Accepting the challenge to reclaim medical anthropology from biomedicine, in all of its various incarnations, does not mean, however, that one rejects the call for salience in the realm of healing and suffering. As I began this chapter with recognition of the ever-present "second audience," I end with the conviction that it is possible to produce work that is as relevant as it is resonant, and that is as applicable as it is anthropological.

Acknowledgments

I am grateful for a Junior Faculty Development Award from the University of North Carolina that funded the ten-year follow-up study. Ongoing research reported here is supported by grant number MH 40314 from the National Institute of Mental Health. I wish also to thank the Department of Social Medicine, UNC, for additional research and travel support associated with the writing of this paper and attendance at the conference. Finally, the paper has been improved by the able assistance of many, especially Ellyn Harris in producing it, the Triangle Mental Health Survey project staff in methodological and substantive areas, and the conference participants in areas of substance and focus.

References

Ablon, Joan
    1984   *Little People in America: The Social Dimensions of Dwarfism.* New York: Praeger.
Albrecht, Gary L. and Judith Levy
    1984   A Sociological Perspective of Physical Disability. In *Advances in Medical Social Science*, J. L. Ruffini, ed., 2:45–105. New York: Gordon and Breach.
APA (American Psychiatric Association)
    1987   *Diagnostic and Statistical Manual of Mental Disorders III—Revised.* Washington, D.C.: American Psychiatric Association Press.
Armstrong, David
    1987   Theoretical Tensions in Biopsychosocial Medicine. *Social Science and Medicine* 25(11):1213–1218.
Bateson, Gregory
    1972   The Cybernetics of "Self": A Theory of Alcoholism. In *Steps to an Ecology of Mind*, pp. 309–337. New York: Ballantine Books.
Beiser, Morton, Nancy Waxler-Morrison, William G. Iacono, Tsung-Yi Lin, Jonathan A. E. Fleming, and Janice Husted
    1987   A Measure of the "Sick" Label in Psychiatric Disorder and Physical Illness. *Social Science and Medicine* 25(3):251–261.
Berkowitz, Monroe
    1986   Illness Behavior and Disability. In *Illness Behavior*, Sean McHugh and T. Michael Ballis, eds., pp. 189–203. New York: Plenum Press.
Blacking, John
    1983   The Concept of Identity and Folk Concepts of Self: A Venda Case Study. In *Identity: Personal and Sociocultural*, Anita Jacobson-

Widding, ed., pp. 47–67. Atlantic Highlands, N.J.: Humanities Press Inc.

Brody, Howard
1987   *Stories of Sickness.* New Haven, Conn.: Yale University Press.

Campbell, Jean S.
1991   Towards Undiscovered Country: Mental Health Clients Speak for Themselves. Ph.D. diss., University of California, Irvine.

Carrithers, Michael, Steven Collins, and Steven Lukes, eds.
1985   *The Category of the Person: Anthropology, Philosophy, History.* London: Cambridge University Press.

Charmaz, Kathy
1983   Loss of Self: A Fundamental Form of Suffering in the Chronically Ill. *The Sociology of Health and Illness* 5(2):168–195.
1987   Struggling for a Self: Identity Levels of the Chronically Ill. *Research in the Sociology of Health Care* 6:283–321.

Chirikos, Thomas
1989   Aggregate Economic Losses from Disability in the United States: A Preliminary Assay. *The Milbank Quarterly* 67(supp. 2, pt. 1):59–91.

Conrad, Peter
1987   The Experience of Illness: Recent and New Directions. *Research in the Sociology of Health Care* 6:1–31.

Corbin, Juliet, and Anselm Strauss
1987   Accompaniments of Chronic Illness: Changes in Body, Self, Biography, and Biographical Time. *Research in the Sociology of Health Care* 6:249–281.

Croce, Nora
1987   Cross-cultural Research, Current Strengths, Future Needs. *Disability Studies Quarterly* 7(3):2.

Denzin, Norman K.
1987   *The Alcoholic Self.* Beverly Hills, Calif.: Sage Publications.

Doherty, Edmund G.
1975   Labeling Effects in Psychiatric Hospitalization: A Study of Diverging Patterns of In-Patient Self-Labeling Processes. *Archives of General Psychiatry* 32:562–568.

Dunham, H. Warren
1968   Society, Culture, and Mental Disorder. *Archives of General Psychiatry* 33:147–156.

Edgerton, Robert B.
1967   *The Cloak of Competence: Stigma in the lives of the mentally retarded.* Berkeley and Los Angeles: University of California Press.

Edgerton, Robert B. and Georges Sabagh
1962   From Mortification to Aggrandizement: Changing Self Concepts in the Careers of the Mentally Retarded. *Psychiatry* 25:263–272.

Erikson, Kai T.
1957   Patient Role and Social Uncertainty: A Dilemma of the Mentally Ill. *Psychiatry* 20(3):263–274.

Estroff, Sue E.
    1984   Who Are You? Why Are You Here? Anthropology and Human
            Suffering. *Human Organization* 43(4):368–370.
    1985   *Making It Crazy: An Ethnography of Psychiatric Clients in an Ameri-
            can Community.* Berkeley, Los Angeles, London: University of Cali-
            fornia Press.
    1989   Self, Identity, and Schizophrenia: In Search of the Subject. *Schizo-
            phrenia Bulletin* 15(4):189–196.
Estroff, Sue E., William Lachicotte, Linda Illingworth, Anna Johnston, and
Bob Ruth
    1991   Everybody's Got a Little Mental Illness: Accounts of Illness and
            Self among People with Severe, Persistent Mental Illness. *Medical
            Anthropology Quarterly* 5(4):331–369.
Ewing, Katherine
    1990   The Illusion of Wholeness: Culture, Self, and the Experience of
            Inconsistency. *Ethos* 18(3):251–278.
Fabrega, Horacio
    1987   Psychiatric Diagnosis: A Cultural Perspective. *Journal of Nervous
            and Mental Disease* 175(7):383–394.
    1989   The Self and Schizophrenia: A Cultural Perspective. *Schizophrenia
            Bulletin* 15(4):277–290.
Fabrega, Horacio, and Peter K. Manning,
    1972   Disease, Illness, and Deviant Careers. In *Theoretical Perspectives
            on Deviance,* Robert Scott and Jack Douglas, eds., pp. 93–116. New
            York: Basic Books.
Finkler, Kaja
    1980   Non-medical Treatments and Their Outcomes. *Culture, Medicine,
            and Psychiatry* 4(3):271–310.
Fisher, Lawrence E.
    1985   *Colonial Madness: Mental Health in the Barbadian Social Order.*
            New Brunswick, N.J.: Rutgers University Press.
Foucault, Michel
    1965   *Madness and Civilization: A History of Insanity in an Age of Rea-
            son.* New York: Random House.
Gara, Michael A., Seymour Rosenberg, and Bertram D. Cohen
    1987   Personal Identity and the Schizophrenic Process: An Integration.
            Psychiatry 50:267–279.
Gerhardt, Uta, ed.
    1990   Qualitative Research on Chronic Illness. *Social Science and Medi-
            cine* 30(11).
Glass, James
    1987   Schizophrenia and Rationality: On the Function of the Unconscious
            Fantasy. In *Pathologies of the Modern Self,* David M. Levin, ed.,
            pp. 405–438. New York: New York University Press.
Goffman, Erving
    1961   *Asylums.* New York: Doubleday-Anchor.

1963   *Stigma: Notes on the Management of Spoiled Identity.* Englewood Cliffs: Prentice-Hall.

Gordon, Deborah R.
1988   Tenacious assumptions in western medicine. In *Biomedicine Examined,* Margaret Lock and Deborah R. Gordon, eds., pp. 19–56. Boston: Kluwer Academic Publishers.

Harding, Courtenay M., George W. Brooks, Takamaru Ashikaga, John S. Strauss, and Alan Breier
1987*a*   The Vermont Longitudinal Study of Persons with Severe Mental Illness, I: Methodology, Study Sample and Overall Status 32 Years Later. *American Journal of Psychiatry* 144(6):718–724.
1987*b*   The Vermont Longitudinal Study of Persons with Severe Mental Illness, II: Long-Term Outcome of Subjects Who Retrospectively Met DSM-III Criteria for Schizophrenia. *American Journal of Psychiatry* 144(6):727–735.
1988   Course Types in Schizophrenia: An Analysis of European and American Studies. *Schizophrenia Bulletin* 14(4):633–644.

Hatfield, Agnes
1987   Expressed Emotion: A Family Perspective. *Schizophrenia Bulletin* 13(2):221–226.

Hatfield, Agnes, Leroy Spaniol, and Anthony M. Zipple
1986   Semantic Barriers to Family and Professional Collaboration. *Schizophrenia Bulletin* 12(3):325–333.

Herzlich, Claudine, and Janine Pierret
1987   *Illness and Self in Society.* Baltimore: Johns Hopkins University Press.

Hopper, Kim, and Jill Hamberg
1984   The Making of America's Homeless: From Skid Row to New Poor, 1945–1984. New York: Community Service Society, Working Papers in Social Policy.

Ingleby, David
1982   The Social Construction of Mental Illness. In *The Problem of Medical Knowledge,* Peter Wright and Andrew Treacher, eds. pp. 123–143. Edinburgh: Edinburgh University Press.

Institute of Medicine
1990   Chronic disease and disability: Beyond the acute medical model. Papers commissioned for the Pew Health Policy Program ed.

Jacobson-Widding, Anita, ed.
1983   *Identity: Personal and Socio-Cultural.* Atlantic Highlands, N.J.: Humanities Press.

Jefferson, Lara
1974   *These Are My Sisters: A Journal from the Inside of Insanity.* Garden City, N.Y.: Anchor Press/Doubleday.

Kapferer, Bruce
1979   Mind, Self, and Other in Demonic Illness: The Negation and Reconstruction of Self. *American Ethnologist* 6:110–133.

Kasl, Stanislav V.
    1983   Social and Psychological Factors Affecting the Course of Disease:
            An Epidemiological Perspective. In *Handbook of Health, Health
            Care, and the Health Professions,* David Mechanic, ed., pp. 683–
            708. New York: The Free Press.
Kaufert, Patricia L., and Joseph M. Kaufert
    1984   Methodological and Conceptual Issues in Measuring the Long Term
            Impact of Disability: The Experience of Polio-Myelitis Patients in
            Manitoba. *Social Science and Medicine* 19(6):609–618.
Kaufman, Sharon
    1988   Toward a Phenomenology of Boundaries in Medicine: Chronic Ill-
            ness Experience in the Case of Stroke. *Medical Anthropology Quar-
            terly* 2(4):338–354.
Kennard, David
    1974   The newly Admitted Psychiatric Patient as Seen by Self and Others.
            British Journal of Medical Psychology 47:27–41.
Kleinman, Arthur
    1988   *The Illness Narratives: Suffering, Healing and the Human Condition.*
            New York: Basic Books.
Kohut, Heinz, and Ernest S. Wolf
    1978   The Disorders of the Self and Their Treatment: An Outline. *Interna-
            tional Journal of Psychoanalysis* 59:413–425.
Kovel, Joel
    1987   Schizophrenic Being and Technocratic Society. In *Pathologies of
            the Modern Self,* pp. 330–348. New York: New York University
            Press.
Kuckelman, Ann, and Edna Hamera
    1986   Illness experience in a Chronic Disease—ALS. *Social Science and
            Medicine* 23(7):641–650.
LaFontaine, Jean S.
    1985   Person and Individual: Some Anthropological Reflections. In *The
            Category of the Person,* Michael Carrithers, Steven Collins, and
            Steven Lukes, eds., pp. 122–140. London: Cambridge University
            Press.
Landy, David
    1983   Medical Anthropology: A Critical Appraisal. In *Advances in Medi-
            cal Social Science,* Julio Ruffini, ed., pp. 185–314. New York: Gor-
            don and Breach Science Publishers.
Lally, Steven
    1989   Does Being in Here Mean There Is Something Wrong with Me?
            Schizophrenia Bulletin 15(4):253–266.
Leff, Julian, Norman Sartorius, Aaron Jablensky, A. Korten, and G. Ernberg
    1992   The International Pilot Study of Schizophrenia: Five Year Follow-
            up Findings. *Psychological Medicine* 22:131–145.
Lefley, Harriet
    1985   Families of the Mentally Ill in Cross Cultural Perspective. *Psychoso-
            cial Rehabilitation Journal* 8(4):57–76.

Link, Bruce
1982   Mental Patient Status, Work, and Income: An Examination of the Effects of a Psychiatric Label. *American Sociological Review* 47: 202–215.
Lofland, John
1969   *Deviance and Identity.* Englewood Cliffs, N.J.: Prentice-Hall.
Luckmann, Thomas
1983   Remarks on Personal Identity: Inner, Social and Historical Time. In *Identity: Personal and Sociocultural,* Anita Jacobson-Widding, ed., pp. 66–92. Atlantic Highlands, N.J.: Humanities Press.
Marmor, Theodore, and Kenneth Gill
1989   The Political and Economic Context of Mental Health Care in the United States. *Journal of Health Politics, Policy and Law* 14(3):459–475.
Marsella, Anthony
1980   Depressive Experience and Disorder Across Cultures. In *Handbook of Cross-Cultural Psychology,* Jurisg Draguns and Harry Triandis, eds., 6:237–290. New York: Allyn Bacon.
McGlashan, Thomas H.
1987   Recovery Style from Mental Illness and Long-Term Outcome. *Journal of Nervous Mental Disease* 175(11):681–685.
1988   A Selective Review of Recent North American Long-Term Follow-up Studies of Schizophrenia. *Schizophrenia Bulletin* 14:515–542.
McLean, Athena
1990   Contradictions in the Social Construction of Clinical Knowledge: The Case of Schizophrenia. *Social Science and Medicine* 30(9):969–985.
Mechanic, David
1987   Correcting Misconceptions in Mental Health Policy: Strategies for Improved Care of the Seriously Mentally Ill. *The Milbank Quarterly* 65(2):203–230.
Mechanic, David, and Linda H. Aiken
1987   Improving the Care of Patients with Chronic Mental Illness. *New England Journal of Medicine* 317(26):1634–1638.
Mollica, Richard
1987   Upside-Down Psychiatry: A Genealogy of Mental Health Services. In *Pathologies of the Modern Self,* David M. Levin, ed., pp. 363–384. New York: New York University Press.
Murphy, H. B. M., and A. C. Raman
1971   The Chronicity of Schizophrenia in Indigenous Tropical Peoples: 12 Year Follow-up in Mauritius. *British Journal of Psychiatry* 118:489–497.
Murphy, Robert M., Jessica S. Scheer, Yolanda Murphy, and Richard Mack
1988   Physical Disability and Social Liminality: A Study in the Rituals of Adversity. *Social Science and Medicine* 26(2):235–242.
Nagi, Saad Z., and Lynn W. Hadley
1972   Disability Behavior: Income Change and Motivation to Work. *Industrial and Labor Relations Review* 25(2):223–233.

Navarro, Vincente
1976   *Medicine Under Capitalism.* New York: Neale Watson.
1987   Federal Health Policies in the United States: An Alternative Explanation. *The Milbank Quarterly* 65(1):81–110.
Noh, Samuel and Ralph J. Turner
1987   Living with Psychiatric Patients: Implications for the Mental Health of Family Members. *Social Science and Medicine* 25(3):263–271.
O'Mahoney, P. D.
1982   Psychiatric Patient Denial of Mental Illness as a Normal Process. *British Journal of Medical Psychology* (55):109–118.
Phillips, Marilyn
1990   Damaged Goods: Oral Narratives of the Experience of Disability in American Culture. *Social Science and Medicine* 30(8):849–857.
Robbins, Richard H.
1973   Identity, culture, and behavior. In *Handbook of Social and Cultural Anthropology,* John Honigmann, ed., pp. 1199–1222. Chicago: Rand McNally.
Rosenberg, Morris
1984   A Symbolic Interactionist View of Psychosis. *Journal of Health and Social Behavior* 25:289–302.
Rosenberg, Morris, and Howard B. Kaplan, eds.
1982   *Social Psychology of the Self Concept.* Arlington Heights, Ill.: Harlan Davidson, Inc.
Scheff, Thomas
1984   *Being Mentally Ill: A Sociological Theory.* 2nd ed. Chicago: Alsine.
Scheper-Hughes, Nancy, ed.
1987   *Child Survival: Anthropological Approaches to the Treatment and Maltreatment of Children.* Dordrecht, Netherlands: Reidel.
Schneier, Frank R., and Samuel G. Siris
1987   A Review of Psychoactive Substance Use and Abuse in Schizophrenia Patterns of Drug Choice. *Journal of Nervous and Mental Diseases* 175(11):641–652.
Schrauger, J. Sidney, and Thomas J. Schoeneman
1979   Symbolic Interactionist View of Self Concept: Thru the Looking Glass Darkly. *Psychology Bulletin* 86:549–573.
Shweder, Richard A., and Edmund J. Bourne
1984   Does the Concept of the Person Vary Cross-Culturally? In *Culture Theory: Essays on Mind, Self, and Emotion,* Richard A. Shweder and Robert A. LeVine, eds. pp. 158–199. London: Cambridge University Press.
Snow, David, and Leon Anderson
1987   Identity Work Among the Homeless: The Verbal Construction and Avowal of Personal Identities. *American Journal of Sociology* 92(6):1336–1371.
Stein, Howard F.
1979   Rehabilitation and Chronic Illness in American Culture: The Cul-

tural Psychodynamics of a Medical and Social Problem. *Journal of Psychological Anthropology* 2(2):153–176.

Stone, Deborah A.
1979   Illness and the Dole: The Function of Illness in American Distributive Politics. *Journal of Health Politics, Policy, and Law* 4(3):507–521.
1984   *The Disabled State.* Philadelphia: Temple University Press.

Strauss, Anselm, and Bernard Glaser
1975   *Chronic Illness and the Quality of Life.* St. Louis: C. V. Mosby.

Strauss, Anselm, and Juliet M. Corbin
1988   *Shaping a New Health Care System: The Explosion of Chronic Illness as a Catalyst for Change.* San Francisco: Jossey-Bass.

Swann, William B.
1987   Identity Negotiation: Where Two Roads Meet. *Journal of Personality and Social Psychology* 53(6):1038–1051.

Swann, William B., and S. C. Predmore
1985   Intimates as Agents of Social Support: Sources of Consolation or Despair? *Journal of Personality and Social Psychology* 49:1609–1617.

Thoits, Peggy A.
1983   Multiple Identities and Psychological Well-being: A Reformulation of the Social Isolation Hypothesis. *American Sociological Review* 48:174–187.
1985   Self Labelling Processes in Mental Illness: The Role of Emotional Deviance. *American Journal of Sociology* 91(2):221–249.

Townsend, John M.
1979   Self-Concept and the Institutionalization of Mental Patients: An Overview and Critique. *Journal of Health and Social Behavior* 17(3):263–271.

Townsend John M., and Jaak Rakfeldt
1985   Hospitalization and First-Contact Mental Patients: Stigma and Changes in Self Concept. *Research in Community and Mental Health* 5:269–301.

Warner, Richard
1985   *Recovery from Schizophrenia: Psychiatry and Political Economy.* London: Routledge and Kegan Paul.

Warner, Richard, Dawn Taylor, Moira Powers, and Joel Hyman
1989   Acceptance of the Mental Illness Label by Psychotic Patients: Effects of Functioning. *American Journal of Orthopsychiatry* 59(3): 398–409.

Wasow, Mona
1982   *Coping with Schizophrenia: A Family Survival Manual.* Palo Alto, Calif.: Science and Behavior Books, Inc.

Watt, D. L., K. Katz, and M. Shepherd
1983   The Natural History of Schizophrenia: A Five-year Prospective Follow-up of a Representative Sample of Schizophrenics. *Psychological Medicine* 13:663–670.

Waxler, Nancy
    1979   Is Outcome for Schizophrenia Better in Non-industrialized Soci-
            eties: The Case of Sri Lanka. *Journal of Nervous and Mental Disease*
            167:144–158.
Weinreich, Peter
    1983   Psychodynamics of Personal and Social Identity: Theoretical Con-
            cepts and Their Measurement in Adolescents from Belfast Sectarian
            and Bristol Minority Groups. In *Identity: Personal and Sociocul-
            tural,* Anita Jacobson-Widding, ed., pp. 159–186. Atlantic High-
            lands, N.J.: Humanities Press, Inc.
Westermeyer, Joseph, and Ronald Wintrob
    1979   "Folk" Criteria for the Diagnosis for Mental Illness in Rural Laos:
            On Being Insane in Sane Places. *American Journal of Psychiatry*
            136(6):755–761.
Witkin, Michael J., Joanne E. Atay, Adele S. Fell, and Ronald W.
Manderscheid
    1987   Specialty Mental Health System Characteristics in NIMH. Mental
            Health, US, 1987. Ronald W. Manderscheid and Sally A. Barrett,
            eds. Department of Health and Human Services (Alcohol, Drug
            Abuse, and Mental Illness Administration) pub. no. 87-1518. Wash-
            ington D.C.: U.S. Government Printing Office. pp. 14–27.
Wolfe, Barbara, and Robert Haveman
    1990   Trends in the Prevalence of Work Disability from 1962 to 1984, and
            their Correlates. *The Milbank Quarterly* 68(1):53–80.
WHO (World Health Organization)
    1979   *Schizophrenia: An International Follow-up Study.* New York: John
            Wiley and Sons.
Yelin, Edward
    1986   The Myth of Malingering: Why Individuals Withdraw from Work in
            the Presence of Illness. *The Milbank Quarterly* 64(4):622–649.
    1989   Misplaced Concern: The Social Context of the Work-Disability
            Problem. *The Milbank Quarterly,* 67(supp. 2, pt. 1):114–165.
Young, Allan
    1982   The Anthropologies of Illness and Sickness. *Annual Review of An-
            thropology* 11:257–285.
Zola, Irving K., ed.
    1982   *Ordinary Lives: Voices of Disability and Disease.* Cambridge/Water-
            town, N.J.: Apple-wood Books.
Zubin, Joseph, Jay Magaziner, and Stuart R. Steinhauer
    1983   The Metamorphosis of Schizophrenia: From Chronicity to Vulnera-
            bility. *Psychological Medicine* 13:551–571.

12

Social Aspects
of Chagas Disease

Roberto Briceño-León

Chagas disease is a parasitic disease that affects the heart and the hollow viscera, causing an increase in their size and thereby affecting their functioning (Novoa Montero 1985; Garcia-Zapata and Marsden 1986). The disease begins with an infection caused by the parasite *Trypanosoma cruzi,* and can be transmitted by the feces of the triatomine bug, by blood transfusion or congenitally. Of the three forms of transmission that involve contact between the vector and humans, the first is the most important: during the night the infected vector bites the human host in order to feed itself, and at the same time defecates. When the human responds by scratching, the parasite, with the feces, enters into the system.

The disease is only found in the New World. It is estimated that 7.6 percent of the population of Latin America, around 24 million people, are infected (OPS 1984), and a further 65 million are at risk of becoming infected (WHO 1985; OPS 1982). However, not everyone who is infected develops the disease. In its acute phase the disease has a mortality rate between 5 and 10 percent, affecting mainly children, but if mortality does not result, the disease enters a chronic phase in which the parasites disappear from the bloodstream and symptoms reappear ten or twenty years later. Nevertheless, during this time, and for reasons as yet unknown, myocardial damage continues. It is estimated that 30 percent of the population previously infected develops the disease, which is characterized by a chronic cardiomyopathy or enlargement of the esophagus and colon. The most important complications are severe constipation and intestinal obstruction from the form of the disease that involves the digestive tract, and systemic and pulmonary embolism and sudden death from the form that involves the heart (Andrade 1983; Carrasco et al. 1983; MSAS 1986).

The disease has two cycles (modes of existence): one is sylvatic; the other is domestic. The disease has existed since ancient times in animals; in its sylvatic cycle it does not affect humans because the insects who are its vector live in palm trees, birds' nests, or animals' burrows, and the parasite moves from one animal to another, never coming into touch with a human host (Zeldon 1974, 1983). The problem began when the forest was cleared and certain animals became domestic. The insect moved to the human household and changed its source of food from animals to humans (Rodriguez Coura et al. 1966). This process seems to have started with the consolidation of the first Indian communities in South America, and mummies more than 1,500 years old have been found with the symptoms in northern Chile (Rothhammer et al. 1984). When the disease occurs in the domestic area a serious health problem arises.

Social Conditions of Transmission

Since its discovery, the disease has been described as a social disease. The social and environmental conditions in which rural populations of Latin America live have been related to the incidence of disease, and in particular to poverty and the state of dwellings (Tejera 1919; Romaña 1952; Gamboa 1965; Torrealba 1956, 1958).

The dwelling, which should provide protection, becomes an aid to transmission of the disease when conditions are present that permit colonization by the disease vector. Palm roof and unplastered mud walls, a mud floor, and the presence of harvested grains inside the house allow different vectors to lodge in the home. Hiding during the day, they come out at night to bite (Pifano and Guerrero 1965; Rocha et al. 1971; Minter 1977; Carcavallo 1978; Marsden et al. 1982; Schofield and Marsden 1982; Maekelt 1983; Schofield and White 1984; Schofield 1985; Velasco 1985).

Now, why is it that conditions that allow the presence of the insect are found in the dwelling? Why do the campesinos build a house that allows the transmission of the disease when they could, hypothetically, have built one in which these conditions were not found and which did not permit disease transmission? This is the question that leads us to look at social conditions. Underdevelopment, poverty, latifundismo, and the lack of education have all been given as explanations, but which of these factors are the most important? (Dias and Dias 1985*b;* Dias and Dias 1986; Briceño-León 1986*a*)

We need first to differentiate between the different levels of analysis and theories that might explain the situation from a social point of view (Sevilla Casas 1987; Mendez-Dominguez 1988; Kleinman 1987). In most analyses carried out with respect to Chagas disease, as with other tropical diseases (malaria, schistosomiasis, leishmaniasis), the macro- and microsocial levels are mixed and confused, and thus two theories of human behavior and action have been used indiscriminately (Garcia 1976; Miles 1976; Celis 1980; Carcavallo 1978). For example, the macrosocial variables considered include underdevelopment, which keeps rural populations in Latin America in a state of misery and impoverishment; or latifundismo, which prevents the campesino from settling productively on the land (Dias and Dias 1982). At the same time, microvariables are applied, such as the physical state of the dwelling, or education. Brief mention is made of the economic circumstances preventing the campesinos from improving their homes, since they cannot afford to buy the products necessary to do so, and of resignation, helplessness, or the lack of motivation to overcome the miserable circumstances that foster transmission of the disease (Torrealba 1980*a;* Ribera 1985; OPS/OMS, 1979).

The debate concerning the macro- and microsocial aspects of a problem cannot be ignored in studying tropical disease, but given the present level of knowledge of vector-transmitted diseases, it is important to grasp the relation between human action or nonaction and disease transmission. By studying microsocial factors, therefore, we can arrive at a better understanding of the phenomenon, and we can also design policies with the participation of the persons at risk (Rosenfield 1986).

Chagas Disease and the Dwelling

To determine why conditions that expose the residents to the disease vector prevail in the homes, we decided to work with two explanatory models. The first is a situation explanation model, which uses three socioeconomic variables: ownership of the land worked, status of the dwelling, and occupation of the male heads of household. The second is a psychosocial model, which identifies three variables: locus of control, beliefs about the control of disease, and rootedness. The entire array of variables seeks to bring together the actual circumstances in which the poor live, their impact on individual self-confidence, and the person's expectations and beliefs, and then to relate these factors to the state of the dwelling.

The first three variables were designed to examine the living conditions.

1. *Ownership of land:*
    Land is basic to the life of the campesinos, and reflects the degree of security and control they have over their work. It was expected that those who did not own land would be more exposed to the disease, since their homes would be in a worse condition.

2. *Status of the dwelling:*
    The ownership or marketability of the dwelling could result in changes being made in the house, since the owner of a saleable house would invest time and money improving it, expecting a return on the investment.

3. *Occupation:*
    This reflects both social status and the financial means to obtain market goods. Conditions in the homes of those with poorer occupations would be more favorable for the transmission of the disease.

Consideration of the psychosocial factors leads to the following inquiries:

1. *General expections with respect to the control of one's destiny:*
    If the individuals believed that their destiny lay in their own hands, their houses would be in better sanitary condition than if they believed that their destiny was controlled by external forces, such as fate or chance (Rotter 1966; Valecha and Ostrom 1974; Levenson 1981; Romero-Garcia 1980; Seligman 1975).

2. *Beliefs about the disease:*
    If the head of the family believed that he or she could do something to control the disease, his or her house would not present conditions favorable to the transmission and contraction of the disease.

3. *Rootedness:*
    If the person interviewed believed that his stay was not permanent, he would not finish his house, but if he intended to stay for a long time, he would build a sanitary dwelling.

We interviewed all the heads of family of the municipality of Tinaquillo, Venezuela (n:556) and sketched descriptive plans of the houses (Sequeda et al. 1982; Tonn, 1978). In order to analyze the results, we worked with the following predictions: we hypothesized that the stronger belief in the possibility of controlling the disease, the fewer the conditions in the dwelling favorable to transmission and contraction of the disease. The less the individual believed in the possibility of controlling the disease, on the other hand, the more conditions would favor disease transmission. The Goodman-Kruskall coefficient and Mann statistics were used in carrying out these calculations.

The results showed the occupation, locus of control, and rootedness variables to be highly significant: housing conditions that might or might not permit transmission of the disease varied together with changes in occupation, expectations with respect to the control of one's destiny, and level of rootedness. The ownership of land and status of the dwelling did not prove to be significant: houses did or did not reveal conditions favorable to the transmission of the disease independent of these variables. The belief about the control of the disease proved to be moderately significant.

The result of the investigation showed that a combination of objective factors (economic means to really improve the house) and subjective factors (belief in the capacity to control one's destiny and rootedness) act together to favor or prevent the transmission of the disease. But there were also factors that were not significant, and which I feel deserve additional explanation. Contrary to what has often been proposed, neither the ownership of land nor of the dwelling proved to be important, and I believe this is due to two factors. First, ownership of farm land is of no great weight in the lives of the poorest in the Venezuelan countryside, since Venezuelan social legislation grants considerable protection even in cases of nonownership. Second, the majority of people interviewed were house owners. Renting hardly exists, and the problem lies in the quality of the house, not in whether or not it is owned. With respect to beliefs about the control of the disease, these proved only moderately significant, because it is far from easy to develop specific expectations of control of a disease such as Chagas, which is asymptomatic and slow to take effect. It is thus difficult to establish a link between the process of transmission and its result, between action taken for its control and the effect of that action.

For these reasons, any attempt to control the disease should be made from a viewpoint of global social improvement, and not limited to the disease alone. The variables that emerged as significant should also be taken into consideration.

Control of the Disease and Community Participation

We wanted later to ascertain how these results could be of use for a disease control program, and at the same time to test their efficacy. The result of the survey enabled us to look into the past and to understand why something had been done or had been left undone, but we did not know if this was valid for the future, or for future action.

We therefore set up an action research program and chose a community of twenty-three families, to whom we proposed a housing improvement program in the name of the state government. The program planned to manipulate two variables that had proved significant in the survey: income and self-confidence. An intervention plan was thus proposed to build and improve the mud and wattle daub houses (Romaña 1952; MSAS 1966, 1969, 1976; Raadt 1976; OPS/OMS 1981, 1982; Romero and Mara 1986; Velloso 1979; Schofield 1984; Webb 1985; Dias and Dias 1985). Small loans from the state in the form of materials were granted according to the evaluation of the campesinos' work. The campesinos also contributed their own labor. Messages of confidence were given in his ability to improve his house. Clear rules applying to everyone were established. Everything had to be accounted for, and nothing was free (Briceño-León 1987).

Participation in the program was voluntary, and sixteen families decided to take part. Five were opposed to the program since they hoped to be given another type of house free of charge by the state housing agency, and two were neither opposed nor took part.

Throughout the whole process the researchers acted as government social workers. They had to act like any official, but were required to keep meticulous records of the whole process in a field diary. The houses were photographed and meetings and interviews with people from outside the community were recorded. All the information recorded by the researchers had to be cross-checked and discussed in meetings of the research group.

The families taking part managed to improve some houses in four months, although these houses had been unfinished for ten years. The program was thus a success. The community decided that the process had been so important for them that they should change the name of the village from Caño Muerto (Dead Creek) to Caño Nuevo (New Creek).

With the project finished, the researchers returned to the community to apply a posttest of the social and psychological variables under study as well as the conditions of the dwelling. They showed each family a photographic record of their home, and discussed the characteristics of the program with them.

Of all the variables considered in this analysis, it could be seen that the individuals who did not take part were those with better jobs and who, therefore, had their own means to improve their homes. The locus of control variable did not turn out to be significant in the decision to take part in the program. In comparing the pretest and posttest, however, it could be seen that the participants increased their level of self-confidence, and that those whose results were more positive showed a greater increase in self-confidence than those whose results were less so.

On the other hand, we observed that the campesinos' vision of the world was important in the decision to take part in the program. Those who decided to take part and who showed the best results were people who had lived outside the community in nearby towns. Although the proposal to build in mud (wattle and daub) is a traditional one—as opposed to modern-day thinking, which considers mud to be a step backwards, and cement to be modern—here traditional techniques become innovative, and paradoxically, those who had lived away were the ones who were more receptive to traditional techniques.

Two other factors were of significance: the encouragement by the woman of the household and the support in the form of labor of children over fifteen years of age. The woman sometimes did work on the house, but what was more important was her decision to persuade her husband to take part in its improvement.

Conclusion

In the case of Chagas disease, one can see that human action (in cutting palm and using it for rooting) or nonaction (in leaving the walls of the house unplastered) allows for the transmission of the disease. It is also in human action, therefore, that the means of control lies, and not in biological solutions to control the insect vector.

This action or nonaction depends on the subjective and objective circumstances of a distinct type. The campesino's perception of the disease is impeded since, even with all the relevant information, it is difficult to understand a disease whose symptoms may take ten or twenty years to be felt. So, despite the fact that Chagas exists as a "disease" in a biological and physical sense, there is no culture about the disease, and so the "illness" does not exist (Kleinman 1978; Young 1982).

Furthermore, since the disease is hard to diagnose and is incurable, medical staff do not inform patients that they are suffering from the disease so as not to cause unnecessary worry, and in autopsies they do not state that a possible relation may exist between a cardiac arrest and Chagas disease. All these factors result in a somewhat contradictory situation in which the Ministry of Health maintains that the disease is important, while the campesinos know hardly anyone who has suffered from it, and even less, anyone who has died of it.

In this case, paradoxically, the absence of "medicalization" has prevented an awareness of the risk of contracting such a disease and, perhaps, has also prevented the participation of people in its control.

An important part of the work that we have done and that is still necessary to do is thus oriented to the production of an "illness," that is, to the construction of a culture about the disease. The campesino has a cultural approach toward snakes, because he knows quite well that snakes are dangerous, but he does not have a cultural approach to the triatomine bug.

These difficulties concerning the perception of the disease are compounded by the conditions in which the poor campesino finds himself. He wonders, and perhaps he is right, why he should be concerned about a disease that will only affect him in several years' time, when he has more immediate problems of daily living to solve. The disease, therefore, is of secondary importance.

Even if the individual does decide to do something to improve his house despite these circumstances, he confronts the problem of obtaining commercial products, which until now have been presented as the only way to achieve a salubrious dwelling. If he cannot obtain these materials, and the government decides to protect him from the disease by giving him a house, the problem is only temporarily solved. When he comes to enlarge the house, he will use traditional materials and technology, once again allowing the transmission of the disease.

If the individual is given the dwelling, or if the disease is controlled by means of insecticide spraying carried out by the government, the message being transmitted is that it is the state that can do something to control the disease and not the campesinos themselves. Such "positive discrimination" produces negative effects. By trying to help in this manner, a greater lack of confidence in oneself is being created.

Moreover, when a representative of the Ministry of Health arrives in a town, looks for the houses in the worst condition, and improves these houses, the message to the population is that if you do nothing for yourself the Ministry will do it. Thus, people who fail to take care of their houses are rewarded, and those who try to improve their living conditions are punished. It is thus essential to consider the unexpected or undesirable effects that a goodwill policy could produce, as the example of Chagas disease illustrates.

One can rightly assume that the campesino and the disease control program have different goals: the health organizations want to control the disease, while the campesino wants to improve his standard of living. This difference can be overcome by modifying the dwelling, since it is both the means of transmission of the disease and its control. It is therefore possible to develop policies that combine both interests.

What is important is that in controlling a disease of this nature, different levels of social reality must be dealt with, making limited action again impossible. Thus, in order to combine the goals of the health organizations with those of the campesinos, the social structure must be taken into account, and the expectations of the campesinos modified so as to increase their confidence in their own efforts. Certain technological solutions are also necessary in order to meet these goals, as well as a reorganization of the administrative procedures in such a way that the poorest do not end up being penalized or treated unfairly. For all this to come about requires both a change in the behavior of the campesinos as well as in that of the personnel of the disease control organizations.

In this particular exercise, theoretical approaches and different methodologies, as well as a combination of basic research and practical application, have been of great help in advancing our knowledge. What is even more noteworthy is that it has brought about a reorientation of the Ministry of Health's program, which could result in a population that has more confidence in achieving its own goals and a more lasting control of the disease. Long-term control of the disease depends also on establishing a new disease category that will allow for the local recognition of illness symptoms and for the development of appropriate sickness behaviors.

Acknowledgments

This research received financial support from the Special Programme for Research and Training in Tropical Diseases UNDP/World Bank/WHO.

References

Briceño-León, Roberto
  1986a   The Social Aspects of Chagas Disease and Health Educational Policies. Paper presented at the seminar, "The Use of Social Science Research in Improving Education for Control of Tropical Diseases," Salvador, Bahia, Brazil, August 3–8.
  1986b   Aspectos psicosomáticos de la enfermedad de Chagas. *Boletín de la Asociación Venezolana de Psicología Social* 9(3):37–41.
  1987   Rural Housing for Control of Chagas Disease in Venezuela. *Parasitology Today* 3:384–387.
Carcavallo, Rodolfo
  1978   Ecología humana y enfermedad de Chagas. *Boletín de la Dirección de Malariología y Saneamiento Ambiental.* 18(4):248–258.
Carrasco, Hugo, Ernesto Palacios Pru, Rosa Mendoza, and Cecilia Dagert de Scorza
  1983   Aspectos clínicos de la enfermedad de Chagas: Diagnóstico del miocardio. *Interciencia* 8(6):342–352.

Celis, Emma L. Rubin
    1980   Community Structures and Dynamics in Rural Areas of Tropical Endemic Countries in Latin America and Their Relationship with the Epidemiology of Chagas' Disease. Paper presented in the workshop on Epidemiological Social and Economic Aspects of Present and Future Methods for Chagas' Disease Control, Mexico City, July 28–August 1.
Dias, Joao Carlos, and Rosinha Borges Dias
    1982   Housing and the Control of Vectors of Human Chagas' Disease in the State of Minas Gerais, Brazil. *Pan American Health Organization Bulletin* 16(2):117–127.
    1985*a*   Participacao da comunidade no controle da doença de Chagas. *Annales de la Societé Belge de Medicine Tropicale* 65 (suppl. 1):127–135.
    1985*b*   Aspectos Socioculturales e Económicos NA expensao e no controle da doença de Chagas Humana. *Annales de la Societé Belge de Medicine Tropicale* 65 (suppl. 1):119–126.
Dias, Rosinha Borges, and Joao Carlos Dias
    1986   Considerations on the mental field of reference of rural people and the control of tropical diseases. *Belo Horizonte,* Brazil. Mimeo.
Gamboa, Jorge
    1965   Comprobación de la presencia de *Rhodnius prolixus* en la vivienda rural. *Boletín Informativo de la Dirección de Malariología y Saneamiento Ambiental* (Maracay, Venezuela) 5(6):270–274.
Garcia, Angelina
    1976   Human Behavior and Chagas Disease. In *American Trypanosomiasis Research,* pp. 319–322. No. 318. Belo Horizonte, Brazil: Pan American Health Organization.
Garcia-Zapata, Marco Tulio A., and Philip D. Marsden
    1986   Chagas Disease. *Clinics in Tropical Medicine and Communicable Diseases* 1(3):557–585.
Kleinman, Arthur
    1978   Concepts and Models for the Comparison of Medical Systems. *Social Science and Medicine* 12:85–93.
    1987   The Conceptual Basis for the Study of Illness Perception and Behaviour in Tropical Diseases. Paper presented at the conference, "Social and Economic Determinants and Consequences of Malaria and Its Control under Changing Conditions," Sitges, Spain, October 26–28.
Levenson, Hanna
    1981   Differentiating among Internality, Powerful Others, and Change. In *Research with the Locus of Control Construct,* Herbert M. Lefcour, ed., 1:15–61. New York: Academic Press.
Maekelt, G. Alberto
    1983.   La epidemiología de la enfermedad de Chagas en relación con el ecosistema domiciliario. *Interciencia* (November–December) 8(6): 353–366.

Marsden, P. D., D. Virgens, I. Magalhaes, J. Tavaraes-Neto, R. Ferreira,
C. H. Costa, C. N. Castro, V. Macedo, and A. Prata
    1982   Ecología doméstica do *Triatoma infestans* em Mambaí, Goiás, Bra-
            sil. *Rev. Instituto Med. Trop. Paulo* (November-December) 24(6):
            364–373.

Marsden, Philip D. and R. Penna
    1982   A 'Vigilance Unit' for Households Subject to Triatomine Control.
            Transactions of the Royal Society of Tropical Medicine and Hygiene
            76(6):790–792.

Mendez-Dominguez, Alfredo
    1988   *Knowledge, Attitudes and Treatment-seeking Behaviour for Malaria
            in Guatemala.* Guatemala: Universidad del Valle.

Miles, M. A.
    1976   Human Behaviour and the Propagation of Chagas' Disease. *Trans-
            actions of the Royal Society of Tropical Medicine and Hygiene* 70(5/
            6):521–522.

Ministerio de Saude, Fundaçao Servicios de Saude Publica
    1975   Melhoria da habitaçao rural para controle da doença de Chagas.
            Mimeo.

Minter, D. M.
    1977   Triatomine Bugs and the Household of Chagas' Disease. Medical
            Entomology Centenary Symposium Proceedings, pp. 85–93. Lon-
            don Royal Society of Tropical Medicine and Hygiene.

MSAS (Ministerio de Sanidad y Asistencia Social)
    1961–   *Informes internos del estado sobre el programa de control de
    1985   Chagas.* Estado Cojedes, San Carlos, Venezuela: Dirección de
            Malariología y Saneamiento Ambiental.
    1966   Campañas contra la enfermedad de Chagas. *Revista Venezolana de
            Sanidad y Asistencia Social* (Caracas) 31(1):114–154.
    1969   *Informe del Primer Seminario Mundial de Vivienda Rural y Servi-
            cios Comunales, 2–9 April 1967.* Maracay, Venezuela: Dirección de
            Malariología y Saneamiento Ambiental.
    1976   *Programa de mejoramiento del rancho campesino.* Maracay-Estado
            Aragua, Venezuela: Dirección de Malariología y Saneamiento Am-
            biental.
    1986   Enfermedad de Chagas. In *7th Congreso Venezolano de Salud Púb-
            lica, February 25–March 1.* Caracas, Venezuela.

Novoa Montero, Dario
    1985   *Miocardiopatía crónica endémica rural venezolana: Chagásica?* Mer-
            ida, Venezuela: Libros de la Universidad de los Andes.

OPS (Organización Panamericana de la Salud)
    1982   Enfermedad de Chagas. *Boletín Epidemiológico de la Oficina Sani-
            taria Panamericana* 3:1–6.
    1984   Situación de la enfermedad de Chagas in las Américas. *Boletín
            Epidemiológico de la Oficina Sanitaria Panamericana* 5:5–9.

OPS/OMS (Organización Panamericana de la Salud/Organización Mundiae de la Salud)
1979   *Enfermedad de Chagas. Los estudios socio-culturales y desarrollo comunitario.* Documento interno. Trujillo, Venezuela: Organización Panamericana de la Salud.
1981   *El control de la enfermedad de Chagas a través del mejoramiento de la vivienda rural.* AMRO-0903. Annual report. Maracay, Venezuela: Organización Panamericana de la Salud.
1982   *El control de la enfermedad de Chagas a través del mejoramiento de la vivienda rural.* AMRO-0903. Annual report. Maracay, Venezuela: Organización Panamericana de la Salud.

PiFano Felix, and Lacenio Guerrero
1963   Campaña contra la enfermedad de Chagas en Venezuela. Aspectos metodológicos, encuestas epidemiológicas de reconocimiento en escala nacional e investigación científica. *Boletín de la Oficina Sanitaria Panamericana* 54:394–411.

Raadt, Peter
1976   Improvement of Rural Housing as a Means of Control of Chagas' Disease. In *American Trypanosomiasis Research,* pp. 323–325. No. 318. Belo Horizonte, Brazil: Pan American Health Organization.

Ribera, B. G.
1985   "Aspectos socioeconómicos y culturales de la enfermedad de Chagas. *Annales de la Societé Belge de Medécine Tropicale* 65 (suppl. 1):1–8.

Rocha e Silva, Eduardo Olavo, José Maluf, and Renato Correa
1971   La enfermedad de Chagas—Vigilancia entomológica en el estado de Sao Paulo, Brasil. *Boletín de la Oficina Sanitaria Panamericana* 71(5):387–401.

Rodriguez Coura, J., Luis Ferreira y Rodriguez da Silva
1966   Triatomineos no estado da Guanabara e suas relaçoes com o domicilio humano. *Revista del Instituto de Medicina Tropical de Sao Paulo* 8:162–166.

Romaña, Cecilio
1952   *Cómo puede construirse un rancho higiénico antivinchuca.* 2d ed. Folleto de divulgación no. 4. Ministerio de Educación de la nación Universidad Nacional de Tucumán, Argentina Instituto de Medicina Regional.

Romero-Garcia, Oswaldo
1980   Locus de control, inteligencia, estatus socioeconómicos y rendimiento académico. Publicación no. 10. Merida, Venezuela: Laboratorio de Psicología, Universidad de los Andes.

Romero, José and D. Mora Marquez
1986   Programa nacional de vivienda rural. In *7th Congreso Venezolano de Salud Pública, February 25–March 1.* Caracas.

Rosenfield, Patricia
1986   The Activist Analyst: The Role of Social Scientist in Tropical Disease Control. Paper prepared for meeting on use of social science

research in improving education for tropical disease control, Salvador, Brazil, August 3–8.

Rothhammer, Francisco, Vivien Standen, Lautaro Nuñez, Marvin J. Allison, and Bernardo Arriaza
1984   Origen y desarrollo de la Tripanosomiasis en el área Centro-Sur Andina. *Revista Chungara.* 12(Agosto 1984):155–160.

Rotter, Julián B.
1966   *Generalized Expectancies for Internal Versus External Control of Reinforcement.* Psychological Monographs General and Applied, vol. 80, no. 1. Gregory A. Kimble, ed. The American Psychological Association, Inc.

Schofield, Chris., and Philip D. Marsden
1982   The Effect of Wall Plaster on a Population of *Triatoma infestans. Pan American Health Organization Bulletin* 16(4):356–360.

Schofield, C. J., and G. B. White
1984   Engineering Against Insect-Borne Disease in the Domestic Environment: House Design and Domestic Vectors of Disease. *Transcriptions of the Royal Society of Tropical Medicine and Hygiene* 78:285–292.

Schofield, C. J.
1985   Control of Chagas' Disease Vector. *British Medical Bulletin* 41(2): 187–194.

Seligman, Martin E. P.
1975   *Helplessness: On Depression, Development and Death.* San Francisco: Freeman.

Sequeda, Milady de, Luis Villalobos, and Andrés Sucre
1982   Enfermedad de Chagas: Resultados en 25,000 pobladores del medio rural venezolano. Sociedad Venezolana de Salud Pública, 29th Annual Assembly, Porlamar, Venezuela, 11–15 May.

Sevilla Casas, Elias
1987   The Study of Social and Economic Determinants of Malaria, Theoretical and Methodological Issues. Paper presented at the conference, Social and Economic Determinants of Malaria and Its Control under Changing Conditions. Sitges, Spain, 26–28 October.

Tejera, Enrique
1919   La Tripanosomiasis Americana o enfermedad de Chagas en Venezuela. *Gaceta Médica de Caracas* 26(10):104–108.

Tonn, Robert, Rosa Hubsch, Efrain Sukerman, Jose W. Torrealba, and Bisremiro Carrasquero
1978   Estudio epidemiológico sobre la enfermedad de Chagas en ocho centros poblados del estado Cojedes, Venezuela. *Boletín de la Dirección de Malariología y Saneamiento Ambiental* 18(1):3–15.

Torrealba, José Witnemundo
1980a   Future Perspectives of Community Involvement for and Control of Chagas' Disease. Paper presented at workshop on "Epidemiological Social and Economic Aspects of Present and Future Methods for

Chagas' Disease Control," World Health Organization, Mexico City, July 28–August 1.

1980*b*   Aspectos médicos sanitarios de la malaria. Enfermedad de Chagas y Leishmaniasis en la región neotropical. Prepared for workshop on "Inmunología de Parásitos," 30th Annual Convention of AsoVac, Merida, Venezuela, 9–14 November.

Investigación y evaluación de estrategias de participación comunitaria en el control integral de la enfermedad de Chagas (Proyecto de Investigación). Departamento de Microbiología y Parasitología, Facultad de Ciencias de la Salud, Universidad de Carabobo, Valencia Venezuela. Mimeo.

Torrealba, José Francisco

1956   *Investigaciones sobre la enfermedad de Chagas en San Juan de Los Morros. Caracas: Imprenta Nacional.*

1958   Alrededor de mis 25 años de investigación sobre la enfermedad de Chagas en Venezuela. In *Investigaciones sobre la enfermedad de Chagas en San Juan de Los Morros,* pp. 415–430. Obras Científicas 5. Recopilación. Fascículo 6. Caracas: Imprenta Nacional.

Valecha, Gopal, and Thomás Ostron

1974   An Abbreviated Measure of Internal-External Locus of Control. *Journal of Personality Assessment* 38(4):369–376.

Velasco, Jorge

1985   Informe epidemiológico. Paper presented at Reunión de Evaluación del Proyecto de Control de la Enfermedad de Chagas a través del Mejoramiento de la Vivienda Rural. Trujillo.

Velloso, Casio H.

1979   *El control de la enfermedad de Chagas (tripanosomiasis americana), mediante el mejoramiento de la vivienda rural en Brasil.* Belo Horizonte, Brazil: Fundação Centro Tecnológico de Minas Gerais.

Webb, D. J. T.

1985   Low Cost Housing and Parasite Vectors. *Parasitology Today* 1(2): 65–66.

WHO (World Health Organization)

1985   Chagas' Disease in the Region of the Americas. *Weekly Epidemiological Record/ Relevé Epidemiologique Hebdomadaire* 60:37–44.

Young, Allan

1982   The Anthropologies of Illness and Sickness. *Annual Review of Anthropology* 11:257–285.

Zeledon, Rodrigo

1974   Epidemiology, Modes of Transmission and Reservoir Hosts of Chagas' Disease. In *Trypanosomiasis and Leishmaniasis with Special Reference to Chagas' Disease.* Ciba Foundation Symposium 20(n.s.):51–85. Amsterdam, London, New York: Elsevier, Excerpta Medica, North Holland: Associated Scientific Publishers.

1983   Vectores de la enfermedad de Chagas y sus características ecofisiológicas. *Interciencia* 8(6):384–395.

Part Five

Body Politics–Past
and Present

Introduction

Body Politics—Past and Present

While each participant in the symposium chose a particular health problem or issue and considered it from the perspectives of human physiology, social setting, and shared meanings, the most difficult bridge to build appears to have been the one linking biology and culture. The three final papers in the volume bring us to the biology-culture dialectic by way of new terrain.

Jean Comaroff's paper shifts our attention from a focus on the body at close range to the intersection of biological and cultural processes viewed historically. Medicine and imperialism in nineteenth-century Africa are seen to be inseparably joined in practice and in concept. The evolving field of biomedicine, introduced by missionary healers, provided images of an ailing human body that would justify the intervention of a colonial state as it imposed its own order of domination (a process similar to the one the Inuit are currently attempting to resist). An era of "humane imperialism" thus drew upon earlier evangelical conceptions of seeing and being, as well as on specific definitions of person, body, health, and society, a bodily inscription of medical categories and healing practices identified in many of the conference papers.

Margaret Lock, for example, writes about the female body as a contested site of symbolic representation and medical practice. The contrasting approaches in North America and Japan to the end of menstruation are seen as evidence of two "local biologies." Many Japanese women do not identify the end of menstruation as a part of menopause, and the physical symptoms usually associated with menopause in North America (hot flashes and night sweats) are not a focus of concern. An explanation for these differences is found in the evaluations of women's place in society, as well as in what is accepted as authentic knowledge in the medical profession in each location. In both, the politics of aging dwells upon biological change and its associated risk of suffering and distress. In North America, however, the aging female is seen as a biological anomaly and a target for medical intervention, whereas in Japan, the anatomy of the middle-aged woman is of less concern than is her potential inability to care for elderly family members in a three-generation household. Thus, while the condition of the aging woman is subject to ideological elaboration and disparagement in both North America and Japan, in the former her physical symptoms are medicalized, while in the latter her symptoms are ignored or suppressed in favor of behavioral discipline.

In Donna Haraway's paper "the body" as a stable, discrete unit of analysis gives way to a postmodern view of the body as a mobile field of strategic differences, depicted in the language of immunology. What constitutes the self, an individual, a unit of analysis, or a subject, is seen to be highly problematic. Our former grasp of such notions as sex, reproduction, race, and disease are loosened as earlier biomedical models phrased in terms of laws of growth and essential properties are replaced by a language of coded systems of recognition and misrecognition. The charge to conference participants that they rethink the relationship of biology to political economy, local context, and symbol are discussed here in terms of a new kind of identity or mutual constitution existing among technology, the body, and signs and symbols.

As the authors in this section underscore, medical anthropology offers many ways to link culture and biology, practice and theory. The intellectual coherence of all the papers is thus not to be found in the objects of study, which are highly variable, but in a common set of questions. In one way or another, all of the contributors attempt to identify the processes that give life to the conceptual frameworks that impose order upon, and give legitimacy to, the voices and beliefs of certain individuals, groups, and institutions rather than others. The intimate relationship of cultural and material production adopted here is now well established in cultural anthropology. The essays in this volume bring matters of health, illness, and human suffering into this critical discussion.

13

The Diseased Heart of Africa

Medicine, Colonialism, and the Black Body

Jean Comaroff

A few years ago a line from Cape Town to Cairo was thought to be a romantic dream, and yet most of us now are hoping to travel that way home before many years have passed; . . . and, what to some of us is more important still, there will be less of human pain and misery and more of healthy enjoyment and progress in the poor, diseased heart of Africa.
Rev. W. C. Willoughby, *Native Life on the Transvaal Border*

Medicine held a special place in the imagination that colonized nineteenth-century Africa. In fact, the rising hegemony of biology in Europe can be traced in the control of threatening populations at home and abroad—and, more generally, in the regulation of relations between the "civil" and the "unruly." But the expanding empire also fed the new science with essential "raw material," and with a natural rationale for its emerging vision of physical man. As an object of European speculation, "Africans" personified suffering and degeneracy, their environment a hothouse of fever and affliction. The rhetoric of the "geographical mission" linked the advance of reason in the interior of the dark continent with the biological thrust into the dim recesses of the human person. Early evangelists in South Africa saw social and political obstacles to their "humane imperialism" as natural contagions, responsive to medical control. As their philanthropic dreams hardened into colonial realities, the black body became ever more specifically associated with degradation, disease, and contagion.

In this paper, I explore the relationship of medicine and imperialism on the South African frontier, focusing on three distinct moments widely separated in time: the shaping of an imperial vision in late eighteenth-century discourses of the afflicted continent; the advent of the mid-nineteenth-century healing mission; and the founding of the colonial state in the early twentieth century. I shall suggest that the development of British colonialism in Africa as a cultural enterprise was inseparable from the rise of biomedicine as science. The frontiers of "civilization" were the margins of a European sense of health as social and bodily order, and the first sustained probe into the ailing heart of Africa was a "mission to the suffering." It followed that the savage natives were the very embodiment of dirt and disorder, their moral affliction all of a piece with their physical degradation and their "pestiferous" surroundings. The early soldiers of Christendom were also the cutting edge of colonialism, and when they tried to domesticate the realities of the "dark" interior, they drew heavily on the iconography and practice of healing. What is more, their accounts of life and affliction in the African "laboratory" served as grist to the mill of a growing natural science.

Yet once they had abetted the rise of the colonial state, missionary healers in South Africa were to find themselves eclipsed by the newly formed agencies of public health. By the turn of this century, their talk of civilizing Africa had given way to a practical concern with the hygiene of black populations—and to the project of taming a native workforce. Here, as elsewhere in the colonized world, persons were disciplined and communities redistributed in the name of sanitation and the control of disease. For as blacks became an essential element in the white industrial world, medicine was called upon to regulate their challenging physical presence. It also crystallized the political threat they posed to that world by linking racial intercourse with the origin of sickness. I shall suggest that, whereas mission healing was little more than a persuasive art, the health regimes of the colonial state rested on a much greater authority, one whose global certainties were the product of the mutually sustaining regimes of science and empire.

The point of my analysis, I stress, is not to argue that imperial expansion determined the rise of biomedical science. Neither do I claim that nineteenth-century medicine was merely an ideology of imperial control. Rather, I seek to show that each played off the other within the unfolding of a particular historical process—that, despite their ostensible independence, they were in fact cut from the same cultural cloth. Each came to verify the other through the categories and metaphors of an underlying vision. Thus, notwithstanding its status as an emerging science, medicine drew upon social images to mediate physical realities, giving colonial power relations an alibi in the ailing human body. And colonial regimes, in turn, drew upon medical icons and practices to impose their domination upon subjects and collectivities.

Biology, Romantic Naturalism, and the African's Place in Nature

Writers on the early nineteenth-century life sciences have observed that the period was marked by a restructuring of the "chain of being," with special reference to its lower half (Figlio 1976:20). The real issue underlying debates about "man's" place in nature was the relationship of the human species to the rest of the living world.

> There was a focusing upon the multi-faceted idea of animality, as opposed to an insistence upon a scalar, uni-dimensional hierarchy, with man at the top of the visible, and God at the top of the invisible, realm. (Figlio 1976:20)

This implied a preoccupation with continuities, with the properties common to all animate beings. Those who sought such properties had to "define the elusive notion of life; to measure and rank the degrees of its expression" (Figlio 1976:28). Rooted in the contrast between the animate and the inanimate, the enterprise fixed upon "man" as the embodiment of perfection—in this debate, the language was unequivocally male—for it was he who had distinguished himself by employing reason to discover his own essence. This, in turn, led inexorably to the concept of "generic human nature" (Stocking 1987:17), a notion that separated man from beast and people from objects, and so rendered anomalous anything—like the slave trade—that confused them. Of course, "human nature" notwithstanding, the chain of being was itself to be differentiated and internally ranked, and it used "the African" to mark out the lowest limits of the human species.

In the epistemology of the time, then, the key to knowledge seemed to lie increasingly within man himself. The essence of life was in the unplumbed depths of organic being, to be grasped through the invasive thrust, the looking and naming, of the new biology (Foucault 1975). Its interior truth—merely signified in outer bodily form—gave rise to meaningful differences in the faculties and functions of living beings. This mode of seeing was becoming increasingly tangible in discourses about exploration in Africa, where the quest for knowledge of the interior likened the continent to the human body (Comaroff and Comaroff 1991: chap. 3). But the newly charted surfaces of the African landscape had an even more direct connection with the human organism, for the geographical mission was also extending European knowledge of the global range of mankind. In investigating the savage, the West set up a mirror in which it might find a tangible, if inverted, self-image. Non-Europeans filled out the nether reaches of the scale of being, providing the contrast against which cultivated man might emerge with clarity. On this scale, moreover, the African was assigned a particularly base position. In treating him as the very embodiment of savagery, the travel literature had given descriptions of his physical form alongside clinical accounts of his "manners and customs" (Pratt 1985). African "nature" was thus grounded in the color, shape, and substance of the black physique.

With the ascendance of comparative anatomy and biology, the reduction of African society and culture to such organic bases took on more authority. For much of the eighteenth century it had been civilization that had separated savage man from his European counterpart—moral and politicoeconomic circumstances rather than physical endowment (Stocking 1987:18). But the vocabulary of natural science was to formalize an existing European association of dark continents with black bodies and dim minds. Comparative anatomical scales and schemes presented the African as the human obverse of the European, the "link" between man and animal (Curtin 1964:38). Late eighteenth-century racial classifications almost invariably placed him at the bottom of the ladder to enlightenment, below such paler peoples as Asians or Native Americans (see White 1799; or Cuvier 1827–1835 1:97, who ranked the "fair or Caucasian variety" above the "yellow or Mongolian," and the latter above the "Negro or Ethiopian"). The hard facts of organic existence, of the ineffable chain of biological being, had come to determine the place of human beings in the world.

The life sciences, then, drew their terms from the current discourse about the human condition that arose out of Europe's encounter with the non-European world. Elevated to a new level of self-consciousness and authority, this "value-free" knowledge found a natural validation for cultural imperialism in the inner secrets of existence. Contemporary naturalists read off the degree of animality and the perfection of life from the external forms of different "organisms," for these forms were a function of the relative complexity, symmetry, and refinement of the faculties within. The influential Dutch scholar Petrus Camper (Cogan 1821), for instance, devised a scale that correlated the shape of the skull with aesthetic appearance and mental capacity. His so-called facial angle measured the projection of the jaw, a protruding profile being associated in the European mind with the long snouts, low brows, and sensory-bound state of animals. Applied to an eclectic array of evidence—including African travelers' accounts—this measurement defined and ranked national character, giving physical shape to the current philosophical concern with the relationship of race, nationality, and civilization (cf. Hume 1854). Camper's scale stretched from dog to ape to Negro, and through the European peoples to the ideal form epitomized in Greek sculpture (Cogan 1821:x; see Figlio 1976:28f). What is more, his pronouncements were publicized beyond the scientific community. The preface to an English translation of his popular lectures addressed a general artistic audience on the practical and aesthetic implications of the science of comparative anatomy:

> [Camper's] grand object was to shew, that national differences may be reduced to rules; of which the different directions of the facial line form a fundamental norma or canon . . . the knowledge of which will prevent the artist from blending the features of different nations in the same individual. (Cogan 1821:x)

Here nationality, culture, and physical type are condensed into the language that, in the nineteenth century, would mature into scientific racism. With his apartheid of the sketchpad, Camper imprinted the physical contours of stereotypic others on the European imagination—and, with them, a host of derogatory associations. The bestiality of the sample African profile, for instance, is quite unmistakable (see fig. 1).

Georges Cuvier, the prestigious Swiss comparative anatomist of the early nineteenth century, took the facial angle and the biological reduction of culture to new levels of sophistication: he developed a scale that purported to evaluate the perfection not only of the intellect but of the introspective self, the moral core of the person. By measuring the proportion of the mid-cranial area to that of the face, he sought to reveal the degree of dependence of an organism upon external sensations; the size of the cranium itself was taken to reflect the development of reason and self-control. On this count, the "Negro" stood between the "most ferocious apes" and the Europeans, who were themselves superseded by the men and deities of ancient Greek sculpture (Figlio 1976:28). But it was the neurological dimension of Cuvier's scheme (1827–1835 1:49) that addressed most explicitly the spiritual and moral capacity of man,

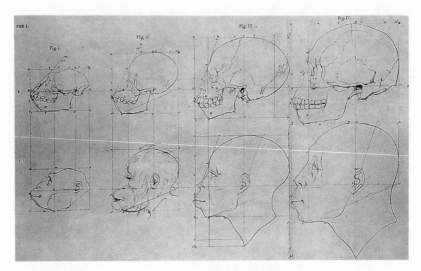

Figure 1.   Petrus Camper: Facial Lines and Angles. Left to right: ape; orang-utang; negro; calmuck. Reproduced from Camper (1821:119).

for the nervous system was the site of internal animation, and its complexity determined the higher faculties of life—intelligence and volition:

> Cuvier associated this compactness quite explicitly with the higher faculties, indeed, with the sense of the 'self.' Just as the nervous system coalesced into a centre from which dependent nerves arose, so too was the sense of self increasingly solidified and distinct. Thus, a grading of this . . . concentrating of the nervous system was simultaneously a grading of animal sentience and selfhood. (Figlio 1976:24)

And so the bourgeois subject, already secure in the ethic of Protestantism and rational philosophy, was given incontestable grounding in biological nature. Needless to say, the inner density and refinement associated by Cuvier with self-awareness and control were underdeveloped among non-Europeans, especially blacks, who were ostensibly bound by the bestial reflexes of survival (Cuvier 1827–1835 1:97; see also Curtin 1964:231).

As Figlio (1976:35) notes, Cuvier's writings were elaborately summarized in the British biomedical press within months of their publication and were widely discussed by scientists, theologians, and literati. In an age when specialist knowledge was not yet set apart by technical language, such work was rapidly directed to a receptive public. Often, as in the case of one widely read translation of Cuvier's *Animal Kingdom*, some "popular and entertaining matter" was added on the "instincts and habits" of animals and primitive man (1827–1835 1:i–ii). The editors in this instance included a description of the "unhappy races" of South Africa, a telling bricolage of current European curiosity substantiated by the accounts of early travelers (Comaroff and Comaroff 1991: chap. 3).

An ingredient of this bricolage was the direct observation made by Cuvier and others of the so-called Hottentot Venus, an unfortunate living exhibit of the "essential black" from the Cape Colony, who died in Paris in 1815 (Cuvier 1827–1835 1:196; see also Gilman 1985:212). These descriptions show early nineteenth-century representations of Africa hardening into stereotypes as travel tales and salon exotica were given scientific credentials and directed toward a seemingly insatiable popular readership. Furthermore, such images had a perceptible effect on the eyes of subsequent European visitors to Southern Africa. The epithets brought into association in the *Animal Kingdom*—the "Hottentots" described as "degraded and disgusting," or as "swarthy, filthy, and greasy"—were to flow from the pens of many later writers who claimed the authority of first-hand observation.

Like others before them, Cuvier and his editors focused on the exotic, simian qualities of the reproductive organs of black women, legitimating as medical inquiry their barely suppressed fascination with such torrid eroticism (Gilman 1985:213). Travelers like John Barrow (1801–1804) had also written in this vein of the "genital aberrations" of Bushman and Hottentot women, and Mungo Park (1799), if in somewhat different idiom, had reduced Africa to the body of a black female yielding herself to white male discovery (Comaroff and Comaroff 1991: chap. 3). This mythic theme also appears in both the poetry of romantic naturalists and the sober prose of our missionary crusaders. But, as the Cuvier text shows, in the early nineteenth century it was science that articulated and authorized such imagery; in fact, the various products of current European fancy at the time sailed under the colors of biological knowledge, knowledge about "nature," health, the body, and the self.

While the internalizing focus of biological science would eventually draw attention away from human transactions with the social and material environment, in the early nineteenth century there was still a lively concern with maintaining an equilibrium between organism and context. There had long been controversy over the role of climate in the origin of human diversity, some early naturalists (e.g., Buffon 1791) and biologists (e.g., Blumenbach 1969 [1775; 1795]) having argued that negro physical characteristics grew out of sustained life in the tropics (Curtin 1964:40). Here, scientific thought drew on European notions of environment dating back at least to the sixteenth and seventeenth centuries; in particular, to the humoral theory that "as the air is, so are the inhabitants" (cf. Hodgen 1964;283). In this legacy, the "southern climes" were associated with heat, sensuality, depletion, and decay, a connection that recurs repeatedly in the perceptions of eighteenth-century Europeans. Lichtenstein (1928–1930 1:58), for instance, blames the Cape Dutchman's "phlegm" on the African climate, quoting Goethe's similar observations about the indolent Neapolitans. Whites in warm climates mediated between the "antipodal constitutions" of the languid Negro and the "sanguinous Anglo-Saxon" (Cartwright 1853; Jones n.d.:48). The virulent effects of febrile disease on those Britons who attempted to establish a colony in West Africa in the late eighteenth century only reaffirmed the image of the "white man's grave," a continent inimical to civilized existence.

Although the writings and actions of the early missionaries to South Africa reveal a sense of contagion lurking in the dark continent and its inhabitants, their vision was most directly informed by the discourses of abolitionism and romantic naturalism, which also drew upon images of corporality and health. Rooted in the early romanticism of the mid-eighteenth century, these discourses expressed a reaction to urban bourgeois society and a celebration of preindustrial rural simplicity. Here the conventionalized savage innocent steps forth. Joseph Warton's "The Enthusiast; or the Love of Nature" (Park 1811:39), written in 1740, captures the mood well:

> Happy is the first of men ere yet confin'd
> To smoky cities; who in sheltering groves,
> Warm caves, and deep-sunk valleys liv'd and lov'd,
> By cares unwounded; what the sun and showers,
> And genial earth untillag'd could produce,
> They gather'd grateful.

But paradise has been blighted by those who, having tasted the fruit of knowledge, can no longer remember simple virtues. By 1750, Warton (Park 1811:52) had put the following words into the mouth of an Andean Indian:

> I see all Europe's children curs'd
> With lucre's universal thirst;
> The rage that sweeps my sons away
> My baneful gold shall well repay.

Africa's gold was its manpower, and, by the closing years of the eighteenth century, the rising strain of abolitionist sympathy had blended with romantic naturalism to depict a vanquished African Eden and an exiled native son. Thus William Roscoe (1787:10) writes of the blissful state from which the royal Cymbello is snatched by the slave-traders:

> Lord of his time, the healthful native rose,
> And seiz'd his faithful bow, and took his way
> Midst tangled woods, or over distant plains,
> To pierce the murd'rous Pard; when glowing noon
> Pour'd its meridian fervours, in cool shades
> He slept away th'uncounted hours . . .

The garden was overtaken by a "foul plague" from Europe—slavery—and "Nature recoiled, and tore with frantic hands her own immortal features" (Roscoe 1787:12). Disease and despoliation follow: Robert Southey's (1815:39) invocation of the "Genius of Africa" recounts the violation of the enchanted landscape. Maternal Africa is despoiled, her offspring torn from her breast by slavery:

> Ah heed the mother's wretchedness
> When in the hot infectious air
> O'er her sick babe she bows opprest,
> Ah hear her when the Traders tear
> The drooping infant from her breast!

Here we encounter a theme that links the romantic poetry of the time to the accounts of famous travelers like Mungo Park, a theme that was to shape the imperial vision of Africa. It is the myth of a continent bereft of its virile manhood, exiled from Eden, awaiting the restorative attentions of the heroic white man. The suffering abandon of Africa cultivated in such romantic poetry, especially when in the service of abolition, provided fertile ground for an ideology of colonial healing.

The Healing Mission

The rhetoric of the first generation of British evangelists in South Africa was to make effective use of the theme of Africa as savage and suffering. Robert Moffat, father-in-law of David Livingstone and illustrious pioneer of the London Missionary Society (LMS) among the Tswana, once addressed a large and admiring philanthropic public as follows:

> Africa still lies in her blood. She wants . . . all the machinery we possess, for ameliorating her wretched condition. Shall we, with a remedy that may safely be applied, neglect to heal her wounds? Shall we, on whom the lamp of life shines, refuse to disperse her darkness? (Moffat 1842:616)

Thus did the metaphors of healing justify "humane imperialism," making of it an heroic response rather than an enterprise of political and economic self-interest.

Is it surprising, then, that those responding to this call should think of their mission in medical terms? Writes Livingstone (1857:5): "I soon resolved to devote my life to the alleviation of human misery . . . and therefore set myself to obtain a medical education, in order to be qualified for that enterprise." While Livingstone was the first, and for many years the only, medically trained missionary among the Tswana, his colleagues all provided some medical aid to their would-be converts (Seeley 1973:75).[1] The early evangelists conceived of themselves as restorers both of body and spirit, bearers not only of salvation, but of a healing civilization.

Within that civilization, however, medicine remained, at least in the middle decades of the nineteenth century, a relatively unrigorous and speculative form of knowledge. For several decades there had been pressure on the British state to regulate the profession (Turner 1959:154). Yet access to formal training remained open to the likes of Livingstone, who started his working life as a piecer in a Scottish mill—though we are told that he almost failed to gain the license of the Faculty of Physicians and Surgeons in Glasgow in 1840 because of his advocacy of the stethoscope, an instrument whose usefulness his examiners disputed (Gelfand 1957: 24). Livingstone had *The Lancet* sent to him during his years in the field so that he might keep abreast of innovations; the ethos of rational discovery was as alive in respect of the "body space" of medicine as it was in the domain of geography. Yet the pharmacopeia at his disposal consisted mainly of herbal compounds, emetics, and purgatives, which he himself saw as close enough to Tswana medicaments to warrant his borrowing the latter to enhance his own stock (Gelfand 1957:63; Seeley 1973:79; Livingstone 1857:692f).

As this suggests, the salience of medical practice in the early mission did not arise from its indisputable and universal status as science. This is confirmed by Livingstone's own reflections on the similarities and differences between European and Tswana healing, presented to us most succinctly in his famous dialogue with a Kwena healer (1857:25; see also Schapera 1960:239–240).[2] The conversation is ostensibly evidence of the fallacious reasoning of the superstitious mind. But, as the following extract demonstrates, the text is structured to convey a more ambivalent message.

Medical Doctor: . . . You can not charm the clouds by medicines. You wait till you see the clouds come, then you use your medicines, and take the credit which belongs to God only.

Rain Doctor: I use my medicines, and you employ yours; we are both doctors, and doctors are not deceivers. You

> give a patient medicine. Sometimes God is pleased to
> heal him by means of your medicine; sometimes
> not—he dies. . . . When he is cured, you take the
> credit of what God does. . . . When a patient dies,
> you don't give up trust in your medicine, neither do I
> when the rain fails. If you wish me to leave off my
> medicines, why continue your own?

MD: I give my medicine to living creatures within my
reach, and can see the effects, though no cure follows; you pretend to charm the clouds, which are so
far above us that your medicines never reach
them. . . . Could you make it rain on one spot and
not on another?

RD: I wouldn't think of trying. I like to see the whole
country green. (Livingstone 1857:25)

Livingstone concludes the dialogue with a remark about the Tswana
genius for argument, and, to be sure, it is he who has had to shift
ontological ground in the exchange. The parallel use of the term "doctor" seems to reinforce the logical equivalence of the two positions. This
conversation, presented in varying versions in Livingstone's writings,
must surely be read as a rhetorical device in which the author rehearses
what he was beginning to see as the intellectual impasse of the mission.
It is not mere evangelical zeal that prevents him from asserting the
indisputable superiority of medical science. At the time, biomedical
knowledge had no clear hegemony and, in the African interior, its practitioners could not be confident that their ability to deal with serious
illness exceeded that of their native counterparts (cf. Jeal 1973:17).

Indeed, if healing was salient on the colonial frontier, it was as a
technique of civilization, carrying with it a pervasive philosophy about
health and contagion, propriety and degeneracy; about the relationship
of bodies and contexts, matter and morality. Ironically, while they continued to foster the image of African affliction, nineteenth-century missionaries acknowledged that Tswana populations tended to be "remarkably" free of disease (Seeley 1973:81; Willoughby 1899).[3] In the eyes of
the churchmen, it was their *spiritual* "suffering"—their "sentence of
death"—that was at issue; and this was a function of their lack of self-
determination, their filthy habits, and their brazen nakedness. The un-
clothed heathen body posed an especially acute threat to the fragile colonial order, and became something of an obsession with the evangelists.
The latter soon declared that it was impossible to open up a spiritual
discourse with the Tswana, who seemed to have hopelessly "carnal views
to all spiritual things" (Broadbent 1865:178), and were captivated by the

white man's goods and techniques. So, instead, the whites commenced their reform of the native person from outside, working on the humble terrain of everyday practice. Here, in the name of decency, cleanliness, and health, they attempted to make the Tswana into Protestant persons, molded by the cultural forms of empire.

Contemporary mission correspondence gives insight into the disquiet that underlay the industrious effort to enclose the African body. It also shows how the churchmen (at the time it was largely a male initiative) tried to intervene in the uncontained physicality that seemed to pervade Tswana life, from their techniques of production and reproduction to their unruly architecture and undisciplined speech (Comaroff and Comaroff 1991: chap. 8). An example can be found in the following passage from the writings of Moffat (1842:287):

> As many men and women as pleased might come into our hut, leaving us not room even to turn ourselves, and making every thing they touched the colour of their greasy red attire. . . . They would keep the housewife a perfect prisoner in a suffocating atmosphere, almost intolerable; and when they departed, they left ten times more than their number behind— company still more offensive.

This may have been a world not yet informed by bacteriology, but there was a persistent association of the African body with noxious organisms that threatened to invade the inviolable world of white order. The image of the infested, "greasy" native—indistinguishable from the pestilential surroundings—had gained currency in the texts of travelers and anatomists in the late eighteenth century. The expression probably derived from the use, especially in the hottest and driest regions of Africa, of animal fat as a moisturizing and beautifying cosmetic. But the epithet carried other derogatory associations. It suggested a body surface that was porous, dirty, and damp—that "gave off" contagion and odor to those with whom it came into contact. Like the "grotesque body" of renaissance representation, the native person was "never closed off from either its social or ecosystemic context" (Stallybrass and White 1986:22).

Nothing could have been further from the discrete, sanitized, conserving individual of the mission ideal. On the African colonial frontier, the "lubricated wild man of the desert" contrasted with the "clean, comfortable and well-dressed believer," as did "filthy" animal fat and skin with the "cotton and woollen manufactures of Manchester and Leeds" (Hughes 1841:523). Creating a need for "healthful" attire was also a self-conscious effort to hitch Africans to the European commodity market, itself perceived as a moral order with cultivating effects (Moffat 1842:605; Livingstone 1857:34). Skin costume was "disgusting" because it failed to separate mankind from bestial nakedness, and could only foster immoderate emission and disease. Moffat (1842:503) writes of the Tswana,

> The child, as may be seen, is carried in a skin on the mother's back, with its chest lying close to her person. When it requires to be removed from that position, it is often wet with perspiration; and from being thus exposed to cold wind, pulmonary complaints are not infrequently brought on.

The style of writing, here, objectifies "native habit," describing it in distancing, almost subhuman terms.

Such observations reveal the cultural logic behind the civilizing mission. They also give insight into the images of Africa relayed to a large and diverse reading public in Britain. When Moffat published his *Missionary Labours and Scenes* in 1842—it was dedicated to Prince Albert—he was a heroic figure whose account was eagerly awaited by adventurers, evangelists, and imperialists (1842:x). Even more influential was Livingstone, whose writings enjoyed enormous circulation, both in the scientific and popular communities. It is interesting that he invoked images of disease very similar to those of his medically untrained colleagues: of illness as the product of exposure and contagion, the result of bodies improperly set off from each other and from the natural elements. Of course, these constructs underpinned European etiological theories of the period, which were still part of the "externalizing discourse" (Young 1978) of humoral pathology. Vital bodily processes were widely held to depend upon outside stimuli—especially heat, a property dense with social and moral value.

Such constructs confirmed established beliefs about the debauched condition of Africa, and they were continually reinforced by the "evidence" collected in the natural laboratory along the colonial frontier. Thus Livingstone asserted that conditions such as inflammation of the bowels, rheumatism, and heart disease seemed to decline among the Tswana with the adoption of decent European dress (Schapera 1961: 129). And he found particularly appealing the current theory of "noxious miasmus," in terms of which fever was caused by the inhalation of emanations from "marshy miasmata," "effluvia, poisons, and human ordure" that fermented into a substrate of contagion in moist, densely vegetated situations (Carlson 1984:38). Livingstone thought Africa especially hospitable to such dank rottenness, and imagined that he had found the cause of the virulent malaria that so threatened whites on the dark continent (Gelfand 1957:297; Schapera 1960:24). These conclusions were transmitted to *The Lancet* by the Hydrographer to the Admiralty, the intense medical interest in tropical fevers at the time being an

apt example of the marriage of imperial concern and biological speculation (Livingstone 1861).

But beneath the "theory" lay a familiar set of associations: disease
arises from dirt, and dirt comes of the confusion of bodies and bodily
secretions—especially in torrid climes, which open the pores and encourage a process of organic and moral degradation. Yet the image of decay
never totally eclipsed the earlier romantic vision of the "healthful native"
(see above). Thus Livingstone was also challenged by the fact that, by
comparison to white men, black women seemed to display a much lower
mortality from malaria (Schapera 1960:24). He speculated (with fellow
evangelist John Mackenzie) that this was due to the women's unusually
heavy menstrual discharge, which flushed the poison from their bodies,
presumably to swell the tide of effluvia in which the disease was held to
grow. In terms of the humoral pathology that obtained in Britain in the
mid–nineteenth century, fever was associated with excess, and menstruation was regarded as a "natural" form of therapeutic bleeding (Jones
1988:81). Again, etiology found meaning in immoderate sexuality, the
uncontained body of the African female seeming a tangible threat to
European male viability. Gilman (1985:231) reminds us that the black
woman served widely as an icon of sexually transmitted illness in the late-
nineteenth-century European imagination. At the time, in fact, some
medical opinion claimed that syphilis was a form of leprosy that had long
been present in Africa and had spread into Europe in the Middle Ages.

Not surprisingly, venereal disease was another of Livingstone's explicit concerns. Though he noted its presence among the Tswana, his
faith in the luxuriance of black fertility led him to the conviction that
syphilis was "incapable of permanence in any form in those of pure
African blood" (Schapera 1961:128). His optimism was ill-founded. The
disease was already following the path of migrant laborers, who left the
region for the colonial towns to the south. By the turn of the century,
communities of black workers were being seen as cesspools of syphilis in
the white man's cities, calling forth the regulatory intervention of public
health authorities (Seeley 1973:124). But, once again, Livingstone's
misperception was not random. It reinforced the contours of a well-
established European mythology. In the late-nineteenth-century vocabulary of sexuality, miscegenation was a particularly threatening source of
pathology, a cause of decline in white populations at home and abroad
(Gilman 1985:237). It was also a matter of particular sensitivity in the
racially marked order of domination established along the frontier. Albeit unwittingly, mission medicine reinforced the ideological bases of
this order by giving it an alibi in the unruly black body.

As this implies, missionary healing had far-reaching effects—although it was more successful in making the blacks into subjects of empire than citizens of Christendom. With the colonial state ever more visibly at their back, the churchmen had a considerable impact upon African modes of production, dress, and architecture. The Tswana, in turn, strove to gain some control over the evident power of the Europeans— power residing in diverse objects and practices, from guns and mirrors to irrigation and literacy. In their own world, power existed in its most condensed form in the diviner's medicine, and they were soon asking the nonconformists for concoctions to make them read, to promote conception, or to ensure successful hunting (Livingstone 1857:146, 622; Moffat 1842:599). In seeking the white man's healing, they attempted to imbibe something of his tangible might. And while his treatment did little to displace indigenous magic, it was so much in demand that the evangelists were sometimes driven to despair.[4] But they encouraged the enthusiasm, for they believed that the African was most impressionable on the "bed of affliction;" and they seldom missed an opportunity to give moral instruction along with their treatment (Seeley 1973:82f). They also seem to have charged "the wealthier natives" for their potions and services, hoping thereby both to cover costs and to teach a useful lesson in monetized value.[5]

Indeed, Western medicine (at least of the sort provided by the missionaries) was one of several civilizing commodities by which the church ushered the Tswana into the marketplace. Perhaps the most blatant example of how this was done is provided by the Rev. Roger Price. In 1880, Price set up a flourishing "hospital" at his station at Molepolole and, from the proceeds, eventually bought himself a farm and handsome herd of cattle.[6] However unsystematic missionary treatment might have been, it was based on the logic of biomedicine, a logic shared by other facets of the culture that colonized nineteenth-century Africa. In this vision, the unit of production was the individual, and values such as health, wealth, and salvation were moral achievements to be secured by hard labor, effective management, and rational consumption. Illness was no longer a sign of disrupted social relations, as it had been for the Tswana. If not caused by natural accident, it was the mark of personal indigence or self-abuse.

In the South African interior of the late nineteenth century, then, the evangelists were the bearers of an expansive European worldview. Their mission was regulated neither by government nor by professional monopoly. But, as they ministered to the peoples of the interior (even to isolated white settlers),[7] they introduced a coherent mode of seeing and being, a specific definition of person, body, health, and society that anticipated the culture and economy of the colonial state.

The Emergence of Colonial
Public Health

But the era of the healing ministry was in fact coming to an end. The expansion of white settlers into the interior took on a new momentum with the discovery of diamonds near Kimberley in 1867. An influx of capital fueled the burgeoning market for goods and labor, and, by 1871, Britain had annexed the diamond fields and surrounding region, including land that was claimed by the southern Tswana. In 1885, after a long period of political struggle among Boers, Britons, and blacks, the Crown Colony of British Bechuanaland was established over the territory of the southern chiefdoms; it was to be transferred to the Cape Colony a decade later. At the same time, the northern Tswana chiefdoms were incorporated into the Bechuanaland Protectorate (which became Botswana in 1966). As part of the government of this protectorate, two medical officers were appointed, and a military hospital was built at the administrative headquarters at Mafeking.

At the level of local practice, biomedicine rapidly ousted missionary healing, its hegemony now being underwritten by the state. Although colonial medical officers provided little actual health care for the Tswana until well into the twentieth century (Seeley 1973:125), their appointment was accompanied by immediate restrictions on the churchmen. By the end of the nineteenth century, government officials were actively discouraging unqualified evangelists from giving treatment where the services of a district surgeon were available, and, in 1894, the LMS issued instructions that no charge should henceforth be levied for care offered by its untrained agents.[8] In their letters from the field, the latter became increasingly apologetic about their healing techniques, bemoaning the burden of the work, their lack of qualifications, and the dearth of "Christian medical men."[9] But there is also the suggestion that, along with their resistance to overrule, some of the peoples of the interior resisted government medicine. The missionaries note that they were frequently consulted—by blacks and whites—in preference to the resident district surgeon.[10]

The first objective of colonial officials was to ensure the well-being both of government employees and of the expanding "European" communities in the interior. But the sine qua non of white welfare in this context was its thoroughgoing dependence upon black labor. Thus the control of the latter loomed large in the public health project from the start, official rhetoric expressing the contradiction built into the very constitution of South African society—that "natives" be central to its economy yet marginal to its political and moral community. The defiling tropes used to distance and subjugate the black other came back to haunt the whites, whose material world was actually dependent on the proximity of native labor.

One of the earliest communications from the medical officer in Mafeking reveals the driving force of this paradox. Writing of the need, in 1890, to enforce the Contagious Diseases Act in the "native location," he says, "The public should have some protection against the spread of syphilis which is frequently effected through the servants attending children as nurses."[11] In parentheses, this statement displays important refinement in lay medical usage: specific infections had replaced the more diffusely conceived contagion of an earlier epoch. Science still found its voice in the contradictory culture of colonization, however: infection continued to emanate from the black female body, a body more immediately threatening because it had been given entrée into the enclosed white world. Indeed, the gateway to infection had become the innocent and vulnerable European infant, whose care, increasingly in the hands of African women, had brought blacks into the most private reaches of colonial life. Tellingly, the medical officer did not acknowledge the possibility that disease might be communicated by sexual congress across the lines of color, although this was an equally present reality of life in settler society. But miscegenation was an inadmissible challenge to the basic premise of inequality on which the entire society was founded: in modern South Africa, at least, until very recently, interracial sex would be known as "immorality" in everyday and legal parlance. Robbed of all other meanings, the term came to imply a crime against humanity itself.

More important still, the report of the medical officer indicates how public health was to serve in the discipline of black populations whose ambiguous physicality was a source of both wealth and danger. Evidence of the relation of state medicine and social control exists—in highly graphic, literal form—in local historical records: the only mention of health facilities for Tswana in the Mafeking district at the turn of the century, for example, was that of the "gaol hospitals" attached to local police stations (Seeley 1973:124). This was merely a refraction of a more embracing disposition of government, however: Maynard Swanson (1977:387) has argued that public authorities in South Africa at the time displayed a noticeable "sanitation syndrome"—a preoccupation with infectious diseases that shaped nationwide policies and practices of racial segregation, especially in the burgeoning cities. Of course, it was a disposition shared with other colonizing regimes (Lyons 1985; Headrick 1987; Cohn 1988), one influenced by nineteenth-century European sanitary reform and discipline imposed—primarily upon indigent urban underclasses—at home (Jephson 1907; Stedman Jones 1971; Foucault 1977).

The actions and interests of the government at the time certainly support Swanson's claim. In 1903, a commission was appointed in response to the need felt for a coherent "native policy"; its members investigated current African "life and habits" and made recommendations for the control of labor relations, taxation, and education. In addressing the problems of building a stable workforce, their report showed a preoccupation with black "hygiene," especially among migrant populations. Where before local health officials had been concerned to limit the threat posed by female servants in the white household, the national administration now focused on the promotion of the "health" and control of black males in the urban workplace. The specter of disease flooding the white cities along with unregulated African labor lurked just below the surface. Nor was any of this new: as early as 1881, Sir Theophilus Shepstone, the influential Secretary for Native Affairs in Natal, had called the mushrooming multiracial towns with their populations of unemployed or casual native labor "the pest spots of our body social and political" (Swanson 1977:391). Not surprisingly, the 1903 commission kept returning to the topic of sanitation, urging that it be given priority in the education of blacks, and that those responsible for transporting and housing migrant workers pay special attention to the control of their toilet arrangements (South Africa 1905:73).

In fact, as Swanson (1977:390) shows, the social and architectural character of South Africa's multiracial cities was already being transformed in response to contagion and medical emergency. The outbreak of bubonic plague in 1900 focused more diffuse notions of danger: while blacks contracted the disease in smaller numbers than did whites or so-called coloureds, they were immediately targeted as the source of infection, to be expelled from the body public. The Medical Officer of Health in Cape Town, for one, declared that "uncontrolled Kafir hordes were at the root of the aggravation of Capetown slumdom brought to light when the plague broke out" (Swanson 1977:392). As an immediate measure, sanitary inspectors were dispatched to rout out such "scattered nests of filth" throughout the city, but the longer-term solution was to be nothing less than the mass removal of the black population (Swanson 1977:393). In the name of medical crisis, a radical plan of racial segregation was passed under the emergency provisions of the Public Health Act. It established an enduring system of black periurban "locations" that were to spread from the cities of the Cape Province to become an enduring feature of the South African landscape. Swanson shows how powerful the sense of medical menace really was: inseparable from the fear of an unregulated "native" presence in the white world, it repeatedly overcame all efforts to resist the social engineering of the regime.

What was the role in all this of the mission? The evangelists were forced to adapt their project to changing circumstances—to the fact that their field had become the rural periphery of South Africa, and now served as a recruiting ground for migrant labor. In the upshot, formal education became their primary civilizing technique; it is, therefore, in the provision of native schooling that we must trace their impact on the everyday world of black South Africans in the early twentieth century. As we have seen, the churchmen had long participated in a moral discourse about pollution and reform. But they, too, were children of their time and their activities also seem to have been organized by an increasingly precise biomedical conception of infection and hygiene. At the turn of the century, their letters display a growing anxiety about effluent and the management of the dirt generated by populations around their stations. It is no coincidence that, when Rev. Willoughby arrived to take command of the mission at Phalapye (Bechuanaland Protectorate) in 1894, he found that the "W.C." (lavatory) built by his predecessor was "the most prominent object" on the skyline.[12] It is also noticeable that specific names were now frequently being given to diseases in missionary correspondence: generic "fever" gave way to "malaria" or "typhoid," conditions that, although rare in Southern Africa, were invoked as a rationale for replacing indigenous residential arrangements with more "hygienic" alternatives (Willoughby 1899:21).

These orientations became particularly evident in the mission school itself. In writing a proposal for the establishment of a training college among the Tswana, LMS evangelists devoted three quarters of their report to issues of hygiene, sanitation, and the regulation of daily ablutions.[13] And, when it was actually founded in 1904, the Tiger Kloof Native Institution (initially for male students alone) was equipped with accommodation specially designed for the close supervision of toilet arrangements (Comaroff and Comaroff n.d.: chap. 10). Furthermore, dormitory chiefs ensured that pupils made their beds "in that neat and uniform manner that prevails in some hospitals;" and a "General Officer of Health" did weekly inspections of student quarters (Willoughby 1912:90). Rules of dress, comportment, and table manners all reinforced these rituals and routines that, even more relentlessly than the formal curriculum, worked to create persons of individual, robust, and uniformly regulated identity. Their stated goal was to instill in the native inmates "moral backbone," the wherewithal to live "clean and healthy" Christian lives (Willoughby 1912:70). Although not altogether intentionally, the desire of the churchmen to produce self-controlled and wholesome subjects resonated well with the politicoeconomic interests of the state: the LMS strove to mold just the kind of disciplined worker of whom policymakers dreamed.

It is no wonder that, over the years, student resistance in South African mission schools would often protest against regimes of bodily discipline. In the Tswana case, its earliest expression in the 1890s took the form of a refusal to comply with sanitary prescriptions, particularly the use of the "privy." It was a practice the black youths deplored, ironically, as "defecation in the house."[14]

Conclusion

> *Medical icons are no more "real" than "aesthetic" ones. Like aesthetic icons, medical icons may (or may not) be rooted in some observed reality. Like them, they are iconographic in that they represent these realities in a manner determined by the historical position of the observers. . . . Medicine uses its categories to structure an image of the diversity of mankind. . . . The power of medicine, at least in the nineteenth century, lies in the rise of the status of science.*
>
> Sander L. Gilman, "Black Bodies,
> White Bodies"

I have tried to show something of the dialectical interplay of nineteenth-century medicine and the colonizing project in South Africa. The two were in many senses inseparable. Both were driven by a global sense of man that had emerged out of the enlightenment. Both concerned the extension of "rational" control over domains of nature that were vital and dangerous. Although ostensibly an autonomous field of knowledge and practice, medicine both informed and was informed by imperialism, in Africa and elsewhere. It gave the validity of science to the humanitarian claims of colonialism, while finding confirmation for its own authority in the living laboratories enclosed by expanding imperial frontiers.

While imperialism and biomedicine have not been engaged in precisely the same reciprocal relationship everywhere, there is any amount of evidence of their elective affinity. Whatever else it might have been, nineteenth-century Western medicine had a powerful ontology, finding confirmation, in bodies at home and abroad, for the universalist claims of European reason. And its role in this regard did not end with formal colonialism. Notwithstanding their contribution to the human condition, biomedical knowledge and technology have played a large part in sustaining the economic and cultural dependency of the non-Western world. What is more, we are still all too ready, in the West, to seek the origins of virulent disease in the uncontained nature of "others"—in the undisciplined sexuality of Africa, for example. In that regard, it might be worthwhile reminding ourselves that, until very recently, the preserved relics of the Hottentot Venus were still on display at the Musée de l'Homme!

Acknowledgments

The National Science Foundation and National Endowment for the Humanities funded the research on which this paper is based; I should like to thank both. Some passages included here are excerpted from *Of Revelation and Revolution: Christianity, Colonialism, and Consciousness in South Africa* (Comaroff and Comaroff 1991: chap. 6). A slightly different version of this piece is published in *Ethnography and the Historical Imagination* (Comaroff and Comaroff 1992: chap. 8).

Notes

1. See also William Charles Willoughby to the Directors of the London Missionary Society (LMS), 21 July 1894 [Council of World Mission (CWM) Archives, LMS Home Correspondence (South Africa), box 51, file 1, jacket D].

2. Similar attempts to "reason" with rainmakers are recorded by several other evangelists from this field (Comaroff and Comaroff 1991: chap. 6).

3. In contrast, mission correspondence gives clear evidence of the toll taken on the health of evangelists and their families; the deaths of infants and women in childbirth were particularly frequent, but dysentery, unidentified "fever," and accidents also took many lives. See, for example, Samuel Broadbent to Wesleyan Methodist Missionary Society (WMMS), 31 December 1823 [WMMS Archives, Home Correspondence (South Africa), 300]; James Archbell to WMMS, 20 March 1832 [WMMS Archives, Home Correspondence (South Africa), 303]. There is also evidence that faithful care was extended to ailing missionaries by their black attendants (Moffat 1842; Gelfand 1957:276ff).

4. See, for example, Livingstone (Schapera 1961:14); Willoughby to the Directors of the LMS, 21 July 1894 [CWM Archives, LMS Home Correspondence (South Africa), box 51, file 1, jacket D].

5. John Brown to LMS, 9 July 1894 [CWM Archives, LMS Home Correspondence (South Africa), box 51, file 1, jacket D].

6. Brown to LMS, 9 July 1894 [CWM Archives, LMS Home Correspondence (South Africa), box 51, file 1, jacket D].

7. Brown to LMS, 9 July 1894 [CWM Archives, LMS Home Correspondence (South Africa), box 51, file 1, jacket D]; Willoughby to the Directors of the LMS, 21 July 1894 [CWM Archives, LMS Home Correspondence (South Africa), box 51, file 1, jacket D].

8. Willoughby to the Directors of the LMS, 21 July 1894 [CWM Archives, LMS Home Correspondence (South Africa), box 51, file 1, jacket D].

9. Willoughby to the Directors of the LMS, 21 July 1894 [CWM Archives, LMS Home Correspondence (South Africa), box 51, file 1, jacket D].

26
The Diseased Heart of Africa

10. Brown to LMS, 9 July 1894 [CWM Archives, LMS Home Correspondence (South Africa), box 51, file 1, jacket D].

11. Great Britain 1891–1892; see also Seeley 1973:124.

12. Willoughby to LMS Bechuanaland District Committee, 1 February 1898, "Proposal for the Establishment of an Institute for the Teaching of Bechuana and Other Native Youth" [CWM Archives, LMS Home Correspondence (South Africa), box 55, file 1, jacket A].

14. Willoughby to LMS Bechuanaland District Committee, 1 February 1898, "Report on a Visit to Certain Native Boarding Schools in South Africa" [CWM Archives, LMS Home Correspondence (South Africa), box 55, file 1, jacket A].

References

Barrow, John
1801–   An Account of Travels into the Interior of Southern Africa in the
1804   Years 1797 and 1798. 2 vols. London: Cadell & Davies.
Blumenbach, Johann Friedrich
1969   On the Natural Variety of Mankind. Trans. by T. Bendyshe from the
         1775 and 1795 eds. New York: Bergman Publishers.
Broadbent, Samuel
1865   A Narrative of the First Introduction of Christianity amongst the
         Barolong tribe of Bechuanas, South Africa. London: Wesleyan Mission House.
Buffon, George Louis Leclerc
1791   Natural History, General and Particular. W. Smellie, trans. London:
         A. Strahan.
Carlson, Dennis G.
1984   African Fever: A Study of British Science, Technology and Politics in
         West Africa, 1787–1864. Canton, Mass.: Science History Publications.
Cartwright, Samuel A.
1853   Philosophy of the Negro Constitution. The New Orleans Medical
         and Surgical Journal 9:195–208.
Cogan, Thomas, ed.
1821   The Works of the Late Professor Camper, on the Connexion between
         the Science of Anatomy and the Arts of Drawing, Painting, Statuary.
         London: J. Hearne.
Comaroff, Jean, and John L. Comaroff
1991   Of Revelation and Revolution: Christianity, Colonialism, and Consciousness in South Africa. Vol. 1. Chicago: University of Chicago Press.
n.d.   Of Revelation and Revolution: Christianity, Colonialism, and Consciousness in South Africa. Vol. 2.
Comaroff, John L. and Jean Comaroff
1992   Ethnography and the Historical Imagination. Boulder: Westview Press.
Cohn, Bernard S.
1988   The Anthropology of a Colonial State and its Forms of Know-

edge. Unpublished paper read at Wenner-Gren Conference, Tensions of Empire: Colonial Control and Visions of Rule, Mijas, Spain, November.

Curtin, Philip D.
1964   *The Image of Africa: British Ideas and Action 1780–1850*. Madison: University of Wisconsin Press.

Cuvier, Georges
1827–   *The Animal Kingdom*. 16 vols. London: Geo. B. Whittaker.
1835

Figlio, Karl
1976   The Metaphor of Organization: An Historiographical Perspective on the Bio-Medical Sciences of the Early Nineteenth Century. *History of Science* 14:17–53.

Foucault, Michel
1975   *The Birth of the Clinic: An Archeology of Medical Perception*. A. M. Sheridan Smith, trans. New York: Vintage Books.
1977   *Discipline and Punish: The Birth of the Prison*. Alan Sheridan, trans. New York: Pantheon Books.

Gelfand, Michael
1957   *Livingstone the Doctor: His Life and Travels*. Oxford: Blackwell.

Gilman, Sander L.
1985   Black Bodies, White Bodies: Toward an Iconography of Female Sexuality in Late Nineteenth Century Art, Medicine, and Literature. *Critical Inquiry* 12:204–242.

Great Britain
1891–   *Bechuanaland Protectorate: Annual Report*. London: Colonial
1892   Office.

Headrick, Rita
1987   *The Impact of Colonialism on Health in French Equatorial Africa, 1880–1940*. Ph.D. diss., University of Chicago.

Hodgen, Margaret T.
1964   *Early Anthropology in the Sixteenth and Seventeenth Centuries*. Philadelphia: University of Pennsylvania Press.

Hughes, Isaac
1841   Missionary Labours among the Batlapi. *Evangelical Magazine and Missionary Chronicle* 19:522–523.

Hume, David
1854   *The Philosophical Works*. 4 vols. Boston: Little, Brown.

Jeal, Tim
1973   *Livingstone*. New York: G. P. Putnam's Sons.

Jephson, Henry
1907   *The Sanitary History of London*. Brooklyn: N. Y. A. Wessels.

Jones, Coby
1988   Leeches on Society: Bloodletting and the Economies of Blood in British Heroic Medicine. Master's thesis, University of Chicago.

Lichtenstein, Henry (Martin Karl Heinrich)
1928–   *Travels in Southern Africa, in the Years 1803, 1804, 1805, and 1806.*
1930   2 vols. Trans. from the 1812–1815 eds. by A. Plumptre. Cape
         Town: The Van Riebeeck Society.
Livingstone, David
1857   *Missionary Travels and Researches in South Africa.* London: Mur-
         ray.
1861   On Fever in the Zambesi. A Note from Dr. Livingstone to Dr.
         M'William. Transmitted by Captain Washington, R.N., F.R.S.,
         Hydrographer to the Admiralty. *The Lancet* no. 1982 (24 Au-
         gust):184.
Lyons, Maryinez
1985   From "Death Camps" to *Cordon Sanitaire:* The Development of
         Sleeping Sickness Policy in the Uele District of the Belgian Congo,
         1903–1914. *Journal of African History* 26:69–91.
Moffat, Robert
1842   *Missionary Labours and Scenes in Southern Africa.* London: Snow.
         Reprint New York: Johnson Reprint Corporation, 1969.
Park, Mungo
1799   *Travels in the Interior Districts of Africa, Performed under the Direc-
         tion and Patronage of the African Association, in the Years 1795,
         1796, and 1797.* London: W. Bulmer.
Park, Thomas, ed.
1811   *The Poetical Works of Joseph Warton.* London: Whittingham & Row-
         land.
Pratt, Mary Louise
1985   Scratches on the Face of the Country; Or, What Mr. Barrow Saw in
         the Land of the Bushmen. *Critical Inquiry* 12:119–143.
Roscoe, William
1787   *The Wrongs of Africa, a Poem.* London: R. Faulder.
Schapera, Isaac, ed.
1960   *Livingstone's Private Journals 1851–53.* London: Chatto & Win-
         dus.
1961   *Livingstone's Missionary Correspondence 1841–56.* London: Chatto
         & Windus.
Seeley, Caroline F.
1973   The Reaction of Batswana to the Practice of Western Medicine.
         Master's thesis, University of London.
South Africa, British Crown Colony of
1905   *Report of the South African Native Affairs Commission 1903–5.*
         Cape Town: Cape Times.
Southey, Robert
1815   *The Minor Poems of Robert Southey.* London: Longman, Hurst,
         Rees, Orme, and Brown.
Stallybrass, Peter and Allon White
1986   *The Politics and Poetics of Transgression.* London: Methuen.

Stedman Jones, Gareth
1971   *Outcast London: A Study of the Relationship between the Classes in Victorian Society.* Oxford: Clarendon Press.
Stocking, George W.
1987   *Victorian Anthropology.* New York: The Free Press.
Swanson, Maynard W.
1977   The Sanitation Syndrome: Bubonic Plague and Urban Native Policy in the Cape Colony, 1900–1909. *Journal of African History,* 18:387–410.
Turner, Ernest S.
1959   *Call the Doctor: A Social History of Medical Men.* New York: St. Martin's Press.
White, Charles
1799   *An Account of the Regular Gradation in Man, and in Different Animals and Vegetables; and from the Former to the Latter . . .* London: Printed for C. Dilly.
Willoughby, William Charles
1899   *Native Life on the Transvaal Border.* London: Simpkin, Marshall, Hamilton, Kent.
1912   *Tiger Kloof: The London Missionary Society's Native Institution in South Africa.* London: London Missionary Society.
Young, Allan A.
1978   Modes of Production of Medical Knowledge. *Medical Anthropology* 2:97–122.

14

The Politics of Mid-Life and Menopause

Ideologies for the Second Sex in North America and Japan

Margaret Lock

The relation between what we see and what we know is never settled.
John Berger, *Ways of Seeing*

Since the mid–nineteenth century female life cycle transitions in Euro-America have been interpreted with increasing insistence by physicians as a series of events that should be subject to medical management. Although passage through the life cycle is simultaneously a social and biological process, the focus of attention within medical circles has been confined ever more intently to the body physical, with the result that both the subjective experience of maturation and associated changes in human relationships have been rendered largely inconsequential in medical discourse.

Of course, women have not sat by passively, willing consumers of each and every new piece of medical technology. On the contrary, the female body has become the site for ever more contentious debate in connection with both its representation and the medical practices performed upon it. However, these contested meanings are not simply responses to the imperialism of a particular medical "gaze" (in Michel Foucault's idiom), nor are they due entirely to the development of new technologies and an urge to maximize their use (Fuchs 1974). The female body, being a potent but malleable signifier, is inevitably a forum for the delineation of sex and gender relations—most notably at this particular historical moment to what extent women should be granted equity in social life (in reality and not simply in name) together with autonomy over their own bodies. The medicalized body, therefore, is not only the product of changing medical knowledge and practice, but is at the same time a manifestation of potent, never settled, partially disguised political contests that contribute to the way in which the female body is "seen" and interpreted.

Donna Haraway has suggested that in the late twentieth century "the universalized natural body remains the gold standard of hegemonic social discourse" (1989:355), and most of us, relativistically inclined anthropologists included, are not willing to seriously confront the question of the body physical with anything other than current scientific wisdom. Anthropologists have, of course, entered sympathetically into an examination of cosmologies where body boundaries are fluid and where ethnoanatomy clearly does not correspond to that of Vesalius, but I suspect that most of us (but not all), no matter how faithful we stay to local accounts, retain a good deal of skepticism about the "accuracy" of informants' knowledge, and implicitly measure local knowledge against the "facts" of science. No doubt, paradoxically, part of the hesitation to relinquish a hold on scientific accounts of the body is *because* of its claim to universality, since any discourse that dwells on biological difference can potentially, after all, be coopted by those of racist and sexist intent.

However, the danger in buying the gold standard, of leaving the universal body intact is that one of the most tenacious assumptions in biomedical knowledge remains unexamined. I propose, through an analysis of some of the current discourse about female aging in North America and Japan, particularly that concerned with the end of menstruation (both medical discourse and that created by women), to contrast the way in which this part of the female life cycle is construed in these two cultures, both of them saturated with scientific knowledge and its practice. The comparison at once makes the permeation of scientific discourse by culture very evident. This should come as no great surprise to anthropologists, but I also want to show as a result of empirical research in Japan, that although these respective discourses are profoundly shaped by unexamined beliefs about the aging female body and its function in society, they are also in part the product of what I shall term "local biologies." In other words, subjective experience associated with physical changes in the body at the end of menstruation appear to be significantly different in Japan and North America, and have a profound effect on the construction of the respective discourses.

My purpose is, therefore, to give an account of the production of local knowledge in two settings. But to rest with contextualized, relativistic interpretations is to stop prematurely because there is, in the end, a reality about growing old and facing death which inevitably colors narratives about menopause, wherever their location in space and time. While no metanarrative can be retrieved, surely there is something more to human aging than that which can be learned from chemistry, numbers, and predictions, or from clinical, epidemiological, and bureaucratic documents? The dominant ideology of our time in North America and Europe focuses almost exclusively on what passes for an accurate account of the chemistry of aging and its implications for future ill-health. The "fact" of menopause becomes a synecdoche for middle-aged women in all their variety, who then disappear from sight to be replaced by estrogen levels, hot flashes, and future heart attacks. Showing how knowledge about the body is historically and culturally situated is the bread and butter of medical anthropologists, but recuperating the experience of middle age in its many colors, and further yet, searching for that which is common about aging to all women—indeed all people—is also part of the story, for only then can one suggest new ways of "seeing" that both coopt local scientific knowledge and, at the same time, transcend it.

Against Nature: Anomalous Female Aging

The "graying" of society is a subject of more than passing interest to politicians and bureaucrats in the so-called developed corners of this world today, most particularly because the baby-boomers are now well into middle age and approaching the "autumn" of their life. In North America and Japan, however, the "problem" is not conceptualized in the same way, and middle-aged women, cast in both locations as the leading figures in this drama, have their roles plotted out for them on remarkably different trajectories.

In North America today discourse about middle-aged women focuses almost obsessively on menopause; moreover, medical literature in particular, with only a few exceptions, is overwhelmingly concerned with pathology and decrepitude.

A progressive physical deterioration of climacteric women is scientifically established. Its course is subtle and often difficult to diagnose, especially in the early stages . . . it is now widely recognized that ovarian deficiency is the cause of these manifestations. (Jern 1973:xiii)

Thus, the end of menstruation is described as the result of "failing ova-ries" (Haspels and van Keep 1979:59; Willson, Beecham, and Carrington 1975:638), or the "inevitable demise" of the "follicular unit" (London and Hammond, 1986:906). Since "follicular atresia" (the gradual loss of the two million primordial follicles present in the ovary), commences in ap-proximately the fifth month of fetal life and continues until the end of menstruation, women are, if one follows this line of argument, on the path to decay even before they are born. There are other, much more positive ways to interpret these biological changes, as at least one gyneco-logical textbook has suggested (Wentz 1988), but the dominant discourse is about loss, failure, and decrepitude (see also Martin 1987).

Why should there be such an emphasis on female decrepitude—for surely aging is a "natural" and unavoidable process common to both men and women? A recent article written by Gail Sheehy for *Vanity Fair* gives us a clue. She states blithely, "At the turn of the century, a woman could expect to live to the age of forty-seven or eight" (1991:227), a sentiment expressed widely not only in popular literature but also in scientific articles. Roger G. Gosden, for example, writing a text for biologists, is explicit that the very existence of postmenopausal women is something of an artifact, the result of our "recent mastery of the environ-ment" (1985:2). He goes on to state,

There are several indications that women are not physiologically well adapted to the postmenopause. . . .
Human menopause is probably a novelty, although its potential has existed for a long time because germ cells are continuously depleted from a non-renewable store. (Gosden 1985:2)

Another frequently expressed opinion, namely, that the human female is the only member of the class Mammalia to live beyond menopause, appears in a gynecological textbook.

The cessation of menstruation, or the menopause, in the human female is . . . a relatively unique [*sic*] phenomenon in the animal kingdom. With increasing longevity modern woman differs from her forebears as well as from other species in that she can look forward to 20 or 30 years . . . after the menopause. (Dewhurst 1981:592)

A picture emerges from arguments such as these which suggests that something contrary to nature's purpose has happened with increasing frequency over the past one hundred years—namely, the regular appearance in society of women over fifty years of age. Grounded in the mischievous and erroneous assumption that until the turn of the century women dropped dead before menopause, linked with the idea that the postmenopausal state goes against nature, and reinforced by the medical description of "senile" reproductive organs and depleted estrogen (the essence of "femaleness"), the picture is indeed insidious and grim.

The thinly disguised assumption inherent in these arguments would seem to be that reproduction of the species is what female life is all about, and that we find ourselves in "advanced" societies with an ever-increasing number of perambulating anomalies: women who can no longer reproduce. Middle-aged women are explicitly contrasted with the animal world and found wanting; they are also compared to their detriment with younger, fertile, women—but of even more significance, perhaps, is that they are different from the male of the species. Haraway, writing about nineteenth-century Europe and North America, asserts that "the 'neutral,' universal body was always the unmarked masculine" (1989:357), that the representative rational subject in the development of a liberal society was embodied in "species Man," leaving women effectively silenced as oddities. Simone de Beauvoir was perhaps the first feminist to elaborate extensively about the way in which woman is constructed as "other," and here in the current literature on aging we find a striking example of this type of discourse, for received wisdom has it, of course, that men have the "natural" potential to reproduce successfully until the day they die. Occasionally this potential is alluded to in passing in the medical literature (Wilson and Wilson 1963), but aside from these innuendos, discussion rarely lights on men at all, and so we are told only that women formerly died in middle age and now live on average for nearly thirty years beyond their "natural" reproductive life span.

That aging affects the reproductive capacities of men so that testicular volume decreases, leading to decelerating spermatogenesis, decreasing sperm motility, and an increased production of defective sperm (Asso 1983) is deftly passed over—so, too, is research that indicates that impotence increases with time such that by age sixty more than 70 percent of men are no longer potent, and by eighty the number approaches 100 percent (Vermeulen et al. 1982). Furthermore, mention is rarely made that men do not live on average as long as women, no speculation is put forward as to why this should be, and no hint that women may have some "natural" advantage here. On the contrary, the very longevity of women is thrown back at them because they are viewed as a liability to society in their latter years.

In the medical literature on menopause it is common these days to start out with a rhetorical flourish that sets the stage right away for coming to terms with the superfluity of older women.

> In contemporary society 95% of women experience the menopause, between 50 and 60% will reach the age of 75 years and a third or more of all women in some countries may be peri- or postmenopausal. (Dewhurst 1981:593)

> More than 30 million women in the United States are more than 50 years old, with an average life expectancy of 81 years. Therefore, a woman in the United States can expect to live more than one third of her life in the postmenopausal state. (Notelovitz 1989)

> More than 40 million American women are menopausal; another 3.5 million will be reaching the climacteric age each year for the next 12 years. These women will have a life expectancy of 30 years after menopause. (Sarrel 1988:2S)

> It is estimated that every day in North America 3,500 new women [sic] experience menopause and that by the end of this century 49 million women will be postmenopausal. . . . Complaints referable to menopausal symptoms have been estimated to initiate approximately one million visits to physicians annually in Canada. (Reid 1988:25)

In a journal for family physicians, the estimated "cost" to society of these potentially decrepit women is explicitly addressed:

> An unwelcome consequence of increased longevity, osteoporosis eventually develops in almost all untreated Caucasian women who reach their 80th year. The direct cost of osteoporotic fractures is estimated to be $7 to $10 billion each year in the United States alone, and the population of postmenopausal women is continually increasing. (Lufkin and Ory 1989:205)

That these figures do not tally with each other is apparently of no great importance; their magnitude is sufficient to make them iconic, and accuracy is not at issue. As this last quote makes patently clear, the concern that drives the production of these figures is not the health of women, but their cost once elderly to society. However, this apparent concern for the welfare of society is, in many cases, a thin disguise for a vested interest in the potential profit that is to be made by attempting to keep women healthy.

The Pathology of Aging

It has been postulated since classical times that ovarian secretions produce a profound effect on many parts of the female body, and, although explanations have changed over the years as to just how this effect is produced, this assumption now has extensive scientific backing and is no longer in dispute. The current medical language describes "target" organs and tissues, and their negative response to "ovarian failure," which includes the pelvic organs (the vulva, vagina, and uterus), breasts, skin, and bones. The heart and cardiovascular system are also implicated, but indirectly, and so too are mental states (although this particular association remains in dispute in medical and social science circles). Medical interest in failing ovaries and dropping estrogen levels is no longer confined, therefore, to what are for most physicians at least, the rather inconsequential symptoms usually associated with menopause, in particular the hot flash. Interest in the menopausal woman is now extended to the remaining thirty years of her life cycle, and to her ongoing "management" so that she will not become an economic liability due to broken bones and an ailing heart.

In recent medical literature on the aging body, with its emphasis on the possible negative long-term impact of menopause on health, it is particularly evident that women are not only the "other" to an unmarked category of white male, but they are doubly marked as the "other" to younger, "normal" women of reproductive age. For example, the World Health Organization has defined the disease of osteoporosis as a state in which the "bone mass/volume ratio" is lower by a designated amount than that of "healthy *young* adults of the appropriate sex" (WHO Scientific Group 1981:42, emphasis added). Body chemistry prior to middle age is taken as the standard measure of what is "normal," and aging is automatically designated as pathological: "If the bone mass/volume ratio is below the young normal age, but within the normal range for the age and sex of the subject, the term 'simple osteoporosis' should be used" (WHO Scientific Group 1981:42). A label of "accelerated osteoporosis" is recommended for those older people who fall outside the range of "normally" abnormal. Since women are more vulnerable to osteoporosis than men, a risk that is directly related to reduced estrogen levels from mid-life onwards according to a good number of experts, and since these definitions appear in a WHO report on menopause, it is clearly women that the writers of this document have in mind, although their language is gender neutral.

Prophylactic Measures

Synthetic estrogens have been available since the early 1930s, and by the 1970s they were among the top five most frequently prescribed drugs in the United States. It was estimated that in 1973 51 percent of women had taken estrogen for at least three months, and that the median use was for ten years (Kaufert and McKinlay 1985). Until the mid-1970s estrogens were usually prescribed to reduce hot flashes and other so-called vasomotor symptoms associated with the end of menstruation. A sudden and sharp decline in the prescription of estrogens occurred after 1975 when four studies were published, three in the *New England Journal of Medicine* and one in the *Journal of the American Medical Association*, linking estrogen replacement therapy to an increased risk for endometrial cancer. A protracted and ever more complex debate has since ensued in the medical literature as to how best to "protect" women from the postulated effects of reduced estrogen in the postmenopausal body (Kaufert and McKinlay 1985). Writers of these articles share an assumption that the female body will be unable to attain its average life expectancy in reasonably good health unless it is regularly fueled with hormones.

> Clinicians abound who believe that the menopause is a physiological event, a normal aging process, therefore estrogen replacement therapy (ERT) is meddlesome and unnecessary. Presbyopia is a normal aging process, but none will deny the need for spectacles. To do nothing other than offer sympathy and assurance that the menopause will pass is tantamount to benign neglect. (Greenblatt and Teran 1987:39)

Many physicians apparently agree with these authors, because throughout the 1980s the use of replacement therapy has increased so that it is once again among the most frequently prescribed drugs, but it is now generally agreed that a second hormone, progesterone, must be added to the medication in order to counter the toxic effects of "unopposed" estrogen. Hence, rather than simply dispensing estrogen, physicians are required to estimate "risks" involved, select the appropriate hormone therapy for each patient, and monitor them accordingly.

Calculating the "Risks and Benefits"

Today the debate about menopausal women in both the medical literature and at conferences is carried forward not only by those gynecologists who are interested in the subject, but also by cardiologists, orthopedic surgeons, geriatricians, breast surgeons, and, above all, clinical epidemiologists who work with physicians in each of the relevant specialities. Articles by clinical epidemiologists have such titles as *Risks and Benefits of Long-Term Treatment with Estrogens, The Use of Hormonal Replacement Therapy and the Risk of Stroke and Myocardial Infarction in Women,* and *Risk of Localized and Widespread Endometrial Cancer in Relation to Recent and Discontinued Use of Conjugated Estrogens.* One recent article starts out with the statement, "The goal of contemporary hormone replacement is to minimize net predictable lifetime risk; success therefore depends upon quantitative assessments of the net quality of life, of net morbidity and of net mortality" (Mack and Ross 1989). This article points out that at present the frequency of eight common conditions is known to be influenced by estrogen usage, including the "climacteric itself," osteoporosis and osteoporotic fractures, acute and chronic ischemic heart disease, stroke, rheumatoid arthritis, gallbladder disease, endometrial cancer, and breast cancer. (In addition to endometrial cancer there is now a major concern that women may be at an increased risk for breast cancer as a result of using hormone replacement therapy, a concern reinforced by findings from several major studies [Bergkvist et al. 1989; Hunt et al. 1987; Jick et al. 1980]).

The authors of this article, Mack and Ross, have created a "model" of a hypothetical cohort of 100,000 women entering menopause at age fifty, who are followed to age seventy-five and treated continuously with a moderate dose of estrogen therapy. They then perform what appear to the uninitiated to be some very complicated statistical manipulations in which the results of more than one hundred actual surveys carried out in connection with estrogen replacement therapy and its effect on the eight common conditions are combined and adjusted to produce data relevant to the hypothetical cohort of 100,000 women. It was concluded from this manipulation that the eight conditions thought to be affected by estrogen account for "slightly more than half of [all] the deaths to be expected in women between 50 and 75, a bit less than half of all the days of disability, and about one in every eight hospitalizations" (Mack and Ross 1989:1815). Mack and Ross continue their analysis by examining the effects that they estimate the administration of estrogen *would have* on morbidity and mortality in this hypothetical cohort.

> We estimate that hospitalizations are made more frequent by an increment of about 75%, and that the days of disability are also more frequent . . . but by a smaller factor of about 17%. More than balancing this net impact on morbidity is a reduction of about 14% in the number of deaths to be expected in members of the cohort, confirming the *net benefit of treatment with estrogen replacement*. (Mack and Ross 1989:1815)

The authors calculate that over half the "anticipated reduction in mortality" would be derived from the prevention of heart disease, that stroke accounts for about one quarter, and osteoporosis for about another eighth. But, if estrogen treatment was stopped after five years, then virtually all the reduction in mortality would be lost. Based on their findings, Mack and Ross reach the following conclusions:

With our limited ability to predict risk, treating a small proportion of the potential beneficiaries is to deny substantial benefits to the majority. With respect to breast cancer, even those with strong risk-factors, such as a family history of breast cancer or a history of benign breast disease, are likely to receive more protection against death from heart disease than they are to be endangered by estrogens. (Mack and Ross 1989:1815)

However, they then go right on to state that today most gynecologists do not use simple estrogen replacement therapy because they are concerned about an increased risk for endometrial cancer when using this regime (for those women who have not had their uterus removed), and hence the majority opt for a combined therapy of estrogens and progesterones, commonly known as "hormone replacement therapy." Mack and Ross point out that reliable empirical estimates of the effect of combined therapy are unavailable, and that there is a "basis for concern about adverse effects on the risk of vascular disease, breast cancer, and gallbladder disease, and about long-term compliance with therapy." But they agree, nevertheless, that evidence suggests that progestin must be given at the same time as estrogen to prevent cancer of the endometrium.

After totting up the possible risks and benefits of hormone replacement therapy in several different ways to produce several different outcomes, the authors then ask rhetorically if there are "any treatment strategies which will provide the valuable benefits while playing it safe?" "Probably not," they answer themselves; neither screening out high-risk women, preferentially treating only those most likely to gain some benefit, treating only those with no uterus, nor using only short-term treatment "will provide major benefit without risk."

In light of these findings it is suggested that for the time being it is perhaps "most prudent" to make use of only estrogen and not a progesterone. This suggestion is in contrast to other physicians who declare that combined therapy must *always* be used (Nachtigall 1990). Mack and Ross remind us, however, that women over fifty with a uterus (only two-thirds of American women!) will then be "patently" at risk for cancer, and patients must be routinely monitored with endometrial biopsies (painful and invasive), as a result of which "large numbers" of them will receive "unnecessary curettage," some under general anesthesia 1989:1818). Mack and Ross close with a caveat similar to others that appear regularly at the end of risk/benefit articles:

Perhaps a prudent course in any event is to assume the role of medical fiduciary [a person to whom property or power is entrusted for the benefit of another] rather than that of decision-maker, to insist that the patient fully participate in the choice of therapy, and to make sure that whatever the choice, she explicitly acknowledge the measure of uncertainty. In any case, both doctor and patient must place high priority on surveillance for unexplained bleeding and breast lumps, emphasizing follow-up and follow-through for the latter. (Mack and Ross, 1989:1818)

Other researchers have shown that even from a purely economic perspective the benefits of replacement therapy are at best tentative. Milton Weinstein and Anna Tosteson asked themselves, for example, if the technology of hormone replacement therapy, including the medical supervision involved, is a prudent investment of healthcare resources. Their article starts out with the usual litany: "In the year 2005 the number of American women between the ages of 50 and 64 will be more than 25 million." They then go on to point out that the national bill for providing hormone replacement drugs and physician monitoring for those women is estimated to be between 3.5 and 5 billion dollars annually. After performing a complex cost-benefit analysis they reach the conclusion that any possible benefits of replacement therapy must be considered as "highly tentative," both in terms of the cost to society and the risk to individual patients (Weinstein and Tosteson 1990:171).

Countering the Hegemony: Women's Responses

Women have not sat silently on the margins while this debate has taken place. The National Women's Health Network in Washington, D.C., put out a paper entitled *Taking Hormones and Women's Health* in the same year as the Mack and Ross article (1989), in which they too reviewed a substantial portion of the literature on menopause and replacement therapy. After stating that they are opposed to the view taken in the majority of the articles, that normal menopause is a deficiency disease, they then point out several of the blind spots and assumptions that are made in virtually all of the articles they reviewed.

For example, researchers usually ignore the fact that the ovary itself continues to secrete hormones "long after menopause" (albeit at a reduced level), and that other sites in the body—the adrenal glands and fatty tissues—also produce estrogen. The Network also points out, as did Mack and Ross, that progesterone has not been in use long enough for evidence to have accrued as to either its risks or benefits, or about the effect of its interaction with the estrogen with which it is combined. Moreover, although the body continues to make estrogen after menopause, it produces very little progesterone (Korenman 1982), and hence there may be some as yet unknown biological reason why this is so. The Network reminds its readers that oral contraceptive pills used in the

1970s (which contained a progesterone) were associated with an increased risk for stroke and heart attacks.

Furthermore, the survey research widely cited in the literature as evidence of reduced risk for heart disease uses, and continues to use, subjects who are for the most part taking only estrogen. Today most women are started out with combined hormone replacement therapy, and hence no long-term predictions can be made from the results of current survey research in connection with present and future generations of women.

The Health Network also points out that less expensive, safer, and "more natural" forms of prevention for heart disease, osteoporosis, and cancer, such as dietary changes, dispensing with cigarette smoking and excessive alcohol use, prevention of falls, and so on, are only rarely discussed in research findings (but see Notelovitz 1989, for example), and they attribute this largely to the fact that most researchers are funded by drug companies. Since dietary changes have proven to be successful in significantly reducing the incidence of heart disease among men, clearly this argument is important.

In addition the Network notes that not all elderly women with fractures have osteoporosis and not all women with osteoporosis have fractures—facts that are often confused in the epidemiological literature. Moreover, there is no simple relationship between estrogen levels, bone mineral density, and the incidence of osteoporosis (Cummings 1985), nor do data exist as to what effect combined hormone replacement therapy has on bones.

The Network goes on to highlight something that none of the researchers themselves discussed in their original articles or apparently take account of—namely, that many women who are now taking hormone therapy were exposed when younger to high-dose birth control pills, and among these women some were given the carcinogenic diethylstilbestrol (DES) while pregnant. The next generation of hormone takers will have been exposed to a lower-dose pill, but from a younger age. It is further argued by the Health Network that it took twenty years for some of the cases of cancer connected with the imbibing of DES to become manifest, and that this experience should encourage the exercise of great caution in connection with replacement therapy (this argument has been countered in the past by the assertion that it was fetal tissue that developed the cancer, and not the pregnant women who were given the medication—and therefore presumably, older women have nothing to fear [Greenblatt 1972]).

Finally, the Health Network points out that women are not usually told about the side reactions they can expect with hormone replacement therapy—most particularly that hot flashes usually reoccur when treatment is stopped—and that combined therapy often causes what is euphe-mistically known as "break-through" bleeding, which not only creates anxiety but entails close monitoring and often painful medical proce-dures to establish its cause. In addition, bloating, "the blues," breast tenderness, and headaches are commonly experienced. Because of these side effects women tend to start and then stop taking medication; many only fill one prescription, or else the pills are not taken regularly— something that it is virtually impossible to monitor carefully and which influences the results of epidemiological studies.

As a result of their review, the Network concluded that it is poor public health practice to "attempt to prevent chronic disease conditions by using drugs of unknown safety and effectiveness;" they added that it is "dangerously misleading" to suggest that the "average" middle-aged woman will experience better health by taking drugs with unknown risks, and that women are, in effect, being urged to take part in a "risky, uncontrolled experiment without their fully informed consent" (Na-tional Women's Health Network 1989:3).

One further criticism passed over by the Health Network can be made of the epidemiological research into replacement therapy—namely, that almost all of the surveys have been conducted with Caucasian middle-class women, and in particular with those who have actively sought out medical care (Kaufert 1988). Extrapolations are then made from these populations to all middle-aged women, in spite of the fact that differ-ences are widely recognized in the incidence of, for example, osteo-porosis, heart disease, and breast cancer among black and Asian women as compared to Caucasians. To complicate things further, there is some evidence to indicate that breast cancer in younger women is not the same disease as that in older women, and, similarly, that the causes and incidence of heart disease are not equivalent among men and women, and younger and older people.

The Network also neglected to discuss the cumulative cost of medica-tion and gynecological check-ups. Given that the experts strongly rec-ommend that virtually all women should take medication and be moni-tored for twenty years or more after the end of menstruation in order to sustain their health, it is odd that no attention is paid to the fact that well over half the population of middle-aged American women cannot possibly afford this kind of care. But it seems these women are the lucky ones, in that they will not be required to juggle with the results of the head-spinning probabilities, regression analyses, risk-benefit analyses, and readjusted and reassessed data with which a middle-class, largely Caucasian population must cope in order to make an "informed decision"—in consultation, of course, with their suitably enlightened physicians.

How *can* an individual woman possibly weigh up and situate in her own life course the risks and benefits of cancerous breasts versus endometrial biopsies and withdrawal bleeding for years? Or a broken hip at age seventy-five versus the doubtful claim that her heart will be protected? How does one assess whether unopposed estrogen replacement therapy is better or worse than combined hormone replacement therapy, when the "experts" cannot agree? Particularly since research has been carried out in both Europe and North America with ever differing dosages and combinations of drugs. And how does one fit the latest and most bizarre of all these drugs into the picture—the antiestrogens, which act as estrogenic agents in some parts of the body and as antiestrogenic agents in other parts? Despite these impenetrable contradictions the clamor for a routinized use of hormone replacement therapy grows louder and louder.

A Triangulation of Interest: Physicians, Pharmaceutical Companies, and the Government

Part of this contest over the long-term use of replacement therapy, becoming ever more heated as the population ages, has to do with the intimate relationship between the medical profession and the major pharmaceutical companies that manufacture estrogen and progesterone. Government concern about the economic "liability" of an aging female population is also evident. But both the pharmaceutical companies and the government only came to recognize the Postmenopausal Woman as a target for their interests many years after her initial creation by the medical profession (in the middle of the last century in Europe [Lock 1993]).

A triangulation of interests among gynecologists, laboratory scientists, and pharmaceutical companies fueled a small replacement therapy industry early this century in which whole ovaries were ground up and injected into patients who had undergone an early menopause, usually due to surgery (Oudshoorn 1990). This practice was simply a small spin-off from another larger research project, however, in which middle-aged men had been injected with ground-up testes as rejuvenation therapy. The pharmaceutical industry did not become involved to any extent in the medicalization of menopause until the 1940s, after the development of synthetic estrogens (Bell 1987). By the late 1930s one or two gynecologists had likened menopause to a deficiency disease—specifically, diabetes and thyroid deficiency disease (Shorr 1940)—but, in spite of the availability of a specific medication to counter the supposed deficiency caused by declining estrogen levels, very few gynecologists actively adopted this way of thinking until relatively recently. On the contrary, most physicians were vociferous in describing menopause as a normal event, and were actively opposed to the use of estrogens except under extenuating circumstances, largely because they were very concerned about iatrogenesis (Bell 1987). Only a very small number of women, therefore—most of them having reached an early menopause due to surgery or for other reasons—were regularly medicated with estrogens prior to the mid-1960s.

It was recognized early in the century that heart disease is a major cause of mortality in postindustrial societies and that men are at a greater risk for heart attacks than women. A large amount of research money has been poured into clinical and epidemiological studies of heart disease, most of it directed at male subjects. Once again, almost as an afterthought, it was noted that young women whose ovaries had been removed were apparently subject to an increased risk for heart disease, and hence it was hypothesized that estrogen must act as a protective factor. As a result of this observation, experiments were carried out in which men were administered estrogen therapy in clinical trials, but "an unexpectedly" large number of heart attacks "often" leading to death were recorded for the subjects of these studies (Furman 1971:47). These experiments were hastily abandoned, but the seeds of the idea that estrogen therapy could be used as a prophylactic against heart disease had been sown. All that remained was to locate a suitable target population, and clearly men would not do!

Sensitivity to an aging population—combined with a growing awareness that although the incidence of heart disease in women at no time in the life cycle exceeds that of men, it nevertheless increases after menopause—provided the impetus to focus on older women as therapeutic subjects. This impetus was doubly reinforced because a link between estrogen decline and an increased risk for osteoporosis became widely accepted. As a result, a major industry more than twenty years in the making was consolidated around the concept of hormone replacement therapy as a prophylactic, although it is still contested in some medical circles and by many feminist groups and other women (Kaufert and McKinlay 1985). The industry is spearheaded not by the research of gynecologists, as was formerly the case, but by clinical epidemiologists, cardiologists, and others funded largely by partisan drug companies, while bewildered family practitioners, GPs, and many gynecologists stand on the fringes wondering what to do in the best interest of their patients (Lock 1993). The government, too, is poised on the sidelines, and sponsors their own analyses and special hearings in which cost-benefit data is no doubt the bottom line.

None of the involved parties—for or against the use of hormone replacement therapy—steps back to question why men so rarely appear in the rhetoric about the decrepit elderly; one or two physicians, but no feminists, I believe, have explicitly questioned the assumption that the young body should be taken as the standard for what is normal in older women. Similarly, a very small number of people, mostly biologists and anthropologists (Weiss 1981), have pointed out that the presence of elderly people in society is by no means a recent phenomenon (an assumption with which only a culture lacking a sense of history could deceive itself). Some women, one or two of them physicians, have tried in their writing to suggest that more "natural" forms of prevention are better than long-term drugging as a prophylactic measure. However, the bulk of the canon on menopause assumes that older women are inherently anomalous; they are conceptualized, usually unconsciously it seems, as the Other to men, apes, and younger women. But the mystification does not end there, because virtually *all* of the discourse is about an essentialized Postmenopausal Body—class and ethnic difference are obliterated; so, too is difference among individual women (Kaufert and Lock 1992). The universalized oddity of the aging, failing, potentially costly, white, middle-class female body is the target of medicalization, and individual women are required to calculate in terms of risks and benefits how they measure up against her.

The "Graying" of Japan

The aging society raises many concerns in Japan too, not the least of which is about a possible decline in the national economy due to the burden that the future elders will, it is assumed, place on society. The "graying" of Japan is particularly disturbing because demographic changes that occurred over the course of about one hundred years in Europe and North America have taken just twenty-five years in Japan. Some official estimates calculate that if present trends continue, by the year 2025 people aged sixty-five and over will make up a remarkable 24 percent of the population, and among the elderly, more than 53 percent will be over seventy-five years of age (Ogawa 1988). Again, if present trends continue, it is estimated that there will be more than 2.25 million Japanese suffering from senile dementia by 2025, of whom 67.5 percent will be women, and more than two million people will be bedridden, of whom 62 percent will be women. It is these figures about bedridden and senile elderly, and not the number of menopausal women, which are iconic in contemporary Japan, and, although women are picked out for special mention (not surprising since Japanese women live longer than anyone else in the world), decrepit men too make an appearance in these predictions.

Since the early 1970s, when the question of the elderly first began to capture the attention of policy-makers in Japan, it has been repeatedly stated that it is preferable for the elderly to be taken care of in their own homes, and family members should be the primary care givers (Kōsei Hakusho 1989). Politicians are concerned that the government is increasingly "expected" by the public to play a larger role in the care of the aging population, and several recent policy changes have been implemented to reverse this trend, as this document on long-term economic planning suggests:

> The home is extremely important to the aged for a secure life of retirement, their health and welfare. In an attempt to form a social environment ideal for future living, it will be necessary to correctly position the home in society [and] the role of people caring for the aged at home will become more important. . . .
>
> Also, it will be necessary to promote a land policy aimed at pressing for three family generations to live in the same place or for family members to live within easy reach. (Keizai Kikaku Chōhen 1982)

Not even the most conservative of politicians resort to the prewar term for the extended family (*ie*) to describe what they are promoting, but the intention is nevertheless clear. The "new residence system" goes under the tag of "living together in three-generation households," and it has been suggested that loans should be made available for such families together with the latest devices to help with nursing the elderly at minimum cost. A recent study showed that out of nearly five hundred people nursing aged relatives in their homes, over 81 percent were women who averaged fifty-six years of age. More than 60 percent of these women had been looking after their relatives for three years or more, 16 percent of them for over ten years (Tokyo Shinbun 1990). A recent study conducted by Japanese women concluded that with the current poor social welfare policies in Japan, the burden of care for the elderly is simply dropped into the laps of younger (that is, middle-aged) women (*Kōrei sha fukushi* 1989).

The Doctrine of Motherhood

A widely shared sentiment exists in Japan today to the effect that although the economic "health" of the country is excellent, this does not extend to the state of the nation itself, nor to the "spiritual" health of its peoples (Mochida 1980). The conservative government and like-minded intellectuals lament what they describe as a loss of traditional values—in particular, the "thinning" of family relationships leading to an undue emphasis on the "Western" value of individualism. The three-generation household, the *ie,* was for three-quarters of a century—from the Meiji

Restoration until the end of the Second World War—recognized as the official family unit in Japan. In this household are enshrined the ancestors, representatives of moral and spiritual values instilled on their behalf in the younger generation by the adult woman of the household, the "pillar" of the family. Modeled on the samurai system of feudal times, and laced with a little late-nineteenth-century European sentiment, the "good wife and wise mother" was expected to discipline herself for service to the household—in particular, for the nurturance and well-being, physical and spiritual, of all other family members (Haga 1990). Whereas feudal Japan exhibited an acute sensitivity to class and occupational differences, with the creation of the early modern state, difference was obliterated and Japanese women were appealed to for the first time as a unified body in terms of gendered social roles to be carried out within the confines of the *ie* (Nolte and Hastings 1991).

As part of such a family, a woman reaches the prime of life in her fifties and at that time enjoys the acme of her responsibility, which, although it gradually wanes, is never extinguished unless she succumbs to severe senility or some other catastrophe. Many Japanese women still live in these circumstances, and their days are filled with monitoring the household economy, care and education of pre-school grandchildren, and care of dependent in-laws, to which is often added piecework done at home, or participation in the household enterprise such as farming or the family business. Although in feudal Japan upper-class women were sometimes described as a "borrowed womb," from the end of the nineteenth century onwards all women came to be thought of primarily as nurturers in addition to economically productive members of society, roles they retained throughout the life cycle, although their specific duties changed through time. Reproduction was obviously important, and the bearing of a son particularly so, but the Japanese have through the years been remarkably flexible about the formal adoption into their families of not only children but even adults should the need arise. Hence, the dominant image of a woman in Japan in recent times has been that of nurturer, a quality with which all women are assumed to be "biologically" endowed (Mitsuda 1985). Emphasis is given in this ideology to dedication to a life-long gendered role, and reproduction is per se rendered less important. Japanese feminists have coined the term *boseishugi* (the doctrine of motherhood) to capture the essence of this ideology.

Social Anomaly: Female Aging and Japanese Modernity

The nuclear household in which approximately 60 percent of Japanese live these days, lacking both enshrined ancestors and the elders, is thought by many commentators to be a fragile, "pathological" conglomeration, particularly because the juridical powers of the household head were stripped away at the end of the war, leaving a vacuum devoid of both an authoritative and a moral voice (Mochida 1980; Eto 1979). Members of the nuclear family—men, women, and children—are thought to be particularly vulnerable to what has been termed "diseases of civilization" or "modernization," including a whole range of neuroses, behavioral disorders, and deviant behavior. These diseases are made factual by catchy diagnostic labels, such as "school refusal syndrome," "high-rise apartment neurosis," "moving day depression," "death from overwork," and so on (Lock 1988*a*). One of them is "menopausal syndrome," a problem believed to have surfaced only in postwar years and which is associated particularly with middle-class, "professional" housewives who live in urban environments. When asked if he thought that all women experience trouble at menopause, a Kobe gynecologist answered,

> No, I don't think so. Women who have no purpose in life [*ikigai*] have the most trouble. Housewives who are relatively well off, who have only one or two children and lots of free time come to see me most often. Menopausal syndrome is a sort of "luxury disease" [*zeitakubyō*]; I'm sure women never used to come running to a doctor before the war with this kind of problem.

A physician who works in the countryside stated emphatically that rural women are much too busy to experience distress at menopause, the implication clearly being that any discomfort they may feel is of minor importance, something that an active and busy woman will "ride over" (*norikoeru*) with ease. Women who are unoccupied, who are not contributing in any obvious way to society, and hence, it is assumed, who have too much time on their hands, are likely to be deficient in the willpower and endurance that was characteristic of their mothers and generations of Japanese women before them, and it is therefore they who will experience distress at menopause (Lock 1988*b*).

The irony of this rhetoric, very evident in popular literature for women, does not pass unnoticed by feminist commentators (Higuchi 1985). Women have systematically been kept out of the full-time work force in postwar Japan despite the fact that large numbers of them put in a full day's work on a regular basis (it is estimated that less than 30 percent of Japanese women are what are known as "professional housewives"). By far the majority of employed women are "temporary" blue-collar workers officially classified as part-time who work long hours with no benefits and are subject to hiring and firing as the national economy waxes and wanes. Aside from the helping professions, married women are rarely found in white-collar and professional jobs because there is enormous social pressure placed on them to resign once they become pregnant. Being rehired into a "good" position at a later date is virtually impossible, even though most women wish to work for financial reasons. Nevertheless, once their children are raised, housewives are subject to stigmatization because while the rest of the nation, with the exception only of some of the elderly, is worked to death (at times literally, it appears [National Defence Counsel for Victims of *Karōshi* 1990]), middle-aged housewives, it is assumed, pass their time by playing tennis and making plastic flowers. There is, of course, *some* truth to this claim, provided one is not responsible for sick elders.

In Japan, therefore, the "homebody" is idealized. She is made into the standard by which all women are measured, but the assumption is that once she becomes middle-aged she is likely to become a social anomaly, no longer of obvious productive use beyond occasionally feeding her husband unless she is prevailed on, as in times past, to carry out her lifelong duties to the extended family. The government, as we have seen, has unveiled plans to ensure that women remain out of the work force by actively encouraging them to fulfill their "natural" duty as unpaid nurses in extended families (and in this manner politicians strive to keep unemployment figures to a minimum, while at the same time avoiding the necessity of providing adequate public facilities for the care of the elderly).

Because those who are financially secure are assumed to represent Japanese women as a whole, it is possible to erase the situation of the majority of women—namely, those who must give up paid labor to look after their relatives, often at great cost to the well-being of other family members—from the national consciousness. Since many Japanese live to be well over ninety years of age, some daughters-in-law in their seventies still have their lives bound over to an incontinent and immobile old person. Furthermore, since stroke is the most usual cause of disability among the elderly in Japan, intensive nursing is often required, and men only very rarely assist in this onerous duty.

It is therefore the issue of home nursing and the three-generation family which takes up the energy of activist women in Japan today. Together with the politically active among the elderly themselves, they question the intransigence of governments national and local on these matters. Against the urgency of this situation the end of menstruation fades into the background, particularly because of the moralistic rhetoric associated with it—in a country driven overwhelmingly by the work ethic, few people relish being accused, even indirectly, of indolence.

The Social Nature of Maturation

Despite a concern about the "graying" of the nation, aging itself is not thought of as an anomaly; on the contrary, Japan is a society exquisitely sensitive to the passing of time, and positively wallows, on occasion, in the ephemeral nature of human life. The life cycle transitions of both men and women were formerly marked and celebrated as social events; continuity with past generations and the presence of the ancestors reinforce the notion that each individual is part of a larger, cosmically ordained order (Smith 1974). Women who are at present age fifty were immersed in this ideology as children and the majority still embrace it (Lebra 1984; Lock in press). Movement through the life cycle is subjectively experienced largely in terms of how one's relationships with other people shift through time, and for women particularly, life is expected to become meaningful according to what they accomplish for others rather than for themselves (Plath 1980:139). Under these circumstances the end of menstruation is not a very potent icon. While there is some mourning for the loss of youth and sexual attractiveness on the part of a few women, emphasis is given by most to what is described as the inevitable process of aging itself: to graying hair, changing eyesight, faulty short-term memory, and so on (Lock 1986). Furthermore these signs of aging, while they obviously represent irretrievable youth, are primarily signifiers for the future—for what may be in store in terms of an enfeebled body, and hence an inability to work and to contribute to society.

Some women do not apparently mark the end of menstruation as part of menopause at all—in a survey I conducted,[1] 24 percent of the sample of women aged forty-five to fifty-five who had ceased menstruating for more than one year reported that they had no sign of menopause (Lock 1986:30). In this discourse about aging, therefore, women are not markedly distinguished from men, for the physical changes associated with middle age that are attributed with significance are common to both sexes.

Signs and Symptoms of Kōnenki

When over one hundred women were interviewed in their homes about the physical symptoms that they associated with *kōnenki* (the term in Japanese that most closely approximates the word menopause), nearly 80 percent of the responses were along the following lines:

I've had no problems at all, no headaches or anything like that. . . . I've heard from other people that their heads felt so heavy that they couldn't get up. A few of my friends complain that they don't exactly have pain, but that they just feel generally bad.

I started to have trouble sleeping when I was about fifty; that was kōnenki, I think. Some people have dizziness, headaches, stiff shoulders, and aching joints.

In my case my eyesight became weak. Some people get sensitive and have headaches.

My shoulders feel as if they are pulled and I get tired easily.

The most common disorders that I've heard about are headaches, shoulder stiffness, and aching joints. Some women get irritable too.

A small number of women—twelve out of the sample of more than one hundred—made statements such as the following:

The most noticeable thing was that I would suddenly feel hot; it happened every day, three times or so. I didn't go to the doctor or take any medication. I wasn't embarrassed and I didn't feel strange; I just thought that it was my age.

In the survey questionnaire a long, culturally appropriate symptom list of fifty-seven items was included, not all of them necessarily associated with *kōnenki,* and women were asked if they had experienced any of these symptoms in the previous two weeks. Overall reporting was low and significantly different from comparable Manitoban and Massachusetts samples (Avis et al. 1993). Most frequently reported symptoms were, in descending order of frequency: shoulder stiffness, headaches, lumbago, constipation, chilliness, irritability, insomnia, aches and pains in the joints, frequent colds, sore throat, feelings of numbness, and then, reported equally, loss of memory and hot flashes (only 10 percent of the sample as opposed to 31 percent and 35 percent in Manitoba and Massachusetts respectively).[2] These were followed closely by "heavy head" (*atama ga omoi*), ringing in the ears, and eventually, almost at the bottom of the list, night sweats (only 4 percent of the sample as opposed to 20 percent in Manitoba and 12% in Massachusetts). The "classical" symptoms of menopause—hot flashes and night sweats—are not, therefore, reported to anything like the same extent as in comparable North American samples.

Over 40 percent of the Japanese women interviewed agreed with the statement made by a Kyoto factory worker: "*Kōnenki* starts at different ages depending on the person. Some start in their late thirties and some never have any symptoms; they don't have *kōnenki* at all." The term *shōgai* (ill effects) has to be added to *kōnenki* ("change of life") before most women start to think in terms of symptoms that could be thought of as distressing.

Creating the Discourse of Kōnenki

The end of menstruation has been recognized for many hundreds of years in traditional Sino/Japanese medicine as an occurrence that can leave "stale blood" in the body, the cause in some women of numerous nonspecific symptoms that often last a few years, including dizziness, palpitations, headaches, chilliness, stiff shoulders, a dry mouth, and so on (Nishimura 1981). Since it was believed that many other events also cause stale blood and associated nonspecific symptoms, no specific term was created to gloss the discomfort some women experience at the end of menstruation. Toward the end of the nineteenth century, when there was a great deal of exchange for the first time between Japan and Europe, the term *kōnenki* was created in Japanese to convey the European concept of the climacterium. Nishimura (1981) has suggested that *kōnenki* could, until recently, be used to refer to all of the life cycle transitions, both male and female, regardless of age. This interpretation is very close to the meaning given to the term climacterium as it was used until the middle of the nineteenth century in Europe. Although usage of this concept has recently been confined to female mid-life, it was originally used throughout Europe to describe the dangers associated with the many critical transitions conceptualized throughout the life cycle, regardless of age or gender (Sears 1986).

Japanese doctors, a good number of whom went to Germany to study Western medicine early in the twentieth century, found a need to invent technical terms in Japanese to gloss the concepts of a female mid-life climacterium (the time span during which menstruation stops) and menopause (the end of menstruation), both of which by the early twentieth century were firmly established in the gynecological literature of Europe and North America. However, the existence of these rather cumbersome terms was short-lived, and by the 1920s they had been dropped in favor of the by now well-established, "ordinary" word of *kōnenki,* which continues to this day to signify a gradual transition period of anything from ten to twenty years' duration. There is still no widely used specific term in contemporary Japanese that expresses in everyday language the event of the end of menstruation, although there is, of course, a technical term, much as menopause was a technical term in English and little used in daily parlance until as recently as forty years ago.

In a 1927 article in a Japanese journal of gynecology a third abstruse term was invented to convey the idea of a hot flash, for which also there was no specific word in Japanese (Yamada 1927), but this technical term, like the others, did not survive for long. The situation remains unchanged today, and those few Japanese women who experience hot flashes have to convey this experience by stating simply that they "suddenly become hot," or that they have *nobose,* which is used to express the rather medical idea of a sudden rush of blood to the head associated with vertigo and dizziness, or alternatively *hoteri,* which is used to talk about the flushed faces that many East Asians experience when they imbibe alcohol. In other words, there is no specific term that specifically designates a hot flash, despite the presence of highly refined discriminators for various body states in the Japanese language in general.

One part of turn-of-the-century German discourse about the climacterium that made good intuitive sense to the Japanese medical world was the concept of the "autonomic nervous system." This idea, when it was first clearly articulated in 1898, caused a stir in medical circles everywhere (Sheehan 1936), but perhaps particularly so in Japan, where it "fitted" with the holistically oriented physiological approach characteristic of Sino/Japanese medicine. Later, in the 1930s, when a close association was postulated between the endocrine system and the autonomic nervous system (Sheehan 1936), Japanese physicians comfortably adopted this idea and postulated a connection between *kōnenki* and disturbances in the autonomic nervous system, an association that the majority of Japanese physicians and women still accept today (Lock, Kaufert, and Gilbert 1988; Rosenberger 1992). The current dominant discourse in Japan is one in which distress is not usually linked directly to a decline in estrogen levels, but is said to be due to a destabilization of the autonomic nervous system to which both sexes are vulnerable with age, but to which women are thought to be more vulnerable than men because of the added impact of declining estrogen levels.

Another factor that no doubt worked in Japan against the construction of a narrowly focused discourse on the aging ovary and declining estrogen levels was that Japanese doctors, unlike their Western counterparts, had never practiced much surgery prior to the twentieth century, a speciality that was disparaged by the powerful, physiologically oriented herbalists of the traditional medical system. Furthermore, anatomy as it was conceived in Enlightenment medical discourse in Europe had relatively little impact in Japan until the twentieth century, and autopsies and dissection were not widely practiced. Japanese gynecologists, therefore, did not have the first-hand experience of removing and dissecting many hundreds of ovaries as was the case for many late nineteenth century European and North American gynecologists (Laqueur 1990) and their "gaze" remained predominantly physiologically rather than anatomically oriented.

One other result of the emphasis given in Japan to physiological changes associated with *kōnenki* has been that until recently the majority of Japanese women, those few who consult with a doctor at this stage of the life cycle, usually go to see an internist and not a gynecologist, since gynecology is primarily a surgical speciality. The combination of this tendency, together with a physiological orientation on the part of both women and physicians, has ensured that the discourse on *kōnenki* is markedly different from that for menopause in North America. Stiff shoulders, headaches, ringing in the ears, tingling sensations, dizziness, and so on are the symptoms that form the core of the *kōnenki* experience. An experience that is also in part contingent upon a "local" biology, where hot flashes and other so-called vasomotor symptoms, thought in the West to be characteristic of menopause, occur rather infrequently. This account of the "unstable" middle-aged body is thought in Japan to be universal (at least to the Japanese archipelago) and is not associated especially with the leisured middle-class housewife, but it is widely accepted that she is the one likely to complain and "fuss" about symptoms, and to seek out medical care rather than simply maintain the correct mental attitude that allows her to "ride over" the distress.

A Japanese gynecologist who has spent many years doing research in connection with *kōnenki* believes that this concept does not coincide with that of the English term menopause; he and all of the thirty physicians whom I interviewed in Japan are of the opinion that hot flashes are not experienced by most Japanese women, and when they do occur they usually cause little distress. That the hot flash is not the key signifier of menopausal distress has meant that there has been relatively little incentive over the years for Japanese doctors to prescribe estrogen therapy for symptom relief, since it is generally agreed both in Japan and North America that hot flashes are rapidly relieved by estrogen replacement therapy. There is, however, one other significant difference between Japan and North America: namely, that the pill is not available in Japan for contraceptive purposes. Both doctors and women regularly report in survey research that they are very concerned about possible iatrogenesis caused by long-term use of the pill (*Mainichi Daily News* 1987), and this fear extends to the use of hormone replacement therapy, the chemical composition of which is very similar to the pill, a fact that the majority of Japanese women apparently appreciate.

The Medical World and Kōnenki

In Japan obstetrics and gynecology have not usually been separated in primary care practice, and individual physicians own and run small hospitals where their income is derived largely from deliveries, abortions, and minor surgery. Recently, however, gynecologists find their medical practices less lucrative than was formerly the case because women now choose to have their babies in tertiary care facilities, and also because the abortion rate is going down due to a more sophisticated use of contraception (despite the unavailability of the pill). Until recently, *kōnenki* has not been medicalized to any great extent in Japan, by either internists or gynecologists, but this is changing due in part to the economic pressures under which many gynecologists in private practice now find themselves. Some of them are currently setting up counseling services for middle-aged patients, while others are busy writing books and articles on the subject for popular consumption. Despite these changing practices, however, and the presence of an aggressive pharmaceutical industry, so far little use is made in Japan of hormone replacement therapy, which is prescribed less frequently than are herbal medications (Japan Pharmaceutical Manufacturers Association 1990).

Japanese physicians keep abreast of the medical literature published in the West, and so one could expect in a country such as Japan, which is actively dedicated to preventive medicine, that there might be some changes in the prescription of replacement therapy to middle-aged women similar to those taking place in North America. Here again, local biology plays a part: Mortality from coronary heart disease for Japanese women is about one-quarter that of American women (WHO 1990), and, although the figures are not altogether reliable, it is estimated that although Japanese women become osteoporotic twice as often as Japanese men, this nevertheless happens about half as often as in North America (Ross et al. 1991). These figures, combined with a mortality rate from breast cancer about one-quarter that of North America, has meant that there is relatively little pressure for Japanese gynecologists to enter into the international arena of debate about the pros and cons of long-term use of replacement therapy, something about which most of them are, in any case, decidedly uncomfortable because of a deep concern about iatrogenesis. The first line of resort of Japanese doctors when dealing with healthy middle-aged women is usually to encourage good dietary practices and plenty of exercise, recommendations that apparently satisfy most of their patients (Lock 1993).

Epidemiologically speaking, *kōnenki* is not, therefore, big news in Japan—all the more so because what springs to the minds of both Japanese physicians and the government in connection with elderly females is not broken hips or heart attacks, but overwhelmingly the image of a semiparalyzed, bedridden, incontinent old lady who has suffered a stroke, and who may well be senile into the bargain. These conditions do not usually figure prominently in the literature on menopause and its long-term effects. All of the above circumstances have contributed in their various ways to a lack of medical interest in *kōnenki* women, a situation not unlike that in North America until twenty-five years ago with respect to menopause.

The Politics of Female Aging

Japanese women, although second class citizens in political terms and until recently legally subordinated to men, have not traditionally been conceptualized in opposition to them, but in a complementary relationship, particularly in terms of family life. Even when elderly, women were not rendered peripheral, but served as vital links between the extended family and the ancestors. The process of aging was thought of as an unavoidable, natural process, with a focus on physiological changes common to both men and women; aging has not been associated with pathology until very recent times. Middle-aged women in Japan were therefore not conceived of historically as either biological or social anomalies, although recent changes in the structure of the Japanese family and in working conditions have meant that today older housewives are at risk for being thought of as social oddities.

In seeking to understand themselves the Japanese have for centuries drawn on an ideology of national unity in which "we Japanese" are set off from the "Other," most often in historical times the Chinese, or else a generalized "barbarian outsider" from further afield. But, since the end of the last century, with the self-conscious opening up of Japan to the rest of the world, the image in contrast to which the Japanese have constructed themselves, always with considerable ambivalence, has been the modernized culture of the "West." However, with ever-growing intensity over the past thirty years, as the Japanese economy has gradually become dominant, it is this same "West" (by which is often understood the worst excesses of America) which is drawn on to create the current discourse about the dangers of unbridled individuality and the fragility of the new Japanese family believed to haunt Japan today. It is this rhetoric of difference between Japan and the West, tradition and modernity, nurturance and individuality, which fuels the moralistic negative discourse associated with *kōnenki*. Thus, middle-aged Japanese women are not found wanting in terms of their biological difference with respect to either men or younger women, nor is their age as such an anomaly. It is their social position that makes *kōnenki* women a target for action, political rather than medical, and in order to make them into a target, middle-aged women are constructed as different from all the generations of properly disciplined and controlled Japanese women who are believed to have gone before them from time immemorial.

The politics of aging, an urgent matter in both Japan and North America, is constructed in both cultural spaces, therefore, out of assumptions about the place of women in society. Although the respective discourses are in part the product of a rhetoric about biological change with its associated risk for distress and even major disease (in North America), this rhetoric is produced from local biologies, specific, historically shaped knowledge, and situated social exigencies. Whereas in North America attention is paid almost exclusively to individual biology and the aging female is set up as a target for medicalization, in Japan thus far it is the care that middle-aged women are expected to give to old people that has captured public attention, and not the middle-aged body *per se*. Any physical distress women may experience in Japan is liable to be largely ignored or suppressed in favor of a display of self-control and discipline designed to be of service to others. However, although the Japanese woman is reduced to the behavioral qualities with which she has been "naturally" endowed and not simply to her anatomy, nevertheless the rhetoric produced in both contexts is cloaked with scientific neutrality.

In both these discourses the subjective experience of aging is ignored; it is assumed to be irrelevant and inaccurate knowledge in political arenas where reality is above all quantitatively constructed. So too are the economic constraints under which women live, and what is more, the fact that many women in North America care for their elderly is pushed to one side, largely unrecognized (Harrington et al. 1985). In both situations women are reduced to a uniform mass, their variety obliterated, but in North America, whereas efforts are made to discipline women indirectly via their internalized sense of individual responsibility to keep fit, in Japan the bureaucratized state enters more directly into the fray. The numerous ways in which the majority of women in both contexts resist, manipulate, and laugh at the ideology is ignored (Lock, in press). Also ignored is the position of men in an aging society, and any suggestion as to how their declining bodies should be medicalized, or alternatively, their habits, hygiene, and behavior "reformed" for the benefit of their families. Thus, in both contexts there is apparently little or no reflection about why women are ideologically targeted while men are not. In North America in particular, although some attention is paid to the health of middle-aged men, we hear almost nothing of older failing male bodies; they are conspicuous by their absence, made invisible in the haze of hot air produced about the opposite sex. It is, above all, this black Pandora's box that remains to be pried open.

Notes

1. A cross-sectional survey was administered to 1,738 Japanese women aged forty-five to fifty-five inclusively. The sample was divided between factory

workers, women who live on and/or run farms, and full-time housewives. A total of 1,316 usable replies were obtained, and the study was comparable with a sample of over 8,000 women in Massachusetts and 2,500 Manitoban women (see Lock 1986 and Avis et al. 1993).

2. This difference holds even when account is taken of the very different rates of hysterectomies in the three settings (Lock 1993).

References

Asso, Doreen
   1983   The Real Menstrual Cycle. New York: John Wiley and Sons.
Avis, Nancy E., Patricia A. Koufert, Margaret Lock, Sonja M. McKinlay, and Kerstin Vass
   1993   The Evolution of Menopausal Symptoms. Ballière's Clinical Endrocrinology and Metabolism 7:17–32.
Avis, Susan
   1987   Changing Ideas: The Medicalization of Menopause. Social Science and Medicine 24:535–543.
Berger, John
   1972   Ways of Seeing. London: Penguin Books.
Bergkvist, Leif, Hans Olav Adanir, Ingemar Persson, Robert Hooves, and Catherine Schairer
   1989   The Risk of Breast Cancer after Estrogen and Estrogen-Progestin Replacement. New England Journal of Medicine 321:293–297.
Cummings, S. R.
   1985   Are Patients with Hip Fractures More Osteoporotic? Review of the Evidence. The American Journal of Medicine 78:487–494.
Dewhurst, John
   1981   Integrated Obstetrics and Gynecology for Postgraduates. Oxford: Blackwell Scientific Publications.
Eto, Jun
   1979   The Breakdown of Motherhood Is Wrecking our Children. Japan Echo 6:102–109.
Fuchs, Victor
   1974   Who Shall Die? Health, Economics and Social Choice. New York: Basic Books.
Furman, Robert H.
   1971   Coronary Heart Disease and the Menopause. In Menopause and Aging, Kenneth J. Ryan and Don C. Gibson, eds., pp. 39–55. Bethesda, Md.: U.S. Department of Health, Education and Welfare.
Gosden, R. G.
   1985   The Biology of Menopause: The Causes and Consequences of Ovarian Aging. London: Academic Press.
Greenblatt, R. B.
   1972   Hormonal Management of the Menopause. Medical Counter-Point 4:19.

Greenblatt, R. B., and A.-Z. Teran
1987   Advice to Post-menopausal women. In *The Climacteric and Beyond,* L. Zichella, M. Whitehead, and P. A. Van Keep, eds. New Jersey: Parthenon Publishing Group.
Haga, Noboru
1990   *Ryōsai kenbo* (Good wives and wise mothers). Tokyo: Yusankaku.
Haraway, Donna
1989   *Primate Visions: Gender, Race, and Nature in the World of Modern Science.* New York: Routledge.
Harrington, Charlene, Robert J. Newcomer, Carroll L. Estes, and associates.
1985   *Long Term Care of the Elderly.* Beverly Hills, Calif.: Sage.
Haspels Ary A., and Pieter A. Van Keep
1979   Endocrinology and Management of the Peri-Menopause. In *Psychosomatics in Peri-Menopause,* Ary A. Haspels and Herman Musaph, eds., Baltimore: University Park Press.
Higuchi, Keiko
1985   Women at Home. *Japan Echo* 12:51–57.
Hunt, Kathryn, Martin Versey, Klim McPherson, and Michael Coleman
1987   Long-Term Surveillance of Mortality and Cancer Incidence in Women Receiving Hormone Replacement Therapy. 94:620–635.
Japan Pharmaceutical Manufacturers Association
1990   *Data Book, 1989.* Tokyo: Japan Pharmaceutical Manufacturers Association.
Jern, Helen
1973   *Hormone Therapy of the Menopause and Aging.* Springfield. Ill.: Charles C. Thomas.
Jick, Hershel, Alexander M. Walker, Richard N. Watkins, Diane C. D'Ewart, Judith R. Hunter, Anne Danforth, Sue Madsen, Barbara J. Dinan, and Kenneth J. Rothman
1980   Replacement Estrogens and Breast Cancer. *American Journal of Epidemiology* 112:586–594.
Kaufert, Patricia
1988   Menopause as Process or Event: The Creation of Definitions in Biomedicine. In *Biomedicine Examined,* Margaret Lock and Deborah Gordon, eds., pp. 331–349. Dordrecht, Netherlands: Kluwer Academic Publishers.
Kaufert, Patricia, and Margaret Lock
1992   "What Are Women For?": Cultural Constructions of Menopausal Women in Japan and Canada. In *In Her Prime: New Views of Middle-Aged Women,* Virginia Kerns and Judith K. Brown, eds., pp. 201–219. Chicago: University of Illinois Press.
Kaufert, Patricia, and Sonja McKinlay
1985   Estrogen-Replacement Therapy: The Production of Medical Knowledge and the Emergence of Policy. In *Women, Health and Healing: Toward a New Perspective,* Ellen Lewin and Virginia Olesen, eds., pp. 113–138. London: Tavistock Publications.

Keizai Kikaku Chōhen
    1982   *Nisen nen no Nihon*. Tokyo: Government Publications Pub.
Korenman, S. G.
    1982   Menopausal Endocrinology and Management. *Archives of Internal Medicine* 142:1131–1136.
Kōrei sha fukushi
    1989   *Kōrei sha fukushi* (Welfare for the elderly). Nihon Fujin Dantai-Rengōkai, ed. Tokyo: Horupu Shuppan.
Kōsei Hakusho
    1989   *Arata na kōreishazō to katsuryoku aru chōju fukushi shakai o mezashite.* Tokyo: Kōseishō.
Laqueur, Thomas
    1990   *Making Sex: Body and Gender from the Greeks to Freud.* Cambridge: Harvard University Press.
Lebra, Takie
    1984   *Japanese Women: Constraint and fulfillment.* Honolulu: University of Hawaii Press.
Lock, Margaret
    1986   Ambiguities of Aging: Japanese Experience and Perceptions of Menopause. *Culture, Medicine and Psychiatry* 10:23–46.
    1988*a*   A Nation at Risk: Interpretations of School Refusal in Japan. In *Biomedicine Examined,* Margaret Lock and Deborah R. Gordon, eds., pp. 391–414. Dordrecht, Netherlands: Kluwer Academic Publishers.
    1988*b*   New Japanese Mythologies: Faltering Discipline and the Ailing Housewife in Japan. *American Ethnologist* 15:43–61.
    1993   Encounters with Aging: *Mythologies of Menopause in Japan and North America,* Berkeley: University of California Press.
Lock, Margaret, Patricia Kaufert, and Penny Gilbert
    1988   Cultural Construction of the Menopausal Syndrome: The Japanese Case. *Maturitas* 10:317–332.
London, Steve, and Charles Hammond
    1986   The Climacteric. *Obstetrics and Gynecology,* In David Danforth and James Scott, eds., pp. 905–926. Philadelphia: J. B. Lippencott.
Lufkin, Edward C., and Steven Ory
    1989   Estrogen Replacement Therapy for the Prevention of Osteoporosis, *American Family Physician* 40:205–212.
Mack, T. M., and R. K. Ross
    1989   Risks and Benefits of Long-Term Treatment with Estrogens. *Schweizensche Medizinische Wochenschrift* 119:1811–1820.
Mainichi Daily News
    1987   Interview with Takuro Kobayashi, "Pill Researcher," February 23.
Martin, Emily
    1987   *The Woman in the Body: A Cultural Analysis of Reproduction.* Boston: Beacon Press.

Mitsuda, Kyōko
    1985   "Kindaiteki Boseikan no Jūyō to henkei: Kyōiku suru hahaoya kara
            ryōsai kenbo e" (The importance and transformation of the condi-
            tion of modern motherhood: From education mother to good wife
            and wise mother). In *Bosei o tou* (What is Motherhood?), Haruko
            Wakita, ed., pp. 100–129. Kyoto: Jinbunshoin.
Mochida, Takeshi
    1980   Focus on the Family. Editorial Comment. *Japan Echo* 3:75–76.
Nachtigall, Lila
    1990   Hormone replacement therapy. In *Highlights from the Sixth Interna-
            tional Congress on the Menopause*, p. 1. Michigan: Beardsley and
            Company.
National Defence Council for Victims of *Karōshi*
    1990   *Karōshi* (Death from overwork). Tokyo: Madosha.
National Women's Health Network
    1989   *Taking Hormones and Women's Health*. Washington, D.C.: Na-
            tional Women's Health Network.
Nishimura, Hideo
    1981   *Josei to Kanpō* (Women and herbal medicine). Osaka: Sōgensha.
Nolte, Sharon, and Sally Ann Hastings
    1991   The Meiji State's Policy. In *Recreating Japanese Women, 1600–1945*,
            Gail Lee Bernstein, ed., pp. 151–174. Berkeley, Los Angeles, Ox-
            ford: University of California Press.
Notelovitz, Morris
    1989   Estrogen Replacement Therapy: Indications, Contraindications and
            Agent Selection. *American Journal of Obstetrics and Gynecology*
            161:8–17.
Ogawa, Naohiro
    1988   Population Aging and Medical Demand: The Case of Japan. In
            *Economic and Social Implications of Population Aging. Proceedings
            of the International Symposium on Population Structure and Devel-
            opment, Tokyo*, pp. 254–275. New York: United Nations.
Oudshoorn, Nelly
    1990   On the Making of Sex Hormones: Research Materials and the Pro-
            duction of Knowledge. *Social Studies of Science* 20:5–33.
Plath, David
    1980   *Long Engagements*. Stanford: Stanford University Press.
Reid, Robert L.
    1988   Menopause: Part I: Hormonal Replacement. *Bulletin: Society of
            Obstetricians and Gynecologists* 10:25–34.
Rosenberger, Nancy
    1992   The Process of Discourse: Usages of a Japanese Medical Term.
            Social Science and Medicine 34:237–247.
Ross, Philip D., Hiromichi Norimatsu, James W. Davis, Katsuhiko Yano, Rich-
ard D. Wasnick, Saeko Fukiwara, Yutaka Hosoda, and L. Hoseph Melton
    1991   A Comparison of Hip Fracture Incidence among Native Japanese,

Japanese Americans, and American Caucasians. *American Journal of Epidemiology* 133:801–809.

Sarrel, Philip M.
1988   Estrogen Replacement Therapy. *Obstetrics and Gynecology* 72 (suppl.):2S–5S.

Shorr, Ephraim
1940   The Menopause. *Bulletin of the New York Academy of Medicine* 16:453–474.

Sears, Elizabeth
1986   *The Ages of Man: Medieval Interpretations of the Life Cycle.* New Jersey: Princeton University Press.

Sheehan, Donald
1936   Discovery of the Autonomic Nervous System. *AMA Archives of Neurology and Psychiatry* 35:1081–1115.

Sheehy, Gail
1991   The Silent Passage: Menopause. *Vanity Fair* (October): 222–263.

Smith, Robert
1974   *Ancestor Worship in Contemporary Japan.* Stanford: Stanford University Press.

Tokyo Shinbun
1990   Rōjin kaigo josei ni zusshiri (Nursing of the elderly lands on women). 13 September.

Vermeulen, A., J. P. Delypere, W. Schelfhout, L. Verdonck, R. Rubens
1982   Androcentrical Function in Old Age: Response to Acute Adrenocorticotropin Stimulation. *Journal of Clinical Endocrinological Metabolism* 54:187–191.

Weinstein, Milton, and Anna Tosteson
1990   Cost Effectiveness of Hormone Replacement. In *Multidisciplinary Perspectives on Menopause,* Marsha Flint, Fredi Kronenberg, and Wulf Utian, eds., pp. 162–171. Annals of the New York Academy of Sciences, vol. 592. New York: New York Academy of Sciences.

Weiss, Kenneth M.
1981   Evolutionary Perspectives on Human Aging. In *Other Ways of Growing Old,* Pamela T. Amoss and Stevan Harrell, eds., pp. 25–58. Stanford: Stanford University Press.

Wentz, Anne Colston
1988   Management of the Menopause. In *Novak's Textbook of Gynecology,* Howard W. Jones, Anne C. Wentz, and Lonnie S. Burnett, eds. 11th ed. Baltimore: Williams & Wilkins.

Willson, James Robert, Clayton T. Beecham, and Elsie R. Carrington
1975   *Obstetrics and Gynecology.* St. Louis: C. V. Mosby.

Wilson, Robert A., and Thelma A. Wilson
1963   The Fate of the Nontreated Postmenopausal Woman: A Plea for the Maintenance of the Adequate Estrogen from Puberty to the Grave. *Journal of the American Geriatrics Society* 11:347–362.

WHO (World Health Organization)
1990   *World Health Statistics Annual.* Geneva.
WHO (World Health Organization) Scientific Group
1981   *Research on the Menopause.* World Health Organization Technical Report series no. 670. Geneva.
Yamada, Kazuo
1927   Kōnenki no rinshōmen (Clinical aspects of menopause). *Rinshōigaku* (Clinical medicine) 9:1095–1102.

15

The Biopolitics of Postmodern Bodies

Determinations of Self in Immune System Discourse

Donna Haraway

If Koch's postulates must be fulfilled to identify a given microbe with a given disease, perhaps it would be helpful, in rewriting the AIDS text, to take "Turner's postulates" into account (1984: 209): 1) disease is a language; 2) the body is a representation; and 3) medicine is a political practice.

Paula Treichler, "AIDS, Homophobia, and Biomedical Discourse: An Epidemic of Signification"

Non-self: A term covering everything which is detectably different from an animal's own constituents.

J. H. L. Playfair, *Immunology at a Glance*

[T]he immune system must recognize self in some manner in order to react to something foreign.

Edward S. Golub, *Immunology: A Synthesis*

Lumpy Discourses and the Denatured Bodies of Biology and Medicine

It has become commonplace to emphasize the multiple and specific cultural dialects interlaced in any social negotiation of disease, illness, and sickness in the contemporary worlds marked by biological research, biotechnology, and scientific medicine. The language of biomedicine is never alone in the field of empowering meanings, and its power does not flow from a consensus about symbols and actions in the face of suffering. Paula Treichler's (1987) excellent phrase in the title of her essay on the constantly contested meanings of AIDS as an "epidemic of signification" could be applied widely to the social text of sickness. The power of biomedical language—with its stunning artifacts, images, architectures, social forms, and technologies—for shaping the unequal experience of sickness and death for millions is a social fact deriving from ongoing heterogeneous social processes. The power of biomedicine and biotechnology is constantly reproduced, or it would cease. This power is not a thing fixed and permanent, embedded in plastic and ready to section for microscopic observation by the historian or critic. The cultural and material authority of biomedicine's productions of bodies and selves is more vulnerable, more dynamic, more elusive, and more powerful than that.

But if there has been recognition of the many non-, para-, anti-, or extrascientific languages in company with biomedicine that structure the embodied semiosis of mortality in the industrialized world, it is much less common to find emphasis on the multiple languages *within* the territory that is often so glibly marked scientific. "Science says" is represented as a univocal language. Yet even the spliced character of the potent words in "science" hints at a barely contained and inharmonious heterogeneity. The words for the overlapping discourses and their objects of knowledge, and for the abstract corporate names for the concrete places where the discourse-building work is done, suggest both the blunt foreshortening of technicist approaches to communication and the uncontainable pressures and confusions at the boundaries of meanings within "science"—biotechnology, biomedicine, psychoneuroimmunology, immunogenetics, immunoendocrinology, neuroendocrinology, monoclonal antibodies, hybridomas, interleukines, Genentech, Embrex, Immunetech, Biogen.

This paper explores some of the contending popular and technical languages constructing biomedical, biotechnical bodies and selves in postmodern scientific culture in the United States in the 1980s. Scientific discourses are "lumpy"; they contain and enact condensed contestations for meanings and practices. The chief object of my attention will be the potent and polymorphous object of belief, knowledge, and practice called the immune system. My thesis is that the immune system is an elaborate icon for principal systems of symbolic and material "difference" in late capitalism. Preeminently a twentieth-century object, the immune system is a map drawn to guide recognition and misrecognition of self and other in the dialectics of Western biopolitics. That is, the immune system is a plan for meaningful action to construct and maintain the boundaries for what may count as self and other in the crucial realms of the normal and the pathological. The immune system is a historically specific terrain, where global and local politics, Nobel prize–winning research, heteroglossic cultural productions from popular dietary practices, feminist science fiction, religious imagery, and children's games to photographic techniques and military strategic theory, clinical medical practice, venture capital investment strategies, world-changing developments in business and technology, and the deepest personal and collective experiences of embodiment, vulnerability, power, and mortality interact with an intensity matched perhaps only in the biopolitics of sex and reproduction.[1]

The immune system is both an iconic, mythic object in high-technology culture and a subject of research and clinical practice of the first importance. Myth, laboratory, and clinic are intimately interwoven. This mundane point was fortuitously captured in the title listings in the 1986–87 *Books in Print,* where I was searching for a particular undergraduate textbook on immunology. The several pages of entries beginning with the prefix "immuno-" were bounded, according to the English rules of alphabetical listing, by a volume called *Immortals of Science Fiction,* near one end, and by *The Immutability of God,* at the other. Examining the last section of the textbook to which *Books in Print* led me, *Immunology: A Synthesis* (Golub 1987), I found what I was looking for: a historical progression of diagrams of theories of immunological regulation and an obituary for their draftsman, an important immunologist, Richard K. Gershon, who "discovered" the suppressor T cell. The standard obituary tropes for the scientist, who "must have had what the earliest explorers had, an insatiable desire to be the first person to see something, to know that you are where no man has been before," set the tone. The hero-scientist "gloried in the layer upon layer of [the immune response's] complexity. He thrilled at seeing a layer of that complexity which no one had seen before" (Golub 1987:531–532). It is reasonable to suppose that all the likely readers of this textbook have been reared within hearing range of the ringing tones of the introduction to the voyages of the Federation starship *Enterprise* in "Star Trek"—to go where no man (or, in the second generation, no *one*) has gone before. Science remains an important genre of Western exploration and travel literature. Similarly, no reader, no matter how literal-minded, could be innocent of the gendered erotic trope that figures the hero's probing nature's laminated secrets, glorying simultaneously in the layered complexity and in his own techno-erotic touch that goes ever deeper. Science as heroic quest and as erotic technique applied to the body of nature are utterly conventional figures. They take on a particular edge in late twentieth-century immune system discourse, where themes of nuclear exterminism, space adventure, extraterrestrialism, exotic invaders, and military high-technology are pervasive.

But Edward Golub's and Gershon's intended and explicit text is not about space invaders and the immune system as a Star Wars prototype. Their theme is the love of complexity and the intimate natural bodily technologies for generating the harmonies of organic life. In four diagrams—dated 1968, 1974, 1977, and 1982—Gershon sketched his conception of "the immunological orchestra" (figs. 1–4). This orchestra is a wonderful picture of the mythic and technical dimensions of the immune system. All of the diagrams are about cooperation and control, the major themes of organismic biology since the late eighteenth century. From his commanding position in the root of a lymph node, "G.O.D." conducts the orchestra of T and B cells and macrophages as they march about the body and play their specific parts. The lymphocytes all look like Casper the ghost with the appropriate distinguishing nuclear morphologies drawn in the center of their shapeless bodies. Baton in hand, G.O.D.'s arms are raised in quotation of a symphonic conductor. G.O.D. recalls the other 1960s bioreligious, Nobel prize–winning "joke" about the coded bodily text of post-DNA biology and medicine—the central dogma of molecular biology, specifying that "information" flows only from DNA to RNA to protein. These three were called the Blessed Trinity of the secularized sacred body, and histories of the great adventures of molecular biology could be titled *The Eighth Day of Creation* (Judson 1979), an image that takes on a certain irony in the venture capital and political environments of current biotechnology companies, like Genentech. In the technical-mythic systems of molecular biology, code rules embodied structure and function, never the reverse. Genesis is a serious joke, when the body is theorized as a coded text whose secrets yield only to the proper reading conventions, and when the laboratory seems best characterized as a vast assemblage of technological and organic inscription devices. The central dogma was about a master control system for information flow in the codes that determine meaning in the great technological communication systems that organisms progressively have become since World War II. The body is an artificial intelligence system, and the relation of copy and original is reversed and then exploded.

G.O.D. is the generator of diversity, the source of the awe-inspiring

*Figure 1.   The immunological orchestra in 1968. The focus was on cell coopera-
tion. The players are B cells, T cells, and macrophages conducted by the Generator of Diversity (G.O.D.). Courtesy of Edward S. Golub.*

multiple specificities of the polymorphous system of recognition and
misrecognition we call the immune system. By the second diagram
(1974), G.O.D. is no longer in front of the immune orchestra, but is
standing, arms folded, looking authoritative but not very busy at the
top of the lymph node, surrounded by the musical lymphocytes. A
special cell, the T suppressor cell, has taken over the role of conductor.
By 1977, the diagram no longer has a single conductor, but is "led" by
three rather mysterious subsets of T cells, who hold a total of twelve ba-
tons signifying their direction-giving surface identity markers; G.O.D.

G.O.D.

Figure 2.   The immunological orchestra in 1974. The role of the thymic cells as helper, cytotoxic, and suppressor is known, and Gershon has made the T cell the conductor of his musical ensemble. Courtesy of Edward S. Golub.

scratches his head in patent confusion. But the immune band plays on. In the final diagram from 1982, "the generator of diversity seems resigned to the conflicting calls of the angels of help and suppression," who perch above his left and right shoulders (Golub 1987:536). Besides G.O.D. and the two angels, there is a T cell conductor and two conflicting prompters, "each urging its own interpretation." The joke of single masterly control of organismic harmony in the symphonic system responsible for the integrity of "self" has become a kind of postmodern

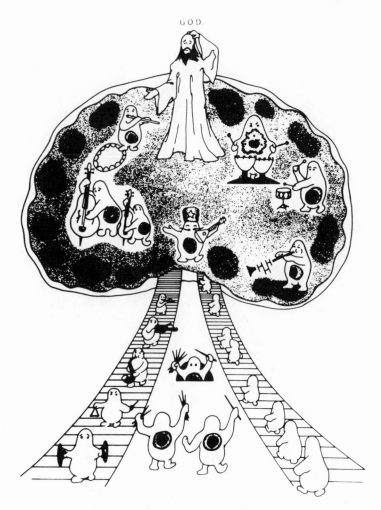

Figure 3.   The immunological orchestra in 1977. With the discovery of subsets of T cells, Ly 1 and Ly 2,3 cells become joint conductors and Ly 1,2,3 becomes the prompter. This complicated situation clearly has distressed the Generator of Diversity. Courtesy of Edward S. Golub.

pastiche of multiple centers and peripheries, where the immune music that the page suggests would surely sound like nursery school space music. All the actors that used to be on the stage set for the unambiguous and coherent biopolitical subject are still present, but their harmonies are definitely a bit problematic.

By the 1980s, the immune system is unambiguously a postmodern object—symbolically, technically, and politically. Katherine Hayles

Figure 4.   The immunological orchestra in 1982. The T cell is the conductor and the Lyt⁺ (helper) and Lyt 2⁺ (suppressor) cells are prompters, each urging its own interpretation. The Generator of Diversity seems resigned to the conflicting calls of the angels of help and suppression. At the sides sit the idiotype network and Ir gene (as impresarios?). The caricatures are of immunologists Niels Jerne and Baruj Benacerraf. Courtesy of Edward S. Golub.

(1987) characterizes postmodernism in terms of "three waves of developments occuring at multiple sites within the culture, including literature and science." Her archaeology begins with Saussurian linguistics, through which symbol systems were "denaturalized." Internally-generated relational difference, rather than mimesis, ruled signification. Hayles sees the culmination of this approach in Claude Shannon's mid-century statistical theory of information, developed for packing the largest number of signals on a transmission line for the Bell Telephone Company and extended to cover communication acts in general, including those directed by the codes of bodily semiosis in ethology or molecular biology. "Information" generating and processing systems, therefore, are postmodern objects, embedded in a theory of internally differentiated signifiers and remote from doctrines of representation as mimesis. A history-changing artifact, "information" exists only in very specific kinds of universes.[2] Progressively, the world and the sign seemed to exist in incommensurable universes—there was literally no *measure* linking them, and the reading conventions for all texts came to resemble those required for science fiction. What emerged was a global technology that "made the separation of text from context an everyday experience." Hayles's second wave, "energized by the rapid development of information technology, made the disappearance of stable, reproducible context an international phenomenon. . . . Context was no longer a natural part of every experience, but an artifact that could be altered at will." Hayles's third wave of denaturalization concerned time. "Beginning with the Special Theory of Relativity, time increasingly came to be seen not as an inevitable progression along a linear scale to which all humans were subject, but as a construct that could be conceived in different ways."

Language is no longer an echo of the *verbum dei,* but a technical construct working on principles of internally generated difference. If the early modern natural philosopher or Renaissance physician conducted an exegesis of the text of nature written in the language of geometry or of cosmic correspondances, the postmodern scientist still reads for a living, but has as a text the coded systems of recognition—prone to the pathologies of misrecognition—embodied in objects like computer networks and immune systems. The extraordinarily close tie of language and technology could hardly be overstressed in postmodernism. The "construct" is at the center of attention; making, reading, writing, and meaning seem to be very close to the same thing. This near-identity between technology, body, and semiosis suggests a particular edge to the mutually constitutive relations of political economy, symbol, and science that "inform" contemporary research trends in medical anthropology.

The Apparatus of Bodily Production:
The Techno-Biopolitics
of Engagement

Bodies, then, are not born; they are made (fig. 5). Bodies have been as thoroughly denaturalized as sign, context, and time. Late-twentieth-century bodies do not grow from internal harmonic principles theorized

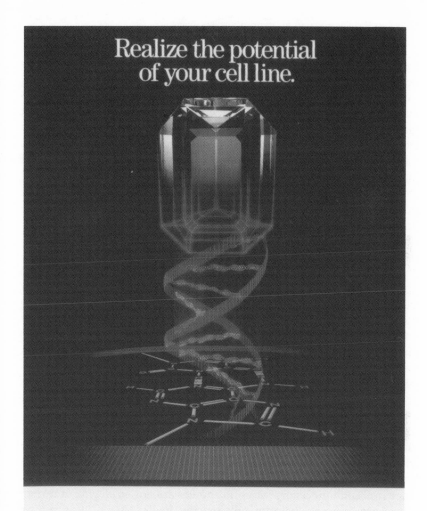

Realize the potential
of your cell line.

Innovators in the many facets
of animal cell culture, Bio-Response advances
your product's commercial success.

Bio
Response

Figure 5.   Taken from Science *magazine, the ad slogan "Realize the Potential of Your Cell Line" picks up echoes from three features on the American cultural landscape: the religious Great Awakenings of the eighteenth and nineteenth centuries; the twentieth-century human potential movement and New Age practices of cultivation of the self; and the drive to efficiency, productivity, and competitiveness in late-capitalist, flexible accumulation strategies. Convicted by the spirit of progress, we are called to testify in a wonderful convergence of religion, science, profit,*

within romanticism. Neither are they discovered in the domains of realism and modernism. One is not born a woman, Simone de Beauvoir correctly insisted. It took the political-epistemological terrain of postmodernism to be able to insist on a co-text to de Beauvoir's: one is not born an organism. Organisms are made; they are constructs of a world-changing kind. The constructions of an organism's boundaries, the job of the discourses of immunology, are particularly potent mediators of the experiences of sickness and death for industrial and postindustrial people.

In this overdetermined context, I will ironically—and inescapably—invoke a constructionist concept as an analytic device to pursue an understanding of what kinds of units, selves, and individuals inhabit the universe structured by immune system discourse: I call the conceptual tool "the apparatus of bodily production." In her analysis of the production of the poem as an object of literary value, Katie King offered tools that clarify the particular historicity of scientific bodies. Partially recalling Louis Althusser's formulation, King suggested the term "apparatus of literary production" to highlight the emergence of what is embodied as literature at the intersection of art, business, and technology. She applied this analytic frame to the relation of women and writing technologies (King 1991).

I would like to adapt her work to the articulation of bodies and other objects of value in scientific productions of knowledge. At first glance, there is a limitation to using King's scheme inherent in the "facticity" of biological discourse absent from literary discourse and its knowledge claims. But, by means of a social/epistemological/ethical operator, I wish to translate the ideological dimension of "facticity" into an entity called a "material-semiotic actor." Scientific bodies are not *ideological* constructions. Always radically historically specific, bodies have a different kind of specificity and effectivity, and so they invite a different kind of engagement and intervention. "Material-semiotic actor" is intended to highlight the object of knowledge as an active part of the apparatus of bodily production, without *ever* implying immediate presence of such objects or, what is the same thing, their final or unique determination of what can

Figure 5. (*continued*) *and self-improvement. Note the New Age crystal, reminiscent of virus and sperm shapes, unwinding into the sacred-secular spiral of the DNA double helix, all against a promising, extraterrestrial, luminescent rainbow of deep blues and purples. Here, one of the new biotechnological firms that rests on the academic-industrial symbioses of molecular biology, so favored by the tax and investment policies of the Reagan-Bush administrations, calls on the core symbols of hegemonic U.S. culture. Here is an "apparatus of bodily production." Be all you can be. Courtesy of BioResponse, Inc.*

count as objective knowledge of a biomedical body at a particular historical juncture. Like King's objects called "poems," sites of literary production where language also is an actor, bodies as objects of knowledge are material-semiotic generative nodes. Their boundaries materialize in social interaction; "objects" like bodies do not preexist as such. Scientific objectivity (the siting/sighting of objects) is not about disengaged discovery, but about mutual and usually unequal structuring, about taking risks. The various contending biological bodies emerge at the intersection of biological research, writing, and publishing; medical and other business practices; cultural productions of all kinds, including available metaphors and narratives; and technology, such as the visualization technologies that bring color-enhanced killer T cells and intimate photographs of the developing fetus into high-gloss art books for every middle-class home (Nilsson 1977, 1987). But also invited into that node of intersection is the analogue to the lively languages that actively intertwine in the production of literary value: the coyote and protean embodiments of a world as witty agent and actor. Perhaps our hopes for accountability in the techno-biopolitics in postmodern frames turn on revisioning the world as coding trickster with whom we must learn to converse. Like a protein subjected to stress, the world for us may be thoroughly denatured, but it is not any less consequential. So while the late-twentieth-century immune system is a construct of an elaborate apparatus of bodily production, neither the immune system nor any other of biomedicine's world-changing bodies—like a virus—is a ghostly fantasy. Coyote is not a ghost, merely a protean trickster.

The following chart abstracts and dichotomizes two historical moments in the biomedical production of bodies from the late nineteenth century to the 1980s. The chart highlights epistemological, cultural, and political aspects of possible contestations for construction of scientific bodies in this century. The chart itself is a traditional little machine for making particular meanings. Not a description, it must be read as an argument, and one which relies on a suspect technology for the production of meanings—binary dichotomization. Note the parallel transitions from the early to the late twentieth century.

Representation	Simulation
Bourgeois novel	Science fiction
Realism and modernism	Postmodernism
Organism	Biotic component, code
Work	Text
Mimesis	Play of signifiers
Depth, integrity	Surface, boundary
Heat	Noise
Biology as clinical practice	Biology as inscription

Physiology	Communications engineering
Microbiology, tuberculosis	Immunology, AIDS
Magic Bullet	Immunomodulation
Small group	Subsystem
Perfection	Optimization
Eugenics	Genetic engineering
Decadence	Obsolescence
Hygiene	Stress Management
Organic division of labor	Ergonomics, cybernetics
Functional specialization	Modular construction
Biological determinism	System constraints
Reproduction	Replication
Individual	Replicon
Community ecology	Ecosystem
Racial chain of being	United Nations humanism
Colonialism	Multinational capitalism
Nature/Culture	Fields of difference
Cooperation	Communications enhancement
Freud	Lacan
Sex	Surrogacy
Labor	Robotics
Mind	Artificial Intelligence
World War II	Star Wars
White Capitalist Patriarchy	Informatics of Domination

It is impossible to see the entries in the right-hand column as "natural," a realization that subverts naturalistic status for the left-hand column as well. From the eighteenth to the mid-twentieth centuries, the great historical constructions of gender, race, and class were embedded in the organically marked bodies of woman, the colonized or enslaved, and the worker. Those inhabiting these marked bodies have been symbolically other to the rational self of universal, and so unmarked, species man, a coherent subject. The marked organic body has been a critical locus of cultural and political contestation, crucial both to the languages of liberatory politics of identity and to systems of domination drawing on widely shared languages of nature as resource for the appropriations of culture. For example, the sexualized bodies of nineteenth-century middle-class medical advice literature in England and the United States, in their female form organized around the maternal function and the physical site of the uterus and in their male form ordered by the spermatic economy tied closely to the nervous system, were part of an elaborate discourse of organic economy. The narrative field in which these bodies moved generated accounts of rational citizenship, bourgeois family life, and prophylaxis against sexual pollution and inefficiency, such as prostitution, criminality, or race suicide. Some feminist politics argued for the full inclusion of women in the body politic on grounds of maternal functions in the domestic economy extended to a public world. Late into the twentieth century, gay and lesbian politics have ironically and critically embraced the marked bodies constructed in nineteenth- and twentieth-century sexologies and gender identity medicines to create a complex humanist discourse of sexual liberation. Negritude, feminine writing, various separatisms, and other recent cultural movements have both drawn on and subverted the logics of naturalization central to biomedical discourse on race and gender in the histories of colonization and male supremacy. In all of these various oppositionally interlinked political and biomedical accounts, the body remained a relatively unambiguous locus of identity, agency, labor, and hierarchicalized function. Both scientific humanisms and biological determinisms could be authorized and contested in terms of the biological organism crafted in post-eighteenth-century life sciences.

But how do narratives of the normal and the pathological work when the biological and medical body is symbolized and operated upon, not as a system of work, organized by the hierarchical division of labor, ordered by a privileged dialectic between highly localized nervous and reproductive functions, but instead as a coded text, organized as an engineered communications system, ordered by a fluid and dispersed command-control-intelligence network? From the mid-twentieth century, biomedical discourses have been progressively organized around a very different set of technologies and practices, which have destabilized the symbolic privilege of the hierarchical, localized, organic body. Concurrently—and out of some of the same historical matrices of decolonization, multinational capitalism, worldwide hi-tech militarization, and the emergence of new collective political actors in local and global politics from among those persons previously consigned to labor in silence—the question of "differences" has destabilized humanist discourses of liberation based on a politics of identity and substantive unity. Feminist theory as a self-conscious discursive practice has been generated in this post–World War II period characterized by the translation of Western scientific and political languages of nature from those based on work, localization, and the marked body to those based on codes, dispersal and networking, and the fragmented postmodern subject. An account of the biomedical, biotechnical body must start from the multiple molecular interfacings of genetic, nervous, endocrine, and immune systems. Biology is about recognition and misrecognition, coding errors, the body's reading practices (e.g., frameshift mutations), and billion dollar projects to sequence the human genome to be published and stored in a national genetic "library." The body is conceived as a strategic system, highly militarized in key arenas of imagery and practice. Sex, sexuality, and reproduction are theorized in terms of local investment strategies; the body ceases to be a stable spatial map of normalized functions and instead emerges as a highly mobile field of strategic differences. The biomedical-biotechnical body is a semiotic system, a complex meaning-producing field, for which the discourse of immunology—that is, the central biomedical discourse on recognition/misrecognition—has become a high-stakes practice in many senses.

In relation to objects like biotic components and codes, one must think not in terms of laws of growth and essential properties, but rather in terms of strategies of design, boundary constraints, rates of flows, system logics, and costs of lowering constraints. Sexual reproduction becomes one possible strategy among many, with costs and benefits theorized as a function of the system environment. Disease is a subspecies of information malfunction or communications pathology; disease is a process of misrecognition or transgression of the boundaries of a strategic assemblage called self. Ideologies of sexual reproduction can no longer easily call upon the notions of unproblematic sex and sex role as organic aspects in "healthy" natural objects like organisms and families. Likewise for race, ideologies of human diversity have to be developed in terms of frequencies of parameters and fields of power-charged differences, not essences and natural origins or homes. Race and sex, like individuals, are artifacts sustained or undermined by the discursive nexus of knowledge and power. Any objects or persons can be reasonably thought of in terms of disassembly and reassembly; no "natural" architectures constrain system design. Design is nonetheless highly constrained. What counts as a "unit," a one, is highly problematic, not a permanent given. Individuality is a strategic defense problem.

One should expect control strategies to concentrate on boundary conditions and interfaces, on rates of flow across boundaries, not on the integrity of natural objects. "Integrity" or "sincerity" of the Western self gives way to decision procedures, expert systems, and resource investment strategies. "Degrees of freedom" becomes a very powerful metaphor for politics. Human beings, like any other component or subsystem, must be localized in a system architecture whose basic modes of operation are probabilistic. No objects, spaces, or bodies are sacred in themselves; any component can be interfaced with any other if the proper standard, the proper code, can be constructed for processing signals in a common language. In particular, there is no ground for ontologically opposing the organic, the technical, and the textual.[3] But neither is there any ground for opposing the *mythical* to the organic, textual, and technical. Their convergences are more important than their residual oppositions. The privileged pathology affecting all kinds of components in this universe is stress—communications breakdown. In the body stress is theorized to operate by "depressing" the immune system. Bodies have become cyborgs—cybernetic organisms—compounds of hybrid techno-organic embodiment and textuality (Haraway 1985*b*). The cyborg is text, machine, body, and metaphor—all theorized and engaged in practice in terms of communications.

Cyborgs for Earthly Survival[4]

However, just as the nineteenth- and twentieth-century organism accommodated a diverse field of cultural, political, financial, theoretic, and technical contestation, so also the cyborg is a contested and heterogeneous construct. It is capable of sustaining oppositional and liberatory projects at the levels of research practice, cultural productions, and political intervention. This large theme may be introduced by examining contrasting constructions of the late-twentieth-century biotechnical body, or of other contemporary postmodern communications systems. These constructs may be conceived and built in at least two opposed modes: (1) in terms of master control principles, articulated within a rationalist paradigm of language and embodiment; or (2) in terms of complex, structurally embedded semiosis with many "generators of diversity" within a counter-rationalist (*not* irrationalist) or hermeneutic/situationist/constructivist discourse readily available within Western science and philosophy. Terry Winograd and Fernando Flores's joint work on *Understanding Computers and Cognition* (1986) is particularly suggestive for thinking about the potentials for cultural/scientific/political contestation over the technologies of representation and embodiment of "difference" within immunological discourse, whose object of knowledge is a kind of "artificial intelligence/language/communication system of the biological body."[5]

Winograd and Flores conduct a detailed critique of the rationalist paradigm for understanding embodied (or "structure-determined") perceptual and language systems and for designing computers that can function as prostheses in human projects. In the simple form of the rationalist model of cognition,

> one takes for granted the existence of an objective reality made up of things bearing properties and entering into relations. A cognitive being gathers "information" about those things and builds up a mental "model" which will be in some respects correct (a faithful representation of reality) and in other respects incorrect. Knowledge is a storehouse of representations that can be called upon to do reasoning and that can be translated

into language. Thinking is a process of manipulating those representations. (Winograd n.d.)

It is this doctrine of representation that Winograd finds wrong in many
senses, including on the plane of political and moral discourse usually
suppressed in scientific writing. The doctrine is also technically wrong
for further guiding research in software design. "Contrary to common
consensus, the "commonsense' understanding of language, thought, and
rationality inherent in this tradition ultimately *hinders* the fruitful application of computer technology to human life and work" (Winograd
n.d.). Drawing on Heidegger, Gadamer, Maturana, and others, Winograd and Flores develop a doctrine of interdependence of interpreter
and interpreted, which are not discrete and independent entities. Situated preunderstandings are critical to all communication and action.
"Structure-determined systems" with histories shaped through processes
of "structural-coupling" give a better approach to perception than doctrines of representation.

> Changes in the environment have the potential of changing the relative
> patterns of activity within the nervous system itself that in turn orient the
> organism's behavior, a perspective that invalidates the assumption that we
> acquire representations of our environment. Interpretation, that is, arises
> as a necessary consequence of the structure of biological beings. (Wino-
> grad n.d.)

Winograd conceives the coupling of the inner and outer worlds of organisms and ecosystems, of organisms with each other, or of organic and
technical structures in terms of metaphors of language, communication,
and construction—but not in terms of a rationalist doctrine of mind and
language or a disembodied instrumentalism. Linguistic acts involve
shared acts of interpretation, and they are fundamentally tied to engaged location in a structured world. Context is a fundamental matter,
not as surrounding "information," but as co-structure or co-text. Cognition, engagement, and situation-dependence are linked concepts for
Winograd, technically and philosophically. Language is not about description, but about commitment. The point applies to "natural" language and to "built" language.

How would such a way of theorizing the technics and biologics of
communication affect immune system discourse about the body's "technology" for recognizing self and other and for mediating between
"mind" and "body" in postmodern culture? Just as computer design is a
map of and for ways of living, the immune system is in some sense a
diagram of relationships and a guide for action in the face of questions

about the boundaries of the self and about morality. Immune system discourse is about constraint and possibility for engaging in a world full of "difference," replete with nonself. Winograd and Flores's approach contains a way to contest for notions of pathology, or "breakdown," without militarizing the terrain of the body.

> Breakdowns play a central role in human understanding. A breakdown is not a negative situation to be avoided, but a situation of nonobviousness, in which some aspect of the network of tools that we are engaged in using is brought forth to visibility. . . . A breakdown reveals the nexus of relations necessary for us to accomplish our task. . . . This creates a clear objective for design—to anticipate the form of breakdowns and provide a space of possibilities for action when they occur. (Winograd n.d.)

This is not a Star Wars or Strategic Computing Initiative relation to vulnerability, but neither does it deny therapeutic action. It insists on locating therapeutic, reconstructive action (and so theoretic understanding) in terms of situated purposes, not fantasies of the utterly defended self in a body as automated militarized factory, a kind of ultimate self as Robotic Battle Manager meeting the enemy (not-self) as it invades in the form of bits of foreign information threatening to take over the master control codes.

Situated purposes are necessarily finite, rooted in partiality and a subtle play of same and different, maintenance and dissolution. Winograd and Flores's linguistic systems are "denaturalized," fully constructivist entities—and in that sense they are postmodern cyborgs that do not rely on impermeable boundaries between the organic, technical, and textual. But their linguistic/communication systems are distinctly oppositional to the AI (artificial intelligence) cyborgs of an "information society," with its exterminist pathologies of final abstraction from vulnerability, and so from embodiment.[6]

The One and the Many: Selves, Individuals, Units, and Subjects

What is constituted as an individual within postmodern biotechnical, biomedical discourse? There is no easy answer to this question, for even the most reliable Western individuated bodies, the mice and men of a well-equipped laboratory, neither stop nor start at the skin, which is itself something of a teeming jungle threatening illicit fusions, especially from the perspective of a scanning electron microscope. The multibillion dollar project to sequence "the human genome" in a definitive genetic library might be seen as one practical answer to the construction of "man" as "subject" of science. The genome project is a kind of technology of post-modern humanism, defining "the" genome by reading and writing it. The technology required for this particular kind of literacy is suggested by the advertisement for MacroGene Workstation. The ad ties the mythical, organic, technical, and textual together particularly literally in its graphic invocation of the "missing link" crawling from the water onto the land, while the text reads, "In the LKB MacroGene Workstation [for sequencing nucleic acids], there are no 'missing links' " (see fig. 6). The monster Ichthyostega crawling out of the deep in one of earth's great transitions is a perfect figure for late twentieth-century bodily and technical metamorphoses. An act of canonization to make the theorists of the humanities pause, the standard reference work called the human genome would be the means through which human diversity and its pathologies could be tamed in the exhaustive code kept by a national or international genetic bureau of standards. Costs of storage of the giant dictionary will probably exceed costs of its production, but this is a mundane matter to any librarian (Roberts 1987*a*, 1987*b*, 1987*c;* Kanigel 1987). Access to this standard for "man" will be a matter of international financial, patent, and similar struggles. The Peoples of the Book will finally have a standard genesis story. In the beginning was the copy.

The Human Genome Project might define postmodern species' being (pacé the philosophers), but what of *individual* being? Richard Dawkins raised this knotty problem in *The Extended Phenotype.* He noted that in 1912, Julian Huxley defined individuality in biological terms as "literally indivisibility—the quality of being sufficiently heterogeneous in form to be rendered non-functional if cut in half" (Dawkins 1982:250). That seems a promising start. In Huxley's terms, surely you or I would count as an individual, while many worms would not. The individuality of worms was not achieved even at the height of bourgeois liberalism, so no cause to worry there. But Huxley's definition does not answer *which function* is at issue. Nothing answers that in the abstract; it depends on what is to be done.[7] You or I (whatever problematic address these pronouns have) might be an individual for some purposes, but not for others. This is a normal ontological state for cyborgs and women, if not for Aristotelians and men. Function is about action. Here is where Dawkins has a radical solution, as he proposes a view of individuality that is strategic at every level of meaning. There are many kinds of individuals for Dawkins, but one kind has primacy. "The whole purpose of our search for a 'unit of selection' is to discover a suitable actor to play the leading role in our metaphors of purpose" (1982:91). The "metaphors of purpose" come down to a single bottom line: replication. "A successful replicator is one that succeeds in lasting, in the form of copies,

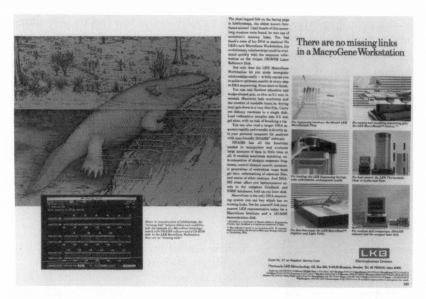

Figure 6.   Echoing themes of religious fullness, evolutionary progress, and labor process design, MacroGene Workstation provides a complete, highly automated apparatus of bodily production. Courtesy of the Electrophoresis Division, Pharmacia LKB Biotechnology, Inc.

for a very long time measured in generations, and succeeds in propogating many copies of itself" (1982:87–88).

The replicator fragment whose individuality finally matters most, in the constructed time of evolutionary theory, is not particularly "unitary." For all that it serves, for Dawkins, as the "unit" of natural selection, the replicator's boundaries are not fixed and its inner reaches remain mutable. But still, these units must be a bit smaller than a "single" gene coding for a protein. Units are only good enough to sustain the technology of copying. Like the replicons' borders, the boundaries of other strategic assemblages are not fixed either—it all has to do with the broad net cast by strategies of replication in a world where self and other are very much at stake.

> The integrated multi-cellular organism is a phenomenon which has emerged as a result of natural selection on primitively selfish replicators. It has paid replicators to behave gregariously [so much for "harmony," in the short run]. The phenotypic power by which they ensure their survival is in principle extended and unbounded. In practice the organism has arisen as a partially bounded local concentration, a shared knot of replicator power. (1982:264)

"In principle extended and unbounded"—this is a remarkable statement of interconnectedness, but of a very particular kind, one that leads to theorizing the living world as one vast arms race. "[P]henotypes that extend outside the body do not have to be inanimate artefacts: they themselves can be built of living tissue. . . . I shall show that it is logically sensible to regard parasite genes as having phenotypic expression in host bodies *and behavior*" (1982:210, emphasis added). But the being who serves as another's phenotype is itself populated by propagules with their own replicative ends. "[A]n animal will not necessarily submit passively to being manipulated, and an evolutionary 'arms race' is expected to develop" (1982:39). This is an arms race that must take account of the stage of the development of the means of bodily production and the costs of maintaining it:

> The many-celled body is a machine for the production of single-celled propagules. Large bodies, like elephants, are best seen as heavy plant and machinery, a temporary resource drain, invested so as to improve later propagule production. In a sense the germ-line would "like" to reduce capital investment in heavy machinery. (1982:254)

Large capital is indeed a drain; small is beautiful. But you and I have required large capital investments, in more than genetic terms. Perhaps we should keep an eye on the germ-line, especially since "we"—the non-germ-line components of adult mammals (unless you identify with your haploid gametes and their contents, and some do)—cannot be copy units. "We" can only aim for a defended self, not copy fidelity, the property of other sorts of units. Within "us" is the most threatening other—the propagules, whose phenotype we, temporarily, are.

What does all this have to do with the discourse of immunology as a map of systems of "difference" in late capitalism? Let me attempt to convey the flavor of representations of the curious bodily object called the human immune system, culled from textbooks and research reports published in the 1980s. The IS is composed of about 10^{12} cells, two orders of magnitude more cells than the nervous system has. These cells are regenerated throughout life from pluripotent stem cells that themselves remain undifferentiated. From embryonic life through adulthood, the immune system is sited in several relatively amorphous tissues and organs, including the thymus, bone marrow, spleen, and lymph nodes, but a large fraction of its cells are in the blood and lymph circulatory systems and in body fluids and spaces. There are two major cell lineages to the system:

1. The first is the *lymphocytes,* which include the several types of T cells (helper, suppressor, killer, and variations of all these) and the B cells (each type of which can produce only one sort of the vast array of potential circulating antibodies). T and B cells have particular specificities capable of recognizing almost any molecular array of the right size that can ever exist, no matter how clever industrial chemistry gets. This specificity is enabled by a baroque somatic mutation mechanism, clonal selection, and a polygenic receptor or marker system.

2. The second immune cell lineage is the *mononuclear phagocyte system,* including the multitalented macrophages, which, in addition to their other recognition skills and connections, also appear to share receptors and some hormonal peptide products with neural cells.

Besides the cellular compartment, the immune system comprises a vast array of circulating acellular products, such as antibodies, lymphokines, and complement components. These molecules mediate communication among components of the immune system, but also between the immune system and the nervous and endocrine systems, thus linking the body's multiple control and coordination sites and functions. The genetics of the immune system cells, with their high rates of somatic mutation and gene product splicings and rearrangings to make finished surface receptors and antibodies, makes a mockery of the notion of a constant genome even within "one" body. The hierarchical body of old has given way to a network-body of truly amazing complexity and specificity. The immune system is everywhere and nowhere. Its specificities are indefinite if not infinite, and they arise randomly—yet these extraordinary variations are the critical means of maintaining individual bodily coherence.

In the early 1970s, the Nobel Prize–winning immunologist Niels Jerne proposed a theory of immune system self-regulation, called the network theory, that must complete this minimalist account (Golub 1987:379–392; Jerne 1985). "The network theory differs from other immunological thinking because it endows the immune system with the ability to regulate itself using only itself" (Golub 1987:379). Jerne's basic idea was that any antibody molecule must be able to act functionally as both antibody to some antigen *and* as antigen for the production of an antibody to itself, albeit at another region of "itself." All these sites have acquired a nomenclature sufficiently daunting to keep popular understanding of the theory at bay indefinitely, but the basic conception is simple. The concatenation of internal recognitions and responses would go on indefinitely, in a series of interior mirrorings of sites on immunoglobulin molecules, such that the immune system would always be in a state of dynamic internal respond-ing. It would never be passive, "at rest," awaiting an activating stimulus from a hostile outside. In a sense, there could be no *exterior* antigenic structure, no "invader," that the immune system had not already "seen" and mirrored internally. Self and other lose their rationalistic oppositional quality and become subtle plays of partially mirrored readings and re-sponses. The notion of the *internal image* is the key to the theory, and it entails the premise that every member of the immune system is capable of interacting with every other member. As with Dawkins's extended pheno-type, a radical conception of *connection* emerges unexpectedly at the heart of postmodern moves. "This is a unique idea, which if correct means that all possible reactions that the immune system can carry out with epitopes in the world outside of the animal are already accounted for in the internal system of paratopes and idiotopes already present inside the animal" (Golub 1987:382–383).

Jerne's conception recalls Winograd and Flores's insistence on structural-coupling and structure-determined systems in their approach to perception. The internal, structured activity of the system is the cru-cial issue, not formal representations of the "outer" world within the "inner" world of the communications system that is the organism. Both Jerne's and Winograd's formulations resist the means of conceptualiza-tion facilitated most readily by a rationalist theory of recognition or representation. In discussing what he called the deep structure and gen-erative grammar of the immune system, Jerne argued that "an identical structure can appear on many structures in many contexts and be re-acted to by the reader or by the immune system" (quoted in Golub 1987:384).[8]

Does the immune system—the fluid, dispersed, networking, techno-organic-textual-mythic system that ties together the more stodgy and localized centers of the body through its acts of recognition—represent the ultimate sign of altruistic evolution toward wholeness, in the form of the means of coordination of a coherent biological self? In a word, no—at least not in Leo Buss's persuasive postmodern theoretic scheme of *The Evolution of Individuality* (1987).

Constituting a kind of technological holism, the earliest cybernetic communications systems theoretic approaches to the biological body from the late 1940s through the 1960s privileged coordination, effected by "circular causal feedback mechanisms." In the 1950s, biological bod-ies became technological communications systems, but they were not quite fully reconstituted as sites of "difference" in its postmodern sense—the play of signifiers and replicators in a strategic field whose significance depended problematically, at best, on a world outside itself. Even the first synthetic proclamations of sociobiology, particularly E. O.

Wilson's *Sociobiology: The New Synthesis* (1975), maintained a fundamentally techno-organicist or holist ontology of the cybernetic organism, or cyborg, repositioned in evolutionary theory by post–World War II extensions and revisions of the principle of natural selection. This "conservative" dimension of Wilson and of several other sociobiologists has been roundly criticized by evolutionary theorists who have gone much further in denaturing the coordinating principles of organismic biology at every level of biotic organization, from gene fragments through ecosystems. The sociobiological theory of inclusive fitness maintained a kind of envelope around the organism and its kin, but that envelope has been opened repeatedly in late 1970s' and 1980s' evolutionary theory.

Dawkins (1976, 1982) has been among the most radical disrupters of cyborg biological holism, and in that sense he is most deeply informed by a postmodern consciousness, in which the logic of the permeability among the textual, the technic, and the biotic and of the deep theorization of all possible texts and bodies as strategic assemblages has made the notions of "organism" or "individual" extremely problematic. He ignores the mythic, but it pervades his texts. "Organism" and "individual" have not disappeared; rather, they have been fully denaturalized. That is, they are ontologically contingent constructs from the point of view of the biologist, not just in the loose ravings of a cultural critic or feminist historian of science.

Leo Buss reinterpreted two important remaining processes or objects that had continued to resist such denaturing: (1) embryonic development, the very process of the construction of an individual, and (2) immune system interactions, the iconic means for maintaining the integrity of the one in the face of the many. His basic argument for the immune system is that it is made up of several variant cell lineages, each engaged in its own replicative "ends." The contending cell lineages serve somatic function because

> the receptors that ensure delivery of growth-enhancing mitogens also compel somatic function. The cytotoxic T-cell recognizes its target with the same receptor arrangement used by the macrophage to activate that cell lineage. It is compelled to attack the infected cell by the same receptor required for it to obtain mitogens from helper cells. . . . The immune system works by exploiting the inherent propensity of cells to further their own rate of replication. (Buss 1987:87)

The individual is a constrained accident, not the highest fruit of earth history's labors. In metazoan organisms, at least two units of selection, cellular and individual, pertain, and their "harmony" is highly contingent. The parts are not *for* the whole. There is no part/whole relation at all, in any sense Aristotle would recognize. Pathology results from a conflict of interests between the cellular and organismic units of selection. Buss has thereby recast the multicellular organisms' means of self-recognition, of the maintenance of "wholes," from an illustration of the priority of coordination in biology's and medicine's ontology to a chief witness for the irreducible vulnerability, multiplicity, and contingency of every construct of individuality.

The potential meanings of such a move for conceptualizations of pathology and therapeutics within Western biomedicine are, to say the least, intriguing. Is there a way to turn the discourse suggested by Jerne, Dawkins, and Buss into an oppositional/alternative/liberatory approach analogous to that of Winograd and Flores in cognition and computer research? Is this postmodern body, this construct of always vulnerable and contingent individuality, *necessarily* an automated Star Wars battlefield in the now extraterrestrial space of the late-twentieth-century Western scientific body's intimate interior? What might we learn about this question by attending to the many contemporary representations of the immune system, in visualization practices, self-help doctrines, biologists' metaphors, discussions of immune system diseases, and science fiction? This is a large inquiry, and in the paragraphs that follow, I will only begin to sketch a few of the sometimes promising but more often profoundly disturbing recent cultural productions of the postmodern immune-system-mediated body.[9] At this stage, the analysis can only serve to sharpen, not to answer, the question.

Immune Power: Images, Fictions, and Fixations

This paper opened with a reminder that science has been a travel discourse, intimately implicated in the other great colonizing and liberatory readings and writings so basic to modern constitutions and dissolutions of the marked bodies of race, sex, and class. The colonizing and the liberatory, and the constituting and the dissolving, are related as internal images. So I continue this tour through the science museum of immunology's cultures with the "Land, ho!" effect described by my colleague, James Clifford, as we waited in our university chancellor's office for a meeting in 1986. The chancellor's office walls featured beautiful color-enhanced photographic portraits of the outer planets of earth's solar system. Each "photograph" created the effect for the viewer of having been there. Some other observer must have been there—with a perceptual system like ours and a good camera, to be sure—but it must have been possible to *see* the land masses of Jupiter and Saturn coming into view of the great ships of *Voyager* as they crossed the empty reaches of space. Twentieth-century people are used to the idea that all photographs are constructs in some sense, and that the appearance that a photograph gives of being a "message without a code," that is, what is pictured being simply *there,* is an effect of many layers of history, including prominently, technology (Barthes 1977; Petchesky 1987; Haraway 1985*a*). But the photographs of the outer planets up the ante on this issue by orders of magnitude. The wonderful pictures have gone through processes of construction that make the metaphor of the "eye of the camera" completely misleading. The chancellor's snapshot of Jupiter is a postmodern photographic portrait—a denatured construct of the first order, which has the effect of utter naturalistic realism. *Someone* was there. Land, ho! But that some*one* was a spaceship that sent back digitalized signals to a whole world of transformers and imagers on a distant place called "earth," where art photographs could be produced to give a reassuring sense of the *thereness* of Jupiter, and, not incidentally, of *space voyagers,* or at least virtual space voyagers, whose eyes would see in the same color spectrum as an earthly primate's.

The same analysis must accompany any viewing of the wonderful photographs and other imaging precipitates of the components of the immune system. The cover of *Immunology: A Synthesis* (Golub 1987) features an iconic replication of its title's allusion to synthesis: a multicolored computer graphic of the three-dimensional structure of insulin showing its antigenic determinants clustered in particular regions. Golub elicits consciousness of the *constructed* quality of such images in his credit: "Image created by John A. Tainer and Elizabeth D. Getzoff." Indeed, the conventional trope of scientist as artist runs throughout Golub's text, such that scientific construction takes on the particular resonances of high art and genius, more than of critical theories of productions of the postmodern body (fig. 7). But the publications of Lennart Nilsson's photographs, in the coffee-table art book *The Body Victorious* (Nilsson 1987) and in *National Geographic* (Jaret 1986), allow the "Land, ho!" effect unmediated scope. The blasted scenes, sumptuous textures, evocative colors, and E.T. monsters of the immune landscape are simply *there,* inside *us.* A white extruding tendril of a peudopodinous macrophage ensnares a bacterium; the hillocks of chromosomes lie flattened on a blue-hued moonscape of some other planet; an infected cell buds myriads of deadly virus particles into the reaches of inner space where more cells will be victimized; the autoimmune disease–ravaged head of a femur glows in a kind of sunset on a nonliving world; cancer cells are surrounded by the lethal mobile squads of killer T cells that throw chemical poisons into the self's malignant traitor cells (figs. 8–9).

Figure 7. Highlighting the cross-linked aesthetic and technical optical fibers of laboratory visual practices, this beautiful "Glowing Coal" photograph represents the solid external molecular surface of an insulin molecule. Solving the structure of insulin is at the narrative heart of the history of molecular biology—as recombinant DNA–derived, microbial insulin was at the heart of the (largely unrealized) hopes for megaprofits in the biotechnology industry in the early 1980s. The combined U.S. and European insulin market in 1981 was about $310 million; capturing a growing world insulin market for r-DNA products was a glowing prospect (Krimsky 1991:28). Courtesy of John A. Tainer and Elizabeth D. Getzoff, the Research Institute of Scripps Clinic, La Jolla, California.

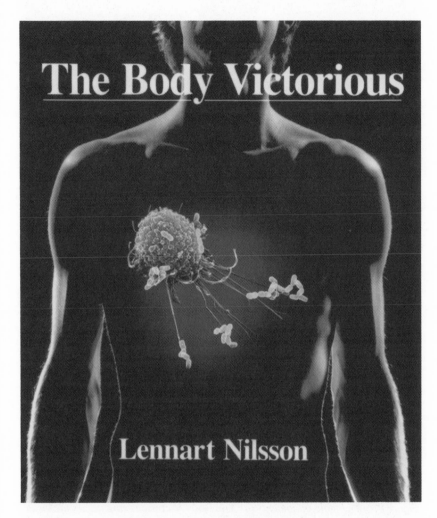

Figure 8. Lennart Nilsson's superb photographic construction of the dynamic macrophage contained within the youthful, nordic, male figure on the cover of the The Body Victorious *announces the complex thematics of the outsider within in this drama of recognition of self and other in the great epics of medical immunology. Courtesy of Lennart Nilsson and Behringer Ingelheim International GmbH, Ingelheim, Germany.*

The equation of outer space and inner space, and of their conjoined discourses of extraterrestrialism, ultimate frontiers, and high technology war, is quite literal in the official history celebrating one hundred years of the National Geographic Society (Bryan 1987). The chapter that recounts *National Geographic*'s coverage of the Mercury, Gemini, Apollo, and

Contents

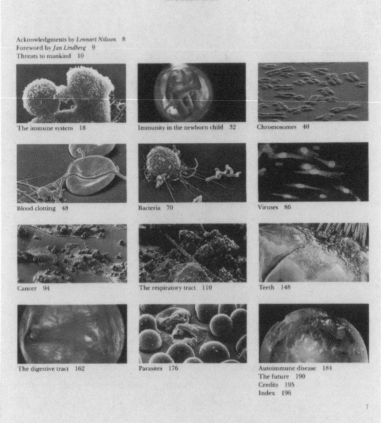

7

Figure 9.   The table of contents for The Body Victorious *emphasizes the visual text in this virtuoso photographic performance of the heterogeneous internal bodily actors and the stages of inner space where their feats take place. The oxymoronic effect of strangeness and intimacy heightens the mythic fascination of the ensuing martial-medical narrative. The etymological kinship of* feat *and* fact *is reaffirmed in this visualizing technological conception and gestation of the biomedical body; realism and extraterrestrialism are the conjoined generic effects. Courtesy of Lennart Nilsson and Behringer Ingelheim International GmbH, Ingelheim, Germany.*

Mariner voyages is called "Space" and is introduced with the epigraph, "The Choice Is the Universe—or Nothing." The final chapter, full of Nilsson's and other biomedical images, is titled "Inner Space" and is introduced with the epigraph, "The Stuff of the Stars Has Come Alive" (Bryan 1987:454, 352). It is photography that convinces the viewer of the fraternal relation of inner and outer space. But curiously, in outer space, we see spacemen fitted into explorer craft or floating about as individuated cosmic fetuses, while in the supposed earthy space of our own interiors we see nonhumanoid strangers who are supposed to be the means by which our bodies sustain our integrity and individuality, indeed our humanity, in the face of a world of others. We seem invaded not just by the threatening "nonselves" that the immune system guards against, but more fundamentally by our own strange parts. No wonder autoimmune disease carries such awful significance, marked from the first suspicion of its existence in 1901 by Julius Morgenroth and Paul Ehrlich's term, *horror autotoxicus.*

The trope of space invaders evokes a particular question about directionality of travel: in which direction is there an invasion? From space to earth? From outside to inside? The reverse? Are boundaries defended symmetrically? Is inner/outer a hierarchalized opposition? Expansionist Western medical discourse in colonizing contexts has been obsessed with the notion of contagion and hostile penetration of the healthy body, as well as of terrorism and mutiny from within. This approach to disease involved a stunning reversal: the colonized was perceived as the invader. In the face of the disease genocides accompanying European "penetration" of the globe, the "colored" body of the colonized was constructed as the dark source of infection, pollution, disorder, and so on, that threatened to overwhelm white manhood (cities, civilization, the family, the white personal body) with its decadent emanations. In establishing the game parks of Africa, European law turned indigenous human inhabitants of the "nature reserves" into poachers—invaders in their own terrain—or into part of the wildlife. The residue of the history of colonial tropical medicine and natural history in late twentieth-century immune discourse should not be underestimated. Discourses on parasitic diseases and AIDS provide a surfeit of examples.

The tones of colonial discourse are also audible in the opening paragraphs of *Immunology: The Science of Non-Self Discrimination,* where the dangers to individuality are almost lasciviously recounted. The first danger is "fusion of individuals":

> In a jungle or at the bottom of the sea, organisms—especially plants, but also all kinds of sessile animals—are often in such close proximity that they are in constant danger of losing their individuality by fusion. . . . But

> only in the imagination of an artist does all-out fusion occur; in reality,
> organisms keep pretty much separate, no matter how near to one another
> they live and grow. (Klein 1982:3)

In those exotic, allotopic places, any manner of contact might occur to
threaten proper mammalian self-definition. Harmony of the organism,
that favorite theme of biologists, is explained in terms of the aggressive
defense of individuality; and Jan Klein advocates devoting as much time
in the undergraduate biology curriculum to defense as to genetics and
evolution. It reads a bit like the defense department fighting the social
services budget for federal funds. Immunology for Klein is "intraorgan-
ismic defense reaction," proceeding by "*recognition, processing,* and
response." Klein defines "*self*" as "everything constituting an integral
part of a given individual" (1982:5, emphasis in original). What counts
as an individual, then, is the nub of the matter. Everything else is "*not-
self*" and elicits a defense reaction if boundaries are crossed. But this
essay has repeatedly tried to make problematic just what does count as
self, within the discourses of biology and medicine, much less in the
postmodern world at large.

A diagram of the "Evolution of Recognition Systems" in a recent
immunology textbook makes clear the intersection of the themes of
literally "wonderful" diversity, escalating complexity, the self as a defended stronghold, and extraterrestrialism (fig. 10). Under a diagram
culminating in the evolution of the mammals, represented without comment by a mouse and a *fully-suited space voyager,*[10] who appears to be
stepping out, perhaps on the surface of the moon, is this explanation:

> From the humble amoeba searching for food (top left) to the mammal
> with its sophisticated humoral and cellular immune mechanisms (bottom
> right), the process of "*self versus non-self recognition*" shows a steady
> development, keeping pace with the increasing need of animals to main-
> tain their integrity in a hostile environment. The decision at which point
> "immunity" appeared is thus a purely semantic one. (Playfair 1984:3;
> emphasis in original)

These are the semantics of defense and invasion. When is a self enough
of a self that its boundaries become central to entire institutionalized
discourses in medicine, war, and business? Immunity and invulnerability
are intersecting concepts, a matter of consequence in a nuclear culture
unable to accommodate the experience of death and finitude within
available liberal discourse on the collective and personal individual. Life
is a window of vulnerability. It seems a mistake to close it. The perfection of the fully defended, "victorious" self is a chilling fantasy, linking
phagocytotic amoeba and moon-voyaging man cannibalizing the earth in

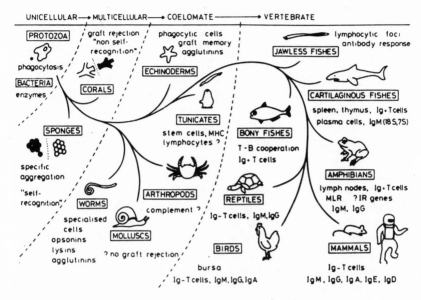

Figure 10.   Pedagogical tools in the apparatus of bodily production include this diagram of the "Evolution of Recognition Systems" from J. H. L. Playfair, Immunology at a Glance *(1984). Courtesy of Blackwell Scientific Publications.*

an evolutionary teleology of postapocalypse extraterrestrialism. It is a chilling fantasy, whether located in the abstract spaces of national discourse or in the equally abstract spaces of our interior bodies.

Images of the immune system as battlefield abound in science sections of daily newspapers and in popular magazines—for instance, *Time* magazine's 1984 graphic for the AIDS virus's "invasion" of the cell-as-factory. The virus is imaged as a tank, and the viruses ready for export from the expropriated cells are lined up as tanks ready to continue their advance on the body as a productive force. *National Geographic* explicitly punned on Star Wars in its graphic entitled "Cell Wars" in Peter Jaret's "The Wars Within" (1986:708–709). The battle imagery is conventional, not unique to a nuclear and Cold War era, but it has taken on all the specific markings of those particular historical crises. The militarized, automated factory is a favorite convention among immune system illustrators and photographic processors. The specific historical markings of a Star Wars maintained individuality[11] are enabled in large measure by high-technology visualization technologies, which are also critical to the material means of conducting postmodern war and business, such as computer-aided graphics, artificial intelligence software, and many kinds of scanning systems.

"Imaging" or "visualization" has also become part of therapeutic practice in both self-help and clinical settings, and here the contradictory possibilities and potent ambiguities over biomedical technology, body, self, and other emerge poignantly. The immune system has become a lucrative terrain of self-development practices, a scene where contending forms of power are evoked and practiced. In *Dr. Berger's Immune Power Diet,* the "invincible you" is urged to "put immune power to work for you" by using your "IQ (Immune Quotient)" (Berger 1985:186). In the great tradition of evangelical preaching, the reader is asked if "you are ready to make the immune power commitment?" (1985:4). In visualization self-help, the sufferer learns in a state of deep relaxation to image the processes of disease and healing, in order both to gain more control in many senses and to engage in a kind of meditation on the meanings of living and dying from an embodied vantage point in the microplaces of the postmodern body. These visualization exercises need not be prototypes for Star Wars, but they often are in the advice literature. *National Geographic* endorses this approach in its description of one such effort: "Combining fun and therapy, a young cancer patient at the M. D. Anderson Hospital in Houston, Texas, zaps cancer cells in the 'Killer T Cell' video game" (Jaret 1986:705). Other researchers have designed protocols to determine if aggressive imagery is effective in mediating the healing work of visualization therapies, or if the relaxation techniques and nonaggressive imagery would "work." As with any function, "work" for *what* cannot remain unexamined, and not just in terms of the statistics of cancer survival. Imaging is one of the vectors in the "epidemics of signification" spreading in the cultures of postmodern therapeutics. What is at stake is the kind of collective and personal selves that will be constructed in this organic-technical-mythic-textual semiosis. As cyborgs in this field of meanings, how can "we," late-twentieth-century Westerners, image our vulnerability as a window onto life?

Immunity can also be conceived in terms of shared specificities; of the semipermeable self able to engage with others (human and nonhuman, inner and outer), but always with finite consequences; of situated possibilities and impossibilities of individuation and identification; and of partial fusions and dangers. The problematic multiplicities of postmodern selves, so potently figured *and* repressed in the lumpy discourses of immunology, must be brought into other emerging Western and multicultural discourses on health, sickness, individuality, humanity, and death.

The science fictions of the black American writer Octavia Butler invite both sobering and hopeful reflections on this large cultural project. Drawing on the resources of black and women's histories and liberatory movements, Butler has been consumed with an interrogation into the boundaries of what counts as human and into the limits of the concept and practices of claiming "property in the self" as the ground of "human" individuality and selfhood. In *Clay's Ark* (1984) Butler explores the consequences of an extraterrestrial disease invading earth in the bodies of returned spacemen. The invaders have become an intimate part of all the cells of the infected bodies, changing human beings at the level of their most basic selves. The invaders have a single imperative that they enforce on their hosts: replication. Indeed, *Clay's Ark* reads like *The Extended Phenotype;* the invaders seem disturbingly like the "ultimate" unit of selection that haunts the biopolitical imaginations of postmodern evolutionary theorists and economic planners. The humans in Butler's profoundly dystopic story struggle to maintain their own areas of choice and self-definition in the face of the disease they have become. Part of their task is to craft a transformed relation to the "other" within themselves and to the children born to infected parents. The offspring's quadruped form archetypically marks them as the Beast itself, but they are also the future of what it will mean to be human. The disease will be global. The task of the multiracial women and men of *Clay's Ark* comes to be to reinvent the dialectics of self and other within the emerging epidemics of signification signaled by extraterrestrialism in inner and outer space. Success is not judged in this book; only the naming of the task is broached.

In *Dawn,* the first novel of Butler's series on *Xenogenesis,* the themes of global holocaust and the threateningly intimate other as self emerge again. Butler's is a fiction predicated on the natural status of adoption and the unnatural violence of kin. Butler explores the interdigitations of human, machine, nonhuman animal or alien, and their mutants, especially in relation to the intimacies of bodily exchange and mental communication. Her fiction in the opening novel of *Xenogenesis* is about the monstrous fear and hope that the child will not, after all, be like the parent. There is never one parent. Monsters share more than the word's root with the verb "to demonstrate"; monsters signify. Butler's fiction is about resistance to the imperative to recreate the sacred image of the same (Butler 1987). Butler is like

> Doris Lessing, Marge Piercy, Joanna Russ, Ursula LeGuin, Margaret Atwood, and Christa Wolf, [for whom] reinscribing the narrative of catastrophe engages them in the invention of an alternate fictional world in which the other (gender, race, species) is no longer subordinated to the same. (Brewer 1987:46)

Catastrophe, survival, and metamorphosis are Butler's constant themes. From the perspective of an ontology based on mutation, metamorphosis, and the diaspora, restoring an original sacred image can be a bad joke. Origins are precisely that to which Butler's people do not have access. But patterns are another matter. At the end of *Dawn,* Butler has Lililth—whose name recalls her original unfaithful double, the repudiated wife of Adam—pregnant with the child of five progenitors who come from two species, at least three genders, two sexes, and an indeterminate number of races. Preoccupied with marked bodies, Butler writes not of Cain or Ham, but of Lililth, the woman of color whose confrontations with the terms of selfhood, survival, and reproduction in the face of repeated ultimate catastrophe presage an ironic salvation history, with a salutary twist on the promise of a woman who will crush the head of the serpent. Butler's salvation history is not utopian, but remains deeply furrowed by the contradictions and questions of power within all communication. Her narrative therefore has the possibility of figuring something other than the Second Coming of the sacred image. Some other order of difference might be possible in *Xenogenesis*—and in immunology.

In the story, Lilith Iyapo is a young American black woman rescued with a motley assortment of remnants of humanity from an earth in the grip of nuclear war. Like all the surviving humans, Lilith has lost everything. Her son and her second-generation, Nigerian-American husband had died in an accident before the war. She had gone back to school, vaguely thinking she might become an anthropologist. But nuclear catastrophe, even more radically and comprehensively than the slave trade and history's other great genocides, ripped all rational and natural connections with past and future from her and from everyone else. Except for intermittent periods of questioning, the human remnant is kept in suspended animation for 250 years by the Oankali, the alien species that originally believed humanity was intent on committing suicide and so would be far too dangerous to try to save. Without human sensory organs, the Oankali are primatoid Medusa figures, their heads and bodies covered with multitalented tentacles like a terrain marine invertebrate's. These humanoid serpent people speak to the woman and urge her to touch them in an intimacy that would lead humanity to a monstrous metamorphosis. Multiply stripped, Lilith fights for survival, agency, and choice on the shifting boundaries that shape the possibility of meaning.

The Oankali do not rescue human beings only to return them unchanged to a restored earth. Their own origins lost to them through an infinitely long series of mergings and exchanges reaching deep into time and space, the Oankali *are* gene traders. Their essence is embodied commerce, conversation, communication—with a vengeance. Their nature is always to be midwife to themselves as other. Their bodies themselves are immune and genetic technologies, driven to exchange, replication, dangerous intimacy across the boundaries of self and other, and the power of images—not unlike us. But unlike us, the Hydra-headed Oankali do not build nonliving technologies to mediate their self-formations and reformations. Rather, they are complexly webbed into a universe of living machines, all of which are partners in their apparatus of bodily production, including the ship on which the action of *Dawn* takes place. However, deracinated captive fragments of humanity packed into the body of the aliens' ship inescapably evoke the terrible Middle Passage of the Atlantic slave trade that brought Lilith's ancestors to a "New World." There also the terms of survival were premised on an unfree "gene trade" that permanently altered meanings of self and other for all the "partners" in the exchange. In Butler's science-fictional "middle passage" the resting humans sleep in tamed, carnivorous, plantlike pods, while the Oankali do what they can to heal the ruined earth. Much is lost forever, but the fragile layer of life able to sustain other life is restored, making earth ready for recolonization by large animals. The Oankali are intensely interested in humans as potential exchange partners partly because humans are built from such beautiful and dangerous genetic structures. The Oankali believe humans to be fatally, but reparably, flawed by their genetic nature as simultaneously intelligent and hierarchical. Instead, the aliens live in the postmodern geometries of vast webs and networks, in which the nodal points of individuals are still intensely important. These webs are hardly innocent of power and violence; hierarchy is not power's only shape—for aliens or humans. The Oankali make "prints" of all their refugees, and they can print out replicas of the humans from these mental-organic-technical images. The replicas allow a great deal of gene trading. The Oankali are also fascinated with Lilith's "talent" for cancer, which killed several of her relatives, but which in Oankali "hands" would become a technology for regeneration and metamorphoses. But the Oankali want more from humanity; they want a full trade, which will require the intimacies of sexual mingling and embodied pregnancy in a shared colonial venture in, of all places, the Amazon valley. Human individuality will be challenged by more than the Oankali communication technology that translates other beings into themselves as signs, images, and memories. Pregnancy raises the tricky question of consent, property in the self, and the humans' love of themselves as the sacred image, the sign of the same. The Oankali intend to return to earth as trading partners with humanity's remnants. In difference is the irretrievable loss of the illusion of the one.

Lilith is chosen to train and lead the first party of awakened humans. She will be a kind of midwife/mother for these radically atomized peoples' emergence from their cocoons. Their task will be to form a community. But first Lilith is paired in an Oankali family with the just-premetamorphic youngster, Nikanj, an ooloi. She is to learn from Nikanj, who alters her mind and body subtly so that she can live more freely among the Oankali, and she is to protect it during its metamorphosis, from which they both emerge deeply bonded to each other. Endowed with a second pair of arms, an adult ooloi is the third gender of the Oankali, a neuter being who uses its special appendages to mediate and engineer the gene trading of the species and of each family. Each child among the Oankali has a male and female parent, usually sister and brother to each other, and an ooloi from another group, race, or moiety. One translation in Oankali languages for ooloi is "treasured strangers." The ooloi will be the mediators among the four other parents of the planned cross-species children. Heterosexuality remains unquestioned, if more complexly mediated. The different social subjects, the different genders that could emerge from another embodiment of resistance to compulsory heterosexual reproductive politics, do not inhabit this *Dawn*.

The treasured strangers can give intense pleasure across the boundaries of group, sex, gender, and species. It is a fatal pleasure that marks Lilith for the other awakened humans, even though she has not yet consented to a pregnancy. Faced with her bodily and mental alterations and her bonding with Nikanj, the other humans do not trust that she is still human, whether or not she bears a human-alien child. Neither does Lilith. Worrying that she is nonetheless a Judas-goat, she undertakes to train the humans with the intention that they will survive and run as soon as they return to earth, keeping their humanity as people before them kept theirs. In the training period, each female human pairs with a male human, and then each pair, willing or not, is adopted by an adult ooloi. Lilith loses her Chinese-American lover, Joseph, who is murdered by the suspicious and enraged humans. At the end, the first group of humans, estranged from their ooloi and hoping to escape, are ready to leave for earth. Whether they can still be fertile without their ooloi is doubtful. Perhaps it is more than the individual of a sexually reproducing species who always has more than one parent; the species too might require multiple mediation of its replicative biopolitics. Lilith finds she must remain behind to train another group, her return to earth indefinitely deferred. But Nikanj has made her pregnant with Joseph's sperm and the genes of its own mates. Lilith has not consented, and the first book of *Xenogenesis* leaves her with the ooloi's uncomprehending comfort that "the differences will be hidden until metamorphosis" (Butler 1987:263). Lilith remains unreconciled: "But they won't be human. That's what matters. You can't understand, but that is what matters." The treasured stranger responds, "The child inside you matters" (1987:

263). Butler does not resolve this dilemma. The contending shapes of sameness and difference in any possible future are at stake in the unfinished narrative of traffic across the specific cultural and political boundaries that separate and link animal, human, and machine in a contemporary global world where survival is at stake. Finally, this is the contested world where, with or without our consent, we are located. "[Lilith] laughed bitterly. 'I suppose I could think of this as fieldwork—but how the hell do I get out of the field?' " (Butler 1987:91).

But do we—or Lilith—really want to get out of the field, out of that richly ambiguous zone in the late twentieth century of imploding mythic, technical, textual, political, and organic forces? Earlier in this chapter, playing with the pervasive, mutually reinforcing secular-sacred resonances in biological discourse, I argued that "genesis" is a serious joke, especially when the body is theorized and materialized as an original coded text, whose secrets yield only to the authorizing reading and writing conventions that constitute laboratory culture. Powerful and heterogeneous practices in biotechnology, molecular biology, and biomedicine have produced the body, illustrated in this chapter on immune system discourse as a highly mobile field of strategic differences, all too like a Star Wars battlefield or a transnational corporate map of investment moves in a regime of flexible accumulation. This is a potent map of differences without identities. But this map is not the only construct of embodiment in modern biological discourse, nor the only way to figure differences without identities in postmodern conditions, and it must not be allowed to establish or deepen its hegemony. The body as contested semiotic object is also the body-in-the-world—that is, the embodied, lived, meaningful locus of signifying power. Always specifically historically situated, always a fiercely material and a relentlessly signifying entity, the body is coyote, a trickster that can be a potent force in the struggle for meanings and lives.

Lilith, in Butler's *Dawn* and in the many stories of the repudiated women of the earth, in which the versions of Lilith still traffic, is such a trickster. She noninnocently refigures stories of coupling, beginnings, diversity, transgression, and freedom. *Dawn* is a serious joke in the SF fields of scientific fact, like those of immune system and genetic discourse. *Dawn* might be read as a hint for refiguring the actors—and the action—in the next editions of *Immunology: The Science of Non-Self Discrimination* (Klein 1982), *Immunology, a Synthesis* (Golub 1987), or *The Extended Phenotype* (Dawkins 1982). The Oankali might be an immunological orchestra playing a very disturbing kind of music for the generator of diversity.

I also argued earlier in this essay that burning questions of "differences"—the global intersections of the demands for respect for radical diversity and fundamental justice—have destabilized the legitimate, conjugal commerce of Western humanist and technicist discourses across large fields of cultural practices, including biology and medicine. Contestations for representations of differences and origins and ends have been at the heart of this essay, as I and others search for less antagonistic, less deadly ways to figure self and other in the painful regions of sickness and mortality, where the coherence of our lives and deaths is at stake. Reproductive, molecular genetic, and immune system biology are particularly important contested terrains for trying to understand and intervene in, as Butler's characters in *Clay's Ark* put it, "this disease we have become" in late-capitalist, new world orders. Writing at a time of resurgent and murderous classist, racist, homophobic, and misogynist hatreds, I end this chapter with a meditation on Butler's SF figuration of the treasured strangers who might mediate a very different new world order of differences. Perhaps our question, as scholars who professionally read and write about cultural and bodily difference, is not so much how we can get out of the field as how we can get into it.

Acknowledgments

This essay is for my friends and house mates of many years, Jaye Miller (1942–1991) and Robert Filomeno (1949–1986). Lovers and spouses to each other, they cherished peace and died of AIDS-related illnesses. This project was supported by the Alpha Fund and the Institute for Advanced Study, Princeton, N.J.; Academic Senate Research Grants of the University of California at Santa Cruz; and the Silicon Valley Research Project, UCSC. Crystal Gray was an excellent research assistant. Special thanks to Scott Gilbert, Rusten Hogness, Katie King, Rayna Rapp, and Joan Scott.

Notes

1. Even without taking much account of questions of consciousness and culture, the extensive importance of immunological discourse and artifacts has many diagnostic signs:

    1. The first Nobel prize in medicine in 1901 was given for an original development, namely, the use of diptheria antitoxin. With many intervening awards, the pace of Nobel awards in immunology since 1970 is stunning, covering work on the generation of antibody diversity, the histocompatibility system, monoclonal antibodies and hybridomas, the network hypothesis of immune regulation, and development of the radioimmunoassay system.

2. The products and processes of immunology enter into present and pro-
    jected medical, pharmaceutical, and other industrial practices. This situa-
    tion is exemplified by monoclonal antibodies, which can be used as ex-
    tremely specific tools to identify, isolate, and manipulate components of
    production at a molecular scale and then gear up to an industrial scale
    with unheard of specificity and purity for a wide array of enterprises—
    from food flavoring technology to design and manufacture of industrial
    chemicals to delivery systems in chemotherapy (see chart on "Applica-
    tions of monoclonal antibodies in immunology and related disciplines,"
    Nicholas 1985:12). The *Research Briefings* for 1983 for the Federal Office
    of Science and Technology Policy and various other federal departments
    and agencies identified immunology, along with artificial intelligence and
    cognitive science, solid earth sciences, computer design and manufac-
    ture, and regions of chemistry, as research areas "that were likely to
    return the highest scientific dividends as a result of incremental federal
    investment" (Committee on Science, Engineering, and Public Policy
    1983). The dividends in such fields are hardly expected to be simply
    "scientific." "In these terms the major money spinner undoubtedly is
    hybridoma technology, and its chief product the monoclonal antibody"
    (Nicholas 1985: preface).

3. The field of immunology is itself an international growth industry. The
    First International Congress of Immunology was held in 1971 in Washing-
    ton, D.C., and was attended by most of the world's leading researchers in
    the field—about 3,500 people from forty-five countries. Over 8,000 peo-
    ple attended the Fourth International Congress in 1980 (Klein 1982:663).
    The number of journals in the field has been expanding since 1970 from
    around twelve to over eighty by 1984. The total number of books and
    monographs on the subject reached well over 1,000 by 1980. The
    industrial-university collaborations characteristic of the new biotechno-
    logy pervade research arrangements in immunology, as in molecular biol-
    ogy, with which it cross-reacts extensively—e.g., the Basel Institute for
    Immunology, entirely financed by Hoffman-La Roche but featuring all
    the benefits of academic practice, including publishing freedoms. The
    International Union of Immunological Societies began in 1969 with ten
    national societies, and increased to thirty-three by 1984 (Nicholas 1985).
    Immunology will be at the heart of global biotechnological inequality and
    "technology transfer" struggles. Its importance approaches that of infor-
    mation technologies in global science politics.

4. Ways of writing about the immune system are also ways of determining
    which diseases—and which interpretations of them—will prevail in
    courts, hospitals, international funding agencies, national policies, memo-
    ries and treatment of war veterans and civilian populations, and so on.
    See for example the efforts of oppositional people, like labor and con-
    sumer advocates, to establish a category called "chemical AIDS" to call
    attention to widespread and unnamed ("amorphous") sickness in late
    industrial societies putatively associated with its products and environ-

ments, and to link this sickness with infectious AIDS as a political strategy (Hayes 1987; Marshall 1986). Discourse on infectious AIDS is part of mechanisms that determine what counts as "the general population," such that over one million infected people in the U.S. alone—not to mention the global dimensions of infection—can be named in terms that make them *not* part of the general population, with important national medical, insurance, and legal policy implications. Many leading textbooks of immunology in the United States give considerably more space to allergies or autoimmune diseases than to parasitic diseases, an allocation that might lead future Nobel Prize winners into some areas of research rather than others and that certainly does nothing to lead undergraduates or medical students to take responsibility for the differences and inequalities of sickness globally. (Contrast Golub 1987 with Desowitz 1987 for the sensitivities of a cellular immunology researcher and a parasitologist.) Who counts as an individual is not unrelated to who counts as the general population.

2. Like the universe inhabited by readers and writers of this essay.

3. This ontological continuity enables the discussion of the growing practical problem of "virus" programs infecting computer software (McLellan 1988). The infective, invading information fragments that parasitize their host code in favor of their own replication and their own program commands are more than metaphorically like biological viruses. And like the body's unwelcome invaders, the software viruses are discussed in terms of pathology as communications terrorism, requiring therapy in the form of strategic security measures. There is a kind of epidemiology of virus infections of artificial intelligence systems, and neither the large corporate and military systems nor the personal computers have good immune defenses. Both are extremely vulnerable to terrorism and rapid proliferation of the foreign code that multiplies silently and subverts normal functions. Immunity programs to kill the viruses, like Data Physicians sold by Digital Dispatch, are being marketed. More than half the buyers of Data Physician in 1985 were military. Everytime I start up, my Macintosh shows the icon for its vaccine program: a hypodermic needle.

4. Thanks to Elizabeth Bird for creating a political button with this slogan, worn by a member of an affinity group called Surrogate Others at the Mothers and Others Day Action at the Nevada Nuclear Test Site in May 1987.

5. The relation of the immune and nervous systems conceived within contemporary neuroimmunology or psychoneuroimmunology would be the ideal place to locate a fuller argument here. With the discovery of receptors and products shared by cells of the neural, endocrine, and immune systems, positing the dispersed and networking immune system as the mediator between mind and body began to make sense to "hard" scientists. The implications for popular and official therapeutics are legion—for example, in relation to the polysemic entity called "stress." See Barnes 1986, 1987; Wechsler 1987; Kanigel 1986. The biological metaphors invoked to name the immune system also facilitate or inhibit notions of the IS as a potent mediator, rather than a master control system or

hyperarmed defense department. For example, developmental biologist and immunologist Scott Gilbert refers in his teaching to the immune system as an ecosystem and neuroimmunology researcher Edwin Blalock (1984) calls the immune system a sensory organ. These metaphors can be oppositional to the hyperrationalistic AI immune body in Star Wars imagery. They can also have multiple effects in research design, as well as teaching and therapeutics.

6. When I begin to think I am paranoid for thinking anyone *really* dreams of transcendent disembodiment as the telos of life and mind, I find such things as the following quote by the computer designer W. Daniel Hillis in the Winter 1988 issue of *Daedalus* on artificial intelligence: "Of course, I understand that this is just a dream, and I will admit that I am propelled more by hope than by the probability of success. But if this artificial mind can sustain itself and grow of its own accord, then for the first time human thought will live free of bones and flesh, giving this child of mind an earthly immortality denied to us" (Hillis 1988:189). Thanks to Evelyn Keller for pointing me to the quote (personal communication). See her "From Secrets of Life, Secrets of Death" (1990). I am indebted to Zoe Sofia (1984; Sofoulis 1988) for analysis of the iconography and mythology of nuclear exterminism, extraterrestrialism, and cannibalism.

7. That, of course, is why women have had so much trouble counting as individuals in modern Western discourses. Their personal, bounded individuality is compromised by their bodies' troubling talent for making other bodies, whose individuality can take precedence over their own, even while the little bodies are fully contained and invisible without major optical technologies (Petchesky 1987). Women can, in a sense, be cut in half and retain their maternal function—witness their bodies maintained after death to sustain the life of another individual. The special ambiguity of female individuality—perhaps more resistant, finally, than worms to full liberal personhood—extends into accounts of immune function during pregnancy. The old biomedical question has been, why does the mother not reject the little invader within as foreign? After all, the embryo and fetus are quite well marked as "other" by all the ordinary immunological criteria; and there is intimate contact between fetal and maternal tissue at the site of certain cells of the placenta, called trophoblasts. Counterintuitively, it turns out that it is women with "underactive immune systems" who end up rejecting their fetuses immunologically by forming antibodies against their tissues. Normally, women make special antibodies that mask the tell-tale foreign signals on the fetal trophoblasts, so that the mother's immune surveillance system remains blind to the fetus's presence. By immunizing the "rejecting" women with cells taken from their "husbands" or other genetically unrelated donors, the women's immune systems can be induced to make blocking antibodies. It appears that most women are induced to make this sort of antibody as a result of "immunization" from their "husband's" sperm during intercourse. But if the "husband" is too genetically close to the potential mother, some women won't recognize the sperm as foreign, and their immune systems won't make blocking antibodies. So the baby gets recognized as foreign. But even this hostile act doesn't make the female a good individual, since it results from her failure to respond properly to the original breach of her boundaries in intercourse (Kolata

1988*a*). It seems pretty clear that the biopolitical discourses of individuation have their limits for feminist purposes!

8. Jerne's debt to Chomsky's structuralism is obvious, as are the difficulties that pertain to any such version of structuralist internal totality. My argument is that there is more to see here than a too rapid criticism would allow. Jerne's and Chomsky's internal image of each other does not constitute the first time theories of the living animal and of language have occupied the same epistemic terrain. See Foucault's *The Order of Things* (1971). Remember that Foucault in *The Archaeology of Knowledge* defines discourses as "practices that systematically form the objects of which they speak" (Foucault 1972:49). The family relation between structuralism and rationalism is something I will avoid for now.

9. Emily Martin has begun a long-term fieldwork project on networks of immunological discourse in laboratories, in the media, and among people with and without AIDS.

10. Mice and "men" are constantly associated in immune discourse because these sibling animal bodies have been best characterized in the immunological laboratory. For example, the Major Histocompatibility Complex (MHC), a complex of genes that encodes a critical array of surface markers involved in almost all of the key immune response recognition events, is well characterized for each species. The complex is called the H2 locus in the mouse and the HLA locus in humans. The MHC codes for what will be recognized as "self." The locus is critically involved in "restriction" of specificities. Highly polygenic and polyallelic, the MHC may be the main system allowing discrimination between self and nonself. "Nonself" must be presented to an immune system cell "in the context of self;" i.e., associated with the surface markers coded by the MHC. Comparative studies of the antigens of the MHC with the molecular structures of other key actors in the immune response (antibodies, T cell differentiation antigens) have led to the concept of the "immunoglobulin superfamily," characterized by its extensive sequence homologies that suggest an evolutionary elaboration from a common genic ancestor (Golub 1987:208–233). The conceptual and laboratory tools developed to construct knowledge of the MHC are a microcosm for understanding the apparatus of production of the bodies of the immune system. Various antigens coded by the MHC confer "public" or "private" specificities, terms that designate degrees of shared versus differentiating antigens against a background of close genetic similarity, but not identity. Immunology could be approached as the science constructing such language-like "distinguishing features" of the organic communications system. Current research on "tolerance" and the ways thymic cells (T cells) "educate" other cells about what is and is not "self" led the biologist Scott Gilbert to ask if that is immunology's equivalent of the injunction to know "thy-self"? (personal communication). Reading immunological language requires both extreme literal-mindedness and a taste for troping. Jennifer Terry examined AIDS as a "trop(olog)ical pandemic" (1988).

11. It is not just imagers of the immune system who learn from military cultures; military cultures draw symbiotically on immune system discourse, just as strategic planners draw directly from and contribute to video game practices

and science fiction. For example, in *Military Review* Colonel Frederick Timmerman argued for an elite corps of special strike force soldiers in the army of the future in these terms:

> The most appropriate example to describe how this system would work is the most complex biological model we know—the body's immune system. Within the body there exists a remarkably complex corps of internal bodyguards. In absolute numbers they are small—only about one percent of the body's cells. Yet they consist of reconnaissance specialists, killers, reconstitution specialists, and communicators that can seek out invaders, sound the alarm, reproduce rapidly, and swarm to the attack to repel the enemy. . . . In this regard, the June 1986 issue of *National Geographic* contains a detailed account of how the body's immune system functions. (Timmerman 1987:52)

References

Barnes, Deborah M.
  1986   Nervous and Immune System Disorders Linked in a Variety of Diseases. *Science* 232:160–161.
  1987   Neuroimmunology Sits on Broad Research Base. *Science* 237:1568–1569.
Barthes, Roland
  1977   The Photographic Message. In *Image Music Text,* Stephen Heath, trans., pp. 15–31. New York: Hill & Wang.
Berger, Stewart
  1985   *Dr. Berger's Immune Power Diet.* New York: New American Library.
Blalock, J. Edwin
  1984   The Immune System as a Sensory Organ. *The Journal of Immunology* 132(3):1067–1070.
Brewer, Mária Minich
  1987   Surviving Fictions: Gender and Difference in Postmodern and Postnuclear Narrative. *Discourse* 9:37–52.
Bryan, C. D. B.
  1987   *The National Geographic Society: 100 Years of Adventure and Discovery.* New York: Harry N. Abrams, Inc.
Buss, Leo
  1987   *The Evolution of Individuality.* Princeton, N.J.: Princeton University Press.
Butler, Octavia
  1984   *Clay's Ark.* New York: St. Martin's Press.
  1987   *Dawn: Xenogenesis.* New York: Warner Books.
Committee on Science, Engineering, and Public Policy
  1983   *Research Briefings.* Committee on Science, Engineering, and Public Policy of the National Academy of Sciences, the National Academy of Medicine, and the Institute of Medicine. Washington, D.C.: National Academy Press.

Dawkins, Richard
    1976   *The Selfish Gene.* Oxford: Oxford University Press.
    1982   *The Extended Phenotype: The Gene as the Unit of Selection.* Oxford:
            Oxford University Press.
Desowitz, Robert S.
    1987   *The Immune System and How It Works.* New York: Norton.
Foucault, Michel
    1971   *The Order of Things.* New York: Pantheon.
    1972   *The Archaeology of Knowledge.* London: Tavistock.
Golub, Edward S.
    1987   *Immunology: A Synthesis.* Sunderland, Mass.: Sinauer Associates.
Haraway, Donna
    1985*a*   Teddy Bear Patriarchy: Taxidermy in the Garden of Eden, New
            York City, 1908–36. *Social Text* 11:20–64.
    1985*b*   A Manifesto for Cyborgs: Science, Technology and Socialist Femi-
            nism in the 1980s. *Socialist Review* 80:65–107.
Hayes, Dennis
    1987   Making Chips with Dust-free Poison. *Science as Culture* 1:89–104.
Hayles, N. Katherine
    1987   Denaturalizing Experience: Postmodern Literature and Science. Ab-
            stract from the conference, "Literature and Science as Modes of
            Expression," sponsored by the Society for Literature and Science,
            October 8–11, Worcester Polytechnic Institute.
Hillis, W. Daniel
    1988   Intelligence as an Emergent Behavior; or, the Songs of Eden. *Dae-
            dalus* (winter):175–189.
Jaret, Peter
    1986   Our Immune System: The Wars Within. *National Geographic* 169(6):
            701–735.
Jerne, Niels K.
    1985   The Generative Grammar of the Immune System. *Science* 229:
            1057–1059.
Judson, Horace Freeland
    1979   *The Eighth Day of Creation.* New York: Simon & Schuster.
Kanigel, Robert
    1986   Where Mind and Body Meet. *Mosaic* 17(2):52–60.
    1987   The Genome Project. *New York Times Sunday Magazine* (Decem-
            ber 13).
Keller, Evelyn Fox
    1990   From Secrets of Life to Secrets of Death. In *Body/Politics: Women
            and the Discourses of Science,* M. Jacobus, E. F. Keller, and S. Shut-
            tleworth, eds., pp. 177–191. New York: Routledge.
King, Katie
    1991   Bibliography and a Feminist Apparatus of Literary Production. *Text*
            5:91–103.

Klein, Jan
   1982   *Immunology: The Science of Non-Self Discrimination.* New York: Wiley-Interscience.
Kolata, Gina
   1988*a*   New Treatments May Aid Women Who Have Miscarriages. *New York Times* (January 5):C3.
   1988*b*   New Research Yields Clues in Fight Against Autoimmune Disease. *New York Times* (January 19):C3.
Krimsky, Sheldon
   1991   *Biotechnics and Society: The Rise of Industrial Genetics.* New York: Praeger.
Marshall, Eliot
   1986   Immune System Theories on Trial. *Science* 234:1490–1492.
McLellan, Vin
   1988   Computer Systems Under Siege. *New York Times,* (January 31) sec. C:1,8.
Nicholas, Robin
   1985   *Immunology: An Information Profile.* London: Mansell.
Nilsson, Lennart
   1977   *A Child Is Born.* New York: Dell.
   1987   *The Body Victorious: The Illustrated Story of Our Immune System and Other Defenses of the Human Body.* New York: Delacorte Press.
Petchesky, Rosalind Pollack
   1987   Fetal Images: The Power of Visual Culture in the Politics of Reproduction. *Feminist Studies* 13(2):263–292.
Playfair, J. H. L.
   1984   *Immunology at a Glance.* 3d ed. Oxford: Blackwell Scientific Publications.
Roberts, Leslie
   1987*a*   Who Owns the Human Genome? *Science* 237:358–361.
   1987*b*   Human Genome: Questions of Cost. *Science* 237:1411–1412.
   1987*c*   New Sequencers Take on the Genome. *Science* 238:271–273.
Sofia, Zoe
   1984   Exterminating Fetuses: Abortion, Disarmament, and the Sexo-Semiotics of Extra-terrestrialism. *Diacritics* 14:47–59.
Sofoulis, Zoe
   1988   Through the Lumen: *Frankenstein* and the Optic of Reorigination. Ph.D. thesis, University of California, Santa Cruz.
Terry, Jennifer
   1988   AIDS, a Trop(olog)ical Pandemic: Figuration and Literality and the Hermeneutics of Lethality. Unpublished manuscript, University of California, Santa Cruz.
Timmerman, Colonel Frederick W., Jr.
   1987   Future Warriors. *Military Review* (September):46–55.

Treichler, Paula
    1987   AIDS, Homophobia, and Biomedical Discourse: An Epidemic of
            Signification. *October* 43:31–70.
Turner, Bryan S.
    1984   *The Body and Society.* New York: Basil Blackwell.
Wechsler, Rob
    1987   A New Prescription: Mind over Malady. *Discover* (February):51–61.
Wilson, E. O.
    1975   *Sociobiology: The New Synthesis.* Cambridge: Belknap Press of Har-
            vard University Press.
Winograd, Terry
    n.d.   Computers and Rationality: The Myths and Realities. Unpublished
            manuscript.
Winograd, Terry, and Fernando Flores
    1985   *Understanding Computers and Cognition: A New Foundation for
            Design.* Norwood, N.J.: Ablex.

Contributors

Roberto Briceño-León is a professor of sociology and the Director of the Social Research Laboratory at the Central University of Venezuela. He has been a visiting professor at Oxford University, and lecturer in several universities in Latin America. His main interest is social and individual behavior, and the use of traditional knowledge, organizations, and appropriate technologies as tools for innovation and change. He has been involved in several grassroots movements in urban and rural areas, is a member of the TDR-WHO Steering Committee on Social and Economic Aspects of Tropical Diseases, and since 1989 has been in charge of an international small grants program designed to attract and support junior social scientists and researchers in the area of tropical diseases. His books include *The Sick House: Sociology of Chagas Disease; The Perverse Effects of Oil; City and Capitalism;* and *The Future of the Venezuelan cities.*

Jean Comaroff is a professor of anthropology at the University of Chicago. She is the author of *Body of Power, Spirit of Resistance: The Culture and History of a South African People,* and co-author, with John Comaroff, of *Of Revelation and Revolution: Christianity, Colonialism, and Consciousness in South Africa, Volume 1,* and *Ethnography and the Historical Imagination.* She has also written widely on healing and the body in Southern Africa.

Sue E. Estroff is an associate professor of social medicine, and an adjunct associate professor of anthropology and psychiatry, at the University of North Carolina at Chapel Hill. Her main research interests are exploring methods and vocabularies for conveying subjectivity in scholarly representations of persons with illnesses; processes of disablement and resistance to chronicity; accounting for different long-term outcomes among persons with severe, persistent mental illnesses; and the roles of social welfare policy and subsistence in the social construction of chronicity.

Horacio Fabrega, Jr. is a professor of psychiatry and anthropology at the University of Pittsburgh. He has been actively involved in the cultural study of medicine and psychiatry for three decades. His areas of interest include the comparison of medical systems and the differences in the way psychiatric and medical concerns are structured and understood across societies. He has focused on social, historical, and cultural anthropological comparisons.

Ronald Frankenberg is a professor emeritus of sociology and social anthropology at Keele University, Staffordshire, England, where he now teaches a master's program as professorial research fellow and Director of the Centre for Medical Social Anthropology. He is also an associate professor in the Centre for the Study of Health, Sickness and Disablement and teaches on the M.Sc. program in medical anthropology at Brunel University in West London. He has taught medical anthropology at Berkeley and Case Western Reserve in the United States, to which he is a frequent visitor. He has also taught for extended periods in Zambia and in India. He was one of the founding editors of *Medical Anthropology Quarterly* in 1986, and of the journal started this year, *Time and Society*. His book-length writings include *Village on the Border* (1957 and 1989), *Communities in Britain* (1966), and the edited volumes, *Custom and Conflict in British Society* (1982) and *Time, Health and Medicine* (1992). He has worked on health care in Lusaka, Zambia, and Italy. His current research interests are AIDS/HIV, the cultural performance of sickness, temporality in biomedicine, and narratives of chronic suffering.

Byron J. Good is associate professor of medical anthropology at Harvard Medical School and lecturer in anthropology at Harvard University. Joint editor-in-chief of *Culture, Medicine and Psychiatry,* he is the author of *Medicine, Rationality and Experience* (Cambridge, forthcoming) and co-editor of *Culture and Depression* (California, 1985).

Mary-Jo DelVecchio Good is associate professor of medical sociology at Harvard Medical School and teaches sociology at Harvard University. She is also joint editor-in-chief (with Byron J. Good) of *Culture, Medicine and Psychiatry.*

Donna Haraway is a professor in the History of Consciousness Board at the University of California at Santa Cruz, where she teaches feminist theory, technoscience studies, and women's studies. She is the author of *Crystals, Fabrics and Fields: Metaphors of Organicism in Twentieth-Century Developmental Biology* (Yale University Press, 1976), *Primate Visions: Gender, Race, and Nature in the World of Modern Science* (Routledge, 1989), and *Simians, Cyborgs, and Women: The Reinvention of Nature* (Routledge and Free Association Books, 1991).

Patricia M. Jeffery studied social anthropology at Cambridge University and received her Ph.D. in sociology from the University of Bristol, for work that later appeared in *Migrants and Refugees: Muslim and Christian Pakistani Migrants in Bristol* (Cambridge University Press, 1976). She has carried out fieldwork in Bristol (England), in Lahore (Pakistan), at the shrine of Hazrat Nizamuddin Auliya in New Delhi, and, since 1982, in Bijnor district, Uttar Pradesh. She is the author of *Frogs in a Well: Indian Women in Purdah* (Zed Press, 1979), and main author (with Roger Jeffery and Andrew Lyon) of *Labour Pains and Labour Power: Women and Childbearing in India* (Zed Press, 1989), and articles on the position of women in north India. She has taught in the social anthropology and sociology departments in the University of Edinburgh, where she is currently a reader in sociology.

Roger Jeffery studied economics at Cambridge University, and received his Ph.D. in sociology from the University of Edinburgh for work that later appeared in *The Politics of Health in India* (University of California Press, 1988). He has carried out fieldwork in Bristol (England), in Lahore (Pakistan), Delhi, and on two occasions in Bijnor district, Uttar Pradesh. He is the second author (with Patricia Jeffery and Andrew Lyon) of *Labour Pains and Labour Power: Women and Childbearing in India* (Zed Press, 1989), and has written articles on health services and health policy in India and Pakistan. He has been teaching in the sociology department at the University of Edinburgh since 1972, and is currently a senior lecturer.

Patricia A. Kaufert earned a Ph.D. in sociology from the University of Birmingham in 1976, and is currently an associate professor in the department of community health sciences at the University of Manitoba. She has published extensively on the topics of childbirth and menopause. Her most recent research is on mammography.

Gilbert Lewis is a lecturer in social anthropology, Cambridge University, England, and Fellow of St. John's College, Cambridge. He received his Ph.D. in 1972 in social anthropology at the London School of Economics, studying the West Sepik Province of Papua New Guinea. He has done field research on medical anthropological themes in this province in 1968–1970, 1975, and 1985, and has also worked in Gambia, West Africa, and in Guinea-Bissau, West Africa. His publications include *Knowledge of Illness in a Sepik Society* (Athlone Press and Humanities Press, 1975), and *Day of Shining Red* (Cambridge University Press, 1980).

Shirley Lindenbaum is a professor of anthropology at the Graduate Center, City University of New York. Fieldwork in Papua New Guinea (on kuru) and in Bangladesh (on cholera) were a prelude to her current study of AIDS in New York City. Her publications include *Kuru Sorcery: Disease and Danger in the New Guinea Highlands* (1979), and a co-edited volume titled *The Time of AIDS* (1992); as a member of a National Academy of Sciences Committee on AIDS Research, she also contributed various segments to *AIDS, Sexual Behavior and Intravenous Drug Use* (1989) and *AIDS, The Second Decade* (1990).

Margaret Lock is a professor of medical anthropology in the departments of humanities and social studies in medicine and anthropology at McGill University. She is the author of *East Asian Medicine in Urban Japan* (1980), and co-editor of *Health, Illness and Medical Care in Japan* (1987) and *Biomedicine Examined* (1988). Her research interests are in the anthropology of the body, the cultural construction of life-cycle transitions, and comparative medical systems. She recently completed a manuscript titled *Encounters with Aging: Mythologies of Menopause in Japan and North America.*

John O'Neil is an associate professor of medical anthropology in the Northern Health Research Unit in the department of community health sciences at the University of Manitoba. He has been engaged in fifteen years of health-policy-oriented research with the Inuit of northern Canada, and has recently expanded these interests to work with indigenous people in Russia and Australia. A recent paper titled "The Cultural and Political Context of Patient Dissatisfaction in Cross-Cultural Clinical Encounters: A Canadian Inuit Study," published in *Medical Anthropology Quarterly,* was the 1990 recipient of the Rudolph Virchow prize in critical medical anthropology.

Tola Olu Pearce received her Ph.D. at Brown University, Providence, Rhode Island, in 1977. Dr. Pearce is a medical sociologist in the Department of sociology/anthropology at the Obafemi Awolowo University (formerly the University of Ife), Nigeria. Her interests include the sociology of knowledge, social change/development, and women and health. Her publications include *Social Change in Nigeria,* an edited book (with

Afonja Longman, 1986); "Professional Interests and the Creation of Medical Knowledge" appearing in *The Professionalisation of African Medicine* (ed. M. Last and G. Chavunduka, University of Manchester Press, 1986); and "Assaulting a Wife: Perspectives on Conjugal Violence Among the Yoruba" appearing in *Women's Health Issues in Nigeria* (ed. M. Kisekka, Tamaza Press, forthcoming).

Rayna Rapp teaches anthropology at the New School for Social Research, helps edit *Feminist Studies,* and has been active in the movements for women's studies, and for reproductive rights, for over twenty years. She is currently completing a book on the social impact and cultural meaning of amniocentesis.

Lorna Amarasingham Rhodes received her Ph.D. in anthropology from Cornell University. She has conducted research in Sri Lanka and in the United States, and is the author of *Emptying Beds: The Work of an Emergency Psychiatric Unit.* She is an associate professor of anthropology at the University of Washington.

Allan Young is a professor of anthropology in the department of humanities and social studies in medicine at McGill University. He has conducted research on a variety of medical and psychiatric subjects in Ethiopia, Nepal, Israel (among Ethiopian immigrants), and the United States. He is co-editor, with Charles Leslie, of *Paths to Asian Medical Knowledge* (University of California Press, 1992).

Index